University of California Press (Berkeley)

Perspectives on Southern Africa

The Rand at War

1899—1902
The Witwatersrand and the
Anglo-Boer War

Diana Cammack

James Currey
LONDON

University of California Press
BERKELEY AND LOS ANGELES

University of Natal Press
PIETERMARITZBURG

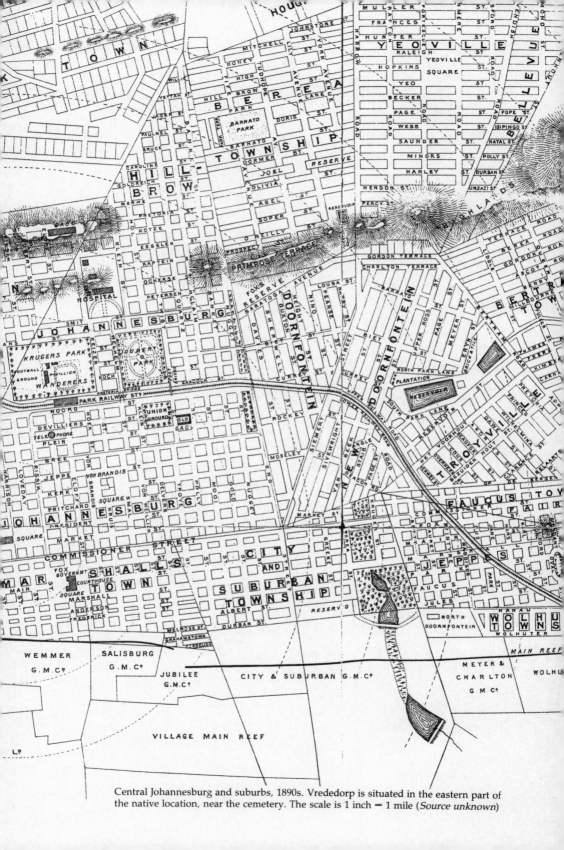

Central Johannesburg and suburbs, 1890s. Vrededorp is situated in the eastern part of the native location, near the cemetery. The scale is 1 inch = 1 mile (*Source unknown*)

Acknowledgements

Several years ago the social historian, Karl Hinthaus, asked me if the Rand had changed much between 1886 and 1902, thus setting me off on a ten-year project which culminated in this book. I am grateful for his interest and support, as I am for that of my other mentors at the University of California: Professors John S. Galbraith, Samuel C. McCulloch and Edward Reynolds.

I also want to thank the Chancellor of the University of California, Irvine, as well as the Department of History at the Rand Afrikaans University in Johannesburg, and especially its chairman, Professor Henning van Aswegen, for their financial assistance without which a year's research in South Africa would have been impossible.

Others in South Africa have also been helpful over the years, including Jill Callinicos, Kevin Knott, Johann Fourie, Digby and Ilse Sales and Charles van Onselen, whom I also wish to thank, while acknowledging his leadership in the field of South African social history. In England, social history Peter Warwick and Guy Routh have been kind in supplying me information while encouraging me in my work. I wish to thank my editor, Selina Cohen for elucidating the obscurities, though no blame for misinterpretation can fall on her.

Numerous librarians and archivists have been patient and forgiving while I rummaged through their documentation and photographs. I thank them for their forbearance and good humour, for without them the historian's work would be even more impossible and time consuming. In particular, I would like to thank:

The Librarian and staff of Rhodes House Library, Oxford for permission to cite portions of the Basil Williams Collection.

The Archivist and staff of the United Society for the Propagation of the Gospel, London, for access to their archive.

The Sisters General of Nazareth House, London, for permission to cite letters held there.

The Librarian, staff, and Trustees of the Liddell Hart Centre for Military Archives, King's College, London, for permission to use and cite the Edmonds and Coverton Papers.

The Keeper and staff of Books and Archives at the National Army Museum, London, for permission to consult and cite documents held there.

The Librarian, Warden and Fellows of New College, Oxford, for access to the Milner papers.

Acknowledgements

Several years ago the social historian, Karl Hufbauer, asked me if the Rand had changed much between 1899 and 1902, thus setting me off on a ten-year project which culminated in this book. I am grateful for his interest and support, as I am for that of my other mentors at the University of California: Professors John S. Galbraith, Samuel C. McCulloch and Edward Reynolds.

I also want to thank the Chancellor of the University of California, Irvine, as well as the Department of History at the Rand Afrikaans University in Johannesburg, and especially its chairman, Professor Henning van Aswegen, for their financial assistance, without which a year's research in South Africa would have been impossible.

Others in South Africa have also been helpful over the years, including Luli Callinicos, Riva Krut, Johann Fourie, Digby and Ilse Sales, and Charles van Onselen, whom I also wish to thank while acknowledging his leadership in the field of South African social history. In England, Shula Marks, Peter Warwick and Guy Routh have been kind in supplying me information while encouraging me in my work. I wish to thank my editor, Selina Cohen, for elucidating the obscurities, though no blame for misinterpretation can fall on her.

Numerous librarians and archivists have been patient and forgiving while I rummaged through their documentation and photographs. I thank them for their forbearance and good humour, for without them, the historian's work would be even more impossible and time consuming. In particular, I would like to thank:

The Librarian and staff of Rhodes House Library, Oxford, for permission to cite portions of the Basil Williams' Collection.

The Archivist and staff of the United Society for the Propagation of the Gospel, London, for access to their archive.

The Sister General of Nazareth House, London, for permission to cite letters held there.

The Librarian, staff, and Trustees of the Liddell Hart Centre for Military Archives, King's College, London, for permission to use and cite the Edmonds and Coverton Papers.

The Keeper and staff of Books and Archives at the National Army Museum, London, for permission to consult and cite documents held there.

The Librarian, Warden and Fellows of New College, Oxford, for access to the Milner papers.

The Librarian and staff of the Bodleian Library, Oxford, for access to the Lady Edward Cecil papers.

The Curator of Manuscripts and Department of Historical Documents, University of the Witwatersrand, for permission to use private papers held there.

The Librarian and staff of the Strange Library of Africana, Johannesburg Public Library, for permission to consult and to cite from their most useful collection.

The staffs of both the Public Records Office in Kew Gardens, London, and the Transvaal Government Archives, Pretoria, for permission to use their facilities.

The Librarian of the South African Jewish Board of Deputies for access to their documentation.

The Librarian of the South African Chamber of Mines, for the use of their collection in Johannesburg.

The Librarian and staff of the London *Times*, for permission to read files held there.

Mr R. O'Brien of Headley, Bordon, Hampshire, for his kind permission to cite the letters of Charles Richard M. O'Brien.

Mr George Lipp and the Librarian of the University of Stellenbosch for their permission to use portions of Isabella Lipp's marvellous diary.

Finally, I wish to acknowledge the great debt I owe my children — Jeff and Chris Cammack — for my hours spent at the typewriter rather than rocking a cradle, or later, playing ball. As the years pass I hope they will understand the importance of combatting apartheid in any little way each of us can. I also wish to thank my husband, Tim, whose support has been demonstrated in very meaningful ways. His love and encouragement have made this book easier to complete.

Introduction

There is a happy land over the Vaal
Chockfull of crooks learning the Taal.
Hear how their bookies yell,
See how their pockets swell.
There is a happy land over the Vaal. [1]

Popular Song

With its few scattered farms, rolling brown hills, streams and pasture land, the Witwatersrand in the mid-1880s was a sleepy sort of place. But within ten years all of this was to change as more than 100,000 people flocked to the veld in search of gold. Colonials, escaping the boredom of small-town life, joined the Indians trekking from the sugar fields of Natal. Cape Coloureds and Chinese shopkeepers mixed with Africans, eager to experience the fast pace of urban life. Artisans and miners from the gold and silver fields of the Americas and Australia, from the coal and tin mines of Europe, joined the wagon loads of men who had learned their craft in the pits of Kimberley. Jews, in search of freedom and employment, headed south to Africa from Eastern Europe and Russia. Mine managers and businessmen, solicitors and engineers, men with skills, education and contacts, confident of their expertise and frequently arrogant in their manner, took up positions in the burgeoning city of Johannesburg and in the new mines along the reef. Mixed in amongst the hard-working labourers, the eager businessmen and acquisitive traders, amongst the wide-eyed newcomers to city life, were pimps and adventurers, crooks and philanderers. A 'Monte Carlo superimposed upon Sodom and Gomorrah': this was Johannesburg in the early years. [2]

Before 1870 the areas of European settlement in southern Africa were almost entirely based upon a pastoral and agricultural economy, with a small export sector specializing in hides, wool, wine and maize. The discovery of diamonds at Kimberley in 1867 began to change all that, as diamond exports came to dominate the economy into the 1890s. But within six years of the discovery of gold on the Witwatersrand (Rand) in 1886, the value of its output exceeded that of diamonds. The miracle of South African economic development was already evident by the end of the century when over a quarter of the world's gold came from the mines within the South African Republic.

Originally gold was extracted from outcrops along the reef, where the gold-bearing rock surfaced and where claims could be worked by men with little capital

1

and relatively little equipment. But in the late 1880s and early 1890s several changes in the methods of mining were initiated, all of which had far-reaching consequences for Rand society. Boreholes driven along the reef in the early 1890s confirmed the view of many engineers that gold in large quantities lay beneath and to the south of the outcrop. Thereafter men began to speak of the Rand having a long and lucrative future — engineers spoke in terms of a man's lifetime then — and a future worth investing in, and fighting for, if need be. Deep-level mining soon came to set the agenda for the whole industry, as profitability was seen in terms of making deep-level mines pay. While only one-third of the Rand mining companies were deep-level concerns by the end of the century, it was none the less clear that that was where the future lay.

Subject to boom—bust cycles, Rand mining in the early years lurched from prosperity to depression, taking all sectors of the economy with it. The first crisis, in the early 1890s, resulted in part from the need for a new method of extracting gold from unoxidized ore brought from below the surface. Inventions culminating in the MacArthur—Forrest cyanide process raised the recovery rate of ore from deep-level mines to upwards of 90 per cent, thus raising outputs and lowering costs per fine ounce. But this first financial crisis was also caused by speculation in property and shares and by over-trading in the latter. Public confidence in Rand mining companies was shaken as a result; European investment dried up and work came to a halt. To attract new money and create the technological and administrative machinery needed to undertake deep-level mining, the industry consolidated its resources and the group system of ownership and control was born.[3] By the late 1890s the two most powerful groups in political and economic terms were Cecil Rhodes's Consolidated Gold Fields and H. Eckstein & Company, which was part of the powerful Wernher, Beit & Company and was represented locally by J. Percy Fitzpatrick among others.

Mining gold put enormous pressures upon the simple economic structure of the Boers' South African Republic. Infrastructural development and economic reforms were necessary to maximize profits and minimize expenditure while extending outcrop operations and developing deep levels. The discovery of coal on the far east Rand at Springs and Boksburg, as well as the construction of the Rand Steam Tram from the colliery to the gold fields and into Johannesburg facilitated the growth of the industry in its early years. Soon, too, the railway arrived from the coast: in September 1892 the Cape railway reached the Rand. Two years later the line from Lourenço Marques (now Maputo) at Delagoa Bay in Portuguese Mozambique — the Rand's closest port — arrived in the Republic, and a third route was opened from Durban the following year. These railway linkages reduced the cost of capital and consumer goods when compared with wagon transport, but the monopoly of all railway lines within the Republic, a monopoly granted by President Paul Kruger to The Netherlands South African Railway Company (NZASM), meant higher carriage rates on all items. This in turn added to the already high cost of living on the Rand, necessitating higher wages for workers. This, along with the fact that material and stores represented 25 per cent of mining costs, pushed the industrialists to advocate a reduction in both customs duties and railway tariffs, pitting employers against the government and NZASM throughout the 1890s.

The industrialists and their colleagues argued that other changes were necessary if the industry and, therefore, the local and the wider Republican economy, were to prosper. Specifically, they complained about the high cost of dynamite — twice the price paid at Kimberley and averaging 10 per cent of the Rand's total mining costs. The high price was again the result of a monopoly granted by Kruger to a foreign concern, a monopoly which insured that the industry had explosives, albeit at a high price, and that the President had a secure local source of ammunition.

Maintaining a dependable supply of cheap African labour was particularly vital to the industry, as the entire unskilled labour force was black. And labour costs were high, averaging 50 to 60 per cent of the total costs. Thus the need for a massive number of cheap black workers put pressure upon the industry and government to enact and strictly enforce measures designed to facilitate African recruitment, halt desertion and exploit African workers more efficiently. While the ratio of white to black mine-workers averaged about 1:7, the total wage bill for whites nearly equalled that of blacks. Thus managers tried to train cheaper non-white labour to replace the more expensive (and unionized) whites, as well as to develop labour-saving devices and introduce different systems of work. Much of the antagonism between white workers and industrialists at the end of the century was predicated upon this fact, just as was much of the racialism displayed by organized labour in its effort to exclude cheaper blacks from skilled work.

High initial capital expenditure, with a long period of development before outputs and profits were realized, put pressure even on the groups with the greatest liquidity. Towards the end of the decade the need to lower costs relating to explosives, fuel, labour, transport and other factors of production, became ever more urgent. As capital from Europe was diverted to new investments elsewhere, some deep-level concerns were forced to slow development. Urban construction ceased and business stagnated, as unemployment rose and demand dropped. Blaming Kruger for his antiquated and inefficient economic system — which may have provided his burghers with ammunition for their rifles and tea for their tables, but which was unequal to the needs of industrial capitalism — the Randlords (the leaders of the industry) demanded economic reforms which, if implemented, would have meant the creation of a totally new economic structure. Though some reforms were introduced in the late 1890s, they were too few and too modest to satisfy the industrialists. Kruger was incapable of doing any more.

While gold was the focus of economic activity on the Rand, there was more to life than mining.[4] At the centre of the 50-mile stretch of mines sat Johannesburg which, within ten years of its founding, was the home of 100,000 people. Less than one in ten of the whites living in or near the city worked on the mines and even fewer Asians and Coloureds were miners. Instead, Johannesburg grew to service the industry and its labourers and became the focus of the Rand's social life. From all along the reef came people to spend money and to drink, gamble and carouse. When someone needed a tailor, a shoemaker or a barber, he came into 'Joburg'. If he wanted to collect post, visit a bank or book a steamship passage, he came to the city. There were large and well-stocked shops and on the streets were hawkers and pedlars, shoulder to shoulder with flower sellers and pimps. Prostitutes, hundreds of them, drawn mostly from America and Europe, congregated in the city centre where they plied their trade from houses established by foreign syndicates. There were bars everywhere and alcohol flowed freely.

The city was full of salesmen, with one-fifth of the population trying to sell something to somebody. Nearly a quarter of the city's traders were Asian, a worry to the white retailers who feared their competition and lower prices. Over 1,000 people worked in the printing trade, and a larger number, several thousand, in construction. Outside the city was an agricultural community which provided 'Johannesburgers' with dairy products, meat and vegetables. In other words, by the mid-1890s Johannesburg had all the characteristics of a modern city, for labour diversification and specialization were far advanced and wage labour was the norm.

The community in Johannesburg, and along the Rand generally, was multi-cultural, multinational, multilingual and multiracial. In and near the city about half the population was black, with most of the urban Africans having come from the Cape, Natal or another of the British territories. On the nearby mines and scattered out along the reef were nearly 100,000 black workers, mostly from Mozambique, but also from the colonies, Protectorates and Boer Republics. Living among the black community in Johannesburg were Coloureds from the Cape, and Asians, mainly from India via Natal. The white community was just as disparate. Two-fifths of the men and two-thirds of the women were African born, while about one-third of the men and a quarter of the women had come from Britain. British subjects, whether from Great Britain or from near or distant colonies, thus formed a large segment of the 'Uitlander' — the foreign — population. Other Uitlanders came from Holland and Germany, Eastern Europe, Italy and America.

Besides its racial and ethnic mix, the population was characterized by two other features: its youthfulness and its maleness. Nearly 80 per cent of the total population in and near Johannesburg was male. The gender imbalance was at its worst in the black community, where there was only one woman resident for every 25 men. In the white community, close to two-thirds of the people were male. Put another way, there were 1.8 men to every woman, though there was a higher ratio of men among whites of working ages, from 20 to 59 years. Among the Asians there were at least six men to every woman, though the Malay community from the nearby Cape was almost equally divided between men and women.

Johannesburg was also a city of the young. This is not to say that it was a city of children, for they made up only 15 per cent of the community. Instead, it was a city of young adults between 20 and 40 years old. About 80 per cent of the Africans were in this age group and about 50 per cent of the whites. The absence of children and the fact that there were relatively few women confirms views expressed in the 1890s that there was little family life on the Rand, especially among black miners.

The conjugal status of Randites supports this view. Of the total population in the city, two-thirds were single and there were three times as many single men as women. In the white community, two-thirds were single and there were about 3,000 more married men than married women in residence. In other words, there was an abundance of young bachelors and single women did not have to wait long before becoming brides. Further, many married men lived a bachelor existence with all the social consequences this entails. Without their wives or children, few men were likely to settle on the Rand — a political and economic problem which plagued those employers who wished to see a permanent skilled British labour force develop. The disproportionate number of men, the absence of wives and the youthfulness of the men, all help to explain why social reformers and, intermittently, the government were unable to stamp out prostitution and drunkenness.

From the first the city had segregated itself spatially in terms of race and class. For instance, Jeppestown became a centre for white working-class family life, with

A group of workers on the Ferreira mine near Johannesburg (*Africana Museum, Johannesburg*)

Underground mining was arduous and dangerous work (*Africana Museum, Johannesburg*)

Black mineworkers heading for the Rand at the turn of the century (*Africana Museum, Johannesburg*)

Johannesburg before the war was known for its busy cosmopolitan atmosphere (*Africana Museum, Johannesburg*)

A JEWISH PEDLAR AND MINE KAFFIRS

BLACK AND WHITE POLICE

AN INDIAN HAWKER AND A KAFFIR NURSE

An Englishman's view of the population of Johannesburg from *The Graphic*, 24 June 1899 (*Africana Museum, Johannesburg*)

The Jewish Helping Hand and Burial Society was asked by the Boers to operate an ambulance
service on the Rand during the war. This picture shows the 1898 committee (*The South African
Jewish Board of Deputies*)

Jews, mostly from eastern Europe and England, maintained their own traditions: a group of
Cheder boys shortly after the war (*The South African Jewish Board of Deputies*)

a relatively large number of women and children. Unlike areas south of the mines and in the west of the city, the children here attended school, indicating both that schools were nearby and that the parents had high aspirations. To the north was Doornfontein. Known as a 'classy' suburb, it housed the professional and commercial men of Johannesburg, many of whom were cultured western Jews. Not surprisingly, their children were present and they attended school. To the west, in Braamfontein, lived white wage earners with families and single white men, people with money enough to move up and out of the heat and away from the blowing dust. Meanwhile, to the north was Parktown, already known for its exclusivity and wealth.

Further west, in Burgersdorp, the Brickfields and Vrededorp, lived the working poor and unemployed, many of whom were landless burghers who had been encouraged to settle there when, as transport riders, they were made redundant by the arrival of the railway. Nearby were the Malay Camp and the 'Kaffir' and 'Coolie' locations, though racial groups tended to mix throughout the area. The close proximity of these 'dangerous classes' — just blocks away from the city centre — along with their crime and violence, vice and disease, worried the city fathers throughout these years. Their interracial living pattern was of further concern to those who sought to differentiate the white working class from the black.

On the mines living conditions were harsh and alienating, particularly for Africans who lived in large compounds on mining properties. Placed in bunk houses, which were overcrowded and cold in winter, where food was tedious and not overly abundant and where pulmonary disease was rife, Africans, deprived of family life, turned to alcohol and homosexual relations for comfort. Generally speaking, the blacks who lived and worked in town, residing in or near one of the locations or with a white employer, were better off than their compatriots on the mines.

White miners lived differently, though not in overwhelming comfort. Those who were single or without their wives lived with at least one other miner in sparsely-furnished rooms in boarding houses near the mines or in the city. Those who stayed on the mines were keenly aware of their isolation, with miles of empty veld and mine dumps separating them from friends on other mines. The few who lived with their families had accommodation in town or resided in roughly-constructed cabins on the mine properties.

Living among mine managers and engineers were wholesalers and building contractors, solicitors and businessmen. They came from similar backgrounds and shared the same visions, attended the same functions and joined the same clubs. Had they expected quick gains from a goldfield with a short life expectancy, they would have been more willing to maximize their short-term profits, cut their losses and move on. But these men, more so than working men who by and large remained transient, were in the process of putting down roots, going so far as to build houses in one of the new northern suburbs and to bring their families from Europe or America. Doctors, journalists, ministers, teachers and other aspiring and educated Uitlanders moved into nearby suburbs and began to think of Johannesburg as home.

From this class of men the reform movement grew. Psychologically incapable of taking a back seat to the Boers, whom they considered inadequate to the task of managing a modern city and industry, they were men who were trained to take command and who expected to be heard. Allied with Dr L.S. Jameson, their first violent attempt to force the Republican government to adapt to their presence had failed. Thereafter, many of the reformers had left the country; others were banished. But many stayed on in Johannesburg, promising Kruger that they would not 'meddle' in Republican politics for three years — a period which was to expire at the end of May 1899. In the intervening years, tension escalated as Kruger's new legislation, his actions and intransigence antagonized the reformers. More importantly, the economic situation had worsened once again — a state of affairs blamed on the Boers. But in May 1897, with the arrival of Sir Alfred Milner as British high commissioner at the Cape, the reformers' prayers were answered.

An ardent imperialist with fine credentials, including three years in the Egyptian administration and good connections in London, Milner was a logical choice for the post. A bachelor with a private life he kept hidden and a bureaucrat rather than a politician, he arrived in South Africa unencumbered by political loyalties or family baggage. Constitutionally inclined to be autocratic — a 'natural dictator', according to Julian Amery — he was none the less a good administrator with a fine and logical mind. During his eight years in South Africa, his major shortcoming was his inability to recognize the validity of arguments posed by people with whom he disagreed. From the beginning of the war, for instance, his policies at the Cape were marred by his inability to get along with W. P. Schreiner; nor later did he work well with General Lord Kitchener.[5] On the Rand, he demonstrated little sympathy for the working man, preferring to have as companions and allies and, more dangerously, as advisers, men whose class backgrounds, whose education and political leanings were much like his own. To make matters worse, these men, not unnaturally, had a tendency to tell the high commissioner what he wanted to hear. By 1905 this style of government would spell disaster for 'Milnerism', for his inability to modify his policies to take into account the fears, needs and desires of his opponents brought an end to his dream of British South Africa.

The views that were to serve as a backdrop to his policies and actions during the years of war and peace were well developed within a year of his arrival at the Cape. Basically he saw 'two wholly antagonistic systems' operating in southern Africa: the Boers' 'mediaeval race oligarchy' and the British population's 'modern industrial state'. More to the point, he thought these inherent differences had led to political antagonisms which could be eliminated only by reform within the South African Republic or by war. As he saw little chance of reform, war seemed inevitable. What he wanted, then, was to 'work up a crisis' in order to mould public and political opinion in Britain and the colonies.[6] A man in search of an issue and an aggrieved community needing a spokesman: Milner and the Uitlander reformers were made for one another.

While the Uitlander élite looked to Milner for support, the more class-conscious members of the white working class looked to President Kruger. The threat they perceived came not from Pretoria, but from the Randlords, the industrialists who sought to replace them with cheaper black labour, to lower wages and impose new conditions unilaterally. While Milner and his reformers aimed to create a new society run by the Randlords, the radical working class spoke against it. Working men from all over the world, men with previous experience of trade unions and the machinations of mining capitalists, brought their expertise, suspicions and fears to the Rand. They organized, went on strike, and, over the years, turned to Pretoria for protection against the industrialists and the encroachment of

Africans. When the time came to support the Republic with arms, some of the Uitlanders, even British miners, were willing to join the commandos. Others, unwilling to fight, remained on the Rand to dig gold for the Boers, gold which enabled Pretoria to pursue its war.

Although the politicized Uitlander community became polarized as war approached, the mass of people remained apathetic and ambivalent. The very nature of their lives and their conditions of labour — their mobility, rootlessness and lack of family life — meant that few concerned themselves with local social and political reform. Instead, they were concerned almost solely with their safety and with earning a living. While some may have gone so far as to sign a petition or two, or even to attend a meeting or a rally out of curiosity or boredom, they were neither Pro-Boer nor Jingoistic. Most of them, uninterested in Kruger's franchise, voted with their feet and left for the coast.

When they returned two or three years later, a new society was in the making — an expansive, rational and efficient society and one which would influence deeply the development of the whole of southern Africa throughout the twentieth century. Racialism, not permitted to die with the old way of life, was given new meaning in the mines, the factories and homes of the Rand. The partnership forged between the reformers and Milner before the war, and fostered and extended during it, was to blossom afterwards. The war, with its destruction of the old order, prepared the way for a new social and political system which would foster the growth of industrial capitalism. It prepared the way for the creation of a very special sort of society: the unique society which characterizes the Republic of South Africa today.

Notes

1. From a popular song, cited in MS/JPL/van der Horst, p. 18.
2. Butler 1911, p. 14.
3. De Kock 1924, pp. 115, 244—5; Kubicek 1979, pp. 23, 43—5; Katzen 1964, pp. 25, 44, 64—5; Richardson and van-Helten 1980, pp. 23—8.
4. The following discussion draws upon data in OP/JHB/15 July 1896.
5. Nimocks 1968, p. 12 (citing Amery); see also Galbraith 1983, pp. 68—84.
6. Nimocks 1968, p. 18; and see Pakenham 1979, chs 1—9.

One

An Illusion of Unity

The first casualty when war comes is truth.
Hiram Johnson

In the late afternoon on a winter's day in early August 1899, angry white artisans on the Robinson Deep gold mine, just to the south of Johannesburg, laid down their tools. Only 150 men were involved in the dispute, which lasted just two days, but the strike was to bring into focus a number of issues important to the white community on the Rand prior to the outbreak of war.

In an attempt to bring the hours of his workers into line with those of other artisans in the area, the manager of the Robinson Deep had posted a notice declaring that, as of the following morning, artisans would work ten instead of the normal nine hours a day. The news spread quickly and the men hurriedly met to choose a delegation to see the manager. Faced with the men's refusal to abide by the new regulations, the manager threatened to fill any 'vacancies' the following morning and ordered those who refused to return to work to vacate their cottages on the mine. The men were angry, not just with the longer hours, but because of the suddenness and temerity with which they had been announced. At the recreation hall the following morning, their anger led to the articulation of further grievances: 7s 6d was being deducted from their monthly wages 'merely for a doctor's attendance and the right to put a man in a bed at the Hospital'. Carpenters complained that their wages were lower than those paid to other artisans, and all felt that the management had tricked them into signing agreements which permitted it to eject workers from their cottages with only 24 hours' notice and with no recourse to the law.

Those who decided to fight stood firm, choosing to ignore the manager's threats and refusing to leave their homes. Soon the workers' delegation visited the firemen and underground miners, to seek their support, as well as that of the engine drivers, who during any strike had the ability to close down a mine by halting the trams which carried men and ore. At a mass meeting the following evening, Rand workers were warned to look to the Simmer & Jack Mine — known locally as the 'white compound' because of the restrictions imposed on white workers there — because that was what was in store for them: the management of the Robinson Deep was trying to create the Rand's second white compound.[1]

The strike on the Robinson Deep was the third along the reef in as many months. This spate of labour unrest followed more than a year of relative industrial peace, a peace which had resulted not from good conditions or amicable industrial relations, but because workers had had to accept worsening conditions to keep their jobs in a period of economic depression. By the time of the Robinson Deep strike, this depression was already three years old. Beginning soon after the Jameson Raid, it deepened in 1897/8 and only started to lift in 1899, when the escalation of political tension leading to war ended any hope of economic recovery.

The depression was uneven and hit various economic sectors differently. For instance, while the gold-mining industry had record production figures, in the city the property market stagnated as sales and new construction ceased. Property speculators maintained a constant vigil for forced sales at bargain prices, but were disappointed as there were few. Instead, when sales were advertised, high prices were asked and no buyers appeared. In other words, first-rate property in the central city and middle-class suburbs retained its value as owners chose to wait rather than sell. On the other hand, as unemployment climbed and emigration increased, rents fell as the number of vacant properties rose. With this collapse in the property market, carpenters, masons and others in the building trades were let go, while those lucky enough to keep work had little choice but to accept lower wages.

Similarly, business was reportedly 'very dull' and commerce generally characterized by 'falling returns, restricted business and reduced establishments'. The only 'brisk' trade was in used furniture, as people sold up before leaving. Credit tightened for those who remained, for there was a marked increase in the number of 'levanting debtors' and tenants 'flitting the moon'. Not surprisingly, there was a rise in the number of small business insolvencies. Still, there was no financial panic.

The rise in unemployment was initially offset by an increase in the number of workers leaving the Rand. By May 1897 the exodus had taken on political connotations, for the numbers departing were now sufficiently high to concern the Uitlander reformers. They worried about the shift in political power in the South African Republic that might result from the departure of so many 'better-class British working men'.[2] Those leaving spread out across southern Africa. For instance, the number of unemployed in Bulawayo rose as Randites arrived seeking work. Building artisans had better luck at the coast, particularly in Durban and Port Elizabeth, where a building boom was under way. Unfortunately for those who went to the Cape, a four-year building boom was just drawing to a close and a situation similar to that in Johannesburg was developing there.[3]

For those who stayed in Johannesburg conditions continued to worsen. Burghers and Coloureds, who dominated taxi-driving, found their wages falling as the number of fares declined. Similarly, hairdressers lost their jobs as custom dropped off. Unemployed dressmakers found work by replacing men in the 'sweating trades', while unionized tailors, who went on strike in late 1897 in an effort to maintain their wage level, were replaced by men or women, union or non-union, in fact by anyone willing to accept the rate of pay on offer.

White workers in other sectors faced not only lower wages, but an increase in non-union and non-white competition as employers hired cheaper non-white labour to cut costs. In bakeries, for instance, blacks were hired as whites were dismissed, a state of affairs which angered unemployed whites. In mid-1898 one man reported that, 'in many bakeries Kafirs are used for mixing dough, whereas whites are working at the oven and baking bread. The Kafirs work cheaper and consequently are liked by the "bosses". The natural consequence is that many white people are out of work and on the point of starvation'. And again in December 1898:

> I would like to draw your attention to the kaffirs who are employed in bakeries. In some of them they not only help at the table to form the bread, but are employed to make the dough . . . and it is only a case of cheap labour. . . . If through your valuable paper you can put a stop to this kind of kaffir labour, you could earn the thanks of the public as well as the bakers, journeymen, many of whom are out of work.

Similarly, hotel employees who were threatened by unemployment and non-white competition joined the local International Hotel Employees' Society, which championed the cause of white protection: 'an appeal [is made] to hotel proprietors and the general public to stand by the white servants of the Rand in preference to the black'.[4] The depression, therefore, had the result of deepening racialism and fostering class conflict, as employers were criticized for taking advantage of the situation by lowering wages, lengthening hours and hiring non-whites, who were then blamed for the rising rate of unemployment.

On the mines the impact of the depression was uneven. For instance, at the same time as the industrialists were complaining to Kruger that his economic policy was ruining them, they were being embarrassed by record profits. Still, a number of marginal mines did close, putting people out of work. And, because this was the period when deep-level mines were leaving the development and entering the production phase, some workers (such as carpenters, fitters, painters and masons) lost their jobs while men concerned with production (assayers, miners, amalgamators and cyaniders) were hired.[5] This came as a double blow to artisans in the building trades, who had left the reef to find that there was no work in the city either.

Mine-workers who kept their jobs found their wages under attack by managements intent on reducing working costs. In 1897 white miners, unwilling to see their wages lowered as those of black miners had been in this period, formed the Witwatersrand Mine Workers' Union, and on a number of occasions went on strike to halt what they viewed as the owners' organized attempt to reduce wages from Randfontein to Boksburg. Unionized workers also fought against managements that tried to raise productivity without increasing wages. For instance, in 1897 they opposed the 'two machine movement' whereby, rather than run one drill with the aid of a black 'helper', white miners were asked to supervise two black drillmen and their machines and, in one instance, four. This was only the beginning of a long-term struggle against deskilling in the industry, i.e. 'the reorganization and socialization of labour processes involving the transfer of productive functions from white artisans to socialized groups of African direct producers'.[6]

In 1907, managements' attempts to introduce three, instead of the then customary two, machine drills led to a strike in which unionized workers expressed their belief that the practice was being initiated by owners in a deliberate attempt to reduce the number of skilled, unionized whites in mining, by dividing up and reallocating tasks to semi-skilled blacks and Chinese, supervised by what unionists saw as an under-skilled white (often Afrikaner) work-force. While trade unionists before the war were not unaware of the long-term implications of a change in labour use, they were more concerned with being paid an additional wage for any additional work. Failing that, they wanted a return to the one-man, one-machine system, which they thought was 'more agreeable to the times, for . . . twice as many men were employed'.[7] Such reasoning — then or later — found little support among owners who were trying to cut working costs while exploiting low-grade ore at increasingly deep levels. Thus, when the time was ripe after the war, they once again pursued the two-, three- and even ten-machine movement.

As the depression deepened in 1897/8, there was very little industrial unrest because workers were willing to accept any wages and conditions on offer. For this reason the Robinson Deep Strike was important — it was one of several in a short space of time to mark the revitalization of the white labour movement. It was also important because, in this period of rising political tension, it took on political overtones — it was a strike about hours, which was an issue that had recently been politicized by radical white workers on the Rand. In fact, in these months before the war, a campaign for the eight-hour workday was successfully waged by the Randites' own International Independent Labour Party (IILP), an organization with its roots in the radical Uitlander working class.

A year before the Robinson Deep strike, an engine driver representing his local union at the Typographical Society banquet rose to toast the Kruger regime: 'there is no Government on the face of this earth', he stated, that is 'more ready to give working men their due than the Transvaal [i.e. the Republican] Government'.[8] This view was widely held by white working men on the Rand, for they felt they could generally count on Pretoria to protect them from their bosses' outrageous demands and from cheap labour competition. They had good reason to believe this, for over the years the Kruger government's policies benefited white labour. For instance, the local typographical union had praised the government for imposing a 100 per cent duty on all imported printed matter and stationery. During early franchise negotiations Kruger had supported labour's demand for a secret ballot, just as he had spoken against the importation of cheaper white labour from overseas. Mine-workers especially favoured the government's stance against the introduction of white compounds and independent mine police in the early 1890s. A few years later the engine drivers, with the support of the Boer government, waged a successful battle against the owners who wanted to certify blacks as skilled engine drivers.[9]

For these and other instances of support, white workers expressed their gratitude. In 1895, in a period when Eckstein's *South African Mining Journal* was on the offensive against white labour, the connection between race, class and politics was well made by an articulate 'stoper'. The Boer government, he stated, was well aware of the:

> difference between the Kaffir and his white brother . . . for which they have the support of all working men on the Rand, especially the white miner. I make no doubt the miner would have been working for starvation wages long before this if the capitalists of Johannesburg had their own will. I make no doubt that the Kaffir would have been tried in the place of white men long ago if it had not been for the timely action of the Government in making it impossible for them to hold responsible positions.[10]

Later, during the depression, white workers accused the Randlords of 'engineering' the economic slump in order to 'squeeze out' competitors and to lower white wages.[11] Thus, by the end of the decade, white labour had several years' experience of Boer support and had had time to develop a healthy distrust of the industrialists. These views took concrete form in mid-1899 with the creation of the Randites' own labour party.

The IILP was launched on 8 May by a small group of white working men. The meeting was chaired by James T. Bain, an outspoken Scots engineer and publisher who had experience organizing labour at the Cape and in Johannesburg, but who was better known on the Rand for his outspokenly anti-imperialist stance at the time of the Jameson Raid. Within a few days a mass meeting was held, where it was agreed to form an 'association to protect the interests of workmen on the Witwatersrand'. Its goals, which reflected a blend of socialist idealism and local realities, were soon set: the 'equitable distribution of wealth' and the elevation of the 'moral and intellectual standard' of its members. It opposed any special privilege, supported a Republican form of government and advocated some form of local self-government for the Rand. It sought the nationalization of property (including the mines), the abolition of monopoly concessionaire companies and public ownership and control of all public works, many of which were then under the control of monopoly companies.

The IILP hoped to achieve its immediate aims through the Republican legislature, the Volksraad, and by methods which sought to improve the conditions of labour: the eight-hour workday, a trade-union rate of wages all round, abolition of all unnecessary Sunday labour on the mines, and the prohibition of the importation of contract labour. As nineteenth-century socialists they wanted the vote for all men, without property or religious qualifications, but they were clearly tainted by their years in southern Africa in that they wished to see the Republic maintained as a 'white man's country'. Equality was to be established between worker and boss, Uitlander and Boer, but not between men and women, blacks and whites.

From its inception, the party was plagued by leadership struggles, personality conflicts, ideological rifts and attacks by rowdies suspected of working for local middle-class opponents of the movement. Internal divisions increased as moderate labour leaders challenged the views of socialist speakers; such dissidents were removed from the party leadership by radicals. Hecklers attended meetings and successfully disrupted them until they were thrown out by the party faithful who could no longer tolerate their interruptions. It is fairly clear that external opposition was generated more by the party's pro-Boer and anti-Randlord stance than by its nominally socialist position and, not surprisingly, it was only after Bain was driven from the leadership by men opposed to his vociferous anti-imperialism that the party could settle down and get some of its more important work done.

The movement for the eight-hour workday mushroomed with the Robinson Deep strike, though the desire for shorter working hours had a wide appeal. (The average workday on the mines was about ten hours and, in the city, still longer.) From its inception the IILP had pushed for an eight-hour day, but was in no position to turn this into an issue until the strike erupted and until Bain resigned. Soon the movement gained the support of the Volksraad representatives, Ben Viljoen and S. Tosen, the latter placing the Bill before the House of Assembly the month before the war began. Had the war not intervened, it may well have become law. In any case, in the years following Kruger's departure, workers used this as an example of how the regime remained the friend of the white working class until the very end.[12]

The rise in white labour unrest in mid-1899 paralleled the deepening political crisis. Not surprisingly, because the reformers were anxious to maintain an illusion of unity among Uitlanders in this period when Milner was pressing Kruger for reforms in their name, events at the Robinson Deep took on political connotations. The local branch of the largely middle-class Uitlander organization, the South African League (SAL), took the very perverse step of denouncing the management of the Robinson Deep and labelling its actions 'high-handed'. The SAL was posing as the workers' friend, a position that only made sense in the context of the political developments on the Rand in these months.

After the Jameson Raid in late 1895, any Uitlander conspirators remaining in the Republic were barred from internal political activity for a period of three years from their sentence, which expired at the end of May 1899. This is not to say that they were inactive, nor to suggest that these men were not secretly conspiring to reform (at best) or overthrow the Kruger government. In fact in these years they formed two organizations which, under Milner's orchestration, led the final assault on the Republic. The first, the SAL, had originated in the Cape as the Loyal Colonial League shortly after the Raid. While it claimed to seek to 'promote good government and amicable relations between the various States and Colonies in South Africa', everywhere it was instrumental in fostering nationalistic divisions within the region.[13]

The local SAL was basically a public-relations organization, generating and distributing information on Rand affairs. Its everyday work consisted of collecting material on Pretoria's actions and on the local economic and political situation and transmitting it to the Cape and Natal, where SAL members and politicians could make use of it. At the same time, it tried to keep the Imperial government and British public appraised of the latest Uitlander 'grievances', while keeping all informed of the needs of the gold-mining industry which, according to the SAL, was the 'axle on which the whole wheel of South Africa's material progress revolved'. It was also involved in municipal affairs, seeking to influence the election of town councillors by working for those in whom it had confidence, and pressuring 'tradespeople' by organizing boycotts of shops owned by those whose views differed from the SAL's.[14]

As for the SAL's work on the Rand, its main goal was to mobilize support for Milner in his struggle with Kruger. This took the form of organizing public meetings and demonstrations, providing speakers and writing articles and letters for the local jingoist press. Its centralized structure was under the firm control of such professional men as Wilfred Wybergh, a mining engineer employed by Consolidated Gold Fields until 1899; J. Douglas Forster, a local attorney; and Clem Webb, a solicitor, stockbroker and labour contractor. The control of the SAL by men such as these ensured that little power devolved to the outlying sections and that major decisions were taken only in the central office. For example, they would cancel section meetings if they thought members might damage Milner's bargaining position with ill-considered utterances. The combination of centralized control and continuity of leadership ensured that the SAL was divided neither in policy nor action in the months leading to war.[15]

The second reform organization of these years, the Uitlander Council (UC), represented the interests of Rand capitalists and originated with J. P. Fitzpatrick, though Milner was well-informed of its inception. In fact, in May 1899, before it took public form, the British vice-consul at Johannesburg, J. Emrys Evans, informed the high commissioner that it would soon be started and that it would be composed of men 'who know what they are about and what is wanted'. In the meantime, according to Milner's imperial secretary, George Fiddes, the 'best men' stayed busy, though, as he explained to Milner, 'what they do — and they do a good deal *sub rosa* — is done with a rope around their necks'.[16]

The UC went public in June 1899 when over 600 'unemployed men' met to choose 24 delegates who were supposed to deliberate on 'proposals for the redress of grievances'.[17] This is not to say that the mass of Johannesburgers, or even those in attendance, had much to do with formulating UC policy. The 'programme to be followed' was 'fixed' and certain men, 'who were not under the government's ban on political activity' arising from the Jameson Raid sentences, had already been 'set to work', so that when the 'leading men' were free to pursue their activities publicly, they could go directly into 'harness'. Since it was important to make it appear that the organization was created by the mass of Uitlanders, delegates had to be chosen from the Uitlander unemployed. Even so, a close look at the list of delegates shows that 15 of the 24 selected that day were already seated on the platform. More importantly, a week later men well-known in reformer circles were appointed to the more prominent UC posts. William Hosken, a major wholesaler in the city, chairman of the Chamber of Commerce and a Jameson Raid conspirator, was appointed the UC's chairman. William St John Carr, another conspirator, and Thomas Dodd, secretary of the Transvaal branch of the SAL, became honorary secretaries, while the confectioner and early reformer, John W. Quinn, took the post of honorary treasurer. Soon a 'special' sub-committee was appointed to draft a reply to Kruger's latest franchise proposals — a sub-committee formed not by the unemployed Uitlander masses, but by Henry Hull, a prominent local attorney and former member of the Reform Committee; J. Douglas Forster of the SAL; and William Dalrymple, already experienced in franchise negotiations. All of these men were as likely as any in Johannesburg to know just 'what was wanted'.[18]

While the SAL acted to mobilize mass sentiment and to generate grist for Milner's political mill, the UC served the high commissioner by representing that portion of the Uitlander community he wished to hear. Its opinions were sought on various important issues and the continual pressure it placed on local British government representatives encouraged the imperial government to take a resolute stand with Kruger. Both organizations sought to raise political consciousness locally — a difficult task at the best of times — but their main aim was to create the impression in Britain and the colonies that the Rand's foreign population was united in its opposition to Kruger. Divisions, such as those along class lines which became startlingly and embarrassingly evident during a strike, could not be tolerated. This, then, explains why the SAL publicly criticized the management of the Robinson Deep during the strike of August 1899 — just weeks after the aborted Bloemfontein conference. In less emotive times the SAL would not have addressed the issue of workers' hours at all and would certainly not have championed any strikers' cause.

Instead, the reformers were preoccupied with their own grievances — a set of issues that mostly reflected the concerns of foreigners who wanted to take up permanent residence in the Republic. While a few of these famous 'Uitlander grievances' concerned the mass of residents, most dealt with issues of interest only to a minority of Randites. None the less, they were presented in Britain by Milner and his subordinates (and by Rand commentators) as though they represented the concerns of the majority of Uitlanders on the Rand.

Basically, there were two types of grievances. The first dealt with economic issues and most of these were aired at the 1897 Industrial Commission which Kruger set up in Johannesburg at the behest of the industrialists. During these months of depression, the government was asked to change its economic policy (and to some extent its system of government) to meet the needs of the mining industry. This, in turn, was to have made the general Republican economy more prosperous. Of specific concern to the industrial and commercial capitalists were the abolition of the concessions system (especially as it affected transport and dynamite costs) and the elimination of duties on food and heavy machinery. Issues such as the price of dynamite had little meaning for ordinary folk until the reformers explained how the high input costs put pressure on the mining companies to reduce working costs (by, for example, lowering wages) or to cease work altogether.

During the Industrial Commission's hearings, as several times before during the industry's ten years of existence, the problem of maintaining a dependable supply of cheap black labour was raised. In late 1896 the industry had reduced black wages and this had resulted in so significant an exodus of African workers that it was not until March the following year that the supply was again deemed to be adequate. In April the mining companies again lowered black wages, with the same consequences as before. It was in the midst of this self-imposed labour shortage that the mining industry asked the government to enact stronger pass laws and to enforce them more rigorously. Also aimed at reducing 'desertion' was its insistence that the government eliminate labour 'touts' who helped blacks, who were dissatisfied with low wage levels, find work on other mines for higher rates of pay. In an effort to raise productivity, the owners sought to contain the flow of illicit liquor consumed by Africans. The moralists on the Rand made common cause with them on this issue, though few others in the Uitlander population had much interest in the topic.

Another set of grievances was more socio-political in nature. Of primary concern to the reformers were the Aliens Expulsion Act and the Immigration Act, which came into effect with the new year of 1897. Both these laws were part of Kruger's effort to bar entry to 'undesirables' (i.e. the destitute, criminals, excess labourers and Indians) and to remove them from the Republic. The new laws were also a threat to any potentially hostile aliens, taking effect as they did only a year after the Jameson Raid. Not surprisingly the SAL took exception to the legislation, agreeing with the colonial secretary, Joseph Chamberlain, that it contravened the London Convention. But this line of reasoning carried little weight with the basically apolitical Randites and the SAL instead pursued a racist argument in public. Now that Uitlanders had to register, they were being taunted by Africans and thus 'lowered . . . in the eyes of Kaffir workmen' for being forced to 'carry a pass'. When pressed by Chamberlain, Kruger repealed the Immigration Act and suspended the Aliens Expulsion Act for a year. The president claimed that he did so not because he was bowing to the wishes of any 'suzerain power', as the reformers claimed, but because neighbouring states were upset because the laws made them the 'dumping ground' of the Republic.[20]

The reformers included in their list of grievances the maltreatment of Asians and the commandeering of Coloureds by the Republican government. Their concern for the non-white community was, however, totally out of character and the grievance wholly specious. On the Rand, as elsewhere in southern Africa, racialism influenced every aspect of daily life. Employment, social mores, residence and the full range of social intercourse were dictated by race. When custom was not strong enough to maintain control over the behaviour of non-whites, legislation was used. Throughout the 1890s the legislative process had been utilized to advance white job protection, to maintain black labour supplies and to restrict non-white residential expansion. Uitlander merchants, opposed to the 'ever growing cut-throat competition springing up in all directions among Indian traders', were in full agreement with the ruling in August 1898 upholding Republican Law 3 (1895) and the 'Bloemfontein Award', which, together, meant that Asians were restricted to residence inside designated locations and that Indian merchants were confined to locations for the purposes of trade.[21]

If the Republican authorities' maltreatment of Indians (as British subjects) was to be included among the grievances, Milner first had to muzzle the Johannesburg racists. In early 1899 he sent his secretary Fiddes to do just that. While on the Rand Fiddes made a point of dining with the leading Uitlanders, putting them in 'good humour' by expressing his sympathetic understanding of their concerns. Then, as he later explained to Milner, he turned to the issue of Asians:

> I put the question: 'As regards Indians and Cape Boys. I know you don't love them much, and I know that there is something to be said on your side which I am sure HMG would take into account if properly approached. But the T.V. [Transvaal] don't approach us properly. I may tell you in strict confidence (I always like to tell people open secrets in strict confidence) that at the moment this question might assume a serious shape. Now if HMG made up their minds that it was necessary to take a firm stand on it, would Johannesburg be likely to take up a hostile or embarrassing attitude on it?

Fiddes's dinner companions 'simply chorused': 'Certainly not. Any stick is good enough to beat Paul Kruger with, and though we don't love the Indian, we wouldn't say a word, and we would use our influence for all it's worth, to prevent others from saying a word against you.'[22]

During his visit to Johannesburg the imperial secretary also managed to get W. F. Monypenny and R. J. Pakeman, editors of the jingoist *Star* and *Transvaal Leader* respectively, to 'strike the right note'. J. Percy Fitzpatrick (of Ecksteins and a leading figure in the reform movement) agreed with this approach and he and Fiddes between them were to ensure that the reformers supported Milner in his handling of the issue of rights for non-white British subjects.[23] In this manner, Republican race relations joined the growing list of Uitlander grievances.

While the elimination of non-white oppression had little meaning for most residents, the problem of educating Uitlander children did. Yet clearly even this issue held the interest of only a minority of Uitlanders — those who were committed to staying in the Republic and had children in residence. The reformers argued that the Republic's educational policy aimed to 'dutchify' their children, with the result that parents wanted not only more schools but schools taught in the English medium. Earlier the Rand reformers had created a 'Council of Education', which raised about £10,000 to fund a few new Uitlander schools. By late 1898 the Council was moribund and Fitzpatrick had to appeal to the 'rich men' of the Chamber of Mines for help: while 'fortune after fortune is made out of the place . . . nothing worth speaking of is put back except reinvestment for bigger profit'. His appeal worked and by the time the war began, over £100,000 had been raised and the invigorated Council had begun to draw up plans and select sites for 20 new schools.[24]

While it is true that more schools were needed in Johannesburg and the other towns along the reef, it is untrue that the government, in the years immediately before the war, was trying to turn the Uitlander children into 'Afrikanders'. As Hugh Evans, the Welsh vice-principal of a local government school, stated in 1899, there is no 'supplanting of the English language . . . at any . . . State school for English-speaking children'. At about the same time the Wesleyans of Clifton (Braamfontein) expressed their satisfaction with Pretoria's educational policy and accepted government assistance for their school. But the reformers, anxious to keep the educational issue alive, were upset by Evans and the Wesleyans' remarks and they, along with Milner, made sure that their views only reached the Colonial Office accompanied by the reformers' disclaimers.[25]

Yet another issue championed by those seeking social change was police reform. Local anxiety centred on the lax enforcement of several laws, the liquor, gold-theft and morality laws among them. Certainly there was reason for concern, for prostitution and the white slave trade were rife, and Johannesburg was notoriously oversupplied with alcohol. But because it was a city that spawned fast living, a city where people fell easily into the ways of drinking, gambling and whoring, any police force would have had difficulty dealing with the cosmopolitan, footloose and free-wheeling population. Further, the South African Republican Police, the 'Zarps', were poorly paid and easily tempted by the money to be made by assisting the scoundrels. The liquor, gold-theft and prostitution scandals that rocked the city in 1897/8 focused attention on the Zarps and, because corruption was widespread and crime prevalent, especially as the numbers of burglaries rose along with unemployment, any issue that dealt with police inefficiency had the potential of gaining mass support. It is no surprise then that an incident such as the 'Edgar affair' could be used by the reformers to whip up Uitlander outrage.

Coming home drunk on a Sunday evening before Christmas, the English-born boilermaker, Tom Jackson Edgar, got into a fight with another Uitlander and knocked him unconscious. Edgar ran home and hid and when the Zarp, Barend Stephanus Jones, arrived on the doorstep, he was refused entry by Edgar's wife. Without a warrant, Jones broke down the door, but was struck by a metal-tipped stick, wielded by Edgar. Jones then shot and killed the Uitlander. Soon the Zarp, Jones, was arrested for murder, but the charge was reduced to culpable homicide and he was freed on bail. In response to the orchestrated public outcry, he was rearrested for murder, but again the charge was reduced. Finally, in February 1899, Jones was acquitted by a jury, with the young Republican judge, Antonie Kock, praising the policeman for having done his duty. The prescient public prosecutor, F. R. M. Cleaver, was correct in his assessment of the verdict: 'we have not heard the last of this', he said. 'The Judge has knocked a big nail into our coffin today'.

While really quite a tawdry affair, it is from such incidents that history is made. The reformers, led by Hosken, Wybergh, Forster, Webb and several others, organized a mass meeting at which they presented J. Emrys Evans with a petition asking for imperial government protection. Unfortunately for the reformers, Milner was not in residence at the Cape. In his stead was General Sir William Butler, commander of the British garrison. Unsympathetic to the methods used by the reformers for generating support for the Uitlander cause, Butler refused to take the petition seriously. The Edgar agitation, he wrote, was 'largely artificial' and 'being worked by a combination in which the action of the Press and the South African League could scarcely be distinguished from each other'.[26] Upon his return Milner tried to rectify the impression Butler had made at the Colonial Office by asserting that the killing of Edgar touched a 'particularly sore place' because there is no grievance that 'rankles more in the breasts of the mass of the Uitlander population than the conduct of the police'.[27]

Certainly there was ample reason for complaining about the Zarps, but it was not as though the situation in Johannesburg had been ignored by Pretoria. Indeed, the Republican government was anxious to rid itself of the corrupt force and, in mid-1898, sent the state attorney, Jan C. Smuts, to lead the effort to clear the 'stables' at Johannesburg. Within a year the young attorney had made a good start, with 'reliable, efficient and uncorrupt officers at the head of the Zarp' in Johannesburg.[28] While there is still reason to believe that the police force was less than professional and that abuses remained, it is clear that the acting high commissioner had been right: the 'Edgar Affair' was being 'worked' by the reformers for their own ends.[29]

During the three years before the war the focus of the reformers' agitation shifted. Whereas in 1897 their emphasis had been on economic issues, as outlined at the Industrial Commission, as their frustration increased they began to concentrate on acquiring the vote, which they considered would enable them to resolve all their other problems. While Milner was eventually able to convince most of the outside world — or that part of it that mattered — that the Uitlanders wanted the vote, close observers were not all that certain that they did. Lionel Phillips, a leader of the reform movement who was banished from the Republic in 1897, had noted earlier, for instance, that 'not many people give a fig about it'.[30] There were several reasons why this was the case.

First was the fact that the Uitlanders were, by and large, more interested in 'making more money than ever before in any other country'.[31] Secondly, having left their famililes at home, few wanted to stay in the Republic for any length of time and were therefore unwilling to abandon their British citizenship to acquire the burghers' franchise. The reformers had a difficult time dealing with this concern, though the British representative in Pretoria, Conyngham Greene, held out the false hope that the Republican law might be modified so that those who wanted to become burghers could do so without relinquishing their British citizenship.[32]

Finally, there were those among the white working class who opposed the enfranchisement of Uitlanders because they feared the creation of a new society where the Randlords would rule. One of them explained:

As regards the franchise, how many men, if full burgher rights were conceded, would accept? Not one in a thousand with their own free will, but the big [mining] houses would compel each and everyone to register, and so enable them (the capitalists) to run the men they wish for the constituency and put pressure upon all hands in their employ to support their candidate. Of course, the men are supposed to vote freely, *but* — and a big but — if there was any opposition to their views the result would be 'voetsac'.[33]

Articulate workmen provided examples of places where situations such as this had already developed: in that 'web of capitalistic vampires . . . that godforsaken Bulawayo' said one, in Broken Hill, Australia, where men were 'sounded individually', said another. Their fear, then, was that the end result of the reformers' agitation would be the fall of the Republic into the 'hands of the capitalist to be used for himself as against us'.[34]

This is not to deny that some (perhaps quite a number) of Uitlanders wanted the

NOTICE.

BRITISH SUBJECTS resident on the Witwatersrand Goldfields

ARE HEREBY NOTIFIED that a

Representation

is to be publicly made to the BRITISH VICE-CONSUL in connection with the SHOOTING of the deceased

TOM JACKSON EDGAR (a British Subject)

by Police Constable Barend Stephanus Jones; the subsequent reduction of the charge against the Policeman from that of Murder to one of Culpable Homicide before the holding of any preliminary examination; and his ultimate liberation on bail totally inadequate to the gravity of the charge against him.

All British Subjects prepared to take part in this Representation are hereby requested to assemble at the

MARKET SQUARE,
— ON —
Saturday Afternoon

NEXT, AT 3·30 p.m. SHARP.

[It is hoped, in order to make the REPRESENTATION as impressive as possible, that a large number of British Subjects will attend.]

A notice urging Rand residents to attend the Edgar Demonstration, which marked a turning point in the pre-war agitation (*Africana Museum, Johannesburg*)

Lord Milner (*With the Flag to Pretoria*, p. 15)

President Kruger, painted by E. Rinaldi (*Africana Museum, Johannesburg*)

In 1899 there were several demonstrations by residents of Johannesburg. This one is outside the British Consulate on Commissioner Street (*Africana Museum, Johannesburg*)

Samuel Evans, in a photograph taken after the war, was central to the reconstruction of Johannesburg during the war period (*Africana Museum, Johannesburg*)

Robert Pakeman, editor of *Transvaal Leader*, was arrested shortly before the war for his jingoist writings (*Africana Museum, Johannesburg*)

Wilfred Wybergh, mining engineer, from a picture in *The African Review*, vol. 21, October—December 1899 (*Africana Museum, Johannesburg*)

J. P. Fitzpatrick took a leading role in the agitation which led to the war, and in the reconstruction of the Transvaal after it (*Africana Museum, Johannesburg*)

William Hosken, 'merchant', from a picture in
The African Review, vol. 21,
October—December 1899

J. Douglas Forster, lawyer, from a picture in
The African Review, vol. 21,
October—December 1899

Leading uitlander agitators were generally businessmen or lawyers, engineers or journalists.
From pictures in *The African Review*, vol. 21, October—December 1899.

Clem D. Webb, solicitor, from a picture in *The
African Review*, vol. 21, October—December
1899

Thomas R. Dodd, mining engineer, from a
picture in *The African Review*, vol. 21,
October—December 1899

vote. But who were these people? Primarily they were men who intended to settle in the Republic, for it had already been established that the city would flourish as the Rand mines had some years to run. Similarly, men who wanted the vote were those who took an interest in social reform, in building a society fit for their children. Property owners, merchants, moralists and industrialists, they all wanted the vote as a guarantee that the Volksraad would consider their grievances.

But after June 1899 the reformers came to realize that the vote would not be enough to ensure a change in the political economy of the Republic: if the Uitlanders were enfranchised, they would still constitute a minority. Hence they would still face the 'same corrupt administration as before, with this disadvantage, that [the Uitlanders could] no longer invoke the assistance of the imperial Government'.[35] This marked an important change in the reformers' position. Where once they had concerned themselves with a variety of issues, from the price of dynamite to Uitlander education, they began to focus on the franchise.[36] After the failure of the Bloemfontein conference in June, they were no longer willing to accept solely the vote. Now, as Kruger well knew, they wanted the country.

Nevertheless, in August Kruger tried again, offering a five-year residency-qualified franchise and 'reasonable representation' in the Volksraad. But the reformers were uninterested. When Milner asked its opinion of Kruger's new proposal, the UC opposed the plan: the five newly-offered Volksraad seats would leave the Randites in a 'hopeless and contemptible position', the councillors argued. What they wanted instead was a two-year residency requirement as well as proportional representation, guaranteed independence of the High Court (as a consequence of the High Court crisis in early 1897) and, to ensure Uitlander control over that section of the Republic that interested them, local government for the Rand.[37] Not content with the major changes implementation of such a programme would bring, the reformers pressed on for equal language rights, the removal of religious disabilities, the disarmament of the Boer population and demolition of the new forts, the abolition of industrial monopolies, the right to vote for the president and commandant general, and the rights of free speech, a free press and freely-held public meetings to be guaranteed. Finally, they demanded that any new franchise law be entrenched for ten years, unless a full 100 per cent of their newly-constituted Volksraad voted for a change. Encouraged by the support of the imperial government, the reformers became increasingly unwilling to compromise.[38] The end result, just seven short weeks after these demands were made, was war.

No simple conclusion can be reached on the extent of Uitlander support for the grievances Milner enumerated for the Colonial Office. Some had mass support because they reflected the fears and needs of the wider population. These included the demand for more schools, an honest and efficient police force, and a lower cost of living. Other issues, such as the harassment of non-whites by Republican officials, had less appeal because they were not directly relevant to the Uitlanders' daily lives. Those people who had long-term commitments and roots, with money invested and families in residence, led the reform movement. Their task, with help from the jingo press, was to mould local public opinion and generate publicity about the infamous grievances, publicity which would encourage the British and colonial populations to support what appeared to be a downtrodden, but united, Uitlander population so obviously in need of their help. By late 1898 the reformers were ready and, the following year, their full-blown campaign ended in a war few had bargained for.[39]

The year 1899 began with the word 'Edgar' on everybody's lips, for the reformers had ensured that the incident would not remain solely a killing, an arrest and an acquittal, but would become a *cause célèbre*. On Christmas-eve 1898, they engineered a public demonstration at which the British vice-consul was present in a prominent position. Several men in the crowd were arrested and charged with violence and assault and a week later the organizers, Thomas Dodd and Clem Webb, were arrested for breach of the Public Meetings Act. All these arrests kept the Edgar affair before the public. Subsequent court cases, where speeches made on Christmas-eve were reiterated and reviewed, as well as the libel case in which the public prosecutor, Dr F. E. T. Krause, sued the editor of the *Transvaal Critic*, were well publicized.

In February Fitzpatrick initiated the circulation of a second and far more famous petition than that refused earlier by Butler. The first one had purported to represent the views of 5,000 people — the number supposedly in the crowd on Christmas-eve — but was only signed by 40. This second petition to the queen carried 21,684 signatures.[40] It reached Greene in March and, almost immediately, the reformers began asking him for the imperial government's response. By early April they were despondent, calling upon the British government to take 'resolute action', which, they felt, would impress upon Pretoria the fact that it would 'enforce if need be, a demand for fair reforms'.[41]

In response to their urgency the reformers were advised from all sides to be patient but to maintain vigilance. Samuel Evans, a leading reformer and economist who worked for Eckstein & Company, explained to them that because it would take some time to mould public opinion in Britain, they could not expect immediate results. At the same time, as Milner instructed Fitzpatrick, they must not allow the agitation to 'fizzle', but should continue their efforts to get the 'damning evidence that lies in the petitions' before the House of Commons and the British public.[42] Fiddes followed Milner's lead:

> I have done what I can on the line which you [Milner] marked out for me: i.e. while disclaiming any knowledge, or even ideas, as to the view wh[ich] HMG would take of the petition, I have indicated to them [leading Uit-landers] as my own, and indeed the obvious, view that if they want effect to be given to their petition they must keep steadily though quietly pegging away.[43]

At his dinner party in Johannesburg in April, Fiddes told the reformers that if they wanted the petition to have 'full effect' they 'mustn't go to sleep'. He, like Sam Evans, cautioned them against assuming that the imperial government would be quick to decide what course of action to follow. In the meantime they ought to continue to mould public opinion; they had two options. They could attack a single issue and use it to crystallize opinion — but he doubted that this would work because the Boer government was too smart to do anything foolish at this juncture. Their other course of action was a better one, he thought: to continue to peg away on all issues in an attempt to educate the people at home. He also suggested they formulate a reform programme just in case they were asked for it.[44]

So, the Uitlander leaders kept 'pegging away'. The best way to increase support for their cause in Britain was to demonstrate the discontent of a united population on the Rand. As a result of Fitzpatrick's instructions (and probably Milner's suggestion)[45] a series of meetings along the reef was planned for April and May

1899. And while they were not as well attended or as representative of mining employees' opinion as the jingoist *Star* and the British government asserted at the time, they were well publicized. The arguments presented by the various speakers were, for the most part, uniform, though personalized, which indicates that they were part of a centralized and well-organized effort. More importantly, they were also carefully tailored to suit an audience of class-conscious working men.

Each of the meetings passed a resolution holding that any constitutional settlement in the Republic must recognize the 'fundamental principle [of] equal political rights for all white [male] inhabitants'. Simply stated this meant the vote. Various reasons were given for why the Uitlanders should be enfranchised, one of which was that the Boers could not manage the affairs of industry and the industrial population and needed the Uitlanders' expertise. The economic stagnation of the previous three years was presented as proof and grievances were listed as specific examples of Boer mismanagement.

In some cases a psychological argument was used to persuade the miners that they should support the reform movement. An audience of white miners might well be told that in the Republic they had 'simply the status of a kaffir' and that 'every man who thought himself a man must feel that he should attain the true status of manhood'. They were told that they had become the 'laughing stock of [the] European powers' because they were a 'body of men in the prime of manhood, at the mercy of a miserable, insignificant and ignorant gathering of farmers'.[46]

Some speakers were clever enough to exploit the deep-seated anti-capitalist sentiment on the Rand rather than allow it to be used against them. Also, it was very important that the reform movement was not seen to be based on particular class interests or to be serving capitalist goals. Audiences were asked to support what was labelled everybody's struggle: the Rand capitalists were the champions of the working men and would not sell out the labourers, one group of miners was told. The industrialists, in their negotiations with the Boers, had represented the working man 'very well' and had remembered that the workers' interests were paramount.[47]

The logical extension of such reasoning was that the Kruger government was not the friend of white labour, as some had said. Instead, the men in Pretoria 'bled the capitalists, and because they had done that they wanted to pose as the friends of the working men. [But] by bleeding the capitalists they were bleeding the working men'.[48] To make this argument credible, the speakers denied being the 'tools of the capitalists' and reiterated their working-class credentials. Other speakers pressed home the view that the interests of labour and capital were, at this point in time, one and the same: they should join together as Uitlanders, not fight as workers and bosses. Further, they were told that if the capitalists were allowed to run the mines at a profit, they would be in a position to hire some of the unemployed. With this demand for additional labour, listeners were assured, it would be a 'freak of political economy' if wage levels were to drop.[49]

The argument that the mining magnates were the friends of labour could in no way be sold to audiences of Rand miners. Well aware of this, some speakers took a different tack. Their task was not made any easier by men such as Kenneth Ferguson, of the soon to be established IILP, who warned the audience from the floor at the Wolhuter mine that 'if they got the vote, they would have to vote for the capitalists, or lose their berths'.[50] One convener argued the case for the SAL, stating that, since voting would be done by ballot, the working class, once enfranchised, would have the country in its hands. 'We the working men', he continued, 'have the power' and will find it 'much easier . . . to make terms with the financiers than with the [Boer] Government'. With bravado, the chairman of a later meeting assured his audience that the enfranchised working man could 'not only keep the present autocratic Government within bounds, but [could] also keep the capitalists in their place'.[51]

What, then, was the SAL asking the workers to do to ensure their rise to power? First, it expected them to support the resolutions put to them by the conveners, resolutions which included a demand for equal political rights. The resolutions asserted that the industrialists represented the interests of all the Uitlanders and sometimes included demands reflecting the points made in the SAL's petition to the queen.

Secondly, it asked them to choose delegates who would assist the capitalists in their negotiations with Pretoria, who would consider what further steps ought to be taken to obtain reforms, who would join together in an 'Uitlander Parliament' (i.e. in the UC in June), and who would 'put such questions to the Government as will force an answer of "yes" or "no" or necessitate an evasion so palpable and disingenuous as to expose Kruger to the whole world'.[52] Hence, from the fifth public meeting along the reef onward, men selected by the conveners for their proven sympathies were publicly 'elected' or 'agreed to' by the audiences of miners. Messrs Ingle, Mosel, Strong and Bottomley sat as miners' representatives on the UC, though it remains unclear which mines they represented and who the other miners' representatives were — if, indeed, any others were 'elected'.[53]

Just as the series of SAL meetings drew to a close, the independent labour movement found its voice. Within a week the IILP was formed and the first strike on the Rand in 15 months erupted. Though it was a minor affair concerning wages and involved only about 100 men for two days on the Crown Reef mine, the pro-Boer press covered it extensively. Soon the miners won their case, thereby setting a precedent for a similar strike a month later by workers on the French Rand Company's works. In a move reflecting the deepening political crisis, the Crown Reef miners also demanded a weekly rather than a monthly wage packet, a scheme that was expected to spread quickly along the reef.[54]

At the same time, action in the political arena quickened as Boer sympathizers took the offensive. First, they tried to discredit the SAL's petition by casting doubt on the authenticity of the signatures and, thereby, its representative nature. Secondly, they distributed their own petitions, which the reformers and British government representatives in turn tried to discredit.

The attack on the queen's petition was spearheaded by the pro-Boer, English-language daily, the *Standard and Diggers' News*, which asserted that the signatures had been 'appended in duplicate and triplicate' to make up the imposing array of over 20,000 names. It printed letters from readers who cited cases of fraud: children signed the petition, women signed their husbands' names, some signed without knowing what it was, while others signed it to 'retain their billets'. In June an official Green Book was published in Pretoria, presenting affidavits swearing to similar infractions.[55]

Milner asked Wybergh of the SAL to answer these charges, which he did to the satisfaction of the high commissioner. Greene and Milner then took it upon themselves to explain to Whitehall that one particular accusation about the petition was quite incorrect: it was the work of the 'Edgar Committee' and the SAL and not of the capitalists as asserted; in fact, Wybergh, president of the local

SAL, had actually been fired by Consolidated Gold Fields for his role in its circulation.[56]

In April at least two different pro-Boer petitions circulated through Johannesburg, both addressed to Kruger and denouncing the SAL's principles, its aims and its petition. One asked for the liberalization of the franchise qualifications, but expressed a desire for peace and goodwill between Uitlander and Boer. A second petition was more pointed, accusing the organizers of the queen's petition of being 'capitalists and not the public' and stating that, while the Republican government had no major faults, if it had, they could be rectified without the intervention of foreign powers or the 'advice of capitalists'.[57]

No sooner was the second of these counter-petitions conceived than the reformers took action. A copy of it was stolen from the printers and leaked to the press before it was circulated. Greene attacked it, stating that it was 'generally discredited' because the 9,000 signatures on it were obtained, he claimed, from government and railway workers, most of the latter being naturalized burghers. The *Star* took up Greene's line, printing a letter from a 'Transvaal resident of thirteen years' who asserted that the signatories of the counter-petition were illicit liquor dealers and gold buyers, railway workers 'under pain of dismissal', indigent Boers and 600 or so 'continental peoples'. Reports of duplicity by canvassers while obtaining signatures were forwarded to Milner as well.[58]

Labour leaders took action in May, sending a petition to Chamberlain through Milner's office, a petition which stated that there might be need of reform, but there were 'no grievances . . . which could justify any extreme measures on the part of Her Majesty's Government'. Several men signed it, but still it did not reach the colonial secretary without prejudice, for appended to it were the opinions of Milner and Greene that the petition had been instigated by an 'anti-Imperialist and advanced Irish nationalist'.[59]

In fact a fair amount of Uitlander support for the Boer government was based upon nationalist sentiment. National, cultural and ethnic origin played an important social role among the Rand's heterogeneous population. For instance, national origin and patriotic sentiment served to break down class antagonisms, at least in the short term, though in at least one instance — that of the Australians — trade union membership actually weakened their national-based organization.[60] Still, by the late 1890s there were at least 20 clubs on the Rand which had regional, national or cultural identity as their focus and which helped to maintain the vitality of their members' national allegiance.

Most of these clubs had at least 50 members. Men, and in the case of the Scandinavians, women as well, joined them for a variety of reasons. Certainly they had a social function, bringing together immigrants who eagerly took part in activities reminiscent of home: for example, an 'Eisteddfod', a 'Bastille Day' celebration, or a 'Fourth of July' party. They met the needs of recent immigrants by giving them a ready-made community upon which to lean and from which to draw support. They also took over the functions of other organizations, such as benevolent societies, insurance companies and trade unions. For example, the Devonian Society, the Caledonian Society, the Society of Danes and Norwegians, and the Irish National Foresters' Benefit Society all distributed aid to their poorest members and attempted to find work for their unemployed. In other cases, clubs served the people in the old country by collecting and forwarding money from their compatriots on the Rand.[61]

With the exception of the Irish organizations, few of these clubs had any explicit political function before 1899. Irish clubs had been formed in the early 1890s to foster 'unity, nationality and benevolence' and, in 1897, the 'Irish Amnesty Association' was established to work for the release of Irish political prisoners in Britain. The release of Dr Jameson by the British government spurred them on.[62]

In the years prior to the Anglo-Boer War, Randites vociferously expressed their Irish nationalist sentiment and, as the political situation deteriorated, their Anglophobia gave rise naturally to their support for the Kruger government. For example, in 1897 when Kruger banned the *Star*, one Irishman expressed his antipathy for the paper by stating that the treatment meted out to it was less severe than that handed out by the British to the Irish press. Certainly, too, the comparison between the Boer and Irish nations was inevitable, for both were being tormented by British imperialists.[63] As war approached and the Irish nationalists became increasingly outspoken in their views, they were watched by the British representative on the Rand. He could hardly have been surprised when shortly before the war they formed the First Irish Brigade, the child of the local '98 Centenary Association.[64]

Anglophobia among continental Europeans was also transformed into Republican sympathy as tension mounted. The Germans were probably the most outspokenly sympathetic, having been given their lead some years before by the 'Kruger Telegram'. Kruger's boasting of his German descent probably helped, but business competition between British and German entrepreneurs locally played a significant role as well. Working-class Germans who belonged to the local socialist 'Vorwaerts Society' raised their voices in support of the Boers for additional reasons.[65] Other Europeans, such as Hollanders and Scandinavians, became increasingly critical of the British, and their organizations served as recruiting grounds for war volunteers. And though the pro-British press claimed that the Americans on the Rand supported the Uitlanders' struggle against Kruger, many did not. In fact, even the US consul in 1900, Stanley Hollis, was known for his Boer sympathies.[66]

It was a difficult task the reformers took upon themselves, mobilizing support for the Uitlanders' grievances and maintaining an illusion of unity in these last months before the war. Their efforts were constantly undermined by nationalist ardour and class conflict. But their alliance with Milner and, especially, their control of several English-language newspapers made a difference in the end, as they were able to use command papers and international press reports to convince the outside world that the vast majority of foreigners on the Rand chafed as 'helots' under Boer mismanagement.

In May the situation deteriorated considerably when seven Uitlanders were arrested for treason. R. F. Nicholls, one of the ringleaders, had been an organizer for the SAL in Fordsburg and SAL officials had warned him and the other 'blundering and indiscreet' leaders that their scheme to overthrow the Kruger government would not help, but would actually harm, the Uitlander cause. But he would not be swayed and assured the SAL that he 'had the confidence of their "chief" . . . [who was] acting under direct Imperial sanction'. Thus convinced, he tried to recruit a force that would be armed and prepared to march against the Boers at 24 hours' notice. During these troubled weeks in May, as Milner and Kruger prepared for the Bloemfontein conference, the fate of the men was uncertain. Two months later, though, they were released after evidence was produced which proved that the Republican government was implicated in the plot.[67]

As winter deepened neither did peace descend nor fear evaporate, for it was in June that the UC took public form and the Bloemfontein conference failed. The IILP became active and the wave of industrial unrest began, culminating in the strike of artisans on the Robinson Deep mine in August. The community was by now polarized, which made it difficult for the SAL to obscure the divisions within Rand society. The *Star*, in an effort to minimize its importance, told its readers that the strike was an 'isolated action'[68] though the reformers knew differently. In fact, they gave a collective sigh of relief when the Robinson Deep management capitulated, as they certainly wished to avoid the danger of a 'growing feud between capital and labour at this most critical juncture'.[69] In this they succeeded. But before many more weeks passed, the political situation overtook the interminable struggle between classes, for now, nine months after the Edgar shooting, fear of war had taken a firm hold on the Uitlander community.

Notes

1. *S & D News*, 3 Aug. 1899; *Star*, 4 Aug. 1899.
2. MS/PRO/DO 119/316, Milner to Chamberlain, 11 May 1897, with enclosure, Conyngham Greene to Milner, 6 May 1897, forwarding a report from William Hosken. See also MS/PRO/DO 119/315, Milner to Chamberlain (draft), 6 March 1897, which forwards a report from Greene, 5 March 1897. For the economic depression, see daily reports in the *Star; S & D News*; and MS/JPL/ACPT, London letterbooks.
3. *S & D News*, 6 Dec. 1897; *Star*, 15 July, 13 Dec. 1898.
4. For bakers, see *S & D News*, 2 July 1898; *Star*, 6 Dec. 1898; and for hotel-workers union, see *Star*, 22 July 1899.
5. OP/SAR/Rapports 1897/8, statement 7.
6. Davies 1978, p. 85.
7. *S & D News*, 2 Sept. 1897. Further information on this controversy may be found in *S & D News*, 11 March 1897; Katz 1976, pp. 131—3; and Cope 1943, p. 48.
8. *Star*, 8 Aug. 1898.
9. *Star*, 8 Sept. 1897; *S & D News*, 8 Sept., 12 Dec. 1897, 5 May 1898, 14, 18 Jan., 6 June 1899. For additional information, see Rose 1902, pp. 30—1; Downes 1952, pp. 25, 804, 814; Katz 1976, pp. 25—6; MacDonald n.d., p. 107; OP/TVL/Transvaal Indigency Commission, minutes of evidence, pp. 95—7, evidence by H. W. Sampson.
10. *South African Mining Journal*, 4 (34) 25 May 1895, p. 720.
11. *S & D News*, 10 Sept., 8, 9 Dec. 1897.
12. Both the *Star* and the *S & D News* carried articles on the IILP and Bain, as well as on the eight-hour workday movement. See these papers from May through Sept. 1899, particularly. The 'Platform of the International Labour Party' may be found in MS/TAD/R&O 540, while information about (and criticism of) Bain may be found in the *South African Mining Journal*, 7 (323) 11 Dec. 1897, p. 249. He later served in the Republican secret service, and was captured by the British outside Johannesburg and sent to Ceylon. After the war he was again active in the labour movement and was one of nine men deported by J.C. Smuts after the 1913 strike. Information on workers' hours is found in the *South African Mining Journal*, 4 (14) 13 July 1897; the *Star*, 26 Jan. 1897; and *S & D News*, 5 Aug. 1899. For a different interpretation of the basis of opposition to the IILP, see Grobler 1968, p. 10.
13. The *Star*, from May 1898 until the beginning of the war, is a good source of information

on the SAL. For a fuller discussion, see Bitensky 1950; and, for its role in events leading to war, see Marais 1961. For an example of the SAL's work in the colonies, see Ovendale 1980, pp. 209—34.

14. *Star*, 23 Feb., 21 April, 23 June and 9 July 1898.

15. *Star*, 12 Feb., 21 April 1898 and 20 July 1899; *African Review*, 21 (316) 21 Oct. 1899, pp. 81—3; Marais 1961, p. 164.

16. MS/BOD/Mss. Milner Dep. 229, J. Emrys Evans to Walrond, 15 May 1899, and Fiddes to Milner (private), 7 April 1899. Cf. Mawby 1974, p. 403, whose view of the UC differs somewhat.

17. *Star*, 10 and 12 June 1899, see MS/PRO/CO 417/262, Milner to Chamberlain, 21 June 1899, and Milner to Chamberlain (confidential), 28 June 1899.

18. MS/BOD/Mss. Milner Dep. 229, J. Emrys Evans to Walrond, 15 May 1899; MS/PRO/CO 417/262, Milner to Chamberlain (confidential). The membership of the UC is difficult to reconstruct, partly because of the secrecy which surrounded the organization. According to MS/PRO/CO 417/262, Milner to Chamberlain (confidential), 28 June 1899, with enclosure, 'minutes of meeting of Uitlander delegates . . . Johannesburg, on . . . 17 June' 1899, those present were: J. Arthur, J. G. Auret, — Bartlett, H. Bottomley, O. Brothers, W. Dalrymple, Dr Davies, D. E. Doveton, G. H. Fison, W. Hardwick, W. Hosken, H. C. Hull, F. Ingle, J. B. Knowles, D. F. Morton, C. H. Mullins, J. Pearson, D. J. Pullinger, H. A. Rogers, W. St John Carr, R. Shanks, E. P. Solomon, H. C. Steadman, A. F. Steward, D. Strachan, J. Strong, T. R. Todd, S. T. Tregaskis, T. Trevor and C. D. Webb. The head of detectives, T. M. Menton, sent a 'compleet lyst van namen . . . van den Uitlander Volksraad' to R. G. Okerse, assistant mining commissioner, 11 Oct. 1899, MS/TAD/R&O 517. In addition to the above names, the following men were listed: — Barkley, R. Currie, H. S. Caldecott, S. Evans, J. D. Foster [sic. Forster], T. Mackenzie, A. Mackie Niven, W. A. Martin, S. Mosel, E. H. Perry, J. W. Quinn, A. Rait[t], J. Roos, — Wells and W. Wybergh. See also Bitensky 1950, p. 117, n.304, for a list of delegates according to W. J. Leyds's information.

19. MS/BOD/Mss. Milner Dep. 229, Greene to Milner (private and confidential), 7 April 1899. 'The truth is', Greene states, 'that the Uitlanders of Johannesburg are lacking now, as before, in cohesion, and it is impossible to hope to hold them, for an indefinite interval, together. . . . The [mining] groups have with some difficulty and skilful engineering on the part of Fitzpatrick been got to make common cause with the Uitlander Community.'

20. For a discussion of the Uitlander grievances generally, see Fitzpatrick 1899; and OP/SAR/Mining Industry 1897. A more recent interpretation of the grievances is given in Marais 1961; for information on the economic grievances, see OP/GB/C. 8423 (1897); and daily reports in the *Star* and *S & D News* from 1897 until the war. For the aliens' expulsion and immigration acts, see OP/GB/C. 8423 (1897) nos 87 and 101; and MS/PRO/DO 119/291, HM agent, Pretoria, to HC, 19 Jan. 1897; 'Uitlander' 1899, pp. 1038—47.

21. For merchant views on Asian competition, see *Star*, 9 Aug. 1898: *S & D News*, 15 Nov. 1897; MS/PRO/CO 417/292, Milner to Chamberlain, 30 July 1900, with enclosure, M. J. Paton to Milner, 21 July 1900. For a more thorough discussion of anti-Asian legislation and policy, see Swan 1985, pp. 80—1, 88; and Pillay 1976, pp. 57—84.

22. MS/BOD/Mss. Milner Dep. 229, Fiddes to Milner (private), 7 April 1899.

23. Ibid., see speech by Fitzpatrick, 13 March 1899, cited in Duminy and Guest (eds) 1976. Clearly the editor of the *Star* took his job seriously, for in May 1899 he explained to Walrond in the HC's office that his task on the Rand was to 'keep the pot boiling' (MS/BOD/Mss., Milner Dep. 229, Monypenny to Walrond, 14 May 1899).

24. Fitzpatrick to S. J. Jennings (private), 26 Sept. 1898, in Duminy and Guest (eds) 1976. For a history of Republican education on the Rand, see *Star*, 16 March, 17 May 1899 and 5 Feb. 1902; Fitzpatrick 1899, pp. 427—8; and OP/GB/C. 9345 (1899) section 2.

25. For Evans's remarks, see MS/PRO/CO 417/264, Milner to Chamberlain, 25 July 1899, with enclosure, H. J. Evans to Milner, 15 July 1899; and *S & D News*, 21 March 1899. For

the Wesleyan school debate, see *Star*, 19 Sept. 1899; and MS/PRO/CO 417/261, Milner to Chamberlain, 25 May 1899, with enclosure, Greene to Milner, 29 April 1899. For a general discussion of educational policy in these years, see Malherbe 1925, pp. 288—90; Marais 1961, *passim*; Hobson 1969, pp. 37—9; OP/GB/C. 9345 (1899) no. 25 and C. 8423 (1897) no. 101.

26. MS/PRO/DO 119/498, Butler to Chamberlain (secret), 25 Jan. 1899; and [Cleaver] 1913, p. 8. The Edgar shooting was not atypical, but other cases did not arouse as much anger as this one did. For instance, see the shooting of Blyth, *Star*, 12 Feb. 1898. For members of the 'Edgar Committee', see MS/PRO/DO 119/498, Greene to Milner (secret), 8 March 1899.

27. MS/PRO/CO 417/261, Milner to Chamberlain, 4 May 1899.

28. Van Onselen 1982, vol. 1, p. 81.

29. During the jingoistic phase before the war, the imperial government demanded £4,000 compensation from Pretoria for Mrs Edgar. Two years later she was no longer considered a 'very deserving person' (PRO/CO 291, Milner to Chamberlain, 6 May 1901).

30. Cited in Leyds 1964, pp. 81—2.

31. Blake 1903, p. 37.

32. *S & D News*, 2 May 1899; *Star*, 17 March 1899; MS/PRO/DO 119/349, Greene to Milner, 6 April 1899; 'Uitlander' 1899, pp. 1040—1; and MS/BOD/Mss. Milner Dep. 229, Monypenny to Walrond, 14 May 1899.

33. *S & D News*, 27 May 1899.

34. *S & D News*, 17, 21 June 1899.

35. *Star*, 9 June 1899.

36. MS/BOD/Mss. Milner Dep. 229, Monypenny to Walrond, 14 May 1899.

37. For a discussion of local government, see OP/GB/C. 9345 (1899) nos. 4, 9, 20; MS/PRO/FO 2/249, memorandum from CO to FO, 15 March 1899, with enclosure, Milner to Chamberlain, 9 March 1899; MS/BOD/Mss. Milner Dep. 229, Fiddes to Milner (private), 7 April 1899; Marais 1961, pp. 192—3; Fitzpatrick 1899, p. 311; and [Smuts] 1899, p. 64.

38. MS/PRO/DO 119/358, Greene to Milner, 26 Aug. 1899, with enclosures, J. D. Forster to Greene, 22 Aug. 1899, William Hosken to Greene, 25 Aug. 1899. Kruger's proposal, aimed at getting the British government's true intentions into the open, seems to have worked. See van Heyningen 1978, p. 244.

39. Rhodes assured Milner that 'Kruger will concede everything HMG demands', while Greene relayed the views of the Uitlander agitators that there would be no war. If Britain announced publicly that it was determined to enforce its demand for reform, a resort to arms would be avoided and the Boer government would 'climb down' (MS/PRO/DO 119/349, Greene to Milner (confidential), 4 April 1899; and MS/BOD/Mss. Milner Dep. 212, Rhodes to Milner, 13 Sept. 1899). On the other hand, Sam Evans thought war 'inevitable'. Milner probably agreed. 'I don't want war', he told Selbourne before the Bloemfontein conference, 'but it may be the only way out. But if so, we must be seen to be forced into it'. Salisbury seemingly agreed. Milner is dragging England into war and so 'we have to act upon a moral field prepared for us by him and his jingoist supporters'. (See van Heyningen 1978, p. 226; and Wheatcroft 1985, p. 202).

40. Pakenham 1979, p. 53; cf. Marais 1961, p. 257. The idea of circulating a memorial to the queen was mooted in the press as far back as June 1898 (*Star*, 21 June 1898). For a copy of the first petition, see *Star*, 24 Dec. 1898; and MS/PRO/DO 119/320, Fraser to Butler, 4 Jan. 1899. For information about the larger petition, see *Star*, 27 March 1899.

41. MS/PRO/DO 119/349, Greene to Milner (confidential), 4 April 1899; see *Star*, 27 March 1899.

42. MS/BOD/Mss. Milner Dep. 229, Greene to Milner (private and confidential), 7 April 1899; and Fitzpatrick to J. Wernher, 6 April 1899, in Duminy and Guest (eds) 1976.

43. MS/BOD/Mss. Milner Dep. 229, Fiddes to Milner (private), 7 April 1899.

44. Ibid.

45. Fitzpatrick to J. Werner, 19 April 1899, in Duminy and Guest (eds) 1976; Fitzpatrick 1899, pp. 360, 364. See also Marais 1961, pp. 263—4.
46. For the meetings, see *Star*, 21 April to 25 May 1899. For speeches cited here, see *Star* 22 and 25 April 1899.
47. *Star*, 22 April 1899; see Pakenham 1979, pp. 54—6; and Duminy and Guest (eds) 1976, ch. 5, *passim*.
48. *Star*, 21 April 1899.
49. *Star*, 21 and 27 April and 11 May 1899.
50. *Star*, 22 April 1899.
51. *Star*, 28 April and 2 May 1899.
52. *Star*, 25 and 27 April 1899; and Fitzpatrick to J. Wernher, 19 April 1899, in Duminy and Guest (eds) 1976.
53. MS/PRO/CO 417/262, Milner to Chamberlain (confidential), 28 June 1899, with enclosure from Greene to Milner, 21 June 1899. For the conservatism of Strong and Bottomley, see MacDonald n.d., pp. 105—6; and Katz 1976, p. 406.
54. *S & D News*, 2 and 26 May 1899; *South African Mining Journal*, 8 (402) 17 June 1899, p. 673.
55. *S & D News*, 28 and 30 March, 14 April, 11 May, 22 and 30 June and 7 July 1899; *Star*, 7 April and 13 May 1899.
56. MS/PRO/CO 417/261, Milner to Chamberlain, 10 May 1899, with enclosure, Greene to Milner, 6 May 1899; MS/PRO/DO 119/352, W. Wybergh to Milner, 21 June 1899; and Fitzpatrick to J. Wernher, 16 Jan. 1899, in Duminy and Guest (eds) 1976.
57. *S & D News*, 21 April 1899; *Star*, 22 April 1899.
58. MS/PRO/DO 119/350, Greene to Milner, 6 May 1899; MS/PRO/DO 119/497, P. J. Meyer to J. Emrys Evans, 20 April 1899; *Star*, 1 June 1899. *S & D News*, 16 May 1899, reported that this petition went to the Boer government with 13,943 signatures of white residents, and that other 'similar petitions' were 'coming in'.
59. MS/PRO/CO 417/261, Milner to Chamberlain, 9 May 1899, with enclosure, Greene to Milner, 9 May 1899. For further information about this petition and the controversy it caused, see *Star*, 10 May 1899. In August, another petition was circulated which stated that the signatories were opposed to taking up the franchise, but the SAL immediately tried to warn off potential signatories by stating that, by signing it, they might render themselves liable for military service. See *Star*, 29 Aug. 1899.
60. For the Australians, see *S & D News*, 28 June, 19 July 1897; Katz 1976, pp. 13, 18—19.
61. For examples of these nationally-based clubs, see *Star*, 15 July 1897, 17 Sept. 1898, 6 March, 24 June and 12 Aug. 1899; *S & D News*, 12 Feb., 19, 22 July, 2, 5, Aug., 15 Nov. 1897, 23 Aug. 1898, 19 July 1899; and *Comet*, 28 March 1897.
62. *Star*, 18 March 1891, 7 March 1899; *S & D News*, 4 Jan. 1897, 10 Feb., 24 May 1898; Ruda 1974, p. 203.
63. *S & D News*, 5 April 1897, 21, 22 and 27 June 1899.
64. MS/PRO/CO 417/261, Milner to Chamberlain, 9 May 1899, with enclosure, Greene to Milner, 9 May 1899; Ruda 1974, p. 204; see also MS/TAD/MGP 205, c/19, confidential list of people travelling through or resident in Lourenço Marques since May 1900, 11 Aug. 1900. For additional information about the Irish population in the Transvaal, see Hennessy 1973, ch. 18.
65. *S & D News*, 24 April, 1 June and 2 Sept. 1899; *Star*, 4 May and 25 Aug. 1899; for business competition, see Jenkin 1902.
66. For instance, see *Star*, 11 and 27 Sept. and 7 Oct. 1899; and *S & D News*, 11 Sept., 6, 19 and 26 Oct. 1899. For the Americans, see *Star*, 4 July 1899, and MS/TAD/MGP 205, c/19, confidential list of people travelling through or resident in Lourenço Marques since May 1900, 11 Aug. 1900. For further information on the American view of the war, see Davis 1901; and Noer 1978.
67. MS/PRO/CO 417/261, Milner to Chamberlain, 15, 17 and 23 May 1899; and CO 417/264, Milner to Chamberlain, 25 and 26 July 1899. See also *Star*, 17 May 1899.
68. *Star*, 4 Aug. 1899.

69. *S & D News*, 5, 7 and 8 Aug. 1899; and *South African Mining Journal*, 8 (409) 5 Aug. 1899, pp. 785, 793 (410); 12 Aug. 1899, p. 812.

Two

Preparing for War

And we are here as on a darkling plain
Swept with confused alarms of struggle and flight . . .
Matthew Arnold

As the cooler and drier weather returned to the highveld once again, worried fathers and husbands hustled their families aboard trains bound for the coast. Euphemisms such as the 'winter season' were used to justify their departures, but no one in Johannesburg was fooled. For, in May 1899, it began to look as though war was a real possibility and the mass of white foreigners, not interested in fighting for Kruger's franchise, headed for Natal and the Cape. The first to leave were those whose menfolk were better able to afford it — middle and upper-class dependants. By June white miners had joined the flight, while unattached Uitlander artisans fled to the coast where they joined the ranks of the unemployed.[1] About the same time, shop assistants and others in the urban economy were notified by their employers that their services would not be required after the end of the month. Thus, at the onset of war several months later, there were only about 10,000 whites in the city and perhaps that many again were scattered along the reef. Any British still there a few weeks after the Boers took over the administration of the district remained either because they were outright Boer supporters, because they were deemed to be indispensable to the smooth running of the economy, because they had been abandoned or because they were too old or weak to travel.

From late 1898 onwards, but especially after it was announced that the mining industry had just had another record year, rumours of an impending economic 'boom' spread along the reef. The longed-for boom never did materialize, however, except in a few towns along the reef where secondary industry and commerce depended almost solely on the mines. In the city, though, queues of men in search of work could still be seen outside offices, while the property market remained 'limp'.[2] Nevertheless, the depression had bottomed out — probably in mid-summer 1898/9 — and in the new year the economy was beginning to show a gradual but marked improvement. But the economic recovery was cut short in the middle of 1899 by a politically-induced slump. Credit began to tighten once again and trade collapsed. In the quarter after the Bloemfontein conference, the number of insolvencies in the city increased threefold over the previous year.[3]

For over two years Uitlander workers had been leaving the Rand. Earlier the depressed job market had forced them to go; now it was fear. A constant stream of rumours gave substance to that fear. In May, for instance, news of a *coup d'état* circulated through the taverns just about the time the conspiracy led by the seven men from Fordsburg collapsed. Ordinary Randites also began to explain to one another how the rural Boers were planning to murder them in their beds, while the reformers became more justifiably anxious over threats received in anonymously written letters.[4] The mass of the population, having nothing specific to warrant its fear, began to focus on the fort atop Hospital Hill.

The recently completed fort became the central feature of Boer intimidation in the minds of the Uitlanders and they would not have been surprised to learn that its purpose was, according to its builder, the German Lieut.-Col. Adolf Schiel, to 'keep the town and more especially the Mines in subjugation'. None the less, the commandant of the Johannesburg Commando and Kruger's grandson, Capt. Sarel Eloff, tried to assure the residents that it would not fire upon a 'defenceless city'. His promise did nothing to alleviate their fears, nor did the introduction of weapons into the city from mid-year onwards.[5] To gain further assurances that the city would be afforded the protection guaranteed by the Geneva Convention, a deputation of Johannesburg merchants approached the government in July. It met with the state secretary, F. W. Reitz, who did little to calm them: the fort, he said, was for the purpose of self-defence and would protect the peaceful inhabitants of the city. This the UC saw as a 'veiled threat'.[6]

While the Boers never did give the community reason to fear a wholesale massacre of Uitlanders, this did not keep the jingo press or the general public from speculating. This, in turn, fostered the exodus. The more stalwart watched them leave:

> Never shall I forget how our poor [Uitlander] refugees left here in vast numbers day after day, in many cases terror-stricken, never caring where to or how they provided for their future, only let them be away with their delicate women and helpless little children, away from the awful frowning fort, whose bristling walls constantly menaced their lives, their homes, all that humanity holds dear.[7]

Soon the possibility of being conscripted by Boer commandos began to worry residents, as did the rumour in September that a 'census' was being taken to determine how many men could be relied upon to fight for the Republic. People were also afraid that food supplies would be disrupted and that starvation would be widespread. Most were also worried that black workers and miners would be left without work and allowed to terrorize the district population.[8] With fears compounding daily, panic took hold of people:

> We must get away, what do our homes, our gardens, our pets matter when our lives are at stake — the Boers are going to level Johannesburg to the ground, walk over the bodies of our wives and children, make us work in trenches and put us in front of commandoes [sic] as targets for our own countrymen to shoot at.[9]

The local press did little to ease such fears:

> The city swayed between panic and suspense. The morning paper decided the takings at the railway office. Rumours of settlement, a chance sentence dropped by Reitz, a kindlier grunt from Kruger, and hundreds of anxious men said to their worried wives, 'I think we will stay on after all'. But an

ominous debate in the [Volks]raad, the raving of some incautious Landrost [sic], and the trains would go out at night crowded.[10]

As the political situation worsened, more and more people were thrown out of work. Now, as in 1898 when the normal relief organizations had been unable to cope with the extraordinary number of unemployed and hungry people, special charities were formed to help carry the load. The first to appear was the Women's Relief Fund, an extension of the women's branch of the SAL. It provided funds for women discharged from employment, most of whom were shop assistants, teachers and office workers. The Fund encouraged them to leave the Rand and tried to find them work at the coast. The *Star* and the Women's Club soon followed suit, starting similar funds.[11]

In late June, with uncertainty and fear gaining ground and with no end to the depression or the political crisis in sight, a group of Johannesburg financiers and businessmen, mostly representatives of large mining groups, decided to form an aid organization. Called the 'Johannesburg Temporary Relief Committee', it was funded by leading financial and mining companies, making public subscription unnecessary. The clergy were given an active role, especially the trusted Revd W. E. Kelly of the Present Help League, as it set about achieving its goal: to aid temporarily the 'deserving poor' — women, children and a few old men — of all nationalities and creeds.[12]

A central committee was formed to raise funds, buy provisions and organize the main storage depot, while distribution fell to the six, later seven, district committees, upon each of which sat at least one clergyman whose task was to determine the extent of the need of the applicants. Those families already known to be needy were given a week's supply of food, while any unknown applicant was granted a few days' supplies while the committee investigated his or her case. A special fund was established for the middle-class poor, which was personally administered by the women distributing relief. To protect forever the anonymity of those who felt the shame of accepting assistance, no records of these recipients were kept.[13]

In August the organization formed a Labour Bureau to help men find work. Within days over 350 men had put their names down and two-thirds of these found jobs. But, as the situation worsened, fewer were able to find employment: only another five found jobs before October although another 175 had applied.[14] Eventually free or assisted passages to the coast were granted to some applicants, although this required delicate handling. First, the committee (it later claimed) did not want to fuel panic by recommending to people that they leave their homes. Further, the committee feared that if it recommended that people leave, this would be construed as an unfriendly political act by Pretoria and might lead to some sort of retaliation. Therefore, it was not until the month before war started that it suggested that people leave and, even then, it advised only women, children and men who had no chance of finding work on the Rand to do so. Until that time, the committee gave assisted passages only to women and children who actually applied for them and who had a place to go to and people to care for them. In July and August this amounted to 38 people.[15]

In August, as a 'nameless terror and vague fear' gained ground, the committee approached the Cape and Natal railways, as well as NZASM in the Republic, to ask them to lower their fares. All refused. The following month a similar request led the Cape, Natal and Orange Free State railway authorities to reduce by one-half the fares of second- and third-class passengers who were in receipt of aid from the Temporary Relief Committee. Finally, less than two weeks before war broke out, NZASM followed suit. In September, the committee helped nearly 5,800 whites and 500 Coloureds — 'people who had just enough to live on but could not find the £4 or £5 required to take them to their friends' — to leave the country.[16]

Not surprisingly, the committee's main work was concentrated in the city centre and western suburbs, where Johannesburg's poorest residents lived. While theoretically willing to assist all the poor, the class bias and nationalism of the committee's members tainted its outlook and work: 'the greatest care was needed [wrote one clergyman] to prevent fraud and imposition. . . . Boer and Briton, Jew and Gentile alike, were helped. Boer women from Vrededorp threatened to monopolise the relief, so insistent and so slim [cunning] were they'.[17] More sympathetic to the burgher population, the burgomaster of Johannesburg approached the Republican government for funds for public relief. In October he was given enough to assist 1,700 families, mostly dependants of men on commando. Work on the government's Main Reef Road project continued and men of all nationalities found work there in the months following.[18]

Even in normal times Rand charities and government relief projects were unable to eliminate want. Now the number of needy grew beyond previous proportions and fear of starvation became widespread. The poor were the least able to leave, for they had no money to set up new homes elsewhere. Consequently, the poorest and most desperate just sat, fearing the worst and praying for peace. In some cases such families were divided, as women and children took assisted passages to the coast while husbands and fathers remained in search of any sort of work. In other cases dependants remained, as menfolk fled to the coast to avoid possible conscription, find employment or join the colonial volunteers.[19] The Temporary Relief Committee's last act was aimed at helping these abandoned dependants. It distributed its excess stores and cash to several local charities and to F. J. Carpenter, with instructions that the money and goods were to be used to aid the needy British left in the city.[20]

The exodus began in earnest about the time the SAL's meetings were being held along the reef. In May and June about 8,000 whites left, but in July, as reports of the government arming 'poor burghers' circulated, the number rose to between 250 and 500 per day. In August the numbers rose again, with between 300 and 800 leaving daily. In September the exodus increased dramatically as the masses followed the reformers who fled as warrants for their arrests were issued. For example, on 9 September, a reported 700 people left the city, and on 20 September, more than 2,000. During the last week of the month the figure dropped to about 1,000 a day, but in the last few days of September — when contracts had expired and monthly wage packets had been collected — it rose to about 4,000 a day. In the first two weeks of October, the number fell again, though upwards of 1,500 continued to leave each day. The final, reluctant but voluntary, refugees left before the 18th — the last day unregistered aliens were allowed to remain. Hence, in the period between May and mid-October, nearly 100,000 white people fled the district.[21]

The task of transporting this number of people — as well as the more than 100,000 non-whites who left — was an enormous one. Unprepared for the exodus and having to compete with the military which took rolling stock out of circulation and dominated the routes east, the railway authorities were unable to accommodate the evacuees. In mid-September NZASM needed more carriages and asked the Cape railways for some, but the officials there, unable or unwilling, declined. As a result, third-class passengers were consigned to 'trucks' which normally carried coal, livestock or Africans. At first, only white men were assigned to these trucks, but as the rush became frantic, people of all races and both sexes were thrown together for the trip to the coast.[22]

NZASM tried to keep pace with the demand. In early September it had managed to send four trains out of Johannesburg daily. On 4 October two coal trucks reserved for men were added each day. On 1 October, just as the peak of the exodus was reached, train travel to Natal was suspended because Republican military trains monopolized the lines to the eastern front. Not until the 11th were these lines reopened to civilians, but after that date the authorities refused to guarantee that any train leaving for Natal would arrive at its destination. Trains to Ressano Garcia, on the Mozambican border, were brought into operation to relieve the pressure and so a large number of Rand refugees — mostly the poorest who had waited until the last to leave — were channelled to Lourenço Marques.[23]

The shipping companies had similar problems providing transport for all those waiting to leave Africa. The companies were also needed to ferry passengers from Delagoa Bay to a British colonial port, normally Durban. By September both the Union and the Castle companies' offices on the Rand had extended their hours to enable miners in outlying districts to book passages after work. By this time third-class ship accommodation was fully booked even before a ship reached port and, to avoid a stay of days or even weeks at the coast, Randites were advised to purchase their outbound tickets before leaving the city.[24]

The trip to safety was a mixture of fear, worry and hardship, but at times there was merriment. Trains were loaded at Braamfontein and Park stations and out on the reef at Elandsfontein near Germiston. At each station the crowds were swelled by well-wishers and onlookers, while pickpockets added to the confusion. People shoved and pushed each other, while tears and anger, exhausted parents and lost children were the order of the day. On some occasions, a commando train would draw near to a refugee train as it loaded, causing considerable excitement as mutual insults added to the noise.[25]

With a cheer from the passengers, the trains would pull out of the last station and people would settle down to face a long and tiring journey. Overcrowding was a problem and occasional disturbances interrupted the trip. Latterly, the mixing of white and non-white refugees caused complaints, though some Europeans found their travelling companions 'amusing'. The Uitlanders' most serious worry was that they might be harassed by Boers *en route* and, indeed, there were instances of refugee trains being stoned and shot at, of money being taken from Uitlanders and of beatings. In one case, where a burgher shot at and broke a train window, the Uitlanders retaliated by whole-heartedly singing 'God Save the Queen' and 'Rule Britannia'.[26]

The men along the reef were not immune to the fear generated by the onrush of war. This was particularly distressing to managements of mines that had worked hard for two years to ensure a constant supply of cheap black labour. By mid-June it had become obvious that 'time-expired' blacks, who might in normal times be expected to re-enlist for another season's work, were departing instead, along with an increasing number of 'deserters'. To make matters worse, Africans were not coming in from the hinterland to replace those who left. By August the scarcity of African labour had become a major problem.[27] Already skilled white workers, especially machine men, were in scant supply. By September the trickle had

1st Class

Transvaal
Crisis.

1st Class Passengers
leaving Johannesburg in
Coal Trucks

Duffus Bros
Photo

THE WAR SCARE — 1000 MILES IN CATTLE TRUCKS

BARNETT

The War Scare — coal and cattle trucks were used to carry uitlanders to the coast, 1899
(*Africana Museum, Johannesburg*)

By and large the Boers were farmers and herdsmen, intent on maintaining their lifestyle and freedom (*Luli Callinicos*)

Colonel John Blake of the Irish Brigade, a pro-Boer unit formed on the Rand, had been an Indian fighter in the western states of America before coming to Africa (*Africana Museum, Johannesburg*)

Boer and pro-Boer uitlander commandos were raised in Johannesburg in the weeks before the war (*Africana Museum, Johannesburg*)

Special Commandant D. E. Schutte with burghers going off to the front at the beginning of the war (*Africana Museum, Johannesburg*)

Families and well-wishers at the station seeing Boer and pro-Boer forces off to the Natal front, 1899 (*With the Flag to Pretoria*, p. 24)

become a flood, as miners withdrew their savings, paid their bills and headed home. The situation on the mines was fast becoming critical.[28]

The first attempt to clarify the position of the mining companies and the mine-workers was undertaken by James Hay, director of several companies and former president of the Chamber of Mines. He told the state secretary, Reitz, that because so many men were leaving, industrial operations were being disrupted. The white workers, he explained, were afraid that if war broke out, they would be prevented from leaving the Republic and might even be killed. They wanted Pretoria's assurance that they would be protected in the event of war. Reitz replied to the men on 11 September: if those who remained behaved in a 'calm and peaceful' way, they would be given a reasonable length of time to leave if they wished to go.[29]

The miners near Heidelberg took their concerns to the mining commissioner, Viljoen, and asked him to promise them that, if war came, they would be allowed to leave and would not be forced to carry arms for the Republic. He reiterated Reitz's assurances, adding that, because all blacks were to be sent away, it would be unnecessary for white miners to carry guns for protection. He was emphatic: the government was opposed only to the 'rich men who want the country', not to the workers, whom it wished to see remain.[30] In the meantime, the companies approached the government and asked it to clarify its intentions regarding the industry.[31]

In fact the government was already in the process of defining its position. State attorney Smuts wrote to the Republican executive council on 4 September outlining his view that the mines would be of the utmost importance in the event of war. He emphasized that they would be a vital source of money if they could be kept open and proposed levying a war tax on their output — he suggested 20 per cent — in exchange for 'special protection'. To guarantee their operation, supplies of material and men had to be maintained and this, in turn, meant that whole staffs, even if British, should be encouraged to stay.[32]

To legalize its intentions, the government introduced for consideration by the Second Volksraad, Article 140 of the Gold Law (Law 15 of 1898), which had previously been rejected. To the consternation of the Randlords, it was adopted on 18 September. Briefly, it stated that after martial law was declared, if a mine partially or wholly ceased operations the government could order it to reopen and, if it did not comply, it could take over the operation itself. The government would be entitled to use any gold thus won for its own benefit. Further, the government would be obliged to return the mine to its owner(s) upon repeal of martial law, providing that the owner(s) had not in the meantime been proven guilty of high treason. Specifically, this meant that an owner would not receive the mine back if it could be shown that he had made a compact with a foreign government with a view to inducing the latter to make war on the Republic. Finally, the government was also obliged to compensate the owner(s) for any damage done to the mine, unless it was destroyed in the 'public interest'.[33] Now the Randlords knew exactly where they stood.

Soon the state mining engineer instructed his staff to obtain from each mine manager a list of all white workers employed on his mine and a statement of the quantity of explosives, coal and provisions in store. The industrialists saw this as the first step towards confiscation and the Chamber of Mines questioned the authority of the inspectors who tried to collect this data. In replying to the Chamber, the authorities cited the Gold Law. Clearly Pretoria was not going to be put off.[34]

Because companies faced not only a loss of revenue but confiscation if the mines closed, they were more than a little anxious to keep the ore-crushing stamps pounding. On 12 September a notice had appeared at the Simmer & Jack mine stating that a bonus of £25 — about a month's wage — would be paid to each white miner who remained at work until compelled to leave. Within a few days all the mining houses, with the exception of the J.B. Robinson group, had agreed to a scheme whereby any white worker who remained was to receive a bonus if war broke out or if the government forced him to leave. In other words, while the directors and their families left 'for the winter season at the coast', their workers were expected to accept £25 as a 'sufficient inducement . . . to run the risk of a little discomfort'.[35]

The loophole that made the promise of bonuses worthless was soon discovered: the government wanted the mines to keep working and had no intention of ordering willing workers to leave, even if war did break out. The miners' 'dissatisfaction' with the owners' conditions spread along the reef. As always, real power lay with the engine drivers, for without them the mines could not operate fully — now especially vital because of the threat of confiscation. On 20 September engine drivers along the reef threatened to strike unless the terms of the bonus were changed.[36]

Even without the threat of a strike, by mid-September managements were on the brink of having to cease operations. Work had been disrupted by the departure of skilled workmen, especially engine drivers, and the managers had asked the government to ease its restrictions on employing uncertified drivers so that they could replace the qualified men who had left.[37] This is not to say that the companies waited to receive permission, for experienced men often left with only a day's notice and managers were forced to replace them with unskilled workers and men of poor quality. This, in turn, caused the remaining experienced miners to fear for their safety, which resulted in the departure of even more skilled workmen. Managements on outlying mines faced the additional problem of having their men quit work to take up new employment on mines closer to town, in the belief that they were safer near urban centres.[38] In addition to these difficulties, coal was hard to come by on the mines whose railway sidings had not yet been constructed and water supplies were low, which was normal in these weeks before the rains.[39]

The government's assurances in mid-September did not stop miners from leaving and, within a week, the state mining engineer had approached the managements for suggestions on how best to keep the mines operational. Specifically, he asked the managers to recommend ways of retaining employees (both black and white) and, in keeping with Smuts's memorandum, to supply information regarding their plans for maintaining food supplies and industrial inputs. He also asked them for the names and nationalities of any men prepared to stay and work.[40]

The Chamber of Mines sent its member companies a form letter, which it suggested ought to be forwarded to the mining engineer in reply to his questions. The letter reflected the owners' frustration with the impact the deteriorating political situation was having on the industry, asserting that the threat of martial law and the lack of government assurances regarding the protection of the mines were the two chief causes of discontent among workers. On a more positive note, the Chamber suggested that the government guarantee protection of food supplies in the event of war and, since skilled workmen were in scarce supply, relax the regulations regarding the operation of winding machines. The transport of coal should be given high priority, the Chamber continued, while neither the mines' draught animals nor their conveyances should be subject to commandeering. Also, merchants who supplied the mines ought to be guaranteed special status and government protection. Finally, all canteens near the mines ought to be closed and any blacks necessary to the continued operation of the mines should be kept on the Rand.[41] The Chamber of Mines followed this up with a delegation to Pretoria, which reiterated most of the industrialists' concerns, but the only assurance the government was prepared to give the owners was that it intended to buy their gold and to reopen the mint.[42]

The government was less short-sighted than many of the Chamber's members feared. On 25 September it appointed a commission to frame a general plan for mining operations and within four days a set of formal guidelines had been published (a move intended to reassure white workers). The commission stated that the government hoped to see the mines continue their work undisturbed. In the event of war, men could apply to remain but would be required to swear that they would behave 'calmly, peacefully and subjectively'. Anyone who wished to leave thereafter would be provided with a visa and any person without funds would be given a free ticket. A permit system for the 'subjects of the nation bringing war against us' was to be introduced and a police force established to protect private property, including the mines. Liquor sales would cease, though permission could be obtained in a few instances to sell alcohol. Finally, the government intended to move all gold that was mined to Pretoria and to return coin to the companies to meet their expenses and wages. Upon termination of the war, after deducting taxes, the remainder of the gold would be returned to the companies.[43]

While the industry's response to the guidelines was mainly favourable — except for the clauses that gave Pretoria the right to use the output of working mines — it felt they were so long in coming that they were little use in persuading miners to remain. The industry's general pessimism really came to the fore when the declaration of dividends, which was then due, was postponed.[44] Events in the first week of October were expected to tell the tale: would there be enough men left on the mines at the end of that week to ensure their continued operation?

Like the railway figures, the list of closing mines shows that the exodus did not slow, but picked up, over the weekend of 30 September/1 October and levelled out the following week. On that weekend some of the better-known mines closed, including the Simmer & Jack, the Wolhuter, the Geldenhuis Deep and the Henry Nourse.[45] The Ferreira, with the highest rate of white 'desertions' at the end of September, closed on the 30th. It had the dubious honour of being the first mine threatened with confiscation. The 'Vierkleur' was hoisted there by its new manager, a government mining inspector from Florida on the west Rand, on 2 October. Job applications were accepted and the mine was expected to reopen under government management on the 4th, but having proved its point, Pretoria instead handed the mine back to its directors on the understanding that they would ensure its continued operation.[46]

The exodus of the Robinson Deep's remaining engine drivers forced it to close on the 3rd. By that time all the Consolidated Gold Fields mines had closed, though only one of the Barnato mines had done so. Eckstein & Company had five working mines and Neumann & Company, two. Daily the number mounted and, by the 7th, the government listed 66 major mines closed. At that time only 17 applications to continue operations had been received.[47]

Business in town was at a virtual standstill. In mid-September some windows had been boarded up, reflecting, and no doubt hastening, the departure of many people. By the first week in October probably two-thirds of the city's businesses had ceased operation and those that remained open found it difficult to deliver goods because most of their draught animals had been commandeered. Anxiety among workers in town paralleled that of miners along the reef. For instance, Scottish bank clerks at the National Bank went on strike twice in an effort to get bank officials to make provisions for their departure if and when they chose to leave. By October 'panic' was the word being used to describe the feelings of those who remained. The city had the appearance of being 'besieged', as many firms had 'battened up' while others had their wood and iron work at the ready. Few people were left to roam the streets.[48]

The mines' black workers continued to leave in small numbers throughout September. At the end of the month the supply was still considered 'adequate', but that was because there were fewer mines working. Since fewer men were coming in to replace those leaving the Rand, 'touts' offered men released from closed mines to managers who were trying to keep their own open.[49] At some mines, 'restlessness' among black workers was reported. In early October Africans at the Robinson Deep were described as 'excited'. On the Simmer & Jack they were 'very excited' especially after a local pass official told them that after September no more travelling passes (which were necessary to leave for home legally) were going to be issued. On the Driefontein mine, angry blacks with Martini—Henry rifles occupied an underground section, while on another mine African workers requested a pay rise of £1 per month to stay on. When the manager refused, they besieged the mine secretary's office and were dispersed only with the aid of nearby armed burghers. On the Jumpers Deep the Africans refused to go underground and the mine was forced to cease operations the following day, 5 October.[50]

In the meantime, white workers on some of the mines were finding out how worthless the promise of the bonus really was. Aurora West miners were irate when they found that the company declined to pay the bonus; on 30 September they threatened to wreck machinery, but to no avail. A week later the Croesus dismissed its men with no advance notice and the promised bonus did not materialize. The men, who felt this a 'mean breach of . . . word' and who were placed in a position of not being able to meet their own debts, were in an 'exasperated mood' and 'freely breathe[d] threats of reprisal'.[51]

Many companies did, however, pay the bonus. Eckstein & Company paid £25 to all the men who remained on condition that they would 'avail themselves of the government permission to remain on the mines unmolested even should hostilities break out'.[52] The Rand Mines Limited paid the bonus willingly because, as the chairman of one of its mines explained, while the bonus might cost the company £1,400, the mine remained open a fortnight longer than would otherwise be possible. J. B. Robinson's companies never did pay the bonus, an injustice felt by the men, who chose to leave his mines early.[53]

In these few weeks before the war the directors and shareholders faced a dilemma: the mines had to be kept open because of the threat of confiscation, even though this meant higher costs and reduced profits because fewer stamps could be kept working.[54] The reformers were also feeling the pressure and urged the government to take a strong stand: labourers were leaving, shops were closing and mining supplies were being held up at the coast. London was urged not to 'waste time . . . on franchise negotiations . . . but bring matters to an early issue and terminate present suspense by taking a firm stand, even at the risk of war'.[55]

Similarly, white miners were in a quandary: their common sense told them to flee like the rest of the population, while their bosses and the press bullied them into staying by saying things such as, 'it would not be right to charge these men with lack of patriotism — this is not a quality which is to be expected from men whose sole object in coming hither or proceeding to other countries is to improve their financial position.' None the less, Eckstein's *South African Mining Journal* continued, it would be more satisfactory if 'as Englishmen, they had stood by their fellow countrymen who are endeavouring to bring about a better state of things'.[56]

Randites were worried about the impact of the increasing tension on the African population. All whites agreed that there was a need to pacify the restless Africans and this, in turn, put pressure on both parties to bring about a quick settlement. As far back as June, the *Standard and Diggers' News* had warned the agitators of Johannesburg that they should very carefully consider the consequences of their actions: 'there are 80,000 adult and able-bodied natives employed on the Witwatersrand . . . [and] there are thousands of others in surrounding districts. . . . Are they going to remain quiet? . . . What they will do no man of the world cares to dwell on'.[57] Thereafter, reports of discontent in the compounds and locations filled the press, fuelling panic. For that reason, the government's plan, announced shortly before the outbreak of war, to remove all excess blacks from the district, found favour in all quarters.[58]

Predictions of unrest were correct. Most of the problems centred on the eastern Rand, for officials in the west had devised a 'perfect system' whereby blacks discharged from the mines were herded together in large numbers by armed police and passed from one field cornet to another until they were safely and peaceably escorted out of the district.[59] On the east Rand, things were rather different, particularly near Rietfontein, where trouble started when the mines ceased operations and released their workers. On 4 October rioting and looting began and, the following day, blacks armed with knobkerries set fire to the compound at the Driefontein mine. Looting of canteens and shops in the vicinity by 'some thousands' followed. The local police, unable to quell the disturbance, called on a commando to assist them. Before the situation was brought under control, two Russians were killed, purportedly for refusing to supply Africans with liquor. Closer to Johannesburg, on the Nourse Deep, shops were looted by men who had been discharged on the 5th. They were finally driven away by the police. On the Rietfontein 'A', black workers, unwilling to leave the property but equally as unwilling to work, were paid off by the management which then led them off the property in batches of 50 to keep them from forming large groups and adding to the already troubled situation.[60]

Looting also spread from the central Rand into the city. In early October blacks from Robinson Deep compound looted Chinese shops at Ophirton and raided a nearby butcher shop. On the 8th, at a 'puza' (drink) shop in the location near Vrededorp, shots were fired and the police called in. Soon other shops nearby were broken into and windows smashed. The looting here and elsewhere along the Rand might in part be explained as an attempt by the discharged Africans to gather stores prior to their departure for home. Still, their riotous behaviour was fuelled by the sale of illicit liquor, just the sort of situation the Randites had feared all along.[61]

Despite the desire to rid the city of Africans, the authorities drove thousands of blacks into Johannesburg in an effort to relieve tension along the reef. In the city, chaos resulted as workers, carrying their only possessions, were kept together long enough to be issued with travel permits and to have their transport arranged. In Marshall Square there were 'immense crowds' of Africans, most of whom had been left without work when the mines closed. There they sat for days with their goods bundled, fed by nervous shopkeepers and vendors. Just a mile or so away at the showgrounds in Braamfontein 4,000 more were camped out under guard, waiting for trains to carry them home.[62] The situation in town threatened to deteriorate seriously each time whites took advantage of the disorder to cheat the Africans. 'Kitchen boys' and others in urban employment complained that they had no funds with which to get home because their employers had left the city without paying them. On at least one occasion an unscrupulous agent bought railway tickets for some 200 mine-workers, which were supposed to carry them to the Mozambican border, but only took them as far as Park Station in central Johannesburg, where they sat without any money to go further.[63]

Generally, though, it was the mining companies that were to blame for the chaos on the reef, for few took any responsibility for repatriating their workers after paying them off and ordering them to leave the compounds. In some cases, African workers were actually forced off properties by employers: blacks were reluctant to leave the relative safety of the compound for fear of being commandeered by burghers, becoming involved with the crowds of looters, or being arrested by the police. They were also not anxious to begin a journey that was neither pre-planned nor well provided for and that would probably necessitate crossing battlelines. But leave they must and, in cases where Africans refused to quit compounds, police were called in to eject them. In the midst of the riots the Boer authorities decided they had no option but to send them away without passes; anything, just to get them out of the district. By the 9th they were at their wits' end and they began to commandeer trains to help them rid the Rand of the 'savages'.[64]

The journey home was more arduous for blacks than for the Uitlander refugees. In many cases they were expected to stand for 12 hours in overcrowded, open cattle cars or coal trucks. The last to leave were reported to have travelled for up to three days without provisions. Not all left by train; some had no choice but to walk home. One large-scale effort — then deemed 'heroic' — to lead some 7,000 Africans back to Natal was undertaken by J. S. Marwick, a representative of the Native Affairs Department in the colony.

From June onwards Marwick had advised his charges to remain at work and assured them that, if the time came for them to leave, they would be cared for by the authorities. In late September he approached the Republican government to get permission to send them home and was advised that, rather than wait for passes, he ought to use train tickets as passes and send as many as he could away as quickly as possible. On 1 October he put 1,000 aboard a Natal-bound train; when the Natal line closed he sought the authorities' permission to take the rest home by foot. When advised to wait for the line to reopen, he chose instead to march east.

Before leaving the city he wired ahead nearly £10,000 belonging to his charges. Then, on 6 October, he and six Republican policemen left with 4,000 people. After marching them out of Johannesburg, he returned for another 3,000. Through the rural areas, three policemen rode ahead of the group to warn the residents that they were coming. Although the burghers were thus protected, little was done to prevent the Africans being cheated by unscrupulous shopkeepers along the route.

The party covered about 35 miles a day. The women, children and sick had been sent ahead by train from Heidelberg. Any recently sick or injured person rode aboard a trolley and stragglers who found no room there limped on miles behind the rest. Supplies, ordered in advance, were generally waiting for the group when it arrived at a site, thus saving the countryside from wide-scale looting. Theft and drunkenness were in part the result of a number of Rand criminals having joined the group as it left the city.

The most dangerous, as opposed to the most arduous, part of the journey was when these 7,000 people on the verge of starvation and complete exhaustion came upon the rear of some 3,000 armed burghers near Laing's Nek and Commandant Trichardt refused to let them pass through the lines. Eventually, after a certain amount of negotiation, they were allowed to move forward and they eventually arrived at Newcastle on 11 October. There they dispersed, some going to the coast by train while others continued their trip to Zululand on foot.[65]

While the Temporary Relief Committee assisted indigent whites, very few of the benevolent in the city cared much about impoverished non-whites. The views of the Revd Kelly, a man praised by the Uitlander élite for his work among the city's poor, were not unlike those of most of his colleagues. In July 1899 he explained how:

> white people had the first claim upon their [the benevolent's] consideration. They all know the difficulties in getting native servants. They knew the difficulties most people had in getting natives to work. They could not get native females to do household work or . . . their washing, whereas they knew there were many white females in the town in great distress, and therefore, to begin to discuss this question of what might come [i.e. blacks dying in hundreds and thousands] . . . would, he thought, be most unwise.[66]

One of the few who did care about the distress in the non-white community was Charles Vincent, secretary of the Temporary Relief Committee. In early July he took a firm stand, threatening to resign if nothing were done to help these people. Those opposing him argued that existing organizations could cope with the problem and besides, Kelly warned, 'if they began to throw open the door, they would have all the Coolie location to feed and all the loafers in Johannesburg'.[67]

Undeterred, Vincent and several ministers organized a 'Coloured People's Relief Committee' a few days later. Vincent explained to the people that if they first tried to help themselves, surely the whites would come to their assistance if necessary. Actually, his promise was kept, for when the distress in the Coloured community became 'acute' at the end of September, the Temporary Relief Committee did step in. It distributed food twice weekly to 'ordinary cases' and daily to those known to be absolutely destitute. Some received assisted railway passages, but, because this assistance was limited, many were forced to turn to the Anglican priest, the Revd John Darragh of St Mary's, who helped with funds so that the poorest could leave.[68]

The Asians had an additional handicap: they were no more welcome in Natal than in the Republic and regulations were in force in the colony that made it mandatory for an Indian to pay a deposit to the government there as a guarantee that he or she would not remain longer than a few weeks. In August, Greene (in Pretoria) asked for the Natal restrictions to be relaxed, for he was worried that several thousand Asians would be stranded in the Republic. The Natal authorities were reluctant to announce publicly that Indians would be welcome, but did agree that 'if things come to a head, there will be no one on the border to ask the question . . . and should the Indians be obliged to seek refuge in Natal, Ministers have no intention of keeping them out'. They also waived the fee for the 'visitor's pass' and agreed that an Asian's visit could now legally be extended from three weeks to six. Officials were posted in Johannesburg and at Charlestown to facilitate the issue of passes and in September Asians in large numbers joined the rush to the coast.[69]

Estimates of the number of non-whites fleeing Johannesburg and the surrounding areas in the weeks before the war vary. It may be safely assumed that at least 60,000 'east coast natives' left between 1 and 24 October, though many went before that. Peter Warwick's number of 78,000 leaving by rail between 1 September and 19 October certainly seems plausible, though many went on foot in those weeks. There is little doubt, then, that nearly 100,000 Africans, Asians and Coloureds joined the mass exodus in the months preceding the war.[70]

It may be recalled that in May the Boers arrested seven minor conspirators, while the real antagonists continued to operate in and out of the public arena. By the middle of the year the SAL's work was virtually complete as public opinion in the colonies and at home had crystallized.[71] But the UC's work was not yet finished. Its opinions were still sought by Milner and it was expected to work as a pressure group. Still, its work was circumscribed from July onwards as its members began to receive anonymous threats. Thereafter, its meetings were kept secret and it was no longer considered safe to keep a register of its members and attendance at its meetings. In July, its president, Hosken, asked the British government to extend its 'special protection' to all UC members, by which he meant that the imperial government ought to inform Pretoria that it would be held responsible for any outrage carried out against the persons or property of these men. The British representative in Pretoria asked for a more detailed report from the UC, but because events overtook them it was never filed. Within two months the UC's papers had been secreted away and its members 'scattered to the four winds'.[72]

The departure of the councillors gave rise to comment, for many Randites blamed them personally for the suffering caused by the increase in political tension and the resulting collapse of the local economy. The parody, 'Mr Funkit has left last night for Durban on a brief visit to his wife and children'[73] did not miss the mark, for, as the political horizons darkened, notices began to appear in the social columns of the press detailing the departures of the wives and families of leading Johannesburgers. Their menfolk followed not long after.[74]

The arrest of the jingoist editor of the *Transvaal Leader*, R. J. Pakeman, for high treason on 1 September, did nothing to alleviate the fears of the UC or, indeed, of the general public. He was held for several days as rumours circulated that warrants for the arrest of several other reformers, including Monypenny of the *Star* and Hosken, were waiting to be served. While Pakeman sat in prison, the police began their search for Monypenny, but he, along with H. C. Hull, had taken refuge in a previously prepared hiding place in an unused shaft on the Ferreira mine. For four days they eluded the police and in the early morning hours they left, disguised as prospectors with buckets and spades and four days' growth, for the Cape. Clem Webb of the SAL, disguised as a doctor, fled soon after. The police were unable to find any other agitators and Pakeman informed them that, had they waited one more day, they would not have found him either. He was soon released on £500 bail and fled to Natal, refusing to return for his court hearing. According to Milner, the object of Pakeman's arrest was to intimidate the Uitlander leadership. Whether or not this was in fact the Boers' intention, the goal was achieved.[75]

On 5 September, the *Standard and Diggers' News* published a 'Rand Roll-Call' which listed about 20 names, most of whom were UC members suspected of having left Johannesburg. The paper's stated purpose was to demonstrate to the public just how these men, after stirring up trouble, had fled leaving the rest of the community to suffer. Letters to the editor in the following weeks echoed this sentiment as people expressed their view that these men had neither the 'stamina nor the manliness' to stay and face the music.[76] But the members of the UC felt justified in leaving, for by early September they considered their work complete[77] and it probably was. Also, they were worried that they would be arrested and possibly even killed by the Boers. None the less, Milner was angry when hearing of their sudden departure, feeling that they had given way to 'excessive panic' in the face of Boer attempts to 'frighten people away in order to break down the firm attitude of Johannesburg, and leave [the imperial government] without advisers in [a] joint enquiry'.[78]

Milner's subordinates, closer to the scene, came to the councillors' defence. Vice-consul Evans explained to Milner that they would be more 'useful to the Uitlander cause' at the coast, while Greene in Pretoria outlined his fear that the Boers might well use the councillors as hostages in the event of war and, for that reason, it was better that they had left: their becoming political prisoners would only exacerbate the situation. Milner accepted this reasoning, though Greene still went in search of councillors. On 9 September he was able to find 21, though by the 27th only half that number remained.[79]

In the meantime arrests continued. In late September David Robertson, a 28-year-old Scot working for the Clydesdale (Transvaal) Colliery, was arrested for recruiting Uitlanders for the Imperial Light Horse. He had been sending men down to Natal to join the unit for some time when the police caught up with him. Little could be done for him and he spent several months in jail before the Boers released him.[80]

Pakeman's and Robertson's arrests, as well as the flight of the reformers, gave evidence of the deepening crisis, which, in turn, motivated ordinary people to leave and the more politicized pro-Boer Uitlanders to organize. On 16 September, J. T. Bain once again entered public life when he called a meeting on Market Square in an attempt to enrol volunteers for the Boer forces. The meeting had to be cancelled because of the size and 'turbulence' of the 'mob' that had come to see him. When he appeared on the platform, he was attacked by a group of men wielding sticks, men whom Bain claimed were hired by the reformers to keep him from speaking, a charge never proven.[81] Though Bain was denied a hearing, volunteers did begin to organize.

Bain served as a recruiter and later a member of the First Irish Brigade, which was formed in September. The 'Irish Manifesto', a document published late in the month, laid out the motives behind its formation. It first discussed the Jameson Raid, which was, it claimed, instigated by a 'member of the Queen's Privy Council', and then turned to the present struggle: a 'number of English capitalists', along with this unnamed cabinet member, had continued their scheming and agitation, bringing the two countries close to war. The depth of the hatred of the British government — the reason why many of these men joined the Boers — is notable:

> Irishmen! The Transvaal Boers have fought for a bravely won Independence. You have seen in your own country the effects of English rule; you have seen your fathers, your mothers, and your sisters suffer in themselves and in their children, poverty, nakedness, hunger, misery and oppression of the most dreadful kinds. You know that English rule has left your country desolate, and driven her children forth, homeless, and penniless, to all the ends of the earth. You know that during the sixty years of Queen Victoria's reign, one and a half million of your countrymen and women have perished of starvation! . . . You know all this, you have seen all this, and we ask you, in the presence of the terrible apparition of your own perishing country, whether you are going to help bring the same curse upon the Transvaal. Vengeance! Irishmen![82]

On 1 October, John Y. F. Blake, an Irish-American who had been born on a Texas cattle ranch, had graduated from West Point in 1880 and had served in the American army as an Indian fighter, but who was now resident on the Rand, was chosen to lead the brigade. An adventurer at heart, his idealism matched that of his men: 'It will be a Chamberlain and Rhodes war', he wrote as the contingent left the city, 'against the principles of right, justice, honour, and humanity. . . The Irish Brigade will do its duty because its members have felt the lash of slavery at the hands of the English soldiery'. About 250 men, many of whom had been born in Italy, Scandinavia, Germany and Russia, entrained for Volksrust on the 6th.[83]

The local Scandinavian organization set up the Scandinavian corps in late September. Its members were motivated by many of the same considerations as the Irish. As E. Olsen-Mandahl put it in a review of the liberation struggles of the Nordic peoples in the local press, 'Can we, Scandinavians, with such a record, stand back . . . and see the dearly-bought independence of this country taken away? Look at the ways and means used during the last years by the capitalists and their tools to ruin the country'. The Scandinavian corps, renowned for its bravery, was active on General Piet Cronje's western front until this bravery turned to foolhardiness at Magersfontein in December and the unit was virtually wiped out.[84]

The Russians already resident in the Republic took an active role in reflecting their government's enthusiastic support for Kruger. (Certainly Moscow's own imperial rivalry with Britain in south Asia had something to do with its position). The original Russian corps was made up of about 60 men, though it was careful to exclude what it called 'Russian Border Israelites'. It was led by the gallant playboy, Count Alexis de Ganetzky, who was soon joined by other nobles and adventurers from Russia.[85]

The French corps, known as the de Korte corps, was also formed in September, with the express purpose of protecting property within a five-mile radius of the city centre. Soon it focused on protecting the mines. Not content with this relatively peaceful role, at the end of the year Viscount Villebois-Mareuil formed a small French force, comprised almost solely of newly-arrived Frenchmen.[86]

While many Italians stayed in Johannesburg to man the ammunition works, others joined the Italian Scouts led by the handsome and romantic figure of Captain Camillo Richiardi, whose military experience had been gained in Ethiopia and later the Philippines. The Italian Scouts, which consisted of men of various (but mostly 'Latin') nationalities, was considered one of the ablest units of its kind during the war.

During the first months of the war, pro-Boer Americans fought in Boer commandos, but after the Natal campaign they were brought together by Captain John Hassell as the American Scouts. Hassell had been in southern Africa for five years (prospecting and with shooting expeditions) and thus had a good understanding of the nature of the countryside. His scouts were soon augmented by men who entered the country especially to fight with the Boers.

Naturally, there was a Hollander corps. It was based in Pretoria, but included many men from government establishments and the railway yard and office in Johannesburg. It was virtually annihilated at Elandslaagte in November, though surviving members joined other commando units thereafter.

A few Greeks living in Johannesburg and along the reef joined commandos, rather than form their own.[87] The Jews of Johannesburg chose not to form a military unit at all. Instead, they were active in public service. In October they offered their services to the government and were asked to organize an ambulance corps. The Johannesburg Jewish Ambulance Unit tended wounded men sent from the front, provided equipment to commandos on patrol, visited at least one battle to give medical assistance and helped the wounded at Begbie's explosion. After the British captured the Rand in late May, it continued to transport sick and wounded to and from Elandsfontein until disbandment in April 1901.[88]

As war approached, German Anglophobia took concrete form in the creation of a German corps. While some Germans organized to protect women and children on the Rand, others joined Colonel Schiel's force. Many signed on, not because of their dislike of all things British, but because of their disgust with the machinations of the Randlords. In any case, some 400 men joined the corps, which was the first to leave the Rand (heading for Volksrust) on 1 October. At Elandslaagte, Schiel was captured and the corps suffered severe losses. Thereafter it was reorganized under Commandant Krantz and fought in Natal and later in the Orange Free State.[89]

How many Rand Uitlanders fought with the Boers is difficult to say — it may have been as many as 1,000 — but most of them, anxious to find a safe place to sit out what was expected to be a short-lived war, left for the coast, or beyond to their homes overseas. Asians clung tenaciously to the African continent, there by the grace of the colonial governments. Coloureds for the most part went back to the Cape, there to wait patiently for an end to the war. Those blacks who managed to avoid conscription by the Boers returned to their kraals, but several thousand remained (generally unwillingly) on the reef to work.

As the population of Johannesburg fell, it took on what one observer called a 'Scotch Sabbath appearance'.[90] An unnatural quiet settled over the city:

> From being a busy, flourishing hive of energetic workers of all descriptions crowded to excess, fearing accidents at every street corner, seething with life, hope and ambition, aided by ferment of political unrest, Johannesburg became a deserted, gloomy empty city with what appeared to our overstrung nervous minds to be a rapacious blood thirsty horde at its gates, anxious and ready to despoil the Egyptian of all the treasures stored up in the 'Curse of the Transvaal'. It is heartrending to see the lovely suburban homes barricaded, in some cases, with corrugated iron, in others with wood, deserted, neglected, their only occupants some poor starving pet dog or cat, who faithful to the last stuck to their posts, though their poor skeleton bodies showed they were more or less starving.[91]

The reformers had done their work well, and now the end had come. Ordinary

Randites had been caught up in a struggle for control of the Republic and its wealth:

> So away they went, poor souls, enduring great hardships on the journey to a place of refuge in British territory — packed like sardines in carriages, coal trucks, animal trucks, scarcely standing room, and when the panic was at its height, foodless, without drinks for their little crying thirsty children — no shelter from the burning South African sun, white and coloured mixed indiscriminately — a journey of hours taking days, stoppages at the sidings and stations for many hours while commando trains filled with Boers passed on. . . . [At] Braamfontein station . . . everywhere little groups of people with small bundles containing a rug or two and perhaps a few sandwiches, with haggard pathetic faces and drooping dejected mien, thinking of the homes they had abandoned, fleeing to an unknown and uncertain future, in most cases quite ruined by the long and protracted course of Diplomacy — talking in subdued heart-broken voices of the situation — crowds of human beings, women, children and men, white and coloured, waiting patiently for the train whose puffings and shrill whistles, told it was close by. Slowly it came on, and before it could be stopped — the patient crowd changed like a kaladeiscope [*sic*] and instead was a frantic, scrambling yelling mass of arms and legs, no matter how obtained a place must be got. 'Father, father, come, come, climb here', a little sobbing voice called out, and we saw a little boy of about 13, his face white and distorted climbing over the wheels into a cattle truck while the train was still in motion, and dragging after him an old white-haired man feeble and tottering. Women with babies in their arms, hardly recovered from the illness of travail, struggled, with two or three little ones clinging to their skirts, into that haven of safety, a bogey or a cattle truck — by and bye — the train could hold no more.[92]

War had come to Johannesburg.

Notes

1. *Star*, 29 April, 7 and 8 July 1899; *S & D News*, 21 and 23 June, 22 July 1899; MS/PRO/DO 119/349, Greene to Milner (confidential), 4 April 1899; and MS/PRO/DO 119/545, Greene to Milner, 6 May 1899, with enclosed report by J. E. Evans. See also MS/JPL/ACPT, London letterbook, reports dated 16 May, 12 June, 3 and 31 July, 7 and 21 Aug. 1899, and 'accounts, Jan. to 30 June 1899', pp. 321—48.
2. *Star*, 17 Nov. 1898, 19 Jan., 16 Feb., 11 and 24 April 1899; MS/JPL/ACPT, reports dated 7 Nov. 1898, 30 Jan. and 3 April 1899; MS/PRO/DO 119/349, Greene to Milner (confidential), 4 April 1899; Marais 1961, p. 256.
3. *Star*, 9 and 29 June, 9 Sept. 1899; *S & D News*, 20 and 21 June 1899.
4. MS/PRO/DO 119/545, Greene to Milner, 6 May 1899, with enclosed report by J. E. Evans; MS/PRO/CO 417/264, Milner to Chamberlain, 26 July 1899, with enclosure Greene to Milner, 19 July 1899, forwarding report from Hosken, 18 July 1899. Also, for the 'war scare', see *S & D News*, 8 May 1899; MS/JPL/ACPT, London letterbooks, reports dated 1 May, 21 Aug. and 4 Sept. 1899.
5. MS/BOD/Mss. Milner Dep. 227, 'Secret Boer documents, 1899', report by S. Schiel to commandant general, Pretoria (confidential), 11 May 1899. *S & D News*, 15 June, 24 July 1899; *Star*, 22 June, 3 July, 24 Aug. and 26 Sept. 1899.
6. MS/PRO/CO 417/264, Milner to Chamberlain, 26 July 1899, with enclosure, Greene to Milner, 19 July 1899, reporting on deputation and Hosken's views.

7. MS/USL/Lipp, p. 2. See also MS/JPL/ACPT, London letterbook, report dated 21 Aug. 1899, for a calmer view.
8. *S & D News*, 1 Sept. 1899; *South African Mining Journal*, 8 (413) 2 Sept. 1899; *Transvaal Critic*, 6 Oct. 1899; MS/TAD/R&O 515, 'Rust en Orde, notule Oktober 1899'.
9. MS/USL/Lipp, p. 2.
10. Harris 1901, p. 23.
11. *Star*, 31 May, 21, 24 and 27 June, 21 July, and 22 Aug. 1899.
12. *Star*, 1 Sept. 1899.
13. Numbers in receipt of relief for the week ending: 18 July (1,194), 25 July (1,690), 1 August (1,919), 8 August (1,486), 15 August (1,325) and 22 August (1,712). From late August until late September the numbers averaged upwards of 2,000 a week, though a peak of 4,000 was reached in the last week of September 1899. (*Star*, 1 and 23 Sept. 1899, 7 May 1902).
14. *Star*, 1 and 23 Sept. 1899, 7 May 1902. The mines, as in 1898, offered work to men at a rate of 5/— plus housing per day.
15. *Star*, 7 May 1902, and see 16 Sept. 1899, when editor suggests that people no longer postpone their departures on account of any feeling of optimism.
16. Harris 1901, pp. 23—4; *Star*, 1, 12 and 29 Sept. 1899; *S & D News*, 11 Sept. 1899; MS/BOD/Mss. Milner Dep. 212, Greene to Milner (private), 5 Sept. 1899, 8 Sept. 1899. See also MS/LHC/Edmonds, Box V/4/5/3, 'The Netherlands Southern African Railway Company and the Transvaal War'.
17. Harris 1901, pp. 23—4.
18. *Star*, 14 July, 11 and 14 Sept. 1899; *S & D News*, 6 and 7 Oct. 1899.
19. For letters from Randites to the Rust en Orde Commission in Johannesburg, see MS/TAD/R&O 540—7; MS/PRO/CO 417/268, Milner to Chamberlain, 25 Oct. 1899, with enclosure, governor of Natal to Milner, 22 Oct. 1899, forwarding letter from Miss K. Orr in Johannesburg; MS/PRO/DO 119/487 and DO 119/497, letters to J. E. Evans; and Harris 1901, p. 26.
20. *Star*, 7 May 1902; and Harris 1901, p. 25, where he notes that the Committee left £500 in cash and foodstuffs valued at £2,000 for the use of British residents.
21. Estimates of the number leaving the Rand vary widely. See *Transvaal Critic*, 29 Sept. 1899, p. 299; and the daily editions of the *Star* and *S & D News*. See also Roos 1949, pp. 1—16.
22. See daily press reports, esp. *S & D News*, 11, 21, 22 and 30 Sept. 1899; and *Star*, 26 Sept. 1899.
23. *Star*, 3 and 9 Oct. 1899; *S & D News*, 11 Sept., 2 and 11 Oct. 1899. For a first-hand account of the journey and the stay in Lourenço Marques, see Froes 1899.
24. *Star*, 8, 11, 18 and 22 Sept., 2 and 6 Oct. 1899; *S & D News*, 13 and 15 Sept., 7 and 13 Oct. 1899.
25. For general descriptions, see daily press, esp. the *Star*, 23 Aug., 1, 22, 26, 29 Sept. 1899; and *S & D News*, 9, 11, 22, 30 Sept., 2 Oct. 1899. For a first-hand account, see MS/JPL/Lennard, entry dated 17 Oct. 1899; and MS/JPL/van der Horst, p. 27.
26. Froes 1899, pp. 14, 23; MS/PRO/CO 417/267, Milner to Chamberlain, 10 Oct. 1897 and CO/417/268, Milner to Chamberlain, 18 Oct. 1899. See also the daily press, esp. the *Star*, 25 Aug. 1899; and *S & D News*, 26 Sept. 1899. At least one novel (Blore 1900) gives an account, somewhat exaggerated, of the exodus.
27. *South African Mining Journal*, 8 (402) 17 June 1899, p. 673; (404) 1 July 1899, p. 703; (405) 8 July 1899, p. 721; (410) 12 Aug. 1899, p. 809; (412) 26 Aug. 1899, p. 846. See also *African Review* 21 (360) 14 Oct. 1899, pp. 6—8.
28. *South African Mining Journal*, 8 (412) 26 Aug. 1899, p. 846; (413) 2 Sept. 1899, p. 858; (415) 16 Sept. 1899, pp. 889, 891. See also *Star*, 29 Aug. 1899.
29. *South African Mining Journal*, 8 (415) 16 Sept. 1899, p. 889; *S & D News*, 12 Sept. 1899.
30. *S & D News*, 18 Sept. 1899; *South African Mining Journal*, 8 (416) 23 Sept. 1899, p. 905.
31. *South African Mining Journal*, 8 (416) 23 Sept. 1899, p. 905.
32. Smuts to Executive Council, SAR, 4 Sept. 1899, in Hancock and van der Poel (eds) 1966, pp. 322 ff.

33. *Star*, 14, 19 Sept. 1899; *African Review*, 21 (315) 14 Oct. 1899, pp. 61—2.
34. *Star*, 15 Sept. 1899; *South African Mining Journal*, 8 (415) 16 Sept. 1899, p. 891.
35. *South African Mining Journal*, 8 (415) 16 Sept. 1899, p. 891; *Star*, 13, 16 Sept. 1899; *S & D News*, 23 Sept. 1899.
36. *Star*, 18, 20, 23 Sept. 1899; *S & D News*, 18, 21, 23 Sept. 1899; *South African Mining Journal*, 8 (416) 23 Sept. 1899, pp. 905—6.
37. *Star*, 22, 30 Sept. 1899; *S & D News*, 23 Sept. 1899.
38. *Star*, 22, 30 Sept., 5 Oct. 1899.
39. *S & D News*, 23 Sept. 1899; *Star*, 30 Sept. 1899.
40. *Star*, 22, 23 Sept. 1899; *South African Mining Journal*, 8 (417) 30 Sept. 1899, pp. 921—2.
41. *Star*, 23 Sept. 1899.
42. *Star*, 25 Sept. 1899; *South African Mining Journal*, 8 (417) 30 Sept. 1899, p. 922.
43. *Star*, 26 Sept., 5 Oct. 1899; *S & D News*, 5, 6 Oct. 1899.
44. *South African Mining Journal*, 8 (417) 30 Sept. 1899, p. 923; *Star*, 29 Sept. 1899.
45. *S & D News*, 2 Oct. 1899, p. 4.
46. *South African Mining Journal*, 8 (417) 30 Sept. 1899, p. 923; *Star*, 2, 3, 4 Oct. 1899; *S & D News*, 5 Oct. 1899.
47. *S & D News*, 9 Oct. 1899; *Star*, 3, 4 Oct. 1899.
48. MS/JPL/ACPT, London letterbook, report dated 2 Oct. 1899; see *Star*, 20 Sept., 4 Oct. 1899.
49. *Star*, 30 Sept. 1899; *South African Mining Journal*, 8 (417) 30 Sept. 1899, pp. 923—4.
50. *Star*, 30 Sept., 6 Oct. 1899; *S & D News*, 2, 7 Oct. 1899; *South African Mining Journal*, 8 (417) 30 Sept. 1899, pp. 923—4; Warwick 1983, pp. 131—2.
51. *S & D News*, 2, 6 Oct. 1899.
52. *S & D News*, 6 Oct. 1899.
53. *S & D News*, 6, 14 Oct. 1899; *Transvaal Critic*, 29 Sept. 1899, p. 312.
54. *Star*, 26 Sept. 1899.
55. MS/PRO/DO 119/542, Greene to Milner, 29 Aug. 1899; DO 119/361, Greene to Milner, 14 Sept. 1899 for further requests by the UC. Henry Lambert at the CO noted about this time that, 'this is why many think that even war would be a relief — it would certainly put money into circulation'. See the note on file MS/PRO/CO 417/265.
56. *South African Mining Journal*, 8 (423), 2 Sept. 1899, p. 858.
57. *S & D News*, 14 June 1899.
58. For instance, see *S & D News*, 6 Oct. 1899; *African Review*, 21 (314) 7 Oct. 1899, pp. 21—2.
59. MS/TAD/R&O 516, file M, report no. 1, 6 Oct. 1899.
60. *Transvaal Critic*, 6 Oct. 1899, p. 319; *S & D News*, 6 Oct. 1899; *Star*, 5, 7 Oct. 1899.
61. *Star*, 4, 5, 9 Oct. 1899; *S & D News*, 9 Oct. 1899. Daily reports provide other instances of rioting.
62. *Star*, 5 Oct. 1899; *S & D News*, 6 Oct. 1899; see Warwick 1983, p. 127.
63. *S & D News*, 9 Oct. 1899; *Star*, 5 Oct. 1899.
64. *S & D News*, 7, 20 Oct. 1899; *Star*, 7 Oct. 1899; MS/JPL/ACPT, London letterbook, report dated 7 Oct. 1899; see Warwick 1983, pp. 127—9; MS/TAD/R&O 516, file M, Consolidated Goldfields of South Africa Ltd to mine commissioner, Johannesburg, 2 Oct. 1899.
65. *S & D News*, 7 Oct. 1899; *African Review*, 21 (318) 4 Nov. 1899, p. 188; and, for Marwick's report, see MS/PRO/DO 119/431, Hely Hutchinson to Milner, 24 Oct. 1899, with enclosed report dated 19 Oct. 1899. See also Warwick 1983, p. 128; van Onselen 1982, vol. 2, p. 178.
66. *Star*, 4 July 1899.
67. Ibid.
68. *S & D News*, 14 July 1899; *Star*, 19 Sept., 4 Oct. 1899, 7 May 1902.
69. MS/PRO/CO 417/266, Milner to Chamberlain, 12 Sept. 1899, with enclosures; and, for the Asian exodus, see *S & D News*, 21 Sept., 2 Oct. 1899.
70. MS/TAD/SNA/11, 'Portuguese labour question', and appendix of report by J. Ivens

Ferrar, 16 June 1900, 'Statistics of the exodus of Portuguese east coast natives from the Transvaal and bound to the kraals in the Province of Mozambique'; also Warwick 1983, p. 127. For reports of exodus with statistics, see *S & D News*, 21 Sept. and 9 Oct. 1899; *Star*, 5 Oct. 1899.

71. For instance, see Ovendale 1980.

72. MS/PRO/CO 417/264, Milner to Chamberlain, 26 Aug. 1899, with enclosure, Greene to Milner, 19 Aug. 1899; MS/PRO/DO 119/363, Greene to Milner, 28 Sept. 1899.

73. *S & D News*, 28 June 1899; see also 6 and 26 Sept. and 13 Oct. 1899.

74. See the social and personal column in the *Star* throughout September and October 1899.

75. *S & D News*, 2 Sept. 1899; *Star*, 2, 5 and 7 Sept. 1899; *African Review*, 21 (314) 7 Oct. 1899, p. 12; MS/BOD/Mss. Milner Dep. 212, Greene to Milner (private), 5 Sept. 1899; Neame (ed.) 1956, pp. 125—7.

76. *S & D News*, 5 , 6 Sept. 1899.

77. MS/BOD/Mss. Milner Dep. 212, Greene to Milner, 8 Sept. 1899. Greene states that the councillors 'consider that they have accomplished their task and that the object for which the council was formed, viz. to put the Uitlander case before the public has been accomplished'.

78. MS/BOD/Mss. Milner Dep. 212, Greene to Milner (private), 9 Sept. 1899, where Greene refers to Milner's displeasure.

79. MS/BOD/Mss. Milner Dep. 212, Greene to Milner (private), 9 Sept. 1899. For further information regarding the departure of the UC, see Greene to Milner, 8 and 27 Sept. 1899.

80. *S & D News*, 28 Sept. 1899; MS/PRO/CO 417/267, Milner to Chamberlain, with enclosure, Greene to Milner, 2 Oct. 1899; and CO 417/269, Milner to Chamberlain, 19 Dec. 1899. See also MS/USL/Lipp, pp. 56—7, for reference to Robertson.

81. *S & D News*, 18 and 19 Sept. 1899.

82. *S & D News*, 28 Sept. 1899; *Star*, 5 Sept. 1899.

83. *S & D News*, 7 Oct. 1899. For additional information about Blake and the First Irish Brigade, as well as other Uitlander corps, see Blake 1903, *passim*; Hennessy 1973, ch. 18; Hillegas 1900, pp. 269—72; MacNab 1975, pp. 165—6; May 1970, pp. 91—3; and MS/JPL/Auson, p. 4.

84. *S & D News*, 29 Sept., 24 Nov., 11 Dec. 1899. See also MS/JPL/Auson, p. 3; MacNab 1975, p. 163; and Hillegas 1900, p. 273.

85. *S & D News*, 2 Nov. 1899; MacNab 1975, pp. 168—70; and MS/JPL/Auson, p. 5.

86. *S & D News*, 30 Sept. 1899; MacNab 1975, p. 87; and Hillegas 1900, pp. 257—61.

87. MS/JPL/Auson, pp. 3—5; *S & D News*, 15 Jan. and 3 March 1900; *Star*, 11 Sept. 1899; May 1970, pp. 103, 115; MacNab 1975, pp. 163—4, 167; and Hillegas 1900, pp. 261, 264—7, 272—3.

88. *S & D News*, 5 and 17 Oct. 1899; Rabinowitz 1989.

89. *S & D News*, 2 Sept. 1899; *Star*, 24, 25 Aug. 1899; MS/JPL/Auson; Hillegas 1900, pp. 262—3; and MacNab 1975, pp. 161—2.

90. MS/JPL/ACPT, London letterbook, report dated 13 Oct. 1899.

91. MS/USL/Lipp, pp. 1—2.

92. MS/USL/Lipp, pp. 2—3.

Three

Johannesburg under the Boers

Let him who desires peace, prepare for war.
Vegetius

While living behind the battle lines for the next eight months, the 40,000 or so people who remained on the Rand over the summer of 1899/1900 saw relatively little of the war. In fact they had to expend considerable effort just to find out what was happening on the battlefields to the south and east. Although periodically a wave of excitement would ripple through the community as refugees from the south arrived with news, or there was an explosion in town, or rumours of a Boer revenge or an African insurrection, most of their energies went into fighting boredom and hunger.

As the mass of people departed, the local Boers gathered into their own hands the reins of power and wealth on the Rand and, for the next eight months, used its vast fortune and reserve of black and white labour to bolster the Republican war effort. To exploit fully the Rand's potential the Boers first had to gain, then maintain, control over what was essentially a foreign district. This entailed making several difficult decisions: for instance, should all Africans be sent off the Rand to guarantee relative peace, or should some be encouraged to remain to work? A similar consideration had to be made with respect to the Uitlanders: could Pretoria take the chance of allowing a number of British subjects to remain to facilitate the operation of the mines and other essential businesses and services? Did not their very presence enable spies and saboteurs to move freely in the district? And, if foreigners and Africans were allowed to remain alongside the burgher dependants, how would they all be fed and clothed, paid and protected?

In late September the executive in Pretoria turned to the problem of governing the Rand. This step was necessary because the local town council was no longer able to manage, partly because the Municipal Act under which it was constituted tended to stifle initiative, but mostly because the town councillors were too frightened and, at times, too officious to take decisive action.[1] Unable to leave the vast wealth of the district without any means of exploiting it and the diverse and adventurous population without any means of controlling it, Pretoria appointed the local Rust en Orde (Peace and Order) Commission in late September.

The Rust en Orde Commission consisted of D. E. Schutte, the peace-time commissioner of police and soon to be appointed special commandant of the

Witwatersrand; Dr F. E. T. Krause, first public prosecutor and Schutte's successor as special commandant; J. L. van der Merwe, the mining commissioner; and N. P. van den Berg, first criminal landdrost. It had the power to add to its membership and, within days, others sat with these men making and implementing decisions.[2] Its two most pressing tasks were to protect property and to gain control of the remaining population.

Few of the departing Uitlanders had made adequate provision for their personal property when they fled. Many had no choice but to leave their things in rented rooms. Some tried to safeguard their belongings by leaving them with black servants, caretakers or neighbours, but all with limited success because Africans were commandeered and some neighbours took to selling goods in their safe-keeping. Those with money were best able to protect their goods and homes by putting things into storage locally or sending them to the coast. This latter course was fraught with its own difficulties: 'it was a common sight . . . to see a commandeering officer stop a trolley, cab, trap or carriage, order the horse or horses to be outspanned, hand the owner a "kommandeer brief" describing their valuation. Compensation was to be paid after the war'.[3]

Shopkeepers and dealers tried to protect their stores by secreting them deep in the shafts of unused mines, while others placed them under the protection of a foreign flag. The most farsighted sent lists of their possessions to the British vice-consul, assuming that after the war one of the belligerents would compensate for property losses. Those who had relied on insurance companies were sorely disappointed because policies rarely offered security in times of war. For most people, though, the only feasible defence against vandalism and theft was to board up their windows and doors. Descriptions of the city and environs in this early phase of the war all mention the quiet streets faced by barricaded shops and homes.[4]

Ironically, boarded windows turned out to be the least protective of measures, for these made it obvious that the closed-up shop or home belonged to an Uitlander-in-exile. Furthermore, in mid-October, a decision (*besluit*) from Pretoria declared that untenanted and closed stores could be commandeered and, in the following months, there was extensive commandeering by Boer officials of abandoned supplies.[5]

Another method used by departing Uitlanders to protect their property was to appoint a caretaker. People who normally had jobs quite unrelated to caretaking now took on the task of guarding abandoned buildings. Some were promised a wage — often to be paid after the war. Women left behind by their menfolk augmented their incomes by looking after exiles' homes and people were often asked to move into the empty houses. Uitlanders in a hurry to leave sometimes simply handed their keys to neighbours who planned to remain behind. Leaving African domestics to keep a watch on houses was generally a failure, for not long after the war began the Republican government took to commandeering 'idle' blacks for service in and outside the city.[6]

None of these methods was foolproof. Goods, particularly pianos, furniture and silver plate, were stolen from abandoned homes and ended up on market stalls. In fact, it was later estimated that over 60 per cent of the houses in the city had been 'visited and looted' in these months. Ironically, the rich were the least inconvenienced, for they had hired reliable caretakers or had put their valuables in storage. Instead, the working-class and petty-bourgeois householders suffered at the hands of the robbers.[7]

While such individual methods of protecting goods were being devised, the Boer authorities decided that a more foolproof system of protection was needed. Hence, in mid-September, the Johannesburg merchant, A. Holt, was summoned to Pretoria by Commandant-General Piet Joubert. There Holt met the general and state secretary, Reitz, and was advised to convene a small meeting of Johannesburg merchants to discuss the 'advisability of forming some sort of guard to protect the interests of the city'. On 20 September a meeting of nearly 40 men was held and a deputation of seven appointed to return to Pretoria to ascertain what arrangements could be made for 'conserving the business of the city'.[8]

Propertied Uitlanders were pleased with developments, if a bit confused in the details. The manager of the African City Properties Trust wrote to London:

It is evident that the Government in Pretoria has little confidence in either the Burgomaster of Johannesburg or the Town Council. Secret Communications have been taking place . . . with a view to arranging proper protection, Lucas Meyer will be appointed protector of Town Properties and will enrol all peaceably disposed persons willing to assist in the protection thereof. . . . I am glad to hear of this movement by the Government.[9]

On 26 September the deputation from the 'Merchants' Committee' waited upon the executive at Pretoria and there Joubert laid out his plans. He wanted the city's property and population to be 'thoroughly protected' in the event of war, so that people could carry on their vocations in a safe and secure manner. He feared that, because the regular police had been withdrawn and sent to the front, the city would fall prey to 'ruffianism and looting' and suggested that all 'objectionable characters' be removed from the city and a force of volunteers be created. The deputation then returned to Johannesburg and set about devising a scheme: a force of 750 or so 'respectable' men would patrol the town and suburbs. This volunteer force was to be under the control of a committee of three merchants as well as van den Berg, Krause and the police commandant, G. M. J. van Dam.[10]

Before the Merchants' Committee had finalized its scheme, the Rust en Orde Commission had acted and the committee had no choice but to place its plan before it. The merchants were informed that their system of joint control was unacceptable, though the Rust en Orde Commission was quite willing to take the names of the 300 or so men the Merchants' Committee had thus far collected. By 6 October the whole matter of protection of persons and property had been assumed by the Rust en Orde Commission.[11]

The Rust en Orde Commission had already drafted its own plan: the city and suburbs would be divided into several administrative units for the purpose of policing. Any reliable (*vertrouwbare*) men could join the special police (*speciale constabels*), but 'under no circumstances could British subjects'. It took some time for this restriction to filter down to recruitment officers and, consequently, some British residents were allowed to join the special police during October. It was not until later that month that all the British who had been enrolled were removed, but not before confusion and hard feelings had been generated.[12]

The 'specials', drawn from the ranks of the un- and under-employed of the city, were a volunteer force in receipt of rations. Although expected to guard the city in all weather, they were not provided with boots or raincoats — a cause for complaint — and were given only badges to identify themselves as police. Not surprisingly, within a couple of months many of these foreigners and burghers, who were for one reason or another unfit for duty at the front, were shirking their duty and their colleagues were forced to cover for them, sometimes by patrolling the streets for up to 14 hours a day, three days a week.[13] The conditions of service and the poverty of the members gave rise to criticism from within the force. At the end of October a Russian 'special' articulated the men's anger:

> The argument advanced by some Government officials that the townspeople are protecting themselves and their property is palpably absurd, as the vast majority of the police are young men who have nothing to protect, while those older inhabitants who are possessed of any means, generally manage to rank as sergeants and corporals, and do duty inside the different Charge Offices.[14]

Ironically, many of the men the Merchants' Committee and General Joubert had wanted to expel from the city as objectionable characters were now enrolled as 'specials' and placed in charge of protecting property. Uitlanders still in residence thought them a 'terrible lot of men', while the foreign press stated that the force was made up of Russian Jews who, in peace-time, supplied blacks with illicit liquor or scavenged bottles for a living. Throughout the eight-month period they were repeatedly accused of looting and unofficially commandeering goods and many were suspected by the authorities of being part of Johannesburg's criminal element. The leadership of the force tried to weed out some of the worst characters in November, but with little success. Not all the members were criminals; many were just poor or unemployed men who found themselves placed in positions in which they could take with impunity goods abandoned by the Uitlanders who, many felt, had caused the war in the first place.[15] The service was poorly rewarded, and the property owners who had fled made no contribution to its upkeep, but it was necessary to the smooth running of the city.

Outside the city, along the reef, the situation was somewhat different. A well-organized and well-supplied force was created there to guard the millions of pounds of abandoned machinery. Early on, the notion of extending the duties of the 'specials' to include the mines had been mooted, but the idea was soon discarded, along with that of enrolling unemployed British miners as guards. In the end the French mining concerns took the initiative:

> During the last days of September when the war seemed about to break out at any moment, a Committee of Frenchmen was formed with the aim of organizing this police force . . . to guarantee the safety of the town from possible destruction and plunder by workers of all nationalities, who, following the closure of a number of mines found themselves unemployed and more or less without resources. The idea . . . was to concern itself with the town only, but the other part of the reef was deserted by white workers . . . and abandoned to the Kafir miners whose enormous numbers, about 90,000, had prevented them from being sent back to their respective countries; it was then that the idea came to three Frenchmen . . . to establish a police corps which would be stationed on the mines and would operate a constant watch there.[16]

Although there was talk at one time of creating a unit of 1,000 men, the mine police, also known as the de Korte corps, had a membership only of about 390 men. The Austrian and German brigades donated men to form the main body of the force and the corps leader, Captain de Korte, a former officer in the Dutch army and a civil judge in peace-time, was an efficient and trusted man. Below de Korte

During the first months of the war, Johannesburg took on a 'Scotch sabbath' appearance. This is 'deserted Pritchard Street' (*Africana Museum, Johannesburg*)

Members of the Johannesburg Special Police, almost all of whom were foreigners, were appointed by the Boers during the first months of the war (*Africana Museum, Johannesburg*)

DIENSTREGLEMENT

DER

Speciale Politie

Afdeeling C.

The Rand Printing Works, Box 3284, Johannesburg.

A Special Police identity card, and the translation of the Special Police regulations of service, January 1900 (*Africana Museum, Johannesburg*)

TRANSLATION.

REGULATIONS OF SERVICE
For the Special Police,   Division C.
Commanding Officer: P. DIETZCH.
Captain: W. Shawe.

Members of the Sub-Commission:
A. Eckart Beckmann. (Chairman)
M. Rothkugel, (Vice Chairman).
G. BRANDON, H. SERLIG, A. I W. VISEE, L. MEYER
W. JAHN, TH. FELBERT.

This Commission which has got instructions from their superiors of "Rust en Orde" to rule and regulate the division of Johannesburg. from Fordsburg to Endstreet and from Commissioner Street to Nord Street, stipulates the following:

1 The Sub - Commission has got supervision of the special Police in their own ward, and all persons belonging to it are subjected to and receive their orders from them.

2 Each night watch is under the command of the officer du jour, and consists of two lieutenants, four sergeants and the ordinary constables.

3 The officer du jour is a member of the commission and has got the sole command of the Night Watch.

4 The Night Watch is divided in two sections, one to the east, the other to the west. The eastern portion is called up in front of the office of the special Police in Kerk Street, the western in Eloff Street.

5 A lieutenant is placed at the head of each section. It is his duty, to prepare the lists of men for night duty according to the form decided upon by the Commission, into whose office they must be returned after duty is over.

6 The officer du jour instructs the lieutenant, when to call the roll.

7 The lieutenant reports to the officer du jour, that the men have fallen in and awaits further instructions.

8 The lieutenant leads the section in marching order with his sergeants and reports to the officer du jour, that the men are properly placed at their posts.

9 It is the duty of the lieutenant to see, that the men remain in their beats, till they are relieved by their sergeant.

10 The lieutenant writes the night report.

11 It is the duty of the sergeants, that at the call of the roll the men fall in in two rows, and that military discipline is observed.

12 The sergeants must inspect the men during the watch, must take them from their beat and lead them back to the office in military fashion, where the men will be relieved by the lieutenant.

13 This will not take place, before the relieving sections have taken their beat.

14 The men must be civil to the public in asking for the night permits, must not shout to them "Stop" from a distance, but walk up to them and ask them civilly for their permits.

15 The men, who through very serious circumstances are prohibited from doing duty, must give written notice hereof to the officer du jour before 4 o'clock p. m.

16 The officer du jour alone has got the right, to grant one nights night-permit.

17 The officer du jour appoints a lieutenant to act for him in his absence, during which this lieutenant may not leave the office.

18 The orders of the officer du jour have to be strictly observed by the lieutenants, sergeants and men.

19 These regulations are drawn up in accordance with Police law No 11 of 1895, to which every member of the special Police is subjected.

In the name of the commission
(Signed) A. ECKART BECKMANN, Chairman.

Acknowledged by me
(Signed) W. Shawe, Captain of the Special Police.

Johannesburg 20 th January 1900.

Officers of the Boers' Special Mine Police, November 1899. Commandant de Korte sits in the centre of the front row. The Mine Police were sometimes known as the 'de Korte corps' (*Africana Museum, Johannesburg*)

Group E5 of the Mine Police in July 1900, with British officers (*Africana Museum, Johannesburg*)

in rank were several *kapiteins* (each in charge of a section of the Rand), and, below them, about a dozen lieutenants, with sergeants taking orders from both.

For purposes of administration, the Rand was divided into ten areas — four to the west and six to the east of the Wemmer mine, which formed the central point. Each district contained between six and ten mines, with one to ten men stationed on each. In this manner, some 345 men patrolled the mines from Benoni to Randfontein — about 50 miles of reef. In addition, 25 men were assigned the duty of guarding the railway lines which passed through the area.[17]

Upon enlistment each man had to show proof of his nationality, for no British were allowed to join, and all had to take an oath similar to that of the special police. Unlike the 'specials', though, they were specifically guaranteed that they would not have to take up arms against any 'nation in a state of peace' with the individual corpsman's country. The pay was originally set at 15s a day, but had been reduced to 10s by 20 October. The central barracks and the headquarters of the corps were at Heath's Hotel, which had been commandeered by the government for this purpose. Khaki uniforms with jaunty hats were distributed to the men and revolvers were issued by the government. Because they offered steady employment, lodging, cheap meals and wages, and because they were away from the front, these posts were highly coveted.[18]

The financing of the corps was undertaken by the mine owners, including those in exile who channelled funds to their representatives still on the Rand. It was estimated that the cost would be about £10,000 per month and this seems to have been accurate, for, after the British took control of Johannesburg at the end of May 1900, the Chamber of Mines reported that £80,000 had been expended on the mines' security for the months of Boer rule.[19] As the war was, in many respects, being fought to decide who would control the Rand's wealth, it is not surprising that the mine owners and the Boer government joined together to ensure that it remained safe until the war decided the issue.

The Rust en Orde Commission's other task was to achieve and maintain control over the heterogeneous population that remained on the Rand. This meant devising and implementing policies to determine who stayed and under what conditions. The Commission began its work by carrying out Kruger's order to expel all 'known criminals and pimps'. The local police drew up a list of 60 or so Randites, which was forwarded to Pretoria on 17 October. A week later a list of about 100 people appeared in the local press with the warning that those enumerated had two days to leave the Republic before being forcibly removed. Some of the names on this list can be traced to earlier arrests for contravention of the 1897 *Ontucht Wet* (the morality act), though other well-known criminals somehow managed to escape expulsion. The 'weeding out' of undesirable residents continued into December.[20]

Pressures on supplies and manpower made it imperative that the Boers reduce the number of criminals already behind bars. Debtors held in the local gaol were some of the first to be freed. Then, on 13 October, Pretoria ordered the release of all 'short term' prisoners with less than a year left to serve. Any burghers among them were expected to join their commandos, while foreigners were ordered to leave the country. At least 900 black and white prisoners were freed under this ruling, including more than 60 prostitutes. Not all were deported, for some blacks were kept in Johannesburg to do manual labour for the local authorities. Long-term prisoners, such as the notorious pimp Joe Silver, were transferred to central prisons. Thereafter, to keep the prison population at a minimum, the Rust en Orde Commission used deportation, sometimes following a short gaol term, as punishment.[21]

The Republican executive committee's policy regarding British residents remaining on the Rand vacillated. The first utterances from Pretoria were conciliatory, urging British people to remain at work. Soon, though, it was clear that only approved people would be allowed to stay. A permit system was thus introduced and, by 4 October, the earlier policy had been reversed: all British subjects were expected to leave except those with 'exceptional circumstances'. This vacillation was partly caused by a difference of opinion within ruling circles about whether any British subjects, needed or not, should be allowed to stay. Those advocating the more pragmatic approach, which was also the more lucrative, won out and a committee was soon formed, consisting of the mining commissioners of Johannesburg, Boksburg and Krugersdorp, along with the commissioner of police and the acting state mining engineer. This committee soon began to review applications from British subjects wishing to 'pursue their avocation at mines, banks, stores, apothecaries and similar institutions' necessary to the smooth running of the society. In the meantime, to ensure the continuation of essential services, temporary residence permits were granted to the staffs of the Waterworks Company, the Cold Storage Company and the fire brigade.[22]

Instructions about the permit system published in the daily press warned non-British Uitlanders to obtain nationality documents from their embassies and ordered British men to send their applications to their local mining commissioner. Initially it was uncertain what provision would be made for British women, but eventually it was decided that the majority would be allowed to stay upon obtaining residential certificates. Women who had been abandoned by their menfolk were ordered to leave, but Krause prevailed with his lenient interpretation of the government's proclamation: 'No undue harshness' need be applied in these cases. Most women, then, were allowed to remain, though the fear of deportation hung over the heads of many during the following months. Those denied residential certificates were placed under the care of the Revd John Darragh of St Mary's, who managed to get them travel documents and, where necessary, railway tickets. The men and women who were allowed to remain had to swear that they would conduct themselves in a 'quiet, calm and submissive manner' and do nothing against the 'independence of the country or people'.[23]

Men wanting to obtain permits were warned to make their applications early, for if they had not received them by 8 p.m. on 19 October they would be liable for arrest and deportation. The same applied to women who failed to get a residential certificate before the 23rd.[24] This threat, coming as it did after months of stress and weeks of indecision, placed the Uitlanders under strain. A young woman, Ada Lennard, recorded the disappointment felt by her family when it was first refused a permit: 'When father came home', she wrote in her diary, 'he felt miserable indeed . . . Poor mother, she did look ill . . . — Well, we had lunch, but none of us could eat anything [as] we were all too upset'.[25]

It is difficult to say with any certainty why any one British resident wanted to remain. Still, from applications extant,[26] it seems to have been British and colonial men who had put down roots and who had lived in the Republic for a number of years, rather than months, who wished to remain. The mean age of those who applied (and who provided their ages to the permit committee) was 40 — i.e. they were not young men, as most in Johannesburg were. Many were also family men who had wives and children with them, also in itself unusual for Johannesburg.

Some had Republican wives and their children had been born in the Boer Republic. Possibly because they thought it might help obtain a permit, but also possibly because it was true, some, about a tenth, expressed definite pro-Boer sympathies in their letters to the permit committee.

Nearly half the applicants had work — many as caretakers — though a considerable number wanted to stay because they had neither the train fare to leave nor the money to set up a new home elsewhere. About a quarter of those who applied were mine-workers, many of whom had recently lost their jobs and were anxious to find new work. Another 25 to 30 per cent were urban artisans and 10 per cent stated that they or their dependants were too old or infirm to hazard a journey to the coast. A significant number of these British applicants — about 20 per cent — were already enrolled in the special police or were willing to join the unit, though this was an option soon barred to them.

Few of the applicants who applied individually were granted permission to remain. Exceptions were made in some instances, though. Applicants who were too ill to go and who had doctors' certificates to prove it, were allowed to stay, as were men who could prove ardent and long-standing support for the Republic. Labour leaders such as J. T. Bain, E. B. Rose and G. Marshall, secretary of the IILP, were thus given permission to stay.[27] Other exceptions included those who had close family ties to burghers, or had a family member on commando. In a few cases men were allowed to remain because well-connected Boers vouched for them. Generally, though, those allowed to stay were given permits because they held jobs deemed necessary to the community: for example, bakers, pharmacists, ministers, teachers, storekeepers and doctors. Some British workers were permitted to remain, but most of those who were had had their names on lists submitted by companies whose services were deemed essential to the war effort or to the smooth functioning of the city: for example, banks, insurance companies and mining companies.

The names of those allowed to stay appeared in the daily press. The disappointed permit-seekers filled to overflowing the trains to the Cape and to Delagoa Bay in the days before the 18 October deadline. Between 14 and 17 October inclusive, about 10,000 people left the area by train. On the 18th several trains pulled out of Park Station, though none was as full as those leaving earlier that week. Even so, the last trainload of reluctant but voluntary refugees consisted of nine packed carriages and 13 coal trucks, carrying over 1,000 people. During this second exodus, the government provided free travel as far as the border to any refugee without the funds to purchase a ticket.[28]

Having cleared away the criminal element and the superfluous population, the Rust en Orde Commission turned its attentions to regulating the affairs of those who remained. First, all British males were required to get permits, while all other residents were to get certificates to prove their nationalities. Secondly, all residents — black, white, male and female — above the age of 12 had to obtain residential certificates. Any white person wishing to be on the street during the hours of curfew (9 p.m. to 5 a.m.) had to obtain a night permit. A curfew for blacks was established (7 p.m. to 5 a.m.), during which all except those special cases where officials or employers had given the African written permission, were to be off the streets. A special permit was needed to travel outside the city, for any resident found in the countryside without documents would be suspected of sabotaging railway lines and other acts of war.

After martial law was declared on 11 October, giving force to all these and other regulations, the police conducted a house-to-house search and a search of the mines to establish the number of men, women and children in residence and to make sure that the regulations were being followed. Martial law gave effect to restrictions, erratically enforced at first, which forbade the general sale of alcohol. It also established special courts with the power to administer summary justice.

Even though the administration had attempted to remove all unwanted persons, some slipped through its net. Anyone caught — and some were found during the first house-to-house search — was deported straight away. Nonetheless, it was later estimated that upwards of 100 British subjects remained illegally in or near the city throughout these months, some hiding in deserted stores and buildings, while others moved about the city freely.

Rioting among blacks in early October gave urgency to the need to gain control of the black population, many of whom were now unemployed and abandoned. The government decided not to expel all of them, but encouraged many to remain long enough for martial law to take effect, at which time their labour could be commandeered.[29] Non-whites who remained were granted residential certificates. Those on the mines had their certificates given to their bosses. Consequently, blacks had to stay on the mines unless given written permission by the management to leave the premises.[30]

Basically, the government felt that no African ought to be 'idle' and if any were, he should be given work. Certain jobs, such as selling newspapers, were forbidden to them as their services were felt to be of more use elsewhere. The Rust en Orde Commission also decreed that any black found without work would be arrested, even if in possession of a residential certificate. Therefore, so-called 'loafers' became targets of police raids into locations and along city streets, while Africans left to guard abandoned houses were commandeered. Domestics still in employment were frightened that they too would be similarly treated by the authorities.[31]

The Africans who remained in Johannesburg and environs served the war effort reluctantly. Informal camps were disrupted and blacks led away by police, while raids into locations, nominally in search of illicit liquor and 'vagabonds', were also used as labour round-ups. In January 1900 about 200 'loafing kafirs' were removed from the city's locations and sent to the front to dig trenches, care for livestock, drive wagons and, in a few cases, tote a rifle. Others were commandeered for work on farms owned by burghers on commando, while 'idle' black women were sent to the nearest field cornet for assignment.[32] In December 1899, according to the diarist Mrs Lipp, 'the various native locations [were] . . . cleared out of women, children and non-workers — those strong and able bodied [were] commandeered to work on the farms'. About 60 men were then marched under guard to the Rose Deep mine, while the women were led away:

> A batch of about 140 passed through town from the George Goch mine, the women were heavily laden with children and home utensils and as they marched they sang a weird dirge like melody, a wailing tune that sounded very sad, for they have a great dread of the Boer and no doubt thought they were being driven to prison or death. Many stories of cruelty and brutality have reached us.[33]

This was not an isolated case, as the Boers raided other locations, seeing their 'inmates [as] a source of danger and a nuisance to inhabitants of adjoining townships'. Thus the police's 'midnight expeditions' continued.[34]

By the time the exodus was complete, there were just over 10,000 whites in the city and about the same number of blacks. For the whole of the Rand, nearly 27,000 residential certificates had been issued to whites by late 1899; 12,900 to men, 8,141 to women, and the remainder to children over 12. Over 15,400 blacks were also legally resident. There were, in addition, some Coloureds in the city, who were mainly women and very poor. Few Indians remained — those who did not leave in the first rush were later denied permits by the Rust en Orde Commission — but there were about 700 Chinese scattered along the length of the reef.[35]

The majority of whites managed to live through these eight months, at least in peace if not without anxiety and boredom. They were able to move about; bicycles were the favoured mode of transport, though a few old cabs, private carriages and some rickshaws could also be seen on the streets. They had some contact with the outside world in that poste restante services were maintained, but mail was censored by the Rust en Orde Commission (specifically F. E. T. Krause's office) and the British authorities censored letters in the colonies. It took about a month for a letter to travel from the Cape to Johannesburg (via Lourenço Marques), but after March 1900 even that service was interrupted. Telegraphic communication from the Republic to Europe was unreliable and was intercepted by the imperial government at Aden. A few residents were so desperate for outside news that they kept carrier pigeons, but this was as dangerous as it was illegal. Most made do with the local press, reading and rereading the *Standard and Diggers' News*, though it too was subject to censorship.

Few public services were disrupted to the point of being unavailable. Electricity was supplied irregularly and water was available to all customers, even those in arrears with their payments. The regular fire brigade was denied permission to remain because of its suspect loyalty, but non-British Uitlanders were recruited at half-pay and, where necessary, the brigade was supplemented by a volunteer force. Wash 'boys' were still available and medical services were provided despite the British doctors and nurses having left the hospital in a huff in mid-October. Banks continued to serve the public with reduced staff hours, though J. B. Robinson's bank was closed for a few weeks in early 1900 when he made overt Anglophile comments for the benefit of the Britsh press.[36]

Most schools closed, though a few reopened to serve a reduced population. The Marist Brothers School reopened in January 1900, with over 100 boys who were preparing for their Cape university exams. The German school, with about 200 pupils, and the Jewish school, with about 50, also stayed open. J. S. Morris, the local Wesleyan minister, was concerned about the number of poor children on the streets and gained permission to open a school for them. It had enrolled 60 children by the end of November 1899. Meanwhile, St Cyprians for non-white children continued to take pupils, even after its headmistress, Miss Holmes Orr, was deported along with many other British residents in April 1900.[37]

Early in October, acting against the wishes and even the threats of the local hotel keepers and bar owners, the Rust en Orde Commission implemented Pretoria's order to stop all liquor sales. It was not until the beginning of the new year that the edict was relaxed and certain clubs and restaurants were allowed to sell liquor. Initially the easing of restrictions caused a 'great deal of intoxication', though at no time before could it really be said that the population was totally without alcohol. Even so, it was harder to obtain and this undoubtedly pleased what remained of the moralists who concerned themselves with the fast-living population in peace-time.[38]

Prohibition, curfew and travel restrictions, transport difficulties and the exodus of entertainers along with the rest of the refugees forced those who remained to create their own fun. Sporting teams were formed and club tournaments held, while small concerts and dances, even a few charity galas, were organized. Clubs remained open — even the famous Rand Club — but were under-staffed and under-utilized. A few prostitutes continued to ply their trade and illicit liquor could be found in brothels.[39] Families found their fun picnicking and bicycling around the area.

Although well away from the front line for most of these months, the people who stayed suffered from anxiety. The overriding fear of the British was that Boer commandos, or even the civilian burgher population, would attack and kill them. Because many held secret pro-British views, they were afraid that even their innermost thoughts might reveal them. Letters to loved ones at the coast went unsent, diaries were carefully hidden and some even censored by their authors. Idle gossip was discouraged and private thoughts shared with only the closest intimates. It was unwise to express pro-British sentiments aloud, for anonymous letters accusing neighbours of overheard anti-Boer utterances were sent to the Rust en Orde Commission, which, in turn, sent investigators to look into the matter. This method of arranging a neighbour's deportation was often an excellent way for people to settle old scores.

As the British army moved north, anxiety increased: fears that the Boers would fire on the city, blow up its largest buildings, imprison or murder the British population filled the timid. Rumours raced through the city, probably at the speed of bicycles: the British are being deported, Ladysmith has surrendered to the Boers, Jameson is on the march to relieve Johannesburg, the British government is suing for peace.[40] When the panic subsided after any one of these scares, people returned to being bored by the stillness, to grass growing in the streets, gardens overly lush with vegetation, and to the dust blowing through boarded-up windows.

The most anxious of the Uitlanders were the members of families that had been separated. Worried about their absent husbands and sons, women lived for months without knowing the whereabouts of their loved ones, who were later often found to have been in one of the irregular corps at the coast or living in poverty somewhere in the colonies. They also feared that the government might decide to enforce its regulation to expel all abandoned women. The many who had been left without money were forced to do odd jobs to keep their children fed; some worked as clerks in shops or cooked and cleaned for bachelors, while others took in sewing or cared for abandoned houses.

Two months before the war began, food prices began to rise, providing evidence that the increase in political turmoil had begun to disrupt farm production and the distribution of goods as men were mobilized. By September, the price of food in Johannesburg had increased by as much as 15 per cent and the cost of certain processed foods, such as sugar, flour and tinned meat, had risen even higher. Items began to disappear from shelves, while some shopkeepers boarded up their stores and left for the coast. Residents who intended to stay began to stockpile goods, though most put away only one or two months' supply, thinking that the war would be over by the end of the year.

Initially the government attempted to regulate prices by proclamation, ordering retailers to maintain pre-war price levels except where increased costs (such as transport) made it necessary to raise them. In fact, the government's need to build up its own store of provisions put pressure on the commercial system. For example, the authorities' buying of meat and grain from local farmers for the commandos caused shortages in the cities. Furthermore, they were unable to convince storekeepers that their goods would be safe from looting or commandeering, so merchants stopped ordering more goods or building up reserves.[41]

After the war began, the situation worsened, since what amounted to a food embargo by the British exacerbated already difficult supply problems. Also, families without their menfolk to provide for them soon ran out of food and had no money to buy more. Looting and theft became commonplace; valuables were taken to sell on the market and the theft of consumer goods, such as food, fuel and clothes, redistributed scarce supplies. Most robberies were carried out by poor burgher women or black men, or sometimes the two working together. Some demonstrated elaborate planning, with shops entered into repeatedly and a constant stream of supplies removed. Others were obviously more spontaneous, with people breaking into shops, grabbing items and fleeing. The Boer authorities were known to turn a blind-eye to thefts and some officials left barricaded shops open after they had commandeered them, thus giving access to women in search of food.[42]

In addition, the authorities had to cope with the food riots that periodically burst forth. Even before the war, poor women at Roodepoort on the west Rand broke into closed and boarded shops and dared the men who stood watching to stop them. In November, the pay packets of the regular Johannesburg police (then at the front) were held up and their wives rioted: women, 'driven by hunger', who had neither food nor cash, broke into shops and successfully repelled the not overly-zealous special police. Again, a month later, when some burgher dependants were reduced to half-rations, food riots ensued. The young prosecutor, F. R. M. Cleaver, intervened in one of the riots and was nearly torn limb from limb by women accusing him of being one of those *verfluckste* (stinking) officials 'who had sent their husbands to the front and left them to starve'. Such riots were reported not only in Roodepoort, but in the western districts of Johannesburg and in Jeppestown in the city.[43]

While the war itself disrupted the production and distribution of food, imperial policy was also to blame for the shortage of supplies on the Rand. The British government held that any British subject trading with the Republic was a traitor. Hence, British-owned ships carrying goods bound for Delagoa Bay were re-routed to colonial ports, where their cargoes were off-loaded. Merchants at Delagoa Bay tried to out-manoeuvre the British by ordering their agents in Europe to ship goods out in non-British owned vessels, but their cables were intercepted by British intelligence at Aden. The British went one step further and ordered nearly a dozen ships — gunboats and cruisers mostly — to the East African coast to detain, board and search foreign-owned ships outside territorial waters. British agents also watched cargo as it was being off-loaded at Lourenço Marques.[44]

While the British searched for arms, ammunition and medical supplies for the commandos, and machinery for the mines, food shipments were disrupted. Food was not formally considered a contraband of war, but the British felt it legitimate to stop any food shipments that could be proven to be destined for commandos. Milner and his subordinates then pressured the Mozambican authorities into seizing shipments, including civil food supplies (which they were reluctant to do)[45] and this created shortages both at Lourenço Marques and in the Republic and fostered the belief that there was a formal food blockade in place.[46] When shortages in the Republic became acute, reports spread that Pretoria was considering the expulsion of all foreigners. Thereafter some Uitlanders approached their consuls, asking them to request their home governments to put pressure on London to halt the embargo. The combination of complaints from European powers and from the Mozambicans, who were themselves faced with their own 'great dearth and consequent dearness of all sort of provisions' in Lourenço Marques, as well as the possibility of indemnity payments, forced the imperial government to rethink its policy.[47]

In February, Prime Minister Salisbury had no choice but to order the blockade to be modified. Instead of ships being denied entry to Delagoa Bay, goods would be allowed to land there, but released to Mozambican officials for use inside the colony only. This new policy did not, however, keep goods from entering the Republic, for, even though boxes of supplies piled up at the port, nothing could stop the steady trickle of contraband across the permeable frontier. Various methods were used. Some goods were shipped to Ressano Garcia on the border and from there smuggled into the Republic, while others were simply loaded into the suitcases of Republican officials and shipped home. The British thought the Portuguese customs officials — 'pro-Boer to the man' — were to blame and this may well have been part of the reason for the smugglers' success.[48] Lourenço Marques had also become a hotbed of British and Republican spies (who spent a great deal of time trying to outwit one another) and British acts of daring certainly curtailed Republican successes in this sideshow to the war.

Not surprisingly, from February onward, the acute shortages on the Rand eased. Thereafter there were periodic shortages and rises in prices, but the goods most noticeably absent in the previous weeks — sugar, coffee, tea and tinned goods — were once again on the shelves of open shops. These goods supplemented a diet of vegetables and fruit, both abundant throughout the war, as well as eggs, mutton, poultry and, after the good harvest of 1900, mealie flour.

With endemic theft and periodic food riots, it was obvious that some sort of public-aid programme was necessary. In October, the Rust en Orde Commission appointed a Johannesburg Commissariat Commission to feed the burgher poor, most of whom lived in the western suburbs and whose menfolk were away at the front. As the commission commandeered buildings to serve as supply depots, a permanent system of distribution was established, with the famous Wanderers' buildings (the home of sportsmen in peacetime) as the central depot and other buildings scattered around the city as the commissariat stores. Very soon they began to distribute grain daily, mainly to burgher women, but also to a few destitute British.[49]

But as the poor soon pointed out, the distribution of grain served no purpose for people poor enough to need free grain were too poor to buy the coal with which to bake it. Thereafter, pressure was put on the coal and gold-mining companies to help the Commissariat Commission. Idle mines were commandeered for their coal, while blackmail was used to induce otherwise niggardly companies to assist the poor. The manager of the Nigel mine reported that:

in February [1900] the Public Prosecutor of Heidelberg instructed by the Acting Mining Commissioner [was going] to prosecute me for pumping [water from the mine] without a permit, though I was not aware that any such permit was necessary. After explaining that the same engines that drove the pump drove the mealie mill, I was allowed to pump and to mine coal on condition that I should supply the poor families with coal. This I agreed to, as they were taking it in any case, and anything else they could lay their hands on to make fire.[50]

The Commissariat Commission also received donations of clothes, bedding and fresh vegetables from people wishing to help. As a result of provisioning the destitute, food riots subsided for the moment. Alongside this effort, the government sought to help paupers by giving men work on the Main Reef Road, a public works project begun during the depression before the war. Men home from the front were hired for a few days or weeks to earn small amounts of food and cash for their families.[51]

To cope with Johannesburg's excessive (and structural) poverty, the Commissariat Commission needed the help of the few remaining charitable Johannesburgers. In November, the *Standard and Diggers' News* spearheaded a drive to collect money for widows and orphans. Meanwhile, the poor were assisted by the van den Berg Fund, which aimed to bring together burgher and foreign — including British — women into a 'Ladies Committee for the Relief of the Destitute Sick of Johannesburg'. Believing that they could significantly change conditions, these idealistic women began to investigate the extent of the poverty in the western suburbs and in Jeppestown. It was only after they had finished their survey that they were forced to accept that, with their limited funds, they could provide only partial relief. Accordingly, they directed their assistance to the worst cases by distributing food, clothes, brandy and wine (where prescribed by a doctor) as well as bread and meat coupons donated by the French Benevolent Society. Doctors were provided for the very ill.[52]

By the end of November there were a handful of charities operating in the city, but the problem had not diminished. In fact, food riots once again broke out and food shortages worsened. Realizing that duplicated efforts brought waste, the government called for the coordination of relief work and cooperation between the civil and government relief groups. Thereafter the government concentrated on procurement and left distribution to the charities. For example, when there was an acute milk shortage the government commandeered nearly 400 cows, but then left it to a 'Milk Commission', which had been set up in December in Fordsburg, Vrededorp and Burgersdorp, to distribute the milk to the poor.[53]

In December the authorities initiated a food census and wholesalers and retailers were ordered to notify the Commissariat Commission of the amount of specified goods they held in stock. Because local shortages were in part a result of the merchants' unwillingness to order goods for fear that they would only be stolen or commandeered, the government now gave them a guarantee that if they restocked their shelves, their goods would not be commandeered. Instead, commandeering officials turned to barricaded shops that were obviously owned by absent Uitlanders. Goods taken from these were distributed to the needy through the van den Berg Fund and the government commissariat stores.[54]

The authorities also provided housing for the destitute. Although this was a contentious issue in that the Rust en Orde Commission upheld the sanctity of private property (proclaiming in March 1900 that 'private property rights must be protected'), Commandant Schutte felt that certain people, such as the wives of burghers in the field, or refugees from the Orange Free State and the Cape, should be provided with housing. Most of those who approached his office were put into abandoned houses in Braamfontein, Fordsburg, Burgersdorp, Doornfontein,

Jeppestown, or in the Joubert Park or central-city areas of the town. When a large number of refugees arrived from the south in March, the city experienced a mini boom as streets filled with people who eagerly shopped for goods with which to set up home in the vacated houses. Some, of course, were destitute and these were integrated into the pre-existing relief programme.[55]

As the middle-class Uitlanders fled, they left behind their poorer compatriots, the British destitute, who (unlike the *arme burghers* who were assisted by local government and charities) had to rely for the most part on what remained of the Temporary Relief Committee the industrialists had formed before the war. As the poorest of the British subjects wondered what was going to happen to them after J. Emrys Evans and Conyngham Greene left the Republic, the local Anglican priest, John Darragh, complained to Milner of the scandalous way in which 'thousands of our destitute fellow subjects were left here derelict — without one official word of advice. . . . They were left to drift rudderless. They were a motley crew, certainly, but as subjects of the Crown they were worthy of a little more notice and attention than they received.'[56] Darragh helped many of these people to the coast by arranging documents and railway tickets and Charles Vincent actually escorted some of them to Lourenço Marques himself. After that over 1,000 destitute British remained and it fell to what remained of the charitable Uitlanders to care for them.

Vincent, Darragh and Carpenter were assisted in their task by goods and money left behind by R. Schumacher. Some of these supplies were, however, confiscated by government agents who went from house to house searching for food hidden away by British women — the British felt that the agents would have seized all the food had they been able to find it — and, having been left with very little cash, the women were going to be in serious trouble when their secret stockpiles were exhausted.[57]

Vincent shared their concern. Before the war, he wrote to the British consul at Lourenço Marques, A. Carnegie Ross, it had been estimated that only about 200 British would be allowed to remain in central Johannesburg and enough food was left with him to feed that number for three months — the time, presumably, the war was expected to last. As it happened, by November there were about 700 destitute British in the central ward alone and only enough food to last for six weeks.[58] And, as predicted, the number of needy increased as their funds were exhausted. There were 800 on Vincent's rolls in October, 1,000 the following month and over 1,200 by the new year.[59]

This deepening crisis led the Temporary Relief Committee to ask the high commissioner if he could send assistance, a request denied because the British government thought it inadvisable to send food into the Republic. The destitute were to rely instead upon £5,000 made available by Eckstein & Company through its agent who remained on the Rand. Until January money was advanced to the Temporary Relief Committee, but that month it was informed that funding would cease because the British government had told Eckstein & Company not to 'interfere' in Rand affairs. Actually, no such order seems to have been given, at least formally, and the high commissioner's staff was surprised when the endowment was cancelled. Instead, the staff claimed that the grant was stopped by Eckstein himself because he felt that the destitute British ought to be 'got out' of the Republic and 'not encouraged to remain' any longer.[60] This may well have been the first step towards what was to become a programme by the authorities and Randlords to create what Milner later called a new 'social order' on the Rand.

While it remains unclear who ordered the funds cut and for what purpose, agreement was fairly widespread that the destitute should not be permitted to remain much longer. Some Boers thought that all of them ought to be 'got out' because they were either of no use to the state or downright dangerous. Several local administrators felt that only the excess (*voerbordige*) ought to go — which in the light of the food crisis was understandable — but that the rest should remain so that essential services and industries were not disrupted. In January the Rust en Orde Commission, acting on instructions from the State Secretary, Reitz, decided to review permits and concluded that the British ought to be sent away. This decision was reportedly reversed by Kruger.[61]

But in April the decision to expel a number of British was again reached and this time it was carried out. Late that month the US consul, acting for the British government, informed the Temporary Relief Committee that the Boers had ordered about 700 destitute British to leave. Among those told to go were women abandoned by their husbands and people in receipt of aid.[62] For months the Temporary Relief Committee had been afraid that these people would be forced off the highveld onto the steamy, disease-ridden coast. Many had remained because of their delicate health and the possibility of having to spend weeks in Lourenço Marques led the Committee to fear for their lives. But the Boers were not heartless and, after listening to these concerns, agreed that the destitute would not be sent down until a ship was waiting there to receive them. About 700 whites and 500 Coloureds were ordered away, leaving several hundred British subjects on the Rand. Shortly afterwards, however, an explosion rocked the city and, because sabotage was suspected, all but a handful were ordered to go. Consequently, by the time the British army arrived on the Rand a few weeks later, barely 100 British remained and probably not a dozen of these were destitute.[63]

Johannesburg was relatively unaffected by the first eight months of the war. There were of course disrupted services, shortages and a certain amount of fear, tension and boredom. Also, many resident Boers and pro-Boer Uitlanders lost friends and relatives at Elangslaagte, Magersfontein and elsewhere on the veld. But, considering there was a war going on, it seemed very far away and had little real meaning for most people. Safe behind the lines, Johannesburg could serve the Boers. Its homes could house displaced people and the poor; its shops could provide food and clothes for the destitute; but the Rand's most vital resources were its labour and its gold and the Republicans used both in their effort to win the war.

Notes

1. *Star,* 22 Sept., 4 and 5 Oct. 1899; *African Review,* 21 (321) 25 Nov. 1899, p. 301.
2. *S & D News,* 26 and 29 Sept. and 11 Oct. 1899; MS/TAD/R&O 515, 'Rust en Orde, notule Oktober 1899', p. 1 for the rest of the members.
3. MS/JPL/van der Horst, p. 27; and see DO 119/497, H. C. Marshall to J. E. Evans, 2 Sept. 1899; Froes 1899, p. 21; and MS/JPL/ACPT, London letterbook, report dated 25 Sept. 1899.
4. MS/PRO/DO 119/487, 'British agent Pretoria: inventories'; MS/JPL/ACPT, London letterbook, reports dated 25 Aug., 4 Sept., 2 and 7 Oct. 1899; MS/JPL/ERPM, general manager, Hellman, to chairman and board of directors, 2 Aug. 1900; MS/TAD/R&O 515,

file C, US consular agent, Gordon, to Joubert, field-cornet of Jeppestown, 29 Sept. 1900; MS/JPL/Lennard, entry dated 23 Nov. 1899; *African Review*, 21 (360) 14 Oct. 1899; 25 (421) 15 Dec. 1900, p. 391; and *S & D News*, 16 and 19 Oct. 1899.

5. *S & D News*, 19 Oct. 1899; *African Review*, 25 (421) 15 Dec. 1900, p. 391; MS/TAD/R&O 515, file C, US consular agent, Gordon, to Joubert, field-cornet of Jeppestown, 29 Sept. 1900.

6. MS/JPL/Lennard, entries dated 8, 11 and 23 Nov., and 26 Dec. 1899 and 2 and 8 Jan. 1900; MS/JPL/ACPT, London letterbook, reports dated 11 Sept., 7 and 13 Oct., 22 Nov. 1899, 25 April 1900; MS/USL/Lipp, pp. 2, 87; MS/JPL/Potts, pp. 92—3; MS/UWL/Walker, p. 167; MS/PRO/DO 119/487, Afrika van Louw to British agent, 6 Oct. 1899; and PRO/CO 291/27, Milner to Chamberlain, 27 Feb. 1901, re. 'payments of rents, interests on mortgage during martial law', letter from J. A. Hamilton, n.d.; and see *S & D News*, 18 Nov. 1899.

7. PRO/CO 291/39, Milner to Chamberlain, 17 May 1902, with enclosed report by H. J. Roberts, assistant commissioner of police, Johannesburg, 1 May 1902, where it is noted that between January and 30 April 1902, 350 houses in the city were inspected, of which 64 per cent had been looted. In the outside district, 119 houses were inspected, of which 83.1 per cent had been looted. Most were 'workmen's dwellings'. See also MS/TAD/LAJ/4, 143, affidavit, Wm. W. Cawood, 19 June 1900; and *Star*, 24 Jan. 1902.

8. *Star*, 27 and 28 Sept. 1899.

9. MS/JPL/ACPT, London letterbook, 25 Sept. 1899.

10. *Star*, 27 and 28 Sept. and 8 Oct. 1899.

11. *Star*, 6 Oct. 1899; *S & D News*, 6 Oct. 1899.

12. MS/TAD/R&O 515, 3 Oct. 1899, p. 8 'Notule'. See also MS/JPL/Lennard, entries dated 11, 17, 26, 29 and 30 Oct. 1899 and 1, 14 and 16 Jan. 1900; MS/JPL/van der Horst, p. 866; MS/USL/Lipp, pp. 7—8; and see MS/UWL/Law, pp. 37—8. British subjects were apparently permitted to guard the waterworks and, at least initially, the banks.

13. *S & D News*, 17, 20, 29 and 30 Oct. and 11 Nov. 1899. See also MS/PRO/DO 119/506, Ross diary, 1 April 1900; and MS/TAD/R&O 518, 27 April 1900, petition from the special police.

14. *S & D News*, 29 Oct. 1899.

15. MS/USL/Lipp, pp. 50—1, 60; Roos 1949, pp. 63—6; van den Bergh 1972, pp. 874—5; see *Cape Times*, 26 May 1900; *African Review*, 22 (384) 31 March 1900, p. 472; *S & D News*, 7 and 16 Oct. and 16 Nov. 1899.

16. A translation of an anonymous letter in French addressed to the editor of *Le Temps*, 23 April 1900, pp. 5—6. It may be found in MS/JPL/Mine Police. For a photograph of the corps, see *African Review*, 24 (407) 8 Sept. 1900, p. 332. According to the letter to *Le Temps*, a gold theft on the mines on 2 Oct. precipitated a meeting of about 500 persons interested in forming a guard. According to G. Albu (*African Review*, 26 (427) 26 Jan. 1901, p. 124) the force was formed to protect the machinery and buildings from possible damage by 'rabble and Kaffirs'.

17. MS/TAD/R&O 532, 'Documenten in verband met speciale politie voor de mijnen'. See also MS/JPL/Mine Police, 'Sermant', which provides a list of some of the men in the corps. Of the 295 who signed this book after 31 Jan. 1900, and who entered their nationalities, the following breakdown may be made: Burgher (110), German (95), Hollander (22), Austrian (17), Russian (14), American (7), Swedish (4), French (2), Belgian (2), Colonial (2), Swiss (2), Dane (2), Portuguese (2), Italian (1), and unknown or illegible (13). See also MS/JPL/Mine Police, minute book, vol. 1, pp. 115—16; *Star*, 7 Oct. 1899; *Cape Times* (weekly) 18 Oct. 1899.

18. For the oath, see MS/JPL/Mine Police, 'Sermant'. See also *S & D News*, 28 and 30 Nov. 1899, 25 Jan. 1900; *African Review*, 22 (328) 13 Jan. 1900, p. 61; *Cape Times* (weekly) 8 Nov. 1899.

19. *African Review*, 21 (317) 28 Oct. 1899, p. 150; OP/CM 1900/1, p. xxxi. For an example of the cost to one mine, the Wemmer, see *Star*, 21 March 1902.

20. MS/TAD/R&O 515, 'Notule', 5 Oct. 1899, p. 31; see *S & D News*, 19 and 24 Oct., 16 and

22 Nov. and 5 Dec. 1899. For the continuation of prostitution throughout the war, see MS/TAD/R&O 522, p. 8; R&O 528, 4 May 1900; R&O 529, no. 995, 26 April 1900. For an excellent discussion of pre-war prostitution, see van Onselen 1982, vol. 1, pp. 103—62.

21. For reports on criminals and prisons, see *S & D News*, 9, 16, 17, 19 and 23 Oct. 1899, 22 Jan. 1900; *Cape Times*, 5 May 1900; *Cape Times* (weekly) 15 Nov. 1899; *African Review*, 21 (321) 25 Nov. 1899, p. 301; 22 (334) 24 Feb. 1900, p. 268. See also Roos 1949, pp. 10, 18; MS/USL/Lipp, p. 43, where she notes deportations to 'Synor Garcia' (i.e. Ressano Garcia).

22. *Star*, 27 and 29 Sept. and 2, 4 and 5 Oct. 1899; *S & D News*, 5, 6, 7 Oct. 1899.

23. *S & D News*, 10, 12, 18, 29 and 30 Oct. 1899. Anglophobes, then and since, have considered these terms too lenient. See Roos 1949, ch. 1.

24. *S & D News*, 19 Oct. 1899.

25. MS/JPL/Lennard, 14 Oct. 1899. She and her family were eventually given permission to remain.

26. MS/TAD/R&O 540—7. These volumes contain approximately 1,000 individual applications. Only 161 men gave their ages in their letters. Applications from businesses, which also provide lists of staff, may be found in R&O 542.

27. Rose's application may be found in MS/TAD/R&O 540, as can Marshall's. The latter sent a copy of the IILP's platform to the commissioners.

28. See the daily press for October, but particularly, *S & D News*, 10, 12, 13, 14, 16, 17, 18 and 19 Oct. 1899.

29. MS/TAD/R&O 515, 3 Oct. 1899, 'Notule', p. 6; and *Star*, 4 Oct. 1899.

30. For a list of permits issued, see MS/TAD/R&O 547 and, for regulations, see R&O 544, file U, re. 'certification to natives on mines', n.d.

31. *S & D News*, 13 and 23 Nov. 1899; and see MS/USL/Lipp, p. 87; MS/JPL/Lennard, 8 Jan. 1900; and MS/PRO/DO 119/541, Hely Hutchinson to Milner (confidential), 2 May 1900, with report by J. Pitts.

32. MS/USL/Lipp, p. 2; MS/UWL/Walker, p. 165; *S & D News*, 5 and 6 Oct., 13 and 23 Nov. and 9 Dec. 1899, 3 and 25 Jan. 1900; *Cape Times*, 1 May 1900. For a discussion on the use of Africans at the front, see Warwick 1983; and Siwundhla 1977.

33. MS/USL/Lipp, p. 111.

34. *S & D News*, 9 Dec. and 12 Jan. 1900; *Cape Times*, 1 May 1900. For raids by the mine police, see MS/JPL/Mine Police, minute book 3, 'Rapports quotidiens'.

35. MS/TAD/R&O 547, 'Staat van uitgerikte verblyf certificaten van personen woonachtig op de Witwatersrand goudvelden totop 15 Dec. 1899'. See also MS/PRO/DO 119/431, Ross to Milner, 9 Nov. 1899, with letter from Charles Vincent to Ross, 4 Nov. 1899 re. Coloureds. For Asians, see MS/TAD/R&O 541—2, which include many denied requests for permission to remain. For Chinese, see *S & D News*, 20 and 21 Oct. 1899. The *S & D News*, 9 Dec. 1899 notes that the district pass office reported at least 20,000 blacks in the city and area, while the *Cape Times* (weekly) 29 Nov. 1899 suggests that about 13,000 were in the city.

36. *S & D News*, 13, 16, 19 and 20 Oct. 1899, 5 May 1900; *Cape Times*, 2 May 1900; *Cape Times* (weekly) 8 and 29 Nov. 1899; *African Review*, 21 (321) 25 Nov. 1899, p. 301. Good first-hand sources of information on Johannesburg in this period may be found in MS/USL/Lipp; MS/JPL/van der Horst; and MS/JPL/Mann. See also MS/JPL/ACPT, London letterbook, 31 Jan., 8 March and 4 April 1900; MS/PRO/DO 119/582, postmaster general, Cape Colony, to Milner, strictly confidential, 3 Nov. 1899; MS/PRO/CO 417/268, Milner to Chamberlain, 25 Oct. 1899, with enclosure, governor of Natal to Milner, 22 Oct. 1899; MS/PRO/FO 2/399, managing director of Robinson South African Banking Company to FO, 24 Feb. 1900; MS/TAD/R&O 516, file L, 12 Dec. 1899; R&O 518, 13 Feb. and 1 May 1900; and MS/JPL/Johannesburg, correspondence 1900, Smithers to burgomaster, 1 March 1900.

37. For schools during this period, see *Cape Times* (weekly) 29 Nov. 1899; *African Review*, 22 (327) 6 Jan. 1900; *Star*, 7 Oct. 1899; *S & D News*, 29 Nov. 1899, 5, 8, 10 and 19 Jan., 2 Feb. and 28 March 1900; and *Johannesburg Gazette*, 27 Sept. and 3 Oct. 1901. See also

MS/TAD/R&O 516, J. S. Morris to R & O Commission, 2 Nov. 1899; R&O 547, 3 April 1900; PRO/CO 291/39, Milner to Chamberlain, n.d.; and MS/USPG/Letters, K. Orr to secretary, n.d. Government schools were closed.

38. *S & D News*, 6, 7, 9, 14 and 19 Oct. 1899; *Cape Times*, 13 March 1900; *Star*, 7 Oct. 1899; *African Review*, 22 (334) 24 Feb. 1900, p. 268.

39. *S & D News*, 8 Nov. and 20 Dec. 1899; MS/TAD/R&O 522, p. 8, 23 March 1900; R&O 528, 4 May 1900; R&O 529, no. 995, 26 April 1900; *African Review*, 25 (415) 3 Nov. 1899, p. 157; Vera 1902, ch. 5. For other first-hand accounts, see MS/JPL/Lennard, 25 Nov. and 15 and 30 Dec. 1899; and MS/JPL/Mann, p. 11.

40. MS/TAD/R&O 517—8, passim, for accusations against neighbours. For fears and rumours, see MS/USL/Lipp; Vera 1902, ch. 5; MS/JPL/Leslie (b), vol. 1, p. 41; *Cape Times* (weekly) 8 Nov. 1899; and *S & D News*, 28 Oct. 1899.

41. *Star*, 8 Sept. 1899; *S & D News*, 31 Oct., 29 Dec. 1899, 13 Jan. and 12 April 1900; *African Review*, 22 (13) Jan. 1900, pp. 67—8. See also MS/TAD/R&O 543, letter from George [Anderson] to Barbara, 19 Oct. 1899; MS/JPL/Johannesburg, correspondence 1900, A. Eckart-Beckmann to M. Aldolfs, 20 April 1900. For stockpiling of goods, see MS/JPL/Potts; MS/USL/Lipp; MS/UWL/Walker; and MS/SN, letter dated 10 June 1900.

42. MS/TAD/R&O 536; see daily reports in *S & D News* for endemic looting and theft. See also MS/USL/Lipp, 3—9 April 1900; and *S & D News*, 5 April 1900 for a particular theft. For cases of police connivance, see PRO/CO 291/27, Milner to Chamberlain, 19 April 1901, forwarding the 'Report of committee for commandeered, looted and stolen property'.

43. [Cleaver] 1913, p. 15. And see MS/TAD/R&O 536, p. 83, 15 Nov. 1899. Report from district 1; PRO/CO 291/39, Milner to Chamberlain, 17 May 1902, with enclosed report by H. J. Roberts, 1 May 1902; *S & D News*, 28 Oct., 10 Nov. 1899, 11 April 1900; *African Review*, 21 (326) 30 Dec. 1899; and 22 (331) 3 Feb. 1900; *Star*, 24 Jan. 1902; MS/USL/Lipp, pp. 70, 81.

44. MS/PRO/DO 119/506, Ross diary (confidential), 8 and 16 Jan. 1900; OP/GB/Cd. 33 (1900) and Cd. 43 (1900); [Anon.] 1901. For the impact on Johannesburg, see *S & D News*, 13 and 22 Jan. 1900; *Cape Times*, 10 Jan. 1900; MS/UWL/Law, entries for 6—10 Jan. and 8—9 Feb. 1900.

45. MS/PRO/DO 119/547, British consul at Lourenço Marques to Milner, 21 Oct. 1899; DO 119/431, Milner to Ross (draft), 4 Dec. 1899; DO 119/506, Ross diary (confidential), 8, 16 Jan. 1900. See also MS/PRO/FO 2/279, Salisbury to Lascelles, 31 Dec. 1899; MS/PRO/CO 417/285, Milner to Chamberlain (secret), 24 Jan. 1900; *Cape Times*, 10 Jan. 1900.

46. For instance, see MS/USL/Lipp, pp. 54, 115; MS/UWL/Law, pp. 47, 58, 63; *S & D News*, 13 and 22 Jan. 1900.

47. MS/PRO/DO 119/431, Ross to Milner, 9 Nov. 1899, with enclosure, Charles Vincent to Ross, 4 Nov. 1899; MS/PRO/FO 2/399, FO to CO (draft), 24 Feb. 1900 re. Mozambicans' complaints. See also *S & D News*, 13 Jan. 1900.

48. MS/PRO/FO 2/399, FO to CO (draft), 24 Feb. 1900 with Salisbury's recommendations. See also *S & D News*, 6 Jan. 1900 and *Cape Times*, 10 July 1900. Further information about the blockade may be found in [Anon.] 1901; and Moody (ed.) 1977, p. 18.

49. *Star*, 7 Oct. 1899; *S & D News*, 6 Oct. 1899. For a fuller account of the activities of this commission, see Roos 1949, ch. 6.

50. *African Review*, 24 (409) 22 Sept. 1900, p. 421; and 23 (394) 9 June 1900, pp. 351—2; *S & D News*, 17, 18 Oct. 1899; MS/PRO/DO 119/431, Ross to Milner, 9 Nov. 1899, with enclosure, Vincent to Ross, 4 Nov. 1899.

51. *S & D News*, 20, 27 Oct., 8 Nov. 1899. For pre-war charity, see van Onselen 1982, vol. 2, pp. 111—70.

52. *S & D News*, 23 and 24 Nov. 1899.

53. *S & D News*, 18 Nov. and 5 Dec. 1899; PRO/CO 291/27, Milner to Chamberlain, 19 April 1901, with 'Report of committee for commandeered, looted and stolen property'.

54. *S & D News*, 10 Nov., 1, 5, 8 and 25 Dec. 1899, 7 April 1900; MS/USL/Lipp, pp. 81,

103—4, 130—6; MS/UWL/Law, *passim*, for commandeering.

55. MS/TAD/R&O 542, 'Circulaire aan veld-cornetten en sub-commissies van Rust en Orde', 20 March 1900; *S & D News*, 20 Jan., 5 and 23 March, 7 April 1900; MS/PRO/DO 119/405, Hely Hutchinson to Milner, 12 May (confidential), with enclosure, commandant of Durban to governor of Natal (confidential), 12 May 1900; DO 119/541, Hely Hutchinson to Milner, 2 May 1900 (confidential), with report by John Potts, commandant of Durban, 17 April 1900; MS/PRO/FO 2/411, CO to FO, 18 July 1900, with enclosure, governor of Natal to CO, 31 May 1900, forwarding a letter from the commandant of Durban, 28 May 1900, and a report by D. L. Woolf, 26 May 1900. For an increase in business with the arrival of the refugees, see MS/JPL/Johannesburg, correspondence 1900, A. Eckart-Beckmann to M. Aldolfs, 20 April 1900.

56. MS/BOD/Mss. Milner Dep. 212, Darragh to Milner, 17 Oct. 1899. For assistance, see also Harris 1901, pp. 23—5; *S & D News*, 30 Sept. and 10, 16 and 30 Oct. 1899; *African Review*, 21 (320) 18 Nov. 1899, p. 261; and MS/PRO/DO 119/431, Ross to Milner, 9 Nov. 1899.

57. MS/PRO/CO 417/268, Milner to Chamberlain, 25 Oct. 1899, with enclosure, governor of Natal to Milner, 22 Oct. 1899, relaying information from K. Orr to a friend in Durban, n.d.

58. MS/PRO/DO 119/431, Ross to Milner, 9 Nov. 1899, with enclosure, Vincent to Ross, 4 Nov. 1899.

59. MS/PRO/DO 119/431, Ross to Milner, 9 Feb. 1900, with enclosure, Vincent et al. to Ross, 24 Jan. 1900.

60. MS/PRO/DO 119/431, Ross to Milner, 9 Feb. 1900, with enclosure, Vincent et al. to Ross, 24 Jan. 1900, with note on file to the HC. See also MS/PRO/CO 417/285, Milner to Chamberlain (secret), 24 Jan. 1900, with confidential report by Samuel Evans, n.d.

61. MS/TAD/R&O 548, 'Notulen de vergadering revisie permitten', 18 Jan. 1900, permits minute register. See also MS/USL/Lipp, pp. 161—2.

62. MS/TAD/R&O 548, 'Notulen van de vergadering gehonden de Johannesburg op . . . 28 Maart 1900'; MS/PRO/DO 119/557, Hely Hutchinson to Milner (confidential), 24 April 1900, with report from commandant of Durban, 20 April 1900; MS/PRO/CO 417/289, Milner to Chamberlain, 9 May 1900, with enclosure, consul-general of Lourenço Marques to Milner, 26 April 1900, which mentions ten men, 263 women and 422 children. See also MS/USL/Lipp, p. 213; and *S & D News*, 2, 4 April 1900.

63. MS/USL/Lipp, p. 230; MS/TAD/R&O 532, list of British permitted to remain, 30 April 1900; and R&O 543, 'Toegestan Britische onderdanen', n.d.

Four

The Rand Treasure Chest

The sinews of war, unlimited money.
Cicero

The gold which lay under the brown and rolling hills of the Witwatersrand had been a major factor in causing the war, but it could also become the Boers' salvation. If the wealth which filled the Randlords' coffers could be diverted to the government's treasure chest and if labour could be harnessed to bring the gold out of the ground, then the war could be financed easily. Without it the struggle would surely be lost. But to dig gold profitably a well conceived plan was needed. The administration first had to select which mines to work, then had to recruit clerical and technical staff, as well as black and white miners and artisans. It had to provide them with food and lodgings and build up a supply of materials, including spare parts and coal, dynamite and chemicals. Law and order would be essential to maintain production schedules and to convince white miners, artisans and clerks that they and their families were safe.

As war approached the mining companies had been given assurances by the authorities that if they continued production, Uitlander miners would be safe, black miners policed and properties protected. But these assurances came too late and, as the political situation worsened, the mass exodus continued and properties were forced to close for want of skilled labour. By the time the war started, only one company — the City & Suburban mine, belonging to Eckstein & Company — was working independently of the government and when its British workers were denied permits, it too shut down.[1] But by this time the authorities had formulated their own mining policy, one which would ultimately generate profits well above those forecast by the scoffing jingoist press.[2]

In the first week of September the state attorney, Smuts, laid a discussion paper before the executive council, which addressed the problems as well as the benefits to be derived from operating the mines. It and later reports[3] contributed to the administration's ultimate plan: first, it was necessary to choose which mines to work and in this respect matters of security, working costs and the richness of ore were crucial. This meant weighing carefully such factors as the location of the mines, the completeness of their reduction facilities, the extent of their underground development, the narrowness and unevenness of the gold-bearing reef at any one point along the Rand and the expected yield per ton milled. Further, an administrative board was needed, one whose members were experienced enough to direct Rand mining operations, were patriotic and honest enough to do so in the Republic's interest, but balanced enough to ease the fears of friendly mine owners and nations. Staff appointments had to be made keeping in mind a man's trustworthiness as well as his expertise.

By mid-October the government had taken over and begun to work three mines: the Robinson, the Bonanza and the Ferreira Deep. J. H. Munnik, the acting state mining engineer, was appointed manager of the Robinson and placed in charge of the foundry and gold-refining works set up there. Undoubtedly by over-mining, the Bonanza topped its August 1899 level by November. In the following month the Robinson bettered its August level and, in February, the Ferreira Deep produced more than it had in any month prior to the war. By November the authorities had added the Rose Deep to the list of government-operated mines.[4]

Several other mines were allowed − or (if their directors are to be believed) forced − to remain working. These were nominally under company control, their managements in charge, but with a government representative in a position to ensure compliance with the government's terms of operation. The Ferreira was one of these. It had earlier been threatened with confiscation but, in early October, was returned to company control with a government mining inspector acting as manager. It continued to operate throughout this period, dropping only half its normal complement of stamps. Others run by their owners were the Village Main Reef, the Wemmer, the Johannesburg Pioneer (which ceased operations before the end of the year) and the Worcester. About the same time, November 1899, the Langlaagte Deep was allowed to crush ore already above ground and the Crown Deep was allowed a similar 'privilege' later. The Geldenhuis Estate started operations in the new year and worked for four months, while the Crown Reef was apparently mined through a Bonanza shaft before December 1899 and later allowed to bring up its own ore. All these mines were near Germiston or Johannesburg, rather than along the open veld − undoubtedly a result of security considerations. They were also situated in what was labelled the 'rich zone', which runs east of the Langlaagte mines.[5]

Ironically, most of the skilled miners who worked on these properties were drawn from the British and colonial community. In September and October British miners debated whether to go or stay: the war was expected to last only a few months − until Christmas, perhaps − and many felt it unwise to give up their jobs. None the less, some were concerned that staying on and working for the Boers would mean working against the interests of the British, but when they asked the vice-consul for advice, he declined to give it.[6] There were other factors to take into consideration. For example, miners worried about accidents becoming more frequent because the managements had hired under-qualified men to replace the skilled workers who had left. Many worried about the possibility of starving, about Boer reprisals, or about being blacklisted by employers after the war. But their bosses and the jingoist press encouraged them to stay − indeed offered them bonuses to do so − and many minds were thus made up. Enough elected to remain and work to ensure that the Republic would be able to mine gold to pay for the war.

At the beginning of the war, the government-run mines sent lists of miners to the local permits committee requesting that the foreigners be allowed to stay and work. These lists indicate that a large percentage of the work-force was British. For instance the government's Bonanza mine requested permits for 57 men, of whom 47 were British; the government's Robinson mine requested permits for 70 white men, of which two-thirds were British; and the government's Ferreira Deep mine asked for over 80 permits, of which 27 were for British men.[7] Although not all these men were allowed to remain, the vast majority — because they were skilled workmen — were. Therefore, at the beginning of the war the percentage of British in the skilled work-force on the government-run mines could not have been less than 50 per cent and was probably even higher. On the company-run mines, such as the Ferreira and the Village Main Reef, the percentage was higher still.[8]

As time passed the composition of the skilled labour force changed, particularly as British workmen left. In a few instances a large group left together, but more often it was as individuals or in small groups that people headed for the coast. Some left after hearing a rumour that it was treasonable to work on the mines. Still, British and colonial miners continued to form the core of the labour force, which was augmented by other foreigners and Boers, many of whom left their units and worked on the mines for a few weeks at a time.[9] On any mine, then, there was a mixture of nationalities. For example, of the 204 whites employed on the Village Main Reef (and whose nationalities were reported to the Rust en Orde Commission), nearly 60 per cent were British. The next largest groups were Scandinavians and burghers, both with 9 per cent of the total. On the Wemmer mine, of the 122 white men recording their nationalities, 57 per cent were British while the Italians, with 14 per cent, were the next largest group. On the Langlaagte Deep, there was an almost equal number of British, American, Scandinavian and burgher workers.[10]

Once having decided to remain, foreign miners were expected to abide by the regulations which governed the lives of the rest of the population, namely curfew and travel restrictions, and liquor and permit regulations. If a man wanted to change jobs, the Rust en Orde Commission had to be consulted. If he wanted to live away from a mine, he had to get a daily travel pass, which meant an application to the Commission as well. Other than that, the miners had little trouble adjusting to life behind the lines. Mine managers had stockpiled goods, including food, and the mines and their staffs were the recipients of government commandeering. It is probable that the men, especially the highly-skilled ones, earned exceptionally good wages during these months. And, other than cases of drunkenness on duty and one recorded incident of miners being forbidden to go above ground during their lunch break, there seems to have been little white labour unrest.

Peace did not, however, characterize the relationship between the authorities and black labour. On the contrary, chronic unrest was punctuated by riots, some of which were particularly fierce. It is difficult to say exactly how many Africans worked on the mines, though most reliable figures suggest between 12,000 and 13,000 on the operational mines.[11] Blacks were also found on non-operational mines, helping to pump water and make simple repairs. There were, besides, black women and children in some locations — how many is unclear, but it may have been as many as 2,000 or 3,000.[12]

Africans were grouped together in 'native' locations along the reef. The largest were on the working mines, such as the Village Main Reef which housed 2,600 and the Robinson, where more than 3,000 lived. Other locations of considerable size were found on the Ferreira, the Bonanza, and between the Simmer & Jack and South Geldenhuis mines near Germiston. But blacks came together into small communities along the whole length of the reef, for a few Africans were working on each of the closed mines.[13] The authorities worried about this wide dispersal of blacks and, particularly, about any who they thought were 'idle'.

The Boers' goal as war approached — a goal which white Randites and mine owners shared — was to rid the district of 'excess' blacks while retaining enough 'boys' to supply the mines and to man the jobs in the service sector. Many of the Africans caught on the Rand at the beginning of the war would have left had they had the chance and had they been guaranteed a safe passage home. As it was, those selected to work were ordered to remain and were assigned to specific mines. Pre-war pass regulations, combined with the new residential certificates, restricted their mobility.

In order to ensure that only employed blacks stayed on the Rand, the mine police and the city's special police carried out house-to-house and mine-to-mine searches throughout the months before the British entered the area. Those blacks arrested for being without proper papers were sent to the local field cornet and, from there, to work, to the front, or, if very lucky, home. Since mine managers kept the documents of their African workers, deserters (when found without their papers) were eligible for conscription to the front — a strong inducement to stay on an assigned mine.

The government's mine managers, like the company men before them, aimed to maximize peace and output, while minimizing costs. As in peace-time, this meant stamping out the illicit liquor trade. Night after night, week after week, compounds turned out 'kafir beer' and received imported 'brandy'. The mine police were thus kept busy raiding suspected manufacturers and suppliers. These raids had only short-term effect, for no sooner was one operation closed down than another would open on a nearby mine and, not long afterwards, the original location would again be manufacturing, storing and selling beer. While the penalty for each liquor offence was three months' imprisonment with hard labour, brewers and shebeens continued to operate more or less undeterred and, in the city and along the reef, liquor was generally available.[14]

The mine police also carried out raids to remove assegais, sticks and clubs from the African work-force. It was supposed that crowd control would be less fraught with danger if weapons were removed, but this was a continual task, like smashing beer-making equipment, for no sooner were the weapons burnt than they were replaced.[15] The police had every reason to get rid of as many weapons as possible, for there was a continual undercurrent of discontent amongst blacks, discontent resulting from conditions of work and life in the compounds.

In peace-time the conditions of black labour were notoriously bad, but they were worse during the war. Where before and after the war methods of recruitment and retention of labour were hardly subtle, now martial law was used to force men to work. So-called 'loafers' were rounded up and sent to the mines. Men were told which mine they would work on and were shifted from one to another to meet the needs of the government. Any informal transfer of men was forbidden, for the Rust en Orde Commission had to approve all reallocations. In spite of this bureaucratic entanglement, the shifting of men from mine to mine was quite common, with most blacks channelled to the Robinson, the Rose Deep and the Village Main Reef.[16] Their passage through Johannesburg or Germiston caused quite a stir:

> Yesterday a crowd of excited natives passed through the back street, overlooked by my little balcony — they were evidently exchanging from one mine to another, a curious sight they presented — Three or four hundred of

them, dressed in all sorts and condition of clothing, the majority of them with a little loin cloth only or a short shirt but nearly all carrying open umbrellas. . . . [T]hey were very excited, gesticulating freely, brandishing their kerries and speaking to one another in high raised voices — two policemen were keeping them in check.[17]

Those no longer needed by the industry and deemed to be of more use elsewhere, were sent to work on Boer farms, especially during the harvest season, or to commando camps near the front. Extensive commandeering of mine labourers for other work caused unrest along the reef and jeopardized the industry's output. For this reason, many in authority, including the acting state mining engineer, Munnik, opposed the practice.[18]

Besides being told where to work and when, black miners had to work for a wage set by the government. While it is true that, before the war, blacks worked for wages that were low because of unilateral reductions by the companies, they still influenced long-term wage levels by withholding their labour — either by leaving the Rand during or at the end of their contracts or, on a few occasions, by striking. Wages for blacks thus rose from less than 45s a month in 1890 to a peak of 63s in 1895. The Chamber of Mines and the government counteracted this trend by better controlling the mobility of workers through revised legislation on 'touting' and passes, and wages consequently fell after 1896.

Not surprisingly, then, when more complete control over blacks was achieved during the war by the use of commandeering and martial law, wages could be lowered significantly, even while, in some cases, hours increased. In December 1899 the government reduced all black wages to a monthly maximum of £1, though it is likely that some miners earned even less — some as little as 5s a month. Some were paid in kind, with clothes and boots.[19] In April the following year Munnik estimated that the average cost of a black worker was between 20s 6d and 23s 6d a month, which meant a real saving of between six and nine shillings per man-month over the post-war period.[20] This was undoubtedly the result of the lower wage bill as well as commandeering, which provided the mines with goods, including food and clothes, free.

Tight control of the labour force did not ensure peace. Rather, restrictions on mobility and the reduction of wages gave rise to discontent. This manifested itself in a number of ways. For instance, drunkenness, always a widespread problem, did not diminish in these months. The combination of liquor and idleness (brought about by restrictions on Sunday mining) created problems for the guards, since unrest spread beyond the compounds into the city, where Africans frequented (and were illegally supplied with liquor in) the brothels and 'kafir eating houses'. Poor conditions also fostered looting, as blacks scavenged for food (especially fresh meat), coal, firewood and groceries.

Industrial action centred on low wages. Although blacks sabotaged at least one mine in October in an effort to 'thwart the State's best effort' by hiding dynamo oil and other supplies,[21] this may have been an attempt to get the mine to close in the hope that they would be sent home. Even before the war started and well before the wage level was officially lowered, blacks expressed their displeasure with their pay and — as some whites did — organized to demand higher wages, which they felt were due to them as a result of the worsening conditions. But most industrial unrest focused on the reduction in wages at the end of the year. In December 1899 and January 1900 they made their anger known, forcing at least one manager — on the Ferreira — to resign because he did 'not like the look of things'. Soon after there was a 'rising' where shots were fired and rumours of policemen having been killed circulated through the city.[22]

The fear of a mass rising forced the government to reconsider its wages policy, at least informally. By mid-January, wages for some workers — such as those on the railways — were allowed to climb.[23] On the mines the policy seems to have been maintained, though informally relaxed in certain cases. The Wemmer mine manager, for instance, told his African workers that their wage reduction was 'only temporary' and that 'after the war the balance of their wages [would] be paid to them'. In the meantime, he assured them, they were being held in the company's safekeeping.[24]

Discontent also resulted from the Boers' use of forced labour. A notable example of this practice took place in early 1900 when 1,000 Basuto were commandeered to work on the mines. These men had been sent out of Kimberley, during the siege there, by the British who feared that the shortage of food would lead to black unrest. The Basuto, thinking they were being led by the Boers to the Basutoland border, marched as far as Klerksdorp, where they boarded a train bound, not south towards home, but to the Republic. The first batch arrived in central Johannesburg in late January and, upon disembarking, was confronted by police who ordered the men to throw down their kerries, iron sticks and other weapons and to proceed to the Robinson mine. They 'refused to obey and immediately commenced to attack the police who fired on them killing two and dangerously wounding others. More specials and many Burghers with rifles, and constables appearing, the natives were disarmed, handcuffed and marched off to the mine, "commandeered" for work'.[25] Thereafter, some attempted to 'escape' across the veld and there is little doubt that these men were among the large number of blacks arrested for desertion in the following months.[26]

Once having acquired a skilled labour-force and taken control of the less skilled black workers, the Boers turned their attention to the acquisition of supplies. Commandeering was the favoured method of obtaining goods. Because some field cornets just took what they wanted, at the beginning of the war the system was rather haphazard. Soon, though, a 'Provision Committee of Supplies' was established, with two subcommittees — the Commissariat Commission, which assisted the needy, and the War Committee, which was placed in charge of distributing goods to men on commando. The work of Mr van Wouw, previously a boiler inspector for the state mining department but now given authority to commandeer goods for the mines, was quite separate. He began by taking an inventory of the stores held on closed mines, with a view to using them if and when needed.

Van Wouw's men had the power to remove goods from a mine by simply handing its caretaker a receipt. Their power was virtually unlimited: the manager of the Bonanza mine was handed a receipt bearing the words 'Received, one mine' from a commandeerer. Most often, though, these men confined themselves to smaller items, such as containers of cyanide, dynamite, fuses and food. But they were known to commandeer horses, locomotives, houses and tons of coal. Machine parts were taken from one mine and installed directly on another.[27]

Although a number of proclamations and regulations governed commandeering procedures, the practice was naturally open to abuse. For example, the special commandant, Schutte, informally gave people power to take things, even though they had no legal right to do so. This was how the Irish Brigade came to commandeering goods. The acting state mining engineer's alleged commandeering of pianos from abandoned mine managers' homes was also regarded with some suspicion, as was the large-scale scheme of commandeering and selling horses, mules, wagons and saddlery. Less spectacular and less well organized, but equally dishonest cases were constantly being reported to the police and by the press during the period.[28]

Hoping either to retrieve the goods, to collect payment from the Republican government, or to win compensation from insurance companies (or the British government) after the war, company representatives and caretakers attempted to keep track of the type, amount and value of the materials commandeered from their mines. The value of goods taken from mines varied considerably — City & Suburban mine, £3,300; Henry Nourse mine, £8,294; East Rand Proprietary Mines Limited, £17,684 17s 4d; and the Nigel mine, £3,000.[29] In the absence of complete and accurate figures, it can only be assumed that state mining engineer, Klimke, was correct when he stated that, for mining purposes, about £100,000 worth of material was commandeered from British firms during these months. Other estimates mention £500,000 as the value of goods commandeered from all mines in these seven and a half months of war.[30] In any case, it is safe to say that the Boers' ability to commandeer essential materials helped lower their working costs and gave them higher profits.

But the government also had high profits because it over-mined — it was, in the words of the press of the time, 'picking the eyes and ears out of the properties'.[31] Furthermore, managements undertook no development work and stopes were left to lie where they fell.[32] By working only high-yield ore and (in the view of the British consul in Mozambique) by stealing 'all the dynamite and cyanide they required [and cutting] . . . down the boys' pay', the Boers were able to work cheaply and generate high profits.[33] It is ironic that the British government was so cynical about many of the Boers' practices in these months because many were merely conforming, albeit in the extreme, to what the Randlords had advocated for the previous decade.

In any event, the Boers' efforts were successful. By working a dozen or so mines off and on from 10 October 1899 to 30 April 1900, gold valued at an estimated £1,710,549 6s 0d was won from the mines. In May another £240,000 was taken from the few mines then at work. Working expenses were put at about £630,000, of which just over two-thirds was actually paid to the companies by the government — the remainder was left owing. The profit accruing to the Republic was therefore at least £1.5 million, which was sufficient to cover Republican war expenditures to that point in time.[34]

Control of the Rand brought Pretoria not only wealth, but power. On the one hand, by having a virtual hold on the Rand, the administration could use the mines as hostages. Could Kruger, for instance, force countries to support his war against Britain by threatening to destroy them? Could he not take them away from their British owners and sell them to foreign speculators, giving the new owners added incentive for helping the Boers win? Certainly the Boer government had plenty of room to manoeuvre: it could create minor, though expensive, irritants for the industrialists, or it could issue major threats, such as confiscation or destruction of the properties.

On the other hand, because it needed the gold they produced, the administration was in a vulnerable position. For instance, any British policy that could be implemented to reduce production — say, by encouraging skilled workers to leave — would hurt the Boer cause. This game, though, could be played only to the point where the Republican government, seeing its gold production falling, would decide there was no longer a reason to save the mines. This set the stage for the struggle for control of the mines and for the power to regulate gold production, a struggle fraught with complexities and dependent upon the whims and temperament of the individuals involved, but one which was pursued with ardour in these months.

Two relatively petty irritants soon became apparent to the companies: that 'de-watering' a mine was a privilege and that mines were subject to searches. When war broke out managers were encouraged to pump water out of their closed mines, but, by November, the policy had changed. Now permission to pump was conferred only upon those companies whose shareholders were residents of friendly nations. Companies denied permission had to have their men, both black and white, off their properties by 1 December. The blacks were assigned work elsewhere, while the whites were told to find new jobs or to leave the Republic. Though some in authority may have been motivated by other than political reasons — the minister of mines argued that such a step would release blacks needed for agriculture — industrialists viewed the pumping policy as an example of the government's bitterness towards certain individuals and mining groups.

Allowing water to flood a mine held little fear for the managements of mines cut into 'blue rock', which were naturally impervious to water, or mines that became drained when a neighbouring mine was pumped. Even for the rest of the mines, flooding was relatively harmless, though it was expected that 'de-watering' would be time-consuming and costly. It would slow down the reopening of mines once mine managers were given the go ahead and it was for this reason that it caused some concern.

Managers also felt harassed by the repeated searches for guns and goods (supposedly secreted before the war), which took place through these months. Before the war companies had been encouraged to remain working and managers ordered machinery and goods to be stored so that equipment could later be repaired and workers fed. When regular managements left the mines, some hid these supplies in shafts deep underground. Some were sealed into bags and placed so that the rising water would ensure they went undiscovered. Suspecting that such goods were hidden, the government ordered the police to visit managers and caretakers. To regularize the procedure, Kruger proclaimed that any goods that had been placed on the mines in conflict with the mining regulations — i.e. unreported and secreted away — were eligible for confiscation.[35]

Detectives working for the special commandant and members of the mine police carried out these searches. Sometimes they were following 'tips' provided by would-be do-gooders. Sometimes they followed up reports of guns stored in mines — some of which were supposedly hidden at the time of the Jameson Raid. Sometimes they encouraged men who had been arrested for stealing gold to lead them to hidden caches of amalgam. In no case was the search of a mine a pleasant experience for a manager.

But Pretoria did not confine itself to these relatively harmless, though sometimes expensive inconveniences, for it had a more valuable, if not always legal, way of harassing the enemy while helping the war effort: confiscation of raw gold. The first instance of a state gold theft came as an 'utterly unforeseen occurrence' on the evening of 2 October, that is, over a week before the war began. The Johannesburg mail train, bound for the Cape with what was reportedly the first instalment of the mines' September output, was stopped at the border station of Vereeniging, where the authorities removed something like £430,000 worth of gold. The gold was off-loaded there and not in Johannesburg because the commandant, who received his orders from Jan Smuts,[36] did not have the proper papers authorizing him to do so — or so it was said at the time. A better explanation for waiting until the train reached Vereeniging to take the gold was that Schutte feared a reaction by company representatives and bank managers if his men had taken so bold a step as to seize gold on the peace-time Rand. So, the train was flagged down at the nearly deserted station instead, and was boarded by three men, only one of whom was armed. The railway guard was presented with a warrant and then told to help unload 16 cases of gold and a case of securities, which were being sent south for safe-keeping. As the train pulled out of the darkened station, leaving the two unarmed men guarding the cases on the platform, bystanders who had seen the operation commented on how down the ages men had 'endured unheard of privation' to get some 'fabulous treasure'. They then came to the 'prosaic conclusion that holding up a gold-laden train with a piece of paper was the easiest' method so far devised.[37] Neither the bankers nor the company directors who owned the gold would have appreciated this wry rural humour, for it was a joke at their expense. For instance, Eckstein & Company reported a loss of £233,500 and Consolidated Gold Fields, £52,691.[38]

In the following weeks the railway authorities refused to carry any more raw gold, unless specifically relieved of any responsibility for its safe-keeping *en route*. Managers then had to decide: should gold be sent south by rail anyway, should it be smuggled out in some other manner, or should it be hidden on the Rand, waiting for the outcome of the war? All three alternatives were tried with varying degrees of success.[39]

Meanwhile the British government had to decide what to do about the gold. Naturally it pressed Pretoria for its release, but to no avail. At the same time it contemplated retaliation. When Salisbury discovered that a shipment of gold worth some £100,000 had left London for the Republic, he ordered it to be seized at the Cape. Very soon the message was passed from Chamberlain to Milner. Foreseeing trouble with Schreiner at the Cape, who was trying in these tense days to keep his colony as a 'little place of peace . . . standing apart and aloof from the struggle', Salisbury informed the Foreign Office that if Schreiner would not seize the gold, the 'Admiral[ty] must'. With exasperation, Salisbury added: 'We shall soon have to blockade our own colony'. On 10 October Milner informed London that the gold had arrived at the Cape.[40]

Milner's reluctance to follow Chamberlain's order to seize gold on land if it were missed at sea had nothing to do with a desire for peace in the colony. He was concerned that the banks would be upset with the imperial government if he confiscated Republican gold, for they were worried that Pretoria would take revenge in some way that affected them. This line of reasoning carried no weight with Chamberlain, who argued that the banks still open in the Republic should have little cash for the Boers to seize, for the Uitlanders must have taken it all with them. As the rest belonged to burghers, retaliatory seizure by Pretoria was of no interest to the British. What mattered, according to the colonial secretary, was to keep all specie from reaching the enemy. Whitehall's orders having gone out to the Cape and Natal, a shipment of £25,000 in gold, bound for the Republic via Delagoa Bay, was taken by the gunboat *Philomel* in Portuguese waters on 17 October.[41]

According to Thomas Law, a National Bank official in Johannesburg, another shipment (worth £150,000) was also seized. He later recalled how it was returned to the National Bank on condition that the bank's Republican branches were totally isolated from outside branches, and that the colonial branches (as well as the one in Lourenço Marques) were managed from London. The penalty for doing otherwise was to have all the bank's assets confiscated. 'The pistol was therefore at our head', Law wrote, and the management agreed: all communication with (and shipments of gold to) Republican branches was cut off.[42]

Meanwhile the Boers continued to confiscate gold. A week after the theft at Vereeniging, Smuts sent a second order to Johannesburg: the Rust en Orde Commission must take possession of all gold in the banks in the city. On the 9th, two police lieutenants and an assayer from the state mining engineer's office visited four banks and carried away nearly 25,000 ounces of gold. Not long afterwards, the Pretoria branch offices of several banks were visited and their raw gold removed.[43]

Again in March the authorities turned to the banks. Apparently in possession of ample raw gold, but short of gold coin — partly because of the success of the British spy network in Lourenço Marques[44] — Pretoria commandeered some half-million pounds sterling from five banks in Johannesburg. It offered to replace the coin with gold. The offer was apparently accepted by four of the banks, while the fifth, the Standard Bank, refused on the grounds that such an exchange would be tantamount to trading with the enemy and was therefore treasonable.[45]

A third source of raw gold was repeatedly exploited in these months: from the plates and cyanide works of closed mines. Throughout this period Pretoria sent men to the Rand to clean the plates and works. In this way, the Meyer & Charlton, for instance, was stripped of about £1,300 worth of gold, while the Roodepoort United had gold valued at about £2,200 taken from its mill. While this might seem negligible, it should be recalled that there were over 70 mines operating before the war, and many could be cleaned this way.[46]

Unable to stop the Boers confiscating raw gold and coin, the imperial government could do nothing until June 1900 other than try to isolate the Republican economy, disrupt it from outside and keep track of the amount of gold being mined, transferred, stolen, stored and spent.[47]

In an effort to exploit the wealth of the Rand more fully and to put pressure on foreign governments to encourage Britain to stop the war, Pretoria decided in late 1899 to introduce a new gold tax. The local press argued that it was 'quite reasonable' to make foreigners, who had profited enormously from the industry in the past, contribute to the war effort. And it was even more reasonable, the editor of the *Standard and Diggers' News* proposed, when 'it is remembered that . . . we have chiefly to thank the gentlemen who control the mining industry for the present war'.[48]

The amount due in taxes now depended on the state of operation of any mine in question, which, in turn, was presumed to reflect the level of the mine owner's friendliness towards the government. If a company worked its own mine, such as the Ferreira, it would owe 30 per cent of its output in taxes — which was what working mines had been paying since the proclamation of martial law — but a mine working under government orders, such as the Bonanza, would be taxed at a rate of 50 per cent. Furthermore, any non-working mine would owe 30 per cent of its probable output, calculated on three months' production prior to the war. And, most importantly, in case of non-payment of the new tax, the government could auction a mine to recover the tax monies due.[49]

Directors were irate, and their representatives approached both the Boers and the British. Of particular concern to some British companies was the fact that there was no one left behind to arrange payment of taxes, for their agents had been expelled from the Rand. Some also worried about their legal position, for, as Consolidated Gold Fields asked, would not a company's payment constitute a 'breach of duty to the Crown'? In an attempt to outmanoeuvre Pretoria, Gold Fields suggested to Chamberlain that the high commissioner proclaim that 'any forfeiture or confiscation of property, or any act of the Transvaal Government, which may be found to operate injuriously to the interests of British subjects, will be regarded as of no force or effect'. In other words, could not all potential buyers of confiscated property be warned that the imperial government would not sanction, condone or accept as valid, any transfer of property arising from such an auction?[50]

The law officers at the Royal Courts supported the Gold Fields' proposal, partly because they believed that title acquired by speculators at any such auction could 'prove a source of embarrassment' at the close of the war. The Colonial Office agreed and Milner issued a notice on 26 January which announced that the imperial government would not recognize as valid, forfeiture of any property in the Republic or Orange Free State, or any fines, charges, encumbrances, etc., or any conveyance, transfer, etc., which had taken place after the war began.[51] Milner's announcement forced prospective buyers to weigh very carefully all the factors — especially the likelihood of the Boers winning the war — before bidding on any property.

In May 1900, in a further effort to raise money and gain the goodwill of continental powers, Pretoria decided to auction the *bewaarplaatsen* — the mines' depositing sites, with their valuable underground rights — in mid-year. These areas had been coveted for years by the mining houses, and now a great deal of interest — and concern by those not in a position to bid — was being shown. The absent mine owners, unwilling to accept that this long sought-after prize was to pass into continental hands, claimed that Milner's proclamation regarding the transfer of property applied in this case as well.[52] In any event, General Lord Roberts's arrival on the Rand precluded any such auction.

During this eight-month struggle over the control of the wealth of the Rand, the British occasionally took the initiative. One such case was an attempt to extend to the mining industry their proclamation which made it treasonable for any British subject to trade with the enemy. This plan, though, had one central flaw: the mine owners were obviously not going to accept that their continued operation of the mines was treasonable. The industry's spokesman at this juncture, the *Financial News*, maintained that a company would be breaking the law only if it 'voluntarily worked its mine for the deliberate purpose of making a profit by selling the product to the Transvaal Government, but not if it worked a mine in order to keep it open' and thus free from the threat of confiscation. Nor, the paper would have it, was the payment of licence fees to the Boers in violation of the law, for this payment was made 'simply in the future interest of the shareholders'.

Clearly a mine being worked by a company's own management — such as the Ferreira — was in mind when the *Financial News* presented the analogy of the maiden and the milk cow:

> Let us suppose a case. A thief surprises a dairymaid who is milking a cow, and gives her a choice of continuing her work, and handing over to him the milk produced, or of vacating her stool, in which case he will perform the operation himself, or at least seize some of the milk already in the pail. Is the

dairymaid performing a voluntary act if she elects to continue milking, handing the thief the product in return for which he will refrain from molesting her or her cow, which there is otherwise a chance of his doing? We do not think the dairymaid's master would regard the act on her part as voluntary, and therefore merit punishment. We think, on the contrary, he would commend her prudence; the loss of the milk would be little, if any, greater, while she and the cow would have been saved from possible injury.[53]

Not surprisingly, the argument that residents of Park Lane were committing treason went no further. Meanwhile, attention turned to the white miners.

In January Milner heard from the consul in Lourenço Marques, who argued that all British subjects still working on the mines were traitors. He suggested issuing a proclamation stating that their activities were treasonable, but pardonable if they left the country. Sam Evans, who had been sent by Milner to Mozambique on a fact-finding mission, supported Ross's view that a proclamation forbidding British subjects from going into the Republic or working on the mines ought to be issued. He reported that, 'A very serious attempt is being made to work more mines and to increase the output of coal and gold' and that recently 'a certain number of men have been induced to leave the Colonies and return to the Rand'. He estimated that at least 70 per cent of the men working on the gold and coal mines were British and concluded that, to ensure that none of the British in Mozambique found their way back to the Rand, they ought to be sent to the Cape or back to Europe.[54]

Milner agreed and sent their proposals on to Whitehall, where Chamberlain's staff rejected the views of these men on the spot. First, Chamberlain explained to the high commissioner, the mining companies were not deemed to be consorting with the enemy by sending money into the Republic to pay the mine police. Secondly, he feared that if such a proclamation were obeyed and the mines became unworkable as a result, the Boers might retaliate in some way, such as by forcing the men to stay and work, or even by destroying the mines. If, in fact, any damage did result, the British government might be held responsible by the owners who would perhaps demand compensation.[55]

Milner disagreed. If a proclamation were issued, he urged, it would not receive the full support of the British community on the Rand and, if any men were to leave the mines, it would benefit the war effort. He also contended that the mines were being damaged anyway — by being stripped of machinery, for instance. Finally, the mining houses could not hold the British government responsible, for the British on the Rand were working the mines, not protecting them, and their departure could in no way be deemed responsible for any damage done by the Boers.[56] Chamberlain was not convinced, arguing that any man who willingly remained would not leave because of a proclamation anyway, and any who wanted to go might not be allowed to leave. In fact, he concluded, such a proclamation might even endanger lives. There was, he ordered, to be no proclamation.[57]

While obeying the order to the letter, Milner ignored its spirit. In February Ross again asked Milner: 'Do you approve my advising all British subjects in the Republics working directly or indirectly for the Governments to leave the Republics?' Milner responded: 'As Her Majesty's Government will not sanction such a course, you must not issue any public notice, but you should, I think, do all you can to get British subjects out of the Transvaal in the way of private advice.'[58] How or when this 'private advice' was transmitted is not clear, though it is certain that a secret communications network linked Ross and various Johannesburg residents.

Sometime in the late summer or autumn this 'advice' became known on the Rand and 'quite a number of men resigned and left the country'. In May the Boers took the initiative and hastened the departure of the rest. Shortly before Roberts's troops arrived from the south and just after the Rust en Orde Commission had ordered the remaining British to leave, the local press addressed a notice to the British working on company-run mines that it would be considered a 'breach of allegiance you owe to your Queen and country' to continue working on these properties.[59] Why the newspaper decided to publish this notice is unclear, though several reasons can be advanced. Because it was obvious that the Rand would soon fall to the British and that most of the gold to be won for the Boer cause was already out of the ground, the authorities may well have wanted the miners off the Rand to ensure that the British did not restart the mines for their own war effort — which was a real concern for some Boers. Certainly, too, they may have feared that the British miners would support the imperial government in the forthcoming battle for Johannesburg. There were also things going on inside the mines which many in authority may not have wanted anyone to see or disturb. Or, the Boers may simply have wanted to warn the British who had helped them, not only about their legal position, but also about the dangers they faced by staying on in what was soon to become (as far as anyone then knew) a battlefield.

The British, American, continental and colonial miners had served the Boers well, but so too had other foreigners and artisans. Some had built a military balloon for the Boers with materials commandeered locally; the men at Quinn's bakery had used commandeered grain to make bread and biscuits for commandos on the front; and a government clothes factory had opened in December, after the daily press notified 'all master tailors, working tailors, cutters, trimmers, basters, and other hands' that they were required under threat of martial law to attend a meeting to discuss the creation of an 'Army Clothing Establishment'.[60] Soon the stock exchange was commandeered and a number of 'sympathetic loyal' tailors were instructed to sew for the Boers. When they 'remonstrated', they were told that 'now was the time to prove their loyalty and should they not do so willingly, the Government would force them to work and they would receive no gratuities whatever, but proving themselves so sympathetic and loyal, the Government *might* by and by consider the matter of payment.'[61] Within a couple of months, using commandeered sewing machines and cloth, the scheme was quite successfully turning out 500 suits of clothes a week.[62]

Also of use to the Boers in these months was Begbie's armaments factory. Thomas Begbie & Company, a foundry situated near the City & Suburban mine just to the south of the city, was commandeered by the government two days after the war began. The government-appointed manager, Mr Grunburg, had come to the Republic four years earlier as a representative of a mining machinery firm. Mr Leon, a government engineer and now inspector at Begbie's, arrived in the Republic shortly after the Jameson Raid. Together, these two men were responsible for the conversion and maintenance of the armaments factory. Machinery was commandeered and explosives collected and stored in a vacant house next to the foundry. 'Lower class Jews' were hired to salvage scrap-iron to make shrapnel. The shortage of skilled labour was the most difficult obstacle Grunburg and Leon faced in turning Begbie's into a well-run armaments factory. According to all reports, the employees were careless and lacked proficiency — a state of affairs that was to have serious, indeed deadly, consequences. The work-force was made up of Britons (about a quarter of the total), Italians, Frenchmen and Austrians. Despite its labour difficulties, it was one of the most successful government enterprises on the Rand, with estimates of the number of shells produced running as high as 1,000 per day.[63]

Johannesburg and its environs were useful to the Boers during these eight months in a variety of ways. The city served as a huge storehouse and refuge. What remained of the population (black and white, skilled and unskilled) contributed to the war effort in several enterprises, most notably in the mining industry. The gold from the ground and in the banks was what enabled the Republic to pursue the war, for the mines provided Pretoria with enough money to pay wages and buy guns. As long as the Rand remained in burgher hands, the commandos had a chance of winning the war.

The British realized this and tried to fight back by disrupting economic life in and near Johannesburg. Their efforts to restrict trade should be seen in this light, for their attempts to blockade food, clothes, weapons, machinery and medicines were all designed to put pressure on the commandos, the population in general and, therefore, the Kruger government. The aim was to bring the war to a close more quickly. Salisbury was reluctant to sanction the extremes of such a policy, primarily because of adverse international opinion. None the less, local imperial officials tried to achieve these ends by going outside the sanctioned methods. Such policies and their erratic and informal implementation meant that the working man was under the most strain, for he was encouraged to leave his job after earlier being encouraged to stay. No one argued that the Rand worker had the virtue of a milk maid or that his future interests paralleled the preservation of a milk cow. And while British miners working in British-owned mines were accused of treason, no one criticized British businessmen for trying to protect their interests by registering their companies with foreign governments and pretending that they belonged to continental Europeans. No one criticized the Randlords for collaborating with the Rust en Orde Commission in working and protecting the mines. The reason was simple: Milner and the imperialists at home foresaw a time when the industry would be used for the good of the empire. The mines would become the milk cows from which all that was good would flow. But first they had to be saved.

Notes

1. *African Review*, 21 (320) 18 Nov. 1899, pp. 311–12; and 23 (386) 14 April 1900, p. 61; MS/PRO/DO 119/372, Hely Hutchinson to Milner, 31 Oct. 1899, with enclosed report by W. M. Hunter, 26 Oct. 1899; and MS/PRO/DO 119/401, Hely Hutchinson to Milner (confidential), 24 April 1900, forwarding confidential and private report by J. Paton, 19 April 1900.
2. 'If there is a net profit on the Government [mining] operations of £50,000 per month, it will be a matter for surprise. If the profit goes beyond this amount and reaches as much as £100,000 for all the richest mines, it will be a matter for profound astonishment.' (*African Review*, 21, 4 Nov. 1899, p. 187.)

3. Smuts to executive council, 4 Sept. 1899 (Hancock and van der Poel (eds) 1966); MS/TAD/PSY 73, political secretary to the FM C-in-C of HM forces in South Africa, 'Discussion as to which of the mines at present shut down would be the most likely to be worked by the government', a confidential Republican memorandum, 12 Oct. 1899.

4. PRO/CO 291/27, Milner to Chamberlain, 19 April 1901, with 'Report of committee for commandeered, looted and stolen property'; *S & D News*, 25 Oct., 8 Nov. 1899, 22 Jan., 10 Feb., 13 March, 7 and 27 April 1900; *African Review*, 21 (323) 9 Dec. 1899, pp. 388, 326; 30 Dec. 1899, p. 508; *Cape Times*, 26 May 1900.

5. In addition to the sources cited in n. 4 above, see *Star*, 3 Oct. 1899, 9 April and 1 May 1902; *African Review*, 12 (318) 4 Nov. 1899, p. 187; 22 (384) 31 March 1900, pp. 470—1; 24 (401) 28 July 1900, pp. 130—1; 24 (403) 11 Aug. 1900, pp. 202—3, 24 (406) 1 Sept. 1900, p.312; 25 (422) 22 Dec. 1900, pp. 437—8. See also OP/TVL/Mining Industry Commission, p. 446, evidence from Thomas Matthews. For mining at Barberton, see *S & D News*, 12 Jan. and 24 April 1900; and, for coal mining at Vereeniging, see MS/JPL/Leslie (a).

6. MS/PRO/DO 119/497, Dr H. B. Maunsell to J. E. Evans, 5 Oct. 1899, and Cecil Clare to J. E. Evans, 13 Sept. 1899; DO 119/541, Hely Hutchinson to Milner (confidential), 2 May 1900, forwarding copy of report by J. Pitts, 17 April 1900.

7. MS/TAD/R&O 542, H. Stark to mining inspector, Florida district, lists from Bonanza mine, 4 and 9 Oct. 1899, and two lists from Robinson mine, n.d. For Ferreira Deep, see R&O 543, 'Lijst van mannen werkzaam op de Ferreira Deep goud mijn . . .', n.d.

8. MS/TAD/R&O 542, Ferreira Gold Mining Company, list of 'names of the men employed since 13 Oct. 1899', dated 17 Oct. 1899. For Village Main Reef, see 'list of employees at 6 Oct. 1899', 'list of British subjects', dated 13 Oct. 1899, and 'further lists of British subjects', dated 17 and 19 Oct. 1899.

9. MS/PRO/CO 417/285, Milner to Chamberlain (secret), 24 Jan. 1900, forwarding report by Sam Evans, n.d.; see OP/CM 1900/1, p. 63; *Cape Times*, 26 May 1900; *African Review*, 22 (372) 6 Jan. 1900, p.4; 25 (423) 29 Dec. 1900, pp. 463—4; and *S & D News*, 7 April 1900. For men leaving, see MS/JPL/Potts, p. 96; and MS/PRO/DO 119/506, Ross diary (confidential), 19 Nov. 1899.

10. MS/TAD/R&O 547, 'Lysten van blanken en kleurlingen op de mynen op de Witwatersrand woonachtig', n.d. And see, MS/PRO/CO 417/285, Milner to Chamberlain (secret), 24 Jan. 1900, forwarding report by Sam Evans, n.d.

11. *African Review*, 23 (387) 21 April 1900, pp. 96—7, information supplied by acting state mining engineer, Munnik; and, in 22 (327) 6 Jan. 1900, p. 23, an Italian correspondent states the number as 10,000. Warwick 1983, p. 133, estimates there were 14,000 on the mines when the British took the Rand in mid-1900.

12. The mine police records (MS/JPL/Mine Police) make reference to black women and children in the locations along the reef. At the beginning of 1901 there were reportedly 1,226 women and 1,752 black children on the Rand (MS/TAD/SNA/1, report dated 13 Aug. 1901). At that time, there were a total of 26,299 blacks in the area.

13. *S & D News*, 12 April 1900; *African Review*, 23 (387) 21 April 1900, pp. 96—7; MS/TAD/R&O 547, 'Lysten van blanken en kleurlingen op de mynen op de Witwatersrand woonachtig', n.d. See also MS/JPL/Mine Police, for repeated mention of African settlements on the reef.

14. MS/JPL/Mine Police, esp. 'Rapports quotidiens' and minute book, for numerous raids; also *S & D News*, 29 Dec. 1899, 3 Jan. 1900.

15. MS/JPL/Mine Police, esp. 'Correspondence: note de service' and 'Rapports quotidiens'.

16. *African Review*, 22 (378) 17 Feb. 1900, p. 249; *Star*, 9 Oct. 1899; *S & D News*, 11 Oct. 1899, 19 Jan. 1900. MS/JPL/Mine Police mentions transfers of Africans to other mines as well.

17. MS/USL/Lipp, p. 51.

18. *Cape Times*, 28 April 1900; MS/JPL/Mine Police, 'Rapports quotidiens', 21 and 22 March 1900; MS/USL/Lipp, p. 142; MS/PRO/CO 417/285, Milner to Chamberlain (secret), 24 Jan. 1900, forwarding report by Sam Evans, n.d.; MS/PRO/DO 119/506, Ross diary (confidential), 20 April 1900.

19. *S & D News*, 13 Dec. 1899; *African Review*, 22 (384) 31 March 1900, p. 473; 24 (401) 28 July 1900, pp. 130—1; 24 (403) 11 Aug. 1900, p. 200; *Cape Times*, 28 April 1900. Lipp notes that the wages of all blacks were reduced, see MS/USL/Lipp, pp. 111, 127, 149; see also Warwick 1983, p. 131.

20. *African Review*, 23 (387) 21 April 1900, pp. 96—7. For post-war costs see OP/TVL/Transvaal Mines Department, 1902, p. 8.

21. *S & D News*, 18 Oct. 1899; *African Review*, 24 (403) 11 Aug. 1900, p. 200.

22. *S & D News*, 2 Oct. 1899; MS/USL/Lipp, pp. 127, 142. See also Warwick 1983, pp. 131—2.

23. MS/USL/Lipp, p. 153.

24. MS/USL/Lipp, p. 127.

25. MS/USL/Lipp, pp. 159—60. The Revd John Darragh wrote about this incident as well, noting that the 'Boers coolly shot three [Africans] to intimidate the others' and added that they were all Basutos, who were 'working for the magnificent wage of five shillings a month' (*Cape Times*, 30 April 1900). For a discussion of blacks being expelled by the British at Kimberley, see Ashe 1900, esp. pp. 119—20.

26. MS/JPL/Mine Police, 'Rapports quotidiens', esp. 2 Feb. 1900, report from section E-8, which states that 'two kafirs [were] arrested without permits or passes, declaring to come from Kimberley; it appears that they escaped from the lot recently arrived at Braamfontein Station from Kimberley'.

27. MS/UWL/Law, pp. 36—7; *African Review*, 21 (323) 9 Dec. 1899, p. 388; and 24 (401) 28 July 1900, pp. 130—1; MS/JPL/ERPM, report by J. B. MacDonald, 6 Sept. 1900; PRO/CO 291/27, Milner to Chamberlain, 19 April 1901, with 'Report of committee for commandeered, looted and stolen property', n.d.; MS/JPL/Mine Police, 'Rapports quotidiens', 27 April 1900; MS/TAD/PSY 73, 'Affidavits in connection with alleged looting, etc.', Lombard, 19 June 1900.

28. PRO/CO 291/27, Milner to Chamberlain, 19 April 1901, with 'Report of committee for commandeered, looted and stolen property', n.d.; *African Review*, 24 (409) 22 Sept. 1900, p. 412; MS/TAD/PSY 73, 'Affidavits in connection with alleged looting, etc.', Lombard, 19 June 1900.

29. *African Review*, 24 (406) 1 Sept. 1900, pp. 310—11; and 26 (435) 23 March 1901, pp. 403—11; MS/JPL/ERPM, report by Hellman, 2 Aug. 1900.

30. *Pretoria Friend*, 7 July 1900; *African Review*, 25 (420) 8 Dec. 1900, p. 350.

31. *Cape Times*, 26 May 1900.

32. *African Review*, 22 (384) 31 March 1900; pp. 470—1; 24 (403) 11 Aug. 1900, p. 200; and (406) 1 Sept. 1900, p. 312; *Cape Times*, 25 June 1900.

33. MS/PRO/DO 119/506, Ross diary (confidential), 12 Nov. 1899. The state mining engineer acknowledged that this is what enabled the Boer government to reach very high yields per ton milled, as well as to generate high profits (*African Review*, 24 (403) 11 Aug. 1900, p. 200).

34. *African Review*, 24 (403) 11 Aug. 1900, p. 200; and 23 (394) 9 June 1900, p. 348; Roos 1949, pp. 115—20. MS/UWL/Law, pp. 53, 56, estimated in December that £250,000 sterling was being taken from the mines. See also Pakenham 1979, p. 429. It was, however, reported that publicised gold outputs were 'very much under the mark' (MS/PRO/DO 119/506, Ross diary (confidential), 11 May 1900) and that gold theft seemed to have been extensive (OP/CM 1900/1, p. xxxvi; MS/PRO/CO 417/285, Milner to Chamberlain (secret), 24 Jan. 1900, forwarding report by Sam Evans, n.d.).

35. For restrictions on pumping, see *S & D News*, 14 Nov. 1899; *African Review*, 21, 'Supplement to "*African Review*"', 25 Nov. 1899, p. 25; 23 (323) 9 Dec. 1900, p. 388; 22 (335) 3 March 1900, pp. 315—16; 24 (402) 4 Aug. 1900, pp. 164—5; and 24 (403) 11 Aug. 1900, p. 200. See also Roos 1949, p. 108. For a list of mines allowed to pump, see MS/JPL/Mine Police, minute book, 'Kennisgeving', n.d., c. Nov. 1899. For mine searches, see *African Review*, 22 (327) 6 Jan. 1900, p. 23; *S & D News*, 18 Sept., 5 Oct. and 15, 24 and 30 Nov. 1899; and Roos 1949, pp. 105—8.

36. *Star*, 5 Oct. 1899. When the historian J. C. Roos questioned Smuts in the late 1940s

about this incident, Smuts denied both that it had taken place and his role in it (Roos 1949, p. 91).

37. MS/JPL/Leslie(a), pp. 104–5, for this first-hand account. Thomas Law later met the conductor of the train commandeered of its gold, who told him that the men who took it had been 'very polite about it' (MS/UWL/Law, p. 33; see also MS/USL/Lipp, p. 5).

38. According to the *Star*, 4 Oct. 1899, the total losses were: Standard Bank (£179,200), National Bank (£100,000), African Banking Co. (£54,955), Bank of Natal (£52,500), Bank of Africa (£35,641) and Robinson Bank (£13,500). PRO/CO 291/27, Milner to Chamberlain, 19 April 1901, forwards 'Report of committee for commandeered, looted and stolen property', which provides a different amount and a list of the mining companies that really owned the gold. For the amounts given here, see MS/PRO/DO 119/367 and DO 119/368.

39. *S & D News*, 10, 16, 17 Oct. 1899; *Star*, 7 Oct. 1899; *African Review*, 21 (366) 25 Nov. 1899, p. 309; and MS/JPL/ERPM, miscellaneous correspondence, secretary Angelo G[old] M[ining] Co. to manager Standard Bank, 6 Oct. 1899.

40. MS/PRO/FO 2/41, Charles Wood to Chamberlain, 5 Oct. 1899, with note to Salisbury from F. B. at FO, 7 Oct. 1899 and reply. See also MS/PRO/FO 2/268, Milner to Chamberlain, 10 Oct. 1899. For Schreiner's attempt to keep the Cape neutral, see van Heyningen 1978, p. 246.

41. MS/PRO/FO 2/268, Milner to Chamberlain, 10 Oct. 1899; Chamberlain to Hely Hutchinson, 11 Oct. 1899; Milner to Chamberlain, 13 Oct. 1899, 15 Oct. 1899. See also FO 2/249, C-in-C Cape Town to the Admiralty, 20 Oct. 1899.

42. MS/UWL/Law, p. 53; and see MS/PRO/FO 2/268, Milner to Chamberlain, 13 Oct. 1899.

43. According to the *Star*, 9 Oct. 1899: Bank of Africa (£20,000), Standard Bank (£50,000), Natal Bank (£12,500) and African Banking Co. (£7,500). See also *S & D News*, 10 and 11 Oct. 1899; and PRO/CO 291/27, Milner to Chamberlain, 19 April 1901, with 'Report of committee for commandeered, looted and stolen property'.

44. According to Sam Evans, the Pretoria mint was using 1898 dies and minting about £60,000 worth of coin each month. He reported that new dies were due from Germany soon. Thomas Law in his diary (MS/UWL/Law, entry 28 Dec. 1899) relates the following tale: For some time the mint had been shut down and the mint master, a Mr Krauss, was in Europe on half-pay. He was instructed to return and arrived at the Cape six weeks earlier. Unable to get to the Republic, he wrote to the bank in Pretoria 'intimating the position and saying that a Mr Grimm was *en route* to Pretoria by the steamer *Koluig* via the east coast, carrying new dies and other requests for the mint.' The letter did not, according to Law, reach its destination and some time later at Delagoa Bay, when the steamer arrived, a 'stranger' boarded the ship and asked for Mr Grimm. The man gave Grimm a letter, 'somewhat as follows: "My plans have been changed and it is not now necessary for you to go to Pretoria, you will therefore please hand the dies to the bearer of this letter and come round to Cape Town by steamer. Signed Krauss.["]' Grimm accepted the letter and promised to deliver the dies to Mr C. H. Ford, supposedly an accountant with the Bank, but a man Law suspected of working for British military intelligence. In any case Grimm was suspicious of Ford and rather than give him the dies, hid them in his sea chest and tried to get ashore. Grimm, unable to get off the ship, and later at lunch, was called away by the British consul, which gave Ford the opportunity to break into Grimm's room and steal the dies. Ford then boarded a British naval ship and carried the dies away, while Grimm eventually reached shore apparently to tell his tale to the financial community in the Republic, of which Law was a part. See MS/UWL/Law, pp. 53–4; and MS/PRO/CO 417/285, Milner to Chamberlain (secret), 24 Jan. 1900, forwarding report by Sam Evans.

45. MS/UWL/Law, p. 70: Standard Bank (£260,000), Bank of Africa (£80,000), African Banking Co. (£70,000), Netherlands Bank (£50,000) and Natal Bank (£40,000). See also *Cape Times*, 5 May 1900, which notes that the amount was £1 million and that the mint was then shut down. Isabella Lipp (MS/USL/Lipp, p. 211) also refers to the incident, putting the figure at half a million.

46. *African Review*, 26 (427) 26 Jan. 1901, p. 124; MS/JPL/Mine Police, 'Correspondance generale, no. 3'; MS/PRO/CO 291/27, Milner to Chamberlain, 19 April 1901, with 'Report of committee for commandeered, looted and stolen property'.

47. This was only one of the tasks set for Sam Evans when he went to Delagoa Bay; MS/PRO/CO 417/285, Milner to Chamberlain (secret), 24 Jan. 1900.

48. *S & D News*, 6 Jan. 1900; MS/PRO/CO 291/299, FO to CO, 23 Jan. 1900, forwarding a copy of a telegram intercepted by military intelligence at Aden, 18 Jan. 1900, part of which read: 'I suspect that one of the inducements for intervention will be a total or partial remission of this tax'.

49. *African Review*, 21 (371) 30 Dec. 1899, p. 508; MS/PRO/FO 2/330, F. Plunkett to FO, 16 Jan. 1900, forwarding clipping from the *Independence Belge*; MS/PRO/FO 2/393, CO to FO (confidential and immediate), 15 Jan. 1900, with enclosures. This act was made retroactive to 11 Oct. 1899.

50. MS/PRO/FO 2/393, CO to FO (confidential and immediate), 15 Jan. 1900, with enclosure, Consolidated Gold Fields of South Africa Ltd to Chamberlain, 8 Jan. 1900.

51. MS/PRO/FO 2/394, Law Officers' Department, Royal Courts of Justice, report dated 24 Jan. 1900. For Milner's proclamation, see FO 2/405. For further information on this proclamation and reactions to it, see MS/PRO/DO 119/400, Chamberlain to Milner, 7 April 1900; F. Eckstein to Fitzpatrick, 20 Dec. 1899, in Duminy and Guest (eds) 1972; and MS/UWL/Law, p. 63, where he calls Milner's proclamation 'Gilbertian': 'Under what authority does John Bull make this declaration. . . . The Boers do what they think correct and they have never been in the habit of asking permission from anyone to legislate. Soon I suppose Mr Milner may be intimating to the world at large that if any Boer fires a shot at the next Tugela battle, he will be arrested and hanged'.

52. *African Review*, 23 (391) 19 May 1900, p. 240; and 24 (401) 28 July 1900, p. 128. For Milner's draft notice, see MS/PRO/DO 119/404, Milner to Roberts (draft), 26 May 1900, forwarding draft notice no. 3.

53. *S & D News*, 14 March 1900 citing *Financial News*, n.d. See also MS/PRO/FO 2/393, CO to FO (confidential and immediate), 15 Jan. 1900, forwarding letter from Sheba G[old] M[ining] Co. to R. G. W. Herbert, 10 Jan. 1900.

54. MS/PRO/CO 417/285, Milner to Chamberlain, 11 Jan. 1900, and Milner to Chamberlain (secret), 24 Jan. 1900, forwarding report by Sam Evans, n.d. Thomas Law (MS/UWL/Law) notes the ease with which people returned in these months.

55. MS/PRO/CO 417/285, Chamberlain to Milner (draft), 16 Jan. 1900, with notes on file.

56. MS/PRO/CO 417/285, Milner to Chamberlain, 27 Jan. 1900.

57. MS/PRO/CO 417/285, Chamberlain to Milner, 8 Feb. 1900 (draft).

58. MS/PRO/CO 417/285, Milner to Chamberlain (confidential), 8 March 1900, forwarding enclosures, Ross to Milner, 19 Feb. 1900 and Milner to Ross, 23 Feb. 1900.

59. *S & D News*, 4 May 1900; and see DO 119/541, Hely Hutchinson to Milner (confidential), 2 May 1900, forwarding copy of report by J. Pitts, 17 April 1900.

60. *Cape Times*, 1 May 1900; and *S & D News*, 9 Dec. 1899.

61. MS/USL/Lipp, p. 105.

62. MS/PRO/DO 119/506, Ross diary (confidential), 27 Jan. 1900; and see *Cape Times*, 1 May 1900.

63. Roos 1949, pp. 360–1; MS/USL/Lipp, pp. 224–9; MS/JPL/Leslie(a), p. 111; MS/PRO/DO 119/506, Ross diary (confidential), 27 Jan., 3 Feb., 9 April and 11 May 1900, where he records information received from Johannesburg sources. See also *Cape Times*, 1 May 1900; and Hillegas 1900, p. 258.

Five

The Fall of Johannesburg

He that makes a good war makes a good peace.
George Herbert

At the end of May 1900, the then special commandant of the Witwatersrand, Dr F. E. T. Krause, ordered the burghers who wanted to continue fighting for their 'land, liberty and independence' to quit the city and rejoin the commando army in the north. As these 'bittereinders' trudged out of the city and toward Pretoria, the British army led by General Lord Roberts marched in. The Rand had fallen. But in the weeks before the British took control of this, the richest prize of the war, the Boers had given the British government and the Randlords a fright. As long as the Boers could work the mines to finance their war effort, they had reason to protect them. But now that it was becoming increasingly apparent that Roberts would enter the Transvaal, that reason had ended. Indeed, it was feared that the mines, if left in working order, would be used to finance the British war effort. Perhaps those Boers who had for months advocated their destruction had been right: should not the owners, who caused the war, be made to suffer as the Boer nation had done? When key members of the Johannesburg and Pretoria administrations adopted this view, the destruction of the Rand mines nearly became a reality.

The order to drill holes to receive dynamite in the shafts of some 25 mines came from Pretoria before the siege of Ladysmith was lifted. The secretary of state, Reitz, was at the centre of the scheme, while President Kruger, the young judge, Antonie Kock, the state attorney, Smuts, and a previous state attorney, Ewald Esselen, supported him. W. J. Leyds, the Republican ambassador to Europe, knew of the plan, as did the minister of mines, Kleynhans.[1] The acting state mining engineer, John Munnik, received his instructions from Reitz and, in turn, ordered several miners and managers of government-run mines to prepare the holes. Captain Ricchardi of the Italian Corps may well have been involved too.[2]

The conspirators put forward several arguments to justify blowing up the mines and a few of Johannesburg's largest buildings. Kruger himself believed that the mere threat of doing so would be enough to force continental shareholders to put pressure on their governments to assist the Republic.[3] Some cited logistical reasons. For example, Munnik ordered the holes to be placed in the shafts so that the mines could be blown up at a moment's notice: they 'must be so destroyed that should the mines fall into the hands of the enemy they will not be able to be worked during the war, even should it last two years'.[4] Others argued that if they were not destroyed, large amounts of material and provisions stored on the properties would fall into the hands of the occupying forces.[5] Critics found these justifications unconvincing, arguing that by destroying the mines, as Holland had her dykes and Russia her capital, the Republic would still not stop the British advance if 'the mauser in the hands of brave burghers' should fail to do so.[6]

There was a more emotive reason for blowing up the mines. People in the administration, from Reitz downward, felt bitter toward the Randlords and the imperial government and thought destruction an appropriate action.[7] Locally, bitterness intensified and anger welled up as Roberts approached the Rand, giving those who were opposed to destroying the mines more reason to fear that the most radical element of the population and the commandos retreating through the district would carry out the deed. Opponents of destruction thus had to worry not only about premeditated sabotage, but also about the spontaneous acts of men motivated by frustration and rage. There were, in fact, two separate but probably related attempts to destroy the mines, the first of which demonstrated extensive calculation and planning.

The conspiracy was hatched sometime in February 1900[8] and acted upon by mid-March. On the 24th a member of the mine police from section E—1 reported that:

> at the Robinson Deep one workman and 8 kafirs came to work at the Main Shaft; as they had no order authorizing them they were refused permission. Later they returned with the following order: 'This is to certify that you are instructed by me to start work at the Main Shaft Robinson Deep' (s) E. Osterloh, certg. Mining Inspector. The men had instructions to make 8 boreholes on each wall of the Shaft (about 40 feet down) each 3 feet, also in the corner holes are to be made.[9]

From section W—1 came a similar report about work on the main shaft of the Langlaagte Estate, work which had also been ordered by Osterloh 'for secret purposes authorized by the Govt'. The report continued:

> Comt. van Diggelen, Capt. Epler, Lieuts Nathan and Vogt inspected the work personally yesterday morning, at first orders given by Comt van Diggelen to stop work, later after having seen Mr Osterloh and Mr Munnik the work was ordered to be allowed to proceed. Special report has been handed to Comt Schutte by Comt van Diggelen stating the facts and protesting against the work and the nature thereof.[10]

Seemingly Krause, Schutte and van Diggelen were taken by surprise and opposed the boring of holes for the destruction of the mines. Their objection was expressed in a letter to Pretoria, which went unanswered for weeks. Sammy Marks, a local businessman, meanwhile approached the local attorney, W. E. Hollard, and chief justice R. Gregorowski, and asked them to appeal to General Louis Botha to stop the drilling. Van Diggelen also approached the minister of mines, Kleynhans, but was unable to establish who had instigated the scheme and why.

A month later van Diggelen received a note from Reitz instructing those who opposed the drilling to say, if anyone asked about the matter, that 'nothing is known'.[11] With no further official explanation to Rand administrators, the drilling continued in about 25 mines.[12] The news could not be contained and soon letters to the editor of the *Standard and Diggers' News* began to come in, expressing a view that was similar to Krause's own: any such destruction would be a 'crime against civilisation and a stain on the Afrikaner nation'.[13]

Nor could the news be contained within the Rand. On 29 March the 'Association for the Protection of Proprietors of Shares and Debentures in Gold Mines and Other Industrial Enterprises on the Witwatersrand' wired associates in Berlin, stating that holes had been bored in some shafts with a view to destroying the mines. By that date Milner had received word from at least two different sources that the mines were in danger. The share market reflected the news with a drop in prices. This led the astute G. W. Nicholson, then marching north with Roberts, to comment that there was possibly some truth to the rumour of planned sabotage because the drop in prices was probably caused by French selling and he suspected that 'French operations' were 'better informed regarding the Boer plans than we are'.[14]

While the outside world held its breath, those in Johannesburg who opposed the drilling considered how to stop it. Krause contemplated arresting the men boring the holes, with the specific intention of bringing the matter into the public arena. This would, he thought, 'give publicity to the designs of these [highly-placed officials] and thereby bring the matter before the various Generals on commando and give them an opportunity of saying what should be done'.[15] About the same time the attorney, Hollard, received a letter from Smuts denying that the government had any plans to destroy the mines. This Hollard had printed in the *Standard and Diggers' News*.[16] The letter and the subsequent publicity about the secret happenings along the reef were the result of what appears to have been a fortuitous accident.

In January the war-time manager of the City & Suburban mine hired Fred Dempsey, alias Desmond, as watchman and electrician. On 12 March he was discharged for drunkenness and neglect of duty, though he continued to live on the property. Ten days later Dempsey kidnapped the acting state mining engineer, Munnik, and took him to his cottage on the mine. There, several other men joined them, some shots were fired and Munnik agreed to pay the gang £200, though for what reason is unclear. During the fracas, Dempsey induced Munnik to tell him everything he knew about the plan to blow up the mines. Munnik was released by his captors but waited several hours before reporting his abduction. Dempsey, who for some reason had not fled the scene, was then arrested by Krause and held on charges of kidnapping, robbery, attempted murder and high treason.

On 6 April Dempsey was tried, with Krause as the prosecuting attorney and Hollard, the man who only a week before had had Smuts's letter printed in the press, acting in his defence. Hollard examined Munnik about the course of events and the topics he and Dempsey had discussed during the kidnapping, thereby forcing the acting state mining engineer to reveal the plot to blow up the mines. Hollard argued that since Smuts denied the government's involvement in the scheme — and who could doubt Smuts's word — Dempsey could not be guilty of subverting the will of the government, i.e. of treason. He was, though, found guilty of attempted murder and sentenced to seven years imprisonment with hard labour. To this Dempsey reportedly had no objection, for he anticipated that 'on occupation of the town by the British, he would at once be released'.[17]

Meanwhile, as Krause had all along intended, the trial drew the attention of the Boer generals to what was happening on the mines. The Afrikaner historian, J. C. Roos, has suggested that Dempsey worked for British intelligence, but this is unlikely as the British considered him a 'dangerous scoundrel'.[18] If there was a conspiracy, it may well have been between the local officials who opposed the plan and were hoping to bring matters to a head. In any case, the publicity brought the desired reaction. As Steenekamp, chairman of the second Volksraad, related:

> Kruger told us in secret session that [the] Government would blow up Johannesburg, that General Louis Botha, when he heard this, immediately hurried to Pretoria to tell Kruger that unless he engages to countermand the order for such a barbarian act, he and his commandos would cease fighting and fall back on Johannesburg to protect it themselves against such dastardly attempts. Kruger then promised to do so.[19]

A second incident also made it difficult for Munnik to carry out Reitz's orders. This was the return from Europe of his immediate superior, state mining engineer Adolf Klimke. Klimke was as much against the destruction of the mines as were Krause and Botha, and was now in a position to do something about it. He too told Kruger that he opposed the scheme and refused to take up his position again unless the plan was abandoned. Kruger was said to have 'assented but with indifferent grace'[20] and Klimke, on his return to the Rand in April, had the boreholes plugged and the shafts barricaded.[21]

Not long afterwards, though, Klimke quarrelled with the government and, in his own words, was 'given leave of absence without asking for it'.[22] He then left the country and Munnik was reinstated, once again generating anxiety among those who were suspicious of his sentiments and activities. Still, Krause seems to have been satisfied that Munnik had had a change of heart and was now 'anxious to prevent [the mines] from being blown up'. It appeared, then, that at the beginning of May the mines and company buildings in Johannesburg were safe and cables to that effect were sent to Europe, where investors sighed with relief.[23]

The public, already anxious because of the rumour that the mines and buildings had been prepared for destruction, was further shaken by news that a review of residential permits was soon to be undertaken, with a view to expelling some inhabitants. Two months earlier a similar review had been completed, but the decision to deport the British had been reversed.[24] This time the review was seen to be more serious, for, indeed, had not Munnik been kidnapped by a British agent?[25]

The British destitute were the target of the Rust en Orde Commission and several hundred were sent away. But also told to go were British men working on pumping mines and, where these mines were not closed altogether as a result, they were kept working by other foreigners. With businesses operating at a fraction of their former turnover, staffs were once again cut back.[26] In other words, all non-essential British subjects were told to go.

After their departure, the Rand took on an eerie silence for those few hundred British who remained. They had just returned to their routines when they were shaken by an event which literally rocked the city. Mrs Isabella Lipp recalls:

> How am I to describe the awful explosion which took place on Tuesday the 24th of April: at 5.20 p.m. I was near Joubert's Park, looking toward the railway, when suddenly a tremendously loud report shook the city — followed by a brilliant flame shooting upwards like a vast sword, simultaneously a huge column of greenish dirty white smoke arose, gradually spreading out shaped like a vast mushroom. . . . Women pale and terrified rushed out of their rocking homes, children screaming, clung to their mothers' skirts and natives with a wild scared expression on their faces, ran full speed, anywhere away from that horror of smoke, enveloping this ill-fated town. 'The City and Suburban' [mine] cried some, 'no Begbies [armaments] Foundry' cried others, and so it proved.[27]

Bystanders brought additional confusion as the police, fire brigade, the Jewish Ambulance Corps and several doctors rushed to the scene to help the injured. Blacks from the municipal works were loaned to the fire brigade by the authorities to haul out cases of shells which were still afire. The scene was chaotic with dismembered bodies strewn about among still-burning debris and loaded shells. Women and children, families of munitions workers living close to the factory, were among those killed, injured or wandering aimlessly. Many searched for loved ones among the ruins.

To this day the cause of the explosion is unknown, though an eyewitness account may provide a clue:

> We were within 200 yards of the scene. . . . There it lay rent asunder by the awful concussion. Hundreds of neighbouring houses are knocked to pieces. . . . The explosion did not occur in the foundry itself, on the opposite block was a building used for filling the shells and next to this was an empty house in which is now found a great hole in the earth.[28]

Other eyewitness reports also give substance to the view that the explosion took place in a storehouse where explosives were kept.

The critical question facing the authorities was whether it was an accident or sabotage. Immediately, several men were arrested, Thomas Begbie among them. The authorities offered no proof but accused saboteurs, who supposedly tunnelled into the storehouse and there placed dynamite and attached leads to the city's electrical system which, when turned on at 5.17 that evening, ignited the explosives. Both Klimke and Munnik thought it had been the work of British agents, but not everyone shared this view. The carelessness of men filling shells or smoking cigarettes nearby was the alternative explanation.[29]

The explosion at Begbies armaments factory in April 1900 destroyed both the factory building and workers' homes nearby (*Africana Museum, Johannesburg*)

In any case, the explosion crystallized anti-British sentiment locally. While the benevolent of the city opened a special fund to aid the families of those killed and injured, others breathed revenge. E. B. Rose, the Uitlander labour leader, offered a reward for the capture of the suspected saboteurs.[30] Four days later a meeting of between 600 and 700 men, led by Italians, French and Austrians, was convened on Market Square. Threats of 'vendetta' were uttered and knives were brandished as speeches about British treachery filled the air. After the meeting the men marched to Commandant Schutte's office, where they asked him to form a special guard to be posted at any government works where 'Mediterraneans' were employed. Then they demanded that all British still on the Rand be expelled.[31]

The funeral oratory was equally inflammatory, with the burgomaster, de Villiers, voicing the feelings of many of the residents. 'I say', he announced, 'that the time has arrived to declare once and for all no Englishman shall ever re-enter the country which is our God-given right and all that are here shall go out.'[32] The press echoed this sentiment, with letters to the editor demanding the expulsion of the few hundred remaining British. One such correspondent was the former leader of the IILP, J. T. Bain.[33]

On 30 April, only six days after the explosion and less than a month since the previous permit revision, Kruger acted. Stating that he was acting according to the wishes of the burghers and 'other persons favourably disposed towards the Government', the president announced that all British subjects in Pretoria and on the Rand had 36 hours from noon, 30 April 1900, to leave the country. This decision was reported to have had a 'calming effect on the Latin element'.[34]

Especially long trains were prepared to carry away the expected rush of people and a free passage was guaranteed to anyone without funds. The deadline for departure was repeatedly extended, but, by the end of the first week of May, those without permission to stay had left. The only British allowed to remain were those deemed essential to the operation of basic services — certainly no more than 100.[35] These few British were to have the experience of a lifetime, for Boer rule of the South African Republic was drawing to a close — 'Bobs' was on his way.

One other result of the explosion was the removal of Schutte as special commandant of the Witwatersrand. Accused of failing to guard Begbie's works satisfactorily, he was ordered to the front and Dr Krause replaced him. Upon this occasion General Botha told Krause that, as commandant, he would be held personally responsible for the 'preservation of the town' and that he was to 'prevent its destruction by force'. This was in keeping with Krause's own views[36] but Botha's order would be of use to the new commandant before it was all over.

In this last month before Roberts took control of the Rand, the Boers made a final effort to exploit its resources and manpower. Begbie's was reopened and shells were manufactured there; the explosives were now stored well away from the foundry and undoubtedly new safety and security procedures were implemented. In the absence of British miners, some of the mines were kept working by burghers and members of foreign corps who took temporary jobs along the reef. The plates were once again cleaned, and so were some cyanide works. The raw gold taken from these sources was purportedly sent to Pretoria to finance the continued war effort.

For the British who remained in residence, these final weeks were filled with torment. As sporadic reports of Roberts's approach reached Johannesburg, animosity towards the few British there was, for the first time, openly displayed by burghers and foreigners. As rumours circulated that Boer women would be armed and that some buildings in the city were ready for detonation, the British became seriously worried about their safety and their property. Of special concern was the report that the city would be defended by burgher forces and that the government would take no responsibility for any resulting injuries or damage.

Not surprisingly, fears for the safety of the mines once again surfaced. With Klimke's departure and Munnik's reinstatement, with unfounded rumours of Krause's resignation and Schutte's return, and with Roberts's march northward pushing embittered burghers and pro-Boer foreigners before him, residents began to believe that the men who were anxious to 'blow up the mines and destroy the place' had gained ascendancy again.[37] Also, as Roberts approached the city, the black population along the reef became increasingly restive. This in turn fuelled white anxiety, for many feared that the African population would be allowed to run free if the city were endangered from without.[38] When Krause took power on 28 April, he therefore had a surfeit of problems: not only did he have to maintain peace and prevent looting, but he also had to save the mines and the city from being destroyed by those intent upon doing just that.

While few people believed that the government would order the mines to be destroyed at this stage, they still felt that there was a good chance that Boers and foreign commandos would inflict damage as they retreated through the district.[39] Indeed, there was good reason to suppose this to be the case, as ardent Anglophobes were in the process of advocating just such a course. The leader of the First Irish Brigade, John Blake, later recalled how he 'urged the council of war at the Vaal River to allow me to blow up certain mines in Johannesburg, but it was no use talking, not one of them would agree to it. They did not believe in the destruction of property. . . . I regret to this day that we did not destroy them.'[40] Arthur Lynch, a journalist and the leader of the Second Irish Brigade, wrote of the same day:

> At Meyerton, a War Council was held, and here the fate of Johannesburg mines was decided. One of the Generals, Tobias Smuts, suggested that they should be destroyed, on the ground that it was the greed of this gold that had induced the war. Botha, however, replied that we would fight as men, but that we would not do spiteful things, and his opinion carried the day.[41]

Some of the burghers and pro-Boers were not convinced. One such man was Antonie Kock — the young and sensitive judge who had praised the Zarp, Jones, at the time of the Edgar affair — who now led a commando unit. In mid-May Kock arrived at the office of the new special commandant, Krause. He brandished a letter from the state secretary, Reitz, authorizing him to destroy the mines, and told Krause he must help him. This Krause refused to do, telling Kock that he would have him arrested if he set foot on any one of the mines, and produced a letter from Botha to justify his position.[42] Within a few days Krause issued orders to all field cornets and other officials on the Rand:

> Whereas I have been informed that there are many foreign elements, such as Socialists and the like in Johannesburg, I charge you to be strongly on your guard and to begin to make the necessary preparations so that those elements can be properly restrained. I further order you, should you notice that violence might be exercised against life and property, to effectively prevent even the effort, and to stop it, for these elements will spare no efforts to blow up the mines and set fire to the town and it is your duty to prevent this. Finally, I wish to emphasize that from now on I hold you

107

responsible within the working realm of your position for any damage brought to property or life in Johannesburg *and* on the Witwatersrand. Give strict orders to the officers, officials or persons under your authority to follow these orders explicitly.[43]

Not all the local administrators supported Krause's view. For instance, acting state mining engineer Munnik, though now purportedly opposed to the mines' destruction, still conspired to destroy them. According to testimony later given to British military authorities, it was about this time that nine miners, all employed on the Ferreira, were offered £5,000 by one of Munnik's men to blow up the mines. Munnik was in a position to pay these men well, for he had 120,000 ounces of gold, which had supposedly been sent to Pretoria previously.[44] For reasons not known, Munnik's plan never came to fruition.

This was not the case with Kock, who again came to visit Krause on 27 May. He asked the commandant to lend him some horses so that he could go out to the mines 'to view positions' there. When Krause refused, Kock presented him with a letter from 'one of the members of the Government', presumably Reitz, which gave him permission to do 'certain things'. Krause once again responded by producing a letter from Botha, dated 23 May, and a telegram from Kruger dated the 26th, both of which supported Krause's refusal to help. Judge Kock left the office in anger and the next day, the 28th, he and 'his gang of desperadoes' held a meeting and drafted a placard which they posted all over the city and reef:[45]

NOTICE

To all burghers, Friends and inhabitants of Johannesburg.
Men and Brothers.
Much innocent blood has been shed already since this unjust and horrible war started.
For what purpose has this be[sic] done?
Who is the cause of it?
Who will be suffering for it?
Where are the blood-suckers and murderers of our fathers and brothers and friends, who have been slain in this war instigated by capital?
The time has now come to take revenge.
Already it has been resolved, as appears from the Standard and Diggers['] News this morning, by the Government, a few brave men excepted, to give up the riches of our beloved and dearly gained fatherland to the enemy.
Must we, who have now persevered since 8 months in this satanic war, lose courage and fall on our knees before the monster of the stranger and implore for mercy there where no mercy exists.
Shame and dishonour be our lot, if we, after all the innocent blood that has been shed already for our grand and just cause, succumb now as cowards.
Are we rebels or insurgents or murderers or freebooters?
(Remember Jameson, Rhodes, Beit and Chamberlain).
No burghers, we are free but oppressed people. Let us be worthy of our forefathers.
Inhabitants of Johannesburg, have no fear, we do not want to do you any harm. We beg of all, particularly of the mine-police, to withdraw from the mines and from various properties of traitors to avoid any accident to themselves.
We guarantee to all women and children that no harm will be done to them.
They however must conduct themselves quietly.[46]

The following day, Kock went out to the Robinson mine where he set about carrying out his plan. While there he came upon the 120,000 ounces of gold which Munnik had not yet sent to Pretoria. Suspecting that members of the local administration were planning a theft, Kock hurried to Krause to confront him. In so doing he gave himself and his plans away and, in the ensuing struggle, he was disarmed and arrested by van Diggelen and Krause. He was sent to Pretoria where he was released by Schalk Burger and again went to the front.[47]

Although their leader had been arrested, Kock's 'desperadoes' were not finished. Just who was involved in the attack on the Robinson is unclear, though contemporaries reported that the men were 'foreigners' and Krause called them 'socialists'. One Baron van Maltsan was reportedly in a position of leadership, and it is quite possible that the Irish Brigades were involved, for they passed through the district about this time. In any case, the attack was repelled by mine guards and some 70 of Kock's men were captured and led to the front by a captain of the mine police.[48] The mines had been saved.

Nonetheless, panic and alarm remained the order of the day. Fresh produce appeared in great quantities on the market stalls as farmers, fearing expropriation of their land and theft of their produce, attempted to realize immediate profits. There was a run on the National Bank as patrons tried to exchange notes for hard currency. Pro-Boer foreigners and refugees from the south repacked their bags for further flight north, some heading for Lourenço Marques and Europe. Shops were barricaded as rumours spread that the town was to be taken by 'philistines' who would rape and plunder. As the commandos retreated through the city, they carried away provisions previously stored in the commissariat depots around town. At the same time looting, which had never completely disappeared, broke out in fury. Even the Wanderers' central depot was cleared of goods. 'An air of expectancy is over the town', wrote Isabella Lipp in the week before Roberts's arrival, 'and men with wives and children look anxious and worried not knowing which to dread most, British shells, Burgher reprisals or Burgheresses' . . . revenge and anger'.[49]

Cannon fire was first heard on 28 May. Thereafter the foolhardy climbed the hills in an effort to see out on to the veld and to look for the advancing British army.[50] On the 29th Roberts crossed the Vaal River at Viljoen's Drift and by nightfall hungry British soldiers had reached the Rand, where they begged the residents for food. Germiston was soon taken, as was the nearby railway station and its much-prized engines. Rand residents were warned that their water supply might be cut and they went to bed that night expecting to be roused by Johannesburg in flames. Meanwhile the mine police had their hands full searching for saboteurs and trying to restore order in the compounds where riots had broken out. To ease matters, 'kafir eating houses' near the mines were closed once again and an extra guard was enrolled for the Ferreira, the Wemmer and probably other mines nearby.[51]

On the morning of the 30th Roberts's representatives entered the city. It was agreed that the city and district would be handed over peacefully, a decision that suited all concerned. Krause was only following state policy, as he had very specific instructions to protect the city and mines. He was also concerned over the effect a British bombardment might have on the African population.[52] Roberts had his own reasons for agreeing to a handover that permitted the retreat of the 'bittereinders', who took supplies, arms and gold with them, and which extended the war by a full two years.

First, he was averse to street fighting, having seen its effects in Kabul. Secondly, he may well have believed that the war was almost over and that it would be a waste of British soldiers' lives to attack the Boers in Johannesburg. Thirdly, he probably thought the mines would be placed in danger if he rushed the city. And finally, there is every reason to believe that he was worried that if his troops had to fight the 'battle of Johannesburg' they would be tied down for days, or perhaps weeks, and would run out of food. After all, when Roberts's army marched into Germiston on the 30th, it had only one day's supplies on hand.[53]

After meeting with Roberts's men, Krause announced that the British would enter in peace after 10 a.m. the following day, 31 May, on the understanding that, first, there would be 'no hostile movement' by burghers or pro-Boers in the town and, secondly, that any burghers or supporters who chose to continue the fight could leave unharmed. Roberts also promised that women and children would not be molested by his troops.[54]

Not all residents agreed with Krause's decision. For instance, a Mr van Aswegen harangued the crowd which assembled outside the courthouse on the morning of the 30th, telling it that he and Gen. Koos de la Rey had no intention of handing over the city without a struggle. He called upon the bystanders to take up their arms and to defend the town, but found no support among them. Later that day there were reports of a 'band of desperate men' promising to 'leave no Johannesburg remaining for Lord Roberts to enter'. Among them was the retreating Irish Brigade, which, despite orders to stand down, sniped at the British as they moved through the district.[55]

In spite of his plans to transfer power peacefully, Krause had his hands full on the last day of Boer rule. Looting by blacks and whites continued, while sounds of gunfire echoed through the town as burghers and Australian scouts fought a running battle at the waterworks in Doornfontein, a battle which spread into the Barnato Park area, where members of the Irish Brigade were involved. Here Randites with more curiosity than sense ducked between bushes and trees in order to see the war up-close. Meanwhile, streams of Boers carrying their possessions passed through town, ensuring that the war would continue in the north.[56]

The last day of May dawned clear and frosty and inhabitants, some in tears and others euphoric, gathered at the courthouse. The mine police were busy trying to keep order, checking the surges of a sullen and angry crowd. Van Diggelen addressed their officers, thanked them for their months of service, and discharged them from their duties. Captain Brakhan of the mine police in turn praised the authorities for the 'good support' they had given them. And then they waited.[57]

The British troops entered from the east and were surprised by what they saw. Col. H. G. W. Jourdain was particularly diverted

> by the hundreds of natives in all kinds of kits from Adam's garb to an old woman's skirt. They all seemed very amused to see us, and one man shouted out in glee — 'God bless the Queen, may she go straight up.' This was greeted with roars of laughter by our men. We marched down the hill, and up another, when we passed through an awful set of black men, yellowmen, Japs, Zulus, Chinese and Hottentots, in fact the very very scum of all nations.[58]

They marched down Commissioner Street, which was lined with people whom Henry Rawlinson described as 'quite a sort of Port Said population'. Castledown agreed, characterizing those he saw as 'communists in facial type and bearing'. As

Lord Roberts entering Johannesburg with Special Commandant F. E. T. Krause at his side, 31 May 1900 (*Africana Museum, Johannesburg*)

There was silence as the 'Vierkleur' was taken down for the last time: Johannesburg, 31 May 1900 (*Africana Museum, Johannesburg*)

fearful as the white population was to its new masters, it was the blacks who gave them real worries, for there were reports of Africans tearing up their passes in the belief that the British had brought them freedom at last. Meanwhile, looting continued.[59]

At the courthouse the ceremony was short. The Vierkleur was taken down, causing not a few burghers to weep, and the Union Jack raised. Subsequent accounts tended to emphasize the pro-British sentiment expressed that day, but eyewitnesses spoke of the proceedings as having the 'mournfulness and solemnity of a funeral', with only a few voices raised in the singing of 'God Save the Queen'.[60]

After the ceremony, the British army marched towards Pretoria to camp at Orange Grove. Telegrams of congratulations were brought to Roberts, who was already busy planning the capture of Pretoria, which, it was expected, would bring an end to the war. In the city the hotels and restaurants were filled with officers in search of a decent meal and a bottle or two. Barricades were removed from shop windows as stores reopened for business. The *Standard and Diggers' News* was suppressed and a few ardent Boers and pro-Boer Irish were arrested.

Looting by British soldiers in search of food and fuel began, especially in the more remote areas. Civilian volunteers were recruited from the city as hospitals were opened along the reef to treat the many cases of dysentery among the soldiers. The new military commissioner of police, Major Francis Davies of the Grenadier Guards, issued immediate orders that no white civilians were to be out after curfew, set from 7 p.m. to 6.30 a.m., that all jewellery shops were to be closed and that no person was to be on a bicycle without a special permit. All bottle stores, bars and 'kafir eating houses' were closed. The mine police — in a few cases deprived of weapons, only to have them returned once the enormity of their task was realized — were asked to continue to patrol the mines and compounds, which were now filled with an idle and restless, but expectant, black population.[61]

The British now had to figure out how to govern the Rand and its population of blacks (of whom some 13,000 were scattered along the reef) and whites (of whom many, if not most, were hostile to British rule). They were pleased to find that the town was relatively clear of 'undesirables', who had been removed previously.[62] However, they were soon to discover more and had to devise a method of dealing with them. In the meantime, the more urgent problem of feeding the population pressed upon them. Although there was enough food to provide African mine-workers for nearly a month, there was 'scarcely a fortnight's [food]' for the whites in town.[63]

The new regime, then, had immediate problems to face and needed men in Johannesburg to help the military solve them. Two men were already at hand. They had entered the city as Roberts's representatives, to bargain with Krause. It was these two men (Sam Evans and J. Douglas Forster)[64] and their reformer colleagues, who, in the following weeks, set the tenor of the new Rand administration. It had taken almost a decade of agitation and nearly eight months of war, but the Uitlander élite had finally come to power.

Notes

1. For the knowledge and involvement of these men, see MS/PRO/CO 417/287, Milner to Chamberlain, 28 March 1900, secret and confidential, forwarding copy of telegram from Ross; MS/PRO/FO 2/403, CO to WO, 31 March 1900, with enclosure, Milner to CO, 28 March 1900, secret and confidential, forwarding message from Mr Brakhan of Goerz & Co; MS/PRO/CO 417/289, Milner to Chamberlain (confidential), 9 May 1900, with extract of report from military intelligence; MS/TAD/PSY 73, assistant state attorney Jacobs to censor commission, Pretoria, 5 April 1900. Smuts denied in an interview with Roos in the late 1940s that anyone above the level of Munnik and Kock was involved; Roos chose not to believe him. See Roos 1949, ch. 4; also *African Review*, 23 (387) 21 April 1900, pp. 96–7; and May 1970, p. 116.
2. MS/TAD/PSY 50, affidavit by Ernst Frederick Conroy Osterloh, 30 June 1900. See also DO 119/541, Hely Hutchinson to Milner (confidential), 10 May 1900, forwarding information supplied to the commandant of Durban by Daniel MacMillian, 8 May 1900; MS/PRO/FO 2/403, FO to CO (confidential), 3 May 1900, forwarding report from commandant of Durban with information supplied by A. J. Ridgeway, an employee of the Robinson mine during the war. See also May 1970, p. 115.
3. DO 119/541, Hely Hutchinson to Milner (confidential), 2 May 1900, forwarding report from commandant of Durban drawing on information from Mr Pitts. See also Roos 1949, pp. 128–32; and *Cape Times*, 2 May 1900.
4. MS/TAD/PSY 50, J. Munnik to Mr G. Kubale, mining inspector (confidential), 19 March 1900.
5. Blake 1903, p. 183; and see MS/PRO/CO 417/288, Milner to Chamberlain, 18 April 1900.
6. *S & D News*, 26 March 1900. The *S & D News* opposed the destruction of the mines, while it seems that the *Rand Post* advocated it.
7. MS/PRO/DO 119/506, Ross diary (confidential), 20 April 1900; Blake 1903, p. 183. Even those who opposed the mines' destruction felt that the capitalists had started the war, but thought that their destruction would harm the Boers more than the capitalists. See for this debate, *S & D News*, 20–28 March 1900. The industrialists worried about this 'fanaticism' (MS/PRO/FO 2/346, Lascelles to FO, 30 March 1900 which forwards telegram from German consul in Pretoria to Baron von Richtofen, 29 March 1900).
8. Roos 1949, p. 129, although it should be noted that from mid-January onwards, Munnik ordered a special guard to be placed on several mines, some of which were later designated for destruction (*S & D News*, 19 Jan. 1900).
9. MS/JPL/Mine Police, 'Rapports quotidiens', 24 March 1900.
10. Ibid.
11. Roos 1949, p. 140 and appendix H. For a fuller treatment of this episode, see pp. 135–40; and MS/JPL/Mine Police, 'Correspondance generale, no. 3', 2 April 1900; OP/CM 1900/1, pp. xxxii–xxxiii. See also May 1970, p. 116; and Pakenham 1979, p. 384.
12. Drilling to place dynamite took place on at least the following mines: Bonanza, Crown Reef, Robinson Central Deep, City & Suburban, Ferreira Deep, Crown Deep, Langlaagte Deep, Robinson Deep, Simmer & Jack, Simmer & Jack East, Simmer & Jack West, Langlaagte Estate, Langlaagte Block 'B', Langlaagte Star, New Primrose, Geldenhuis Estate, Glencairn Main Reef, and the May Consolidated. This possibly incomplete list was derived from several sources: MS/JPL/Mine Police, 'Rapports quotidiens'; MS/TAD/PSY 73, transcript of Munnik's cross examination; MS/TAD/PSY 50, affidavits of Osterloh and Kubale, with annexures; MS/PRO/FO 2/403, WO intelligence division to FO, 29 March 1900, with enclosed report from GOC Aden to WO, 28 March 1900 (reporting on private telegrams from Lourenço Marques to London); MS/PRO/CO 417/289, Milner to Chamberlain (confidential), 1 May 1900, with enclosed report from Sgt Brooke to commandant of Durban, 11 April 1900,

forwarding information from Mr Mitchell, and with enclosed report from J. A. Nicol to commandant of Durban, 11 April 1900; MS/PRO/DO 119/506, Ross diary (confidential), 9 May 1900.

13. *African Review*, 24 (408) 15 Sept. 1900, p. 382 for Krause's view; and see *S & D News*, 20—28 March 1900.
14. MS/PRO/PRO 30/40, G. W. Nicholson to Ardagh, 4 April 1900. Still, he noted that neither he nor Roberts believed that arrangements had been made to destroy the mines. See also MS/PRO/FO 2/346, Lascelles to FO, 30 March 1900 with enclosures; and MS/PRO/CO 417/287, GOC Aden to secretary of state for war, 22 March 1900. Milner heard from both the consul, Ross, at Lourenço Marques and Mr Brakhan of Goerz & Co.
15. *African Review*, 24 (408) 15 Sept. 1900, p. 382.
16. *S & D News*, 29 March 1900.
17. MS/PRO/DO 119/401, Hely Hutchinson to Milner (confidential), 24 April 1900, with enclosure, H. Bale, attorney-general of Natal to Lt. Col. Hime (confidential), 21 April 1900, forwarding copy of private and confidential report by J. Paton on City & Suburban mine, 19 April 1900. Paton was also arrested for being involved with the kidnapping, but was released after 30 hours. See also 'Munnik's cross examination (which was not permitted to be published in the Diggers['] News)' in MS/TAD/PSY 73; and MS/USL/Lipp, pp. 215—16 for the trial; and Chilvers 1936, pp. 155—7.
18. Roos 1949, pp. 143—5; MS/TAD/LAJ 11/707, legal adviser to the military commissioner of police, 30 Oct. 1900. See also *African Review*, 23 (386) 14 April 1900, p. 45.
19. DO 119/541, Hely Hutchinson to Milner (confidential), 23 May 1900, with enclosure from commandant of Durban, 21 May 1900, forwarding information from Transvaal residents. This tale was related by Steenekamp to A. J. L. Hofmeyr. Botha's views were generally known, see for instance, *African Review*, 24 (408) 15 Sept. 1900, p. 382.
20. Forster to Dalrymple, 2 May 1900, in MS/JPL/Forster. For Klimke's return, see *S & D News*, 7 April 1900; and MS/PRO/FO 2/406, CO to FO, 3 May 1900.
21. *Cape Times*, 2 May 1900; MS/JPL/Mine Police, 'Correspondance generale, no. 3', 11 April 1900; OP/CM 1900/1, p. xxxiii.
22. *Johannesburg Gazette*, 10 July 1900; *African Review*, 24 (408) 15 Sept. 1900, p. 382.
23. *African Review*, 24 (408) 15 Sept. 1900, p. 382 for Krause's feelings and, for investors', see *African Review*, 23 (392) 19 May 1900, p. 240; and MS/PRO/FO 2/406, CO to FO, 3 May 1900, with enclosures.
24. MS/TAD/R&O 548, 'Notulen de vergadering revisie permitten', 18 Jan. 1900.
25. Roos 1949, pp. 142—5, 349—50. This seems to have been Schutte's view.
26. MS/TAD/R&O 548, 'Notulen van de vergadering gehonden de Johannesburg op . . . 28 Maart 1900'. Lipp (MS/USL/Lipp, p. 213) estimates that about 400 were permitted to remain.
27. MS/USL/Lipp, pp. 224—5.
28. MS/UWL/Law, pp. 73—4; Roos 1949, pp. 364—5.
29. *Cape Times*, 16 Aug. 1900; *S & D News*, 25 and 26 April 1900; MS/USL/Lipp, p. 227; MS/JPL/Leslie (a), pp. 110—11. There was a report of a British spy in the area at the time, but no proof was forthcoming that the explosion was the result of sabotage (MS/TAD/R&O 528, minute register, report by Donovan, 30 April 1900).
30. *S & D News*, 27 April 1900 for Rose letter; and see 26 April 1900 for the opening of a relief fund. The government housed the homeless.
31. *S & D News*, 28 April 1900; see 7 May 1900; and *African Review*, 25 (419) 1 Dec. 1900, p. 300.
32. MS/PRO/DO 119/405, Hely Hutchinson to Milner (confidential), 17 May, forwarding reports from commandant of Durban, which provides information supplied by A. W. Morris, 12 May 1900. For a first-hand account of the ceremony, see MS/USL/Lipp, pp. 227—8.
33. *S & D News*, 1 May 1900.
34. *S & D News*, 30 April 1900 and, for their departure, see 28 April—7 May 1900.
35. *S & D News*, 7 May 1900. MS/USL/Lipp, p. 230 notes that 'only some 57 or 60 men

with a few women and children are to remain, these comprise bank managers and a couple of their staff, a secretary or two, and a few others, whom the Government says they consider necessary for the carrying on of public life in Johannesburg'.

36. Roos 1949, p. 365; *S & D News*, 1 May 1900. For Botha's view, see MS/PRO/FO 2/326, Plunkett to FO, 27 Sept. 1900 with report of Krause's interview in *Fremdenblatt*. For Krause's feelings, see *African Review*, 24 (408) 15 Sept. 1900, p. 382.
37. MS/PRO/FO 2/326, Plunkett to FO, 27 Sept. 1900, with report of Krause's interview in *Fremdenblatt*. See also MS/USL/Lipp, pp. 235—6; and L. Phillips to H. Eckstein & Co., 26 May 1900, in Fraser and Jeeves (eds) 1977.
38. MS/JPL/Mine Police, esp. 'Rapports quotidiens', 1, 6, 13 and 25 May 1900; MS/USL/Lipp, p. 22.
39. MS/PRO/FO 2/402, WO, intelligence division, to FO, 17 March 1900, with enclosure, GOC Aden to secretary of state for war, 16 March 1900, forwarding copy of telegram from German consul at Lourenço Marques to FO, Berlin, n.d.; MS/PRO/FO 2/546, CO to FO (confidential), 3 May 1900, with enclosure, commandant of Durban to governor of Natal, forwarding letter written by Wm Stayt, 21 April 1900. And see *African Review*, 23 (385) 7 April 1900, p. 23.
40. Blake 1903, p. 183.
41. Lynch 1924, p. 194.
42. MS/JPL/Roos, p. 4; and cf. *African Review*, 24 (408) 15 Sept. 1900, p. 382. There are some minor discrepancies between the stories told by Krause to Roos in the late 1940s and the *African Review* in 1900. See also MS/PRO/FO 2/326, Plunkett to FO, 27 Sept. 1900, with report of Krause's interview in *Fremdenblatt*, n.d.
43. MS/JPL/Mine Police, 'Sermant'. A copy of the document may also be found in MS/TAD/R&O 548, and a portion of an English translation in MS/PRO/CO 291/27, Milner to Chamberlain, 19 April 1901, with 'Report of committee for commandeered, looted and stolen property'. See also MS/JPL/Krause (a), 'How the mines were saved'.
44. MS/TAD/PSY 50, affidavits by Paul Anhert and Jacobus Petrus Carelse, 18 and 19 June 1900 respectively; see MS/JPL/Krause (a), 'How the mines were saved'; and cf. Chilvers 1936, p. 154.
45. *African Review*, 24 (408) 15 Sept. 1900, p. 382; MS/PRO/FO 2/326, Plunkett to FO, 27 Sept. 1900, with report of Krause's interview in *Fremdenblatt*.
46. MS/JPL/Mine Police, minute book, 'Various documents, original and copies', see also daily report for 29 May 1900 from section E—1.
47. *African Review*, 24 (408) 15 Sept. 1900, p. 382; MS/JPL/Krause (a), 'How the mines were saved'; MS/JPL/Mine Police, 'Rapports quotidiens', p. 157. Kock fought near Pretoria before heading to Lourenço Marques, where he was president of the Boer military court. He then went to Europe where he met Kruger, returned to South Africa in disguise and was captured at Graaff Reinet, only to escape under a sentence of death. After the war he worked for the newspaper, *De Transvaaler*, and wrote poetry. A sensitive and religious man, he spent the last 40 years of his life in a mental institution in Pretoria, where he died in 1949.
48. MS/UWL/Law, p. 76; MS/JPL/Mine Police, 'Rapports quotidiens', 29—30 May 1900; and *African Review*, 24 (406) 1 Sept. 1900, pp. 313, 408; 15 Sept. 1900, p. 382. See also *Johannesburg Gazette*, 18 Feb. 1901.
49. MS/USL/Lipp, p. 235. See also MS/UWL/Law, p. 75; MS/PRO/CO 291/27, Milner to Chamberlain, 19 April 1901, with 'Report of committee for commandeered, looted and stolen property', n.d. and MS/UWL/Walker, pp. 168—9.
50. *Cape Times*, 2 and 5 June 1900; MS/UWL/Law, p. 76; MS/USL/Lipp, pp. 237—8.
51. Pakenham 1979, ch. 34; MS/USL/Lipp, p. 238; MS/SN, letter from Johannesburg, 10 June 1900; and MS/UWL/Walker, pp. 169—70, where she reports feeding the hungry British soldiers. See also *Cape Times*, 30 May, 1, 2, 5 and 7 June 1900; and *African Review*, 23 (394) 9 June 1900, p. 352; and MS/JPL/Mine Police, 'Rapports quotidiens', 29 May 1900.
52. *African Review*, 24 (403) 11 Aug. 1900, p. 191; MS/JPL/Roos, pp. 6—7.

53. MS/JPL/Roos, p. 7; Pakenham 1979, pp. 427–30; MS/NAM/Roberts, correspondence (secret) from South Africa, 1899–1901, Roberts to Lansdowne, 30 May 1900.

54. The formal terms of surrender may be found in MS/JPL/Krause (b).

55. *African Review*, 25 (411) 6 Oct. 1900; MS/USL/Lipp, p. 240; *Cape Times*, 4 June 1900. See also Reitz 1940, pp. 105–6, for mention of de la Rey and 1,000 men who fought against the Boers along the reef.

56. MS/SN, letter from Johannesburg, 10 June 1900; MS/UWL/Law, p. 76; MS/TAD/KC, vol. 4, Krause to commanding officer of British troops, Yeoville, 30 May 1900, where Krause accuses the British of breaking the truce. For looting, see MS/TAD/PSY 73, affidavit by Samuel Hotz, 28 June 1900. Reitz (1940, p. 106) mentions the sightseers, 'and even women [who] came out in cabs and on foot to view the proceedings'.

57. MS/JPL/Mine Police, 'Rapports quotidiens'; MS/JPL/Kearns, p. 1.

58. MS/NAM/Jourdain, vol. 3, 23 June 1900.

59. MS/NAM/Rawlinson, 7–3, 'Journal of South African War', vol. 3, 31 May 1900; Castledown 1923, pp. 197–8. See also *African Review*, 25 (412) 13 Oct. 1900, p. 49; MS/USL/Lipp, *passim*; MS/JPL/Mine Police, 'Rapports quotidiens' for looting in these days.

60. MS/USL/Lipp, p. 242; see MS/JPL/van der Horst, p. 36. For a very different account, see *Cape Times*, 5 June 1900.

61. *Cape Times*, 4 and 29 June 1900; MS/JPL/Mine Police, 'Rapports quotidiens', 31 May 1900 ff.; MS/SN, letter from Johannesburg, 10 June 1900; MS/TAD/LtG 40, 78/2 (Pretoria), L. J. Johnson to Lt. Gov. Lawley, 2 Dec. 1902; MS/UWL/Walker, p. 170; MS/JPL/Potts, pp. 110–11. See also MS/JPL/Battle, specifically a copy of the *Natal Mercury*, war special, 1 June 1900.

62. *Cape Times*, 5 June 1900.

63. Report by Mackenzie, 31 May 1900, which notes there was a supply of three to four weeks' food for black miners (MS/PRO/WO 105, Roberts to Lansdowne, ms. home letterbooks, South Africa and Ireland, 1898–1901, vol. 3, 19 June 1900).

64. MS/UWL/Law, p. 76.

Six

The Uitlander Refugees

To what unknown region borne,
Wilt thou now wing thy distant flight?
No more with wonted humour gay,
But pallid, cheerless and forlorn.
Emperor Hadrian

With the increase in tension in mid-1899 people began to leave the Rand for the coast. Their presence there was felt immediately as a 'glut' of artisans searched for work and prices began to rise. For the refugees and the locals, this was the beginning of three difficult years. For officialdom, the presence of tens of thousands of increasingly impoverished, impatient and vociferous white Randites, only added to the burden of war. Within weeks, local governments and, ultimately, the imperial administration, had no choice but to assist financially the growing number of destitute people, but it was the private and semi-public charities that first came to their rescue.

In the earliest weeks of the exodus from Johannesburg, it was mostly upper and middle-class wives and children who left for the coast. Although most of these people were bewildered and unhappy, few were in need of charitable assistance. Nonetheless, they were met by jingoistic relief groups, comprised of eager and optimistic women from the coastal communities. These Ladies' Relief Committees were formed in Cape Town, East London and Durban in September, and a 'Special Committee' for the 'protection' of refugees was started in Port Elizabeth. Their first goal was to shelter the women and children who arrived with no place to go, and then to find work for the jobless. They saw their duty as helping anyone willing to help herself[1] — the 'idle' were no more welcome at the ports than they had been on the Rand.

The biggest wave of refugee departures took place during the first week of October, when the working poor fled by the trainload. By the end of that week, the magnitude of the task of sheltering and feeding, let alone employing, the exiles had become apparent and the benevolence and optimism of the relief workers began to fade.

Accommodation was in short supply everywhere along the coast. Boarding houses, hotels and vacant homes filled first, but soon very large empty buildings were packed with destitute refugees. In Durban, for instance, the barracks of the African boating company were used to house women and children, as were rooms

117

at the Trappist monastery near Pine Town. By mid-October, some 2,000 men lived in the buildings of the Durban showground. In Cape Town, the city's 'feather market' was used as a male dormitory and later men lived and worked on the Cape Flats, on the grounds of the Groote Schuur and at the Simonstown docks. In Port Elizabeth, the showyard was turned into 'Smithville' and nearly 750 people of all races lived there in tents. On the beaches of East London and Durban, tents were erected to house families.[2] With overcrowding came a change of attitude towards refugees. By 9 October in Port Elizabeth, for instance, charitable assistance had given way to work-for-relief. The press reported:

> The town is receiving large contingents of refugees, and there are now about 300 in the showyard. Many of these are able to pay for accommodation, but are unable to get a place. They are chiefly Polish Jews, and boarding houses will not take them in. The Relief Committee is starting to-day to make each do four hours work a-day, so as to do away with the burden of keeping those who do not want to work.[3]

Relief committees elsewhere were equally reluctant to assist those they considered idle and they tried to remove such people from their rolls.[4]

As the number of destitute continued to climb, it became evident that the Ladies' Committees were not going to be able to cope alone. On 9 October, the mayor of Cape Town called a special meeting of the town council to make arrangements for drawing upon public funds for the relief and provisioning of destitute men, for the Ladies' Committees dealt only with families. The mayor reviewed the worsening situation and stressed that providing for refugees was an absolute necessity, not 'merely [as] a matter of Philanthropy, but one of self-protection for the city'. After a long debate about the use of public as opposed to private funds, it was agreed that the city would donate £1,000 in aid of refugees. But since many felt it wrong to use public monies before private benevolence was exhausted, a Mayor's Fund was started to collect subscriptions.

Immediately after the town council meeting, a meeting of 'citizens' was convened. While a plea for contributions to refugees was made, the most important result of this second meeting was the formation of an 'Uitlander Committee' to take charge of the reception and registration of the exiles, as well as the solicitation and distribution of funds. Thereafter the three organizations — the Ladies' Committee, the Mayor's Fund, and the Uitlander (refugee) Committee — tried to bring order to refugee affairs and assistance to Randites living in or near Cape Town.[5]

The situation continued to deteriorate. By the end of October many refugees' meagre savings were exhausted and still no work could be found. At this point, Milner, already feeling burdened and not a little depressed by the war, expressed the fears of all those in authority: a large number of exiles, he wrote, 'including almost the whole of those who left the South African Republic at the last moment . . . either started entirely destitute or will become so within a very short space of time'. Many, he added, were:

> not only penniless, but belong to a very undesirable class. They include the loafers and hangers on of society, and those who have made a precarious living by mean, and in some cases, illicit, trades — such as the buying of stolen gold and the sale of liquor to natives. A great number of them are the low class of Jews known as 'Peruvians'.

He and others in power worried about the 'immense difficult[ies]' these people would create at colonial ports, as well as about the possibility that their presence would increase the chance of epidemics (including the plague) breaking out. All felt something had to be done.[6]

In Natal[7] the similarly difficult situation was heightened by the steady influx of destitute and 'undesirable' refugees from Lourenço Marques. The rush of Randites to Delagoa Bay had begun in earnest when the railway line to Natal was closed to civilian traffic in early October. Before that date a few refugees had managed to reach the port city, where the cost of living soon began to climb. By 6 October the British consul in Lourenço Marques, A. Carnegie Ross, had several hundred refugees on his hands and notified the high commissioner that he thought it a good idea to shift as many of them to the colonies as possible. Within two weeks Ross's problems were much worse; 5,000 refugees had arrived and overcrowding was critical.[8]

Conditions in Lourenço Marques were poor. The few hotels doubled their rates, but filled quickly anyway. Refugees sought beds and shelter just about anywhere. In at least one instance, a warehouse was fitted out with stretchers which were rented out by the night. Some people found shelter in small huts at Reuben Point, while others stayed with the Bishop of Lebombo. Large thatched huts were erected near the railway station, vacant buildings and houses were donated to the local relief committee, and the governor general lent some small huts which had been built for an exhibition of Mozambican produce. For two weeks 1,000 non-whites and about 100 whites camped at the railway station, before being moved to an area near the fort.[9]

By the third week of October, the situation had become desperate. Ships from the colonies had removed some 3,000 people by the 10th, but more people continued to arrive from the Rand. By sundown on the 19th, Ross had 3,500 people on his hands, but was able to provide relief assistance to less than a third of them. As the situation deteriorated, many refugees became angry, blaming the war on the British capitalists who intended to use it to lower their wages. They also questioned the right of the British government to leave them, abandoned, in Mozambique. A crowd of refugees, buoyed by liquor, marched on the consulate and demanded passages south. Put off by Ross they returned to their camp, which they set alight and razed to the ground. The consul wired the governor of Natal with the news that: 'Without shelter, badly fed, crowded together. Men becoming desperate. Local Authorities impatient. Military called out to maintain order. Several collisions last night. Populace and police both injured.'[10]

The situation was fast becoming an international incident. The governor general complained that there were 5,000 British subjects at the bay and he thought it 'imperative' that they be moved 'at once'. Milner assured him that he was doing his best: two ships were presently in Lourenço Marques and more were on the way.[11] As the days passed, more ships arrived and carried the exiled Randites south. Meanwhile, Milner sent Ross £5,000 and provisions to assist those still stranded on the beach.[12]

Still the situation worsened. Within a week Ross was forced to explain to Milner: there is 'absolutely no means of housing or of sanitation, food [is] becoming scarce, fresh meat [is] already finished [and with the] wet season coming on, fever will claim many victims among [the] badly housed and fed'. In fact for over two weeks many refugees lived on bread and coffee distributed twice daily by the relief committee.[13]

About the same time as Ross reached the point of panic, the colonial authorities began to express their alarm. In early October some 10,000 people (many of whom were destitute and labelled 'undesirables') began to pass through Lourenço Marques on their way to the colonies. By the 24th the mayor of Durban had had enough. He wired the governor of Natal: 'Matters critical. 1,100 Aliens landed yesterday. Prisoners let loose [from the Republic]. Not five percent British. Understand 8,000 more of same class still to come. Absolutely imperative these must not land Durban. . . . Popular feeling running high against landing such class of foreigners. 2,000 at Showground. Matters alarming.'[14]

Milner, upon receiving the news, reported back to the governor that he had no choice: Delagoa Bay had to be cleared of its refugees. Nevertheless, he added sympathetically, he would inform Ross that in the future Durban must 'in self defence' turn away any refugees from Mozambique. Milner then told Ross that his first priority was to do what he could for 'such of them as are destitute and British subjects'. He wanted, if at all possible, to have the remainder of the white refugees sent to Europe, and Asians to India. If this meant leaving a number at Delagoa Bay for a short time, until transport could be arranged, then this could not be helped. The practical result of this policy statement was that the British consulate stopped aiding foreigners. Thereafter foreign destitute people were expected to receive assistance from their own embassies, though Russian Jews, among the poorest of the lot, were refused aid by all of them. To make matters worse, the Mozambican authorities threatened to return to the Republic any person 'not provided for' by his embassy.[15]

In the meantime, Ross responded to the concerns of the Natal authorities. He wired the governor there, explaining that he had already decided not to send any more refugees to Natal. There remained in his charge about 2,000 people, about half of whom were white, and he hoped to send them all to the Cape. But he defended his earlier actions, asserting that no ex-prisoners had been sent south because, to the best of his knowledge, all prisoners deported by the Republic had been refused entrance to Mozambique by the Portuguese. He also informed the high commissioner that all the refugees who had been sent to the colonies from Lourenço Marques in October had been British: his relief committee had personally supervised their embarkation and assured him that this was the case.[16]

Ross's denials did little good, for the rumour that aliens and prisoners had reached Durban and that 8,000 more were on their way spread far and wide. The mayor of Port Elizabeth, upon hearing that the Durban authorities refused to accept more refugees but that more were already on the water heading south, wired Milner for help. But the high commissioner's office explained that the rumour was, according to Ross, unfounded: the men were not prisoners, but were instead of a 'very poor class' and the high commissioner was attempting to distribute them among several port cities until they could be sent to Europe. The mayor then agreed to take his share.[17]

The *Tintagel Castle*, at Durban on 28 October, was dispatched to Delagoa Bay, with Milner's instructions to Ross to select personally any whites who were to board her and to be 'very careful' in doing so, because the colonies 'are simply swamped by refugees of every kind and cannot stand a large influx of [a] large number of undesirables'. The ship left Lourenço Marques on the 31st and, bypassing Durban, headed south towards East London, Port Elizabeth and Cape Town. No sooner had the *Tintagel Castle* left Mozambique than Ross wired Milner to report that more refugees were due to arrive soon.[18]

At the end of October the authorities began a debate about what to do with the non-white refugees. Ross, Milner and the India Office wanted the Asians in Lourenço Marques to be sent to India, but few wished to go. It is therefore no surprise to learn that in the new year complaints reached London from India that some Indians had been 'forcibly deported to India'. With regard to Africans and Coloureds from the colonies, Milner had no objection to their being sent home, though he did not want them dispatched all at once because he hoped to assimilate the white refugees into colonial society first. In the meantime, he promised to give Ross enough money to ward off their starvation.[19]

By early November Ross had about 700 Africans and Asians waiting to return to Natal, as well as 150 Coloureds and about 200 whites. The consul's worries were compounded first by a report that the plague had arrived in Lourenço Marques and then by news that the Republicans were to send another batch of criminals to Ressano Garcia on the Mozambican border. Ross may have preferred to leave the Portuguese to sort out this latter problem, but he had no choice but to warn them not to return any British subject to the Republic without first notifying him.[20]

The last large shipment of refugees to leave the Delagoa Bay in 1899 was aboard the *Braemar Castle* on 11 November. It carried away almost 1,500 people, a quarter of whom were Asians, presumably bound for Natal, and the rest whites and Coloureds who were distributed between the colonial ports. About 50 Natal blacks remained. Ross was unwilling to dispatch them overland, probably because there had been reports of earlier groups arriving in the colonies 'utterly destitute and starving', possibly as a result of attacks on them at Maputa by Portuguese policemen who reportedly stole their blankets, knives and provisions. The Africans who stayed at Delagoa Bay were offered work on the harbour reclamation project in order to earn enough money to pay their sea passages home.[21] A few Asians and 'disreputable' whites stayed on in town, while on the Catembe side of the river, a small community lived peacefully, hoping to remain there until after the war. Ross's relief committee soon closed its shelters and soup kitchens. The crush of refugees had ended, but not before several thousand had passed through the ill-prepared town. Some 6,000 people, excluding Asians, had received assisted passages, which cost the British government about £10,000.[22] By this time, too, the colonies had absorbed the refugees. They had found shelter — some of it pretty poor — and some were in receipt of wages. Many of the men who had neither joined a volunteer corps nor found work had returned to Europe. Some went in search of adventure elsewhere. Others remained a burden on imperial funds.[23]

On the day war was declared the town council in Cape Town approached Milner for assistance. He, in turn, wired the colonial secretary, asking him to send a message to mayors of the leading cities in Britain requesting that funds be raised in aid of Uitlander refugees. In keeping with the prevailing sentiment, Milner asked Chamberlain to assure the mayors that those who would receive aid were, first, British subjects and, secondly, not 'loafers', but people who were willing to work if jobs could be found. The lord mayor of London was thinking along the same lines and on the same day approached the Colonial Office, offering assistance. The result was the creation of the Lord Mayor's Relief Fund, also known as the Mansion House Fund.[24]

To assist with the disbursement of the money, Milner appointed a committee composed of important financial and political figures from the colonies. The committee recruited a staff and then set about determining the number and whereabouts of the destitute refugees. It also discussed policy concerning refugees at Lourenço Marques and undesirables generally, and dispersed funds to local committees.[25]

The first instalment of the Fund — some £25,000 — reached Milner in mid-October. Of this, over two-thirds was distributed to relief committees at Durban, Pietermaritzburg, East London and Cape Town, and to Ross at Delagoa Bay and Godfrey Lagden in Basutoland. By 1 November Milner had received £140,000 from the fund and probably close to 30,000 refugees were in receipt of aid. By the end of the year, £200,000 had been raised and, of that, just over £160,000 remained for disbursement. After the new year, as relief workers and colonial officials had predicted, the burden on the fund grew. People who had previously been financially independent were now added to the rolls. Whereas in October, November and December 1899 the amount dispersed never reached £18,000 per month, in January 1900 the Lord Mayor's Fund distributed over £30,000 to Uitlander refugees. In the following two months over £40,000 was spent and, by 8 April, less than half the money that had been on hand on New Year's Day remained.[26] Furthermore, in April the Rust en Orde Commission in Johannesburg decided to deport the rest of the British there, thus adding to the burden already felt by Ross in Lourenço Marques and by the colonial authorities to the south.

Although the Lord Mayor's Relief Fund began to assume a greater portion of the burden, the local relief committees continued to assist the Randites. For instance, the Ladies' Relief Committee in the Cape organized an appeal for clothes. When Milner forwarded its request to Chamberlain, he dutifully passed on the women's proviso that, because there were 'many cases of better class people' in need, some clothing of a 'superior quality' had to be sent out. Within a month clothes from Britain began to arrive in the Cape, and they were redistributed to women's groups further north along the coast.[27]

The Uitlander Committee also continued its work. It created an Uitlander postal system, opened its own subscription list, liaised with both the Cape Town Mayor's Fund and the Lord Mayor's Fund, and began to house refugees. It also served to bring together men who had been active in the Republic's political affairs before the war. J. Emrys Evans, W. Wybergh, J. Douglas Forster, C. L. Anderson and F. W. Buxton were all active members. In addition, F. Eckstein, W. Dalrymple and J. G. Currey sat on the finance subcommittee, W. van Hulsteyn on the employment subcommittee, and H. Graumann on the reception subcommittee.[28]

Elsewhere in the colonies leading pre-war Randites played prominent roles in refugee politics. For instance, William Hosken was involved in refugee affairs in Natal from September onwards, and T. Mackenzie and A. Mackie Niven, both members of the Uitlander Council, chaired the refugee committees of Port Elizabeth and Durban, respectively.[29] It was the men who dominated reform politics before the war who now tried to lead the refugees — the 'sheep without a shepherd', to use Wybergh's phrase,[30] and to represent their interests in government circles.

The creation of this bureaucratic structure helped Milner handle his two most pressing refugee problems: assisting the destitute and superintending the 'undesirables'. When the war began Milner proposed that the best way to deal with the 'undesirables' was to send them to Europe. Between October and the new year he drew money from the Lord Mayor's Fund to pay for passages to Europe, thus relieving southern Africa of some 600 or 700 destitute or undesirable people. After 1 January, the Castle Shipping Company lowered its fares for passengers in receipt of aid, thus enabling more poor people to book their own passages.[31] Also, it was not until after Christmas 1899 that Milner was able to arrange to send a whole boatload of undesirables home.

On 6 January the *African Review* announced that a number of 'carefully selected' refugees were to be sent to England from Cape Town aboard the *Cheshire* at the expense of the Lord Mayor's Fund. These 'select' passengers were, according to Milner, some 250 British subjects and 350 foreign Jews. The press reported that two-thirds of them were Russian Jews, who, being former illicit liquor sellers, could 'find no scope for their particular talent now that they were exiled from the Rand, and who are, therefore desirous of leaving South Africa'.[32] While the colonial press was well aware of the passenger list of the *Cheshire*, the British press was not and when the ship arrived at Southampton on 2 February a scandal unfolded. The *Daily Mail* reported:

> There landed at Southampton from the transport Cheshire over 600 so-called refugees, their passages having been paid out of the Lord Mayor's Fund,[[33]] and, upon the unanimous testimony of the ship's officers, there was scarce a hundred of them that had, by right, deserved such help, and they were the Englishmen of the party. The rest were Jews. The ship seemed alive with them. . . . The ship's officers . . . told a remarkable tale. . . . 'When we left Cape Town . . . there were hundreds of English people utterly destitute . . . who begged . . . to be allowed to sail. But nobody would listen to them — and the only reason that we can think of is that the people at Cape Town were anxious to get rid of those we brought'.[34]

In the meantime, refugees who wanted to be sent home, and whom Milner wished to oblige, piled up at the coast. On 1 February he asked Chamberlain to send him another transport so that he could send another 400 to 600 people home, but the officials at the Colonial Office, upon reading about the *Cheshire*, refused to comply until the story could be investigated. Milner received his second ship only after he had given his assurances that, in the future, respectable and disreputable refugees would not be mixed together and that the former would be sent home only if they had family or friends who would support them. In March, 118 first-class and 448 third-class passengers — the latter being the bulk of the refugees who wanted to leave and whom the relief committees were willing to assist — were sent home.[35] Unfortunately for Milner and his committees, by March (because of the recent British military victories and the withdrawal of the Boers from certain areas) fewer refugees wanted to return to Britain. They believed that the war would soon end and wanted to be in the first wave of those allowed to return to their homes and work.[36]

If the option of removing destitute British and foreign refugees was closed to Milner, then the alternative was to assist them where they were. But the Lord Mayor's Fund was running low and a second appeal in April 1900 raised very little additional money.[37] In an attempt to reduce the drain on the Fund, the introduction of new (and the expansion of existing) relief projects was recommended. But wages on these works projects were poor and conditions harsh, and, instead of being grateful as the relief workers expected, the refugees complained bitterly. At the Cape Town harbour works, for example, they resented having to work 'cheek by jowl with Kaffirs, with possibly a nigger foreman', all for the sum of 4s 6d a day. At the Cape quarry the men received 3s 6d for a nine-hour workday and were reduced to living in 'dug-outs', i.e. holes in the ground covered with corrugated tin and a foot of sand. And while the men working at the Cape Flats were referred to by their supervisors as being 'filthy and dirty' and 'chronic drunks', the poor facilities and the incessant wind may help to explain their condition.[38] Certainly the men were frustrated with the work, the food and the pay. Walter White, a Rand refugee working at the Umlaas water-works project near Durban, explained to his wife:

> I am sick of being here so long . . . and down here the time crawls along. Work is very scarce. . . . I am working for the Relief Committee, 4/− per day and we have to pay 1/2 for our food which leaves 14/2, lots of money it is not . . . but I would sooner do that than loaf about doing nothing. The work is pick and shovel, laying water pipes to carry the water to Durban; it is Kaffirs work but it is all we can get.[39]

Left with little alternative, Milner decided that, after March 1900, no able-bodied men would receive assistance from the Lord Mayor's Fund. In this way he was able to reduce the number receiving aid by between one-third and one-half.[40] Yet, as the refugees saw their funds exhausted, the number of destitute in the colonies continued to climb and the middle-class now began to join the relief rolls (albeit reluctantly in many cases).

But Milner had other worries. On 4 April Ross, in Lourenço Marques, informed him that there were 80 destitute refugees there and that the number was expected to double in four days. Over the next couple of weeks the Boers in Johannesburg expelled about 1,300 white and coloured residents and, after the explosion at Begbie's foundry, another 300—400 British. The situation soon resembled that of October/November 1899: once again Ross cabled Milner requesting money, while the Natal authorities again sought the high commissioner's 'kind protection'. But the exorbitant cost of living at Delagoa Bay, even in comparison with the high costs of life in a colonial port town in these months, meant both that relief expenditure was higher in Lourenço Marques and that the savings of these new refugees would be more rapidly exhausted. Thus, Ross and Milner agreed that unless they were going to let the destitute starve, they had no choice but to move them south. In late April 1900 the shift began.[41]

It became increasingly clear in these months that charity, whether raised by the mayors of Britain or the women of South Africa, was not going to be sufficient to cover refugee-related expenses. In the first week of May 1900 Milner wrote to Chamberlain explaining that some help from public funds appeared 'inevitable'. He urged that public money be used to bring the refugees from Mozambique and Whitehall agreed. However, the Treasury was adamant that the money could not be used for refugees who were already in the British colonies: their passages and expenses were to be covered by charity, the Lord Mayor's Fund especially, and not by public funds.[42] The shortage of cash in the fund made it unlikely that the increasingly destitute population would be sent home. In southern Africa they were going to stay and Milner had to face the prospect of increased distress and the inevitable unrest which would follow.

Discontent among refugees became apparent in April after able-bodied men were dropped from the relief rolls. Worried that it would get worse if the funds were exhausted, both Milner and Chamberlain began to seek additional assistance from the increasingly parsimonious British public.[43] Problems developed first in East London when Rand artisans — miners, carpenters, masons, blacksmiths and engine drivers — were told that they could no longer collect relief. Ignoring the local Uitlander committee, they marched to the town hall and reported themselves to the local authorities as unemployed and unable to find work. The mayor cabled Milner: 'Section of refugees have taken upon themselves to telegraph you . . . asking for work and assistance. This is being done outside [the] relief committee formed here at your request months back'. Immediately the high commissioner began looking for work for them, even cabling the Railway Pioneer Regiment to see if it needed additional artisans. Two months later in Durban, refugees, after being told they would be taken off the rolls and would be given work at the Umlaas waterworks, 'assailed [the] Relief Committee with violent abuse and threats to bring members before the Supreme Court. They claimed that money was subscribed in London specially for them until the return to Johannesburg, and they meant to have it'.[44] Totally in character for working-class Randites, then, one of their first responses was to reject Uitlander reformer leadership, which worried those in authority who sought to maintain control. Only one thing could make matters worse at this juncture and that was an increase in the number of destitute.

During the second quarter of 1900 it became clear that many who had previously left southern Africa were about to descend on it again. A warning was issued by the *African Review*: 'So soon as Johannesburg is in the hands of the British [Randites will] want to be on the spot to help get things shipshape once again'.[45] By June, as Johannesburg and Pretoria changed hands, the expected rush to southern Africa began. In the months that followed Milner repeatedly tried to stem the tide, warning people that the port cities were already overcrowded and that those who returned would be 'very uncomfortable' and would waste their money in cities where prices were artificially high.[46] His warnings seem to have had little effect, for, throughout the rest of the year, reports from all over the world told of large numbers of people bound for the British South African colonies. It was only in December 1900 — as it became clear that the fall of Johannesburg and Pretoria did not mean an end to the war or a return of refugees to the Rand — that the rush abated. Unfortunately by then thousands of people had been added to the population at the coast, there joining the tens of thousands of refugees already 'loafing about with nothing to do'.[47]

By August 1900 the situation had become critical. The Lord Mayor's Fund was virtually exhausted, while the budgets and the patience of local authorities were strained by the need to finance public works projects to sustain increasingly vociferous refugees. The 'growing impatience' among refugees was, according to Milner, the result of 'considerable and growing destitution'. 'Men are apt to be unreasonable on empty stomachs', he wrote to Lord Roberts.[48] At the beginning the refugees' protests were spontaneous and generally centred on one issue: the fact that the men had been dropped from the relief rolls. Increasingly, though, they turned from bread-and-butter issues to a wide range of topics, yet always focusing upon their imminent return to the Rand as the solution to most of their ills.

After the capture of Johannesburg at the end of May, the Uitlander refugees began to agitate for a return to their homes and work. Milner shared their desire in this regard, for he had three good reasons for wishing them out from under his feet. He explained to Violet Cecil in October 1900 that he wanted to see them back on the Rand where they could be:

> busy and contented, and where they were wanted, instead of being idle and rebellious, where they are not, and above all the Boers must see the hopelessness of the struggle. At present they say 'you can take our country,

but we can prevent its being any good to you'. They would see the folly of this if the Rand were at work again. The smoke of those chimneys will be the end of the war.[49]

Another good reason for sending them home was to eliminate the discontent brewing along the coast. Milner expressed his concerns to his chief of staff in the same month: 'The refugees are showing signs of insubordination', he wrote. 'If they began to give serious trouble, there is no saying what the Dutch [at the Cape] might do'.[50]

But the return, no matter how desirable, was not easy to arrange; the smooth transfer of upwards of 70,000 whites and their possessions required extensive organization. Trains had to be provided — and rolling stock was needed elsewhere in this time of war — and the routes had to be secure from Boer attack. The Rand towns had to have adequate supplies of food, clothing, medicine and, to prevent a repetition of the days of illness which followed the capture of Bloemfontein, fresh water and proper sanitation had to be guaranteed.[51] If men were to have work, then employers had to precede the labour force in order to reopen businesses, or, in some cases such as the mining industry, to recruit black labour, which was an essential prerequisite of white refugee re-employment. Finally, to ensure an orderly transfer of people and to guarantee that the 'undesirables' did not find their way back to the Rand, it was necessary to implement a system of registration and to issue permits to return.

Hence, a complex bureaucratic system was required and the Uitlanders took the initiative. In July, representatives of the Chamber of Mines, the Chamber of Commerce and the Uitlander Committee in Cape Town approached the high commissioner, stating that they were anxious to assist with registration. The result was the formation of the 'Central Registration Committee' (CRC) which undertook to liaise with local Uitlander committees and resident magistrates, to issue them with books of permits and to determine, in conjunction with Milner, which refugees would be permitted to return first. As a result of its control over refugee affairs and because it had Milner's ear, it was a powerful body. Its membership was drawn from the financial and political élite of pre-war Johannesburg: *inter alia*, Harold Strange, Sam Evans, J. G. Currey, Clem Davies, E. P. Solomon, P. J. Pakeman and H. F. Cohen.[52]

Even before Roberts marched into Johannesburg, the Chamber of Mines had drawn up a list of the mining employees it felt should be the first to return to the Rand. On the day Roberts entered the city, this list of 580 names was forwarded to Milner. Major Colin Mackenzie, director of field intelligence and the new military governor of Johannesburg, agreed with the idea in principle: it would be a good idea, he noted, to have mining representatives sent up to Johannesburg to help him deal with the 'native question' — the 'most difficult one' before him. In addition, there were, he told Roberts, no 'reliable principle men' left in the city who could serve as advisers, for they had all fled at the onset of war. In June Milner was still waiting for Roberts's approval of the Chamber's list, but it was more or less assured that it would be forthcoming.[53]

Meanwhile, the Chamber of Mines continued to plan and by mid-June its list topped 1,000 names. But now, as commercial and professional representatives were added, Roberts put his foot down: this number was totally unacceptable, for there were not enough railway engines or provisions to accommodate so large a number of men. He agreed instead to 20 representatives, on condition they provided their own food *en route* and understood that passenger coaches north of

Bloemfontein could not be guaranteed.[54]

On 28 June, 20 men left Cape Town by rail, stopped briefly at Kimberley, and arrived at Bloemfontein on the 30th. There, despite the good intentions of the civil administration and the high hopes of the Chamber of Mines, the train was stopped. When Fiddes, Milner's secretary (who was now acting as Lord Roberts's political secretary), explained to the director of the railways, Lt. Col. P. C. Girouard, that 20 mining men were on their way north to Johannesburg from the Cape, the young engineer exclaimed: 'My God! I'm done! I can never look the [Railway] Pioneer Regiment in the face again. They'll all mutiny to a man. I've promised them that none of the men who sat on their bottoms in Cape Town and did nothing shall return to their billets before the Pioneers.'[55] Girouard was able to convince Roberts of the seriousness of the situation and so the 20 men were held up at Bloemfontein.[56] Within days Milner began pressing Roberts to allow the men to continue their journey north: 'It is of real importance', the high commissioner explained, 'to oblige the Chamber of Mines as they have been most reasonable and helpful throughout and can be of immediate use to us in the future.'[57] Roberts, not unsympathetic to Milner's view, was none the less hesitant. He told Milner:

> I was obliged to delay the departure of the 20 . . . as I found their being allowed to go to Johannesburg was causing great discontent amongst the Railway Pioneers and Imperial Light Horse, the members of which threatened to resign. De Montmorency's Scouts have already resigned and if the Colonial Corps follow this example we should be seriously crippled. I deeply regret having consented to anyone being allowed to return to Johannesburg at present.[58]

Within three days, however, Roberts had relented and the 20 men were allowed to go on to Johannesburg on condition they returned to the coast within ten days to write their reports.[59] But Milner was under pressure from refugees at the coast not to let the matter rest there. At the end of July he explained to Roberts that they were impatient with the 'rather hard bargain' driven by the volunteer regiments, a bargain which insisted that no refugees be permitted to return until the volunteers were disbanded. While the high commissioner understood the volunteers' concern, he explained that until 'a number of people at present excluded are allowed to return, business cannot be restarted' and the volunteers, even if disbanded, would still be unable to find work on the Rand.[60]

Meanwhile Roberts agreed to extend to businessmen the privilege of sending representatives to the Rand to investigate conditions there and to advise the Johannesburg military administration about the best way to provision the district. In June the Durban Uitlander Committee sent a list of 30 men to the Chamber of Commerce in Durban which, expressing 'strong opinions' about the men who drew it up, discarded it. A new one was popularly chosen. But by August the list was cut from 30 to 20 men, drawn not only from Durban but from other colonial towns as well. They were allowed to travel to the Rand for a week before returning to the coast to write their reports.[61]

Meanwhile, Milner and the CRC began to make plans for the return of the mass of refugees. In the second week of July 'Circular A' was issued, which served as a policy statement and a guideline for the registration of refugees. To make registration uniform throughout the colonies, the Uitlander committees were instructed to collect specific data on every male refugee: name, address, former occupation in the Republic and employer's name. The local committees were told to classify the people into different categories: (a) large property owners and important professional and business men; (b) smaller professional and business men; and (c) all other.[62] Of primary concern to Milner and his Uitlander advisers was that 'riff-raff and traitors . . . be given no facilities' to re-enter the Transvaal.[63]

By the time Circular A arrived in Durban, the Uitlander Committee there had already registered some 4,500 people, at least 600 of whom were Asians. An Indian Uitlander Committee was formed in Cape Town in August 1900 and prepared its own separate list, following the guidelines laid down in Circular A.[64] Registration of Coloureds was less well organized for some Uitlander committees allowed them to enrol, while others denied them a place on their lists.[65]

The Durban Uitlander Committee also took the initiative of registering women and, by mid-July, had enrolled some 100 'respectable female refugees' who had worked in the Transvaal as boarding-house keepers, shop assistants and the like. In October the CRC decided to register women and children, probably in response to concerns expressed about what would happen to dependants who were separated from their menfolk. A schedule of priorities was again formulated, with women who owned their own businesses or who employed labour separated from dependent women. The list of dependants was divided into two: those whose menfolk were in business or had work, and those whose menfolk were unemployed. Again it was stressed by Milner and the CRC that registration committees should 'exercise every discretion to prevent, as far as possible, the early return of persons who may be classed as "undesirables" '.[66]

While the refugees were generally quite pleased with being registered for return home, some demonstrated their concern with what they thought was the undue preference given to capitalists on Circular A. The Durban Uitlander Committee, somewhat more responsive that its Cape Town equivalent to working-class and radical opinion, led the opposition to any sort of ordering of people. While the committee agreed that employers of labour, such as mine managers, building contractors, bankers and merchants, ought to be allowed to proceed to the Rand before workers, it demanded to know why property owners ought to be given preference, for instance, over wage-earners. The key, it argued, was to acknowledge the claims of certain trades and professions, in terms of their importance to economic reconstruction, and not permit rich and powerful people to return early only because of their influence. The committee also wanted employers who had returned to send down lists of employees, who could then be included in the second wave of homeward-bound refugees. Milner agreed to these demands: persons on list (a) of Circular A would not have priority over lists (b) and (c), though employers would have precedence.[67]

By the end of July the South African Railway authorities had agreed to let the refugees return to the Transvaal and Orange River Colony at reduced rates. People holding the return portion of tickets bought in 1899 did not have to pay any additional charge, while those without tickets could buy them at lower prices if they swore that they had left the Republic or Free State because of the war. Finally, arrangements were made to give the destitute free passage north if they presented a 'certificate of destitution' (signed by a member of the local refugee committee) to the railway office.[68]

Preparations for the return of the refugees were well under way when, in late September, Roberts agreed to allow a small number to return after 10 October. Milner was jubilant, explaining to the commander-in-chief that it was fine if the return of the Uitlanders was 'slow and gradual', just so long as it was 'regular'. It did not take long for the news to spread: food was going inland and the refugees would soon follow. The number of people returning to southern Africa from other parts of the world rose and refugees already at the coast who had not previously registered did so now.[69]

By October the CRC had a list of nearly 19,000 white males who were living along the coast in Natal and the Cape Colony and who wished to return inland. The committee decided to move 6,000 in the first wave north, of whom half would be mining personnel and the remainder in commerce, the professions and the service sector. These men, who would be sent north in the three weeks following 17 October, would be drawn from these communities along the coast.[70] By the 13th all was prepared: the refugees were going home! But on that day Roberts notified the coastal officials: 'postpone departure of all refugees and others who have been given permission to return to Johannesburg'.[71] The long wait was not yet over.

Notes

1. *Cape Times* (weekly) 14 June, 14 July, 18 Oct. 1899; *S & D News*, 15 June, 7, 8, 9, 12, 14, 15 and 20 Sept. 1899; *Star*, 29 Aug., 7 and 8 Sept. 1899.
2. *Star*, 7, 14, 15, 22, 28 and 29 Sept. 1899; *Cape Times* (weekly) 11, 18 and 25 Oct. and 22 Nov. 1899. See also MS/UWL/Hills, diary vol. 1, 25 Aug. 1900.
3. *Star*, 9 Oct. 1899.
4. *African Review*, 22 (382) 17 March 1900, p. 378.
5. *Cape Times* (weekly) 11 Oct. 1899.
6. MS/PRO/CO 417/268, Milner to Chamberlain, 25 Oct. 1899; and see *S & D News*, 13 Oct. 1899; *Cape Times* (weekly) 1 Nov. 1899.
7. For details of the situation in Natal, see *Star*, 24, 28 and 29 Aug. and 7 Sept. 1899; *S & D News*, 11, 21 and 28 Sept. 1899; *Cape Times* (weekly) 1 Nov. 1899; *African Review*, 21 (366) 25 Nov. 1899, p. 301; (368) 9 Dec. 1899, p. 380. Further information is found in MS/PRO/DO 119/431, Hely Hutchinson to Milner, 16 Nov. 1899, with enclosures; MS/TAD/GOV 327/40, 'Refugee relief: the work in Durban'; MS/PRO/FO 2/268, Hely Hutchinson to Chamberlain (copy), 24 Oct. 1899; MS/PRO/CO 417/268, Milner to Chamberlain, 25 Oct. 1899, and CO 417/269, Milner to Chamberlain, 16 Nov. 1899, with enclosures.
8. MS/PRO/CO 417/268, Milner to Chamberlain, 25 Oct. 1899, with enclosures, Ross to Milner, 6 Oct. 1899, and governor-general of Lourenço Marques to Milner, 20 Oct. 1899.
9. MS/PRO/DO 119/506, Ross diary (confidential), 14 Nov. 1899; MS/PRO/CO 417/268, Milner to Chamberlain, 1 Nov. 1899 with enclosure, Ross to Milner, 12 Oct. 1899; MS/PRO/FO 2/267, Ross to FO, 12 Oct. 1899. See also Froes 1899, pp. 24—6; Barwin 1952, p. 120; *African Review*, 21 (364) 11 Nov. 1899, p. 221; *S & D News*, 10 Oct. 1899.
10. MS/PRO/CO 417/268, Milner to Chamberlain, 25 Oct. 1899, with enclosures, governor of Natal to Milner, 19 Oct. 1899, and governor of Natal to Milner, 20 Oct. 1899, forwarding a copy of a wire from Ross, 19 Oct. 1899. See also Barwin 1952, pp. 123—6 for demonstrations, and for the departure of five ships between 4 and 10 Oct; MS/PRO/FO 2/267, Ross to FO. Each ship was, according to Ross, 'excessively crowded'.
11. MS/PRO/CO 417/268, Milner to Chamberlain, 25 Oct. 1899, with enclosures, governor-general of Lourenço Marques to Milner (and reply), 20 Oct. 1899.
12. MS/PRO/CO 417/269, Milner to Chamberlain, 20 Oct. and 25 Oct. 1899, with enclosures, Milner to Ross, 20 Oct. 1899, and Ross to Milner, 22 Oct. 1899. See also *Cape Times* (weekly) 25 Oct. 1899.
13. MS/PRO/CO 417/268, Milner to Chamberlain, 1 Nov. 1899, with enclosure, Ross to Milner, 25 Oct. 1899; and see Froes 1899, p. 25; Barwin 1952, pp. 127—8, 150, 153; *S & D*

News, 14 Nov. 1899, and reports on conditions in Lourenço Marques.

14. MS/PRO/CO 417/268, Milner to Chamberlain, 25 Oct. 1899, with enclosure, governor of Natal to Milner, 24 Oct. 1899, forwarding cable from the mayor of Durban to the governor of Natal, n.d. The governor agreed with the mayor's feelings.

15. MS/PRO/CO 417/268, Milner to Chamberlain, 25 Oct. 1899, with enclosures, Milner to governor of Natal, 24 Oct. 1899, and Milner to Ross, 24 Oct. 1899. See also Barwin 1952, pp. 127—8; and Froes 1899, p. 25.

16. MS/PRO/CO 417/268, Milner to Chamberlain, 1 Nov. 1899, with enclosures, governor of Natal to Milner, 24 Oct. 1899 (with mention of Ross's telegram), and Ross to Milner, 25 Oct. 1899.

17. MS/PRO/CO 417/268, Milner to Chamberlain, 1 Nov. 1899, with enclosures, mayor of Port Elizabeth to Milner, 25 and 26 Oct., and Milner to mayor of Port Elizabeth, 25 Oct. 1899. See also MS/PRO/FO 2/268, CO to FO, 24 Oct. 1899, with enclosure, Salisbury to Ross, 25 Oct. 1899, and the Admiralty to C-in-C, 25 Oct. 1899.

18. MS/PRO/CO 417/268, Milner to Chamberlain, 1 Nov. 1899, with enclosures, Milner to Ross, 28 Oct. 1899, and Ross to Milner, 31 Oct. 1899.

19. MS/PRO/CO 417/268, Milner to Chamberlain, 1 Nov. 1899, with enclosures, Ross to Milner, 25 Oct. 1899, and Milner to Ross, 26 Oct. 1899; MS/PRO/CO 417/269, Milner to Chamberlain, 16 Nov. 1899, with enclosures, Ross to Milner, 3 Nov. 1899, and Milner to Ross, 3 Nov. 1899. See also MS/PRO/FO 2/398, FO to Sir Mancherjee Bhownaggree (draft), 20 Feb. 1900; MS/PRO/CO 417/268, Milner to Chamberlain, 25 Oct. 1899, with enclosure, Ross to Milner, 19 Oct. 1899; MS/PRO/FO 2/269, under-secretary of state for India to under-secretary of state, FO, 30 Oct. 1899, and CO to FO, 4 Nov. 1899, with enclosure, Chamberlain to Milner, 1 Nov. 1899. See also FO 2/399, FO to Sir Mancherjee Bhownaggree (draft), 26 Feb. 1900.

20. MS/PRO/CO 417/269, Milner to Chamberlain, 16 Nov. 1899, with enclosure, Ross to Milner, 15 Nov. 1899. See also MS/PRO/DO 119/506, Ross diary (confidential), 13 Nov. 1899; MS/PRO/FO 2/269, FO to Ross, 4 Nov. 1899; MS/PRO/CO 291/301, FO to CO, 17 April 1900, with enclosure from Ross, 17 April 1900. Cases of plague were reported from Oct. 1899 to Feb. 1900.

21. MS/PRO/DO 119/506, Ross diary (confidential), 14 and 22 Nov. and 21 Dec. 1899.

22. MS/PRO/CO 417/269, Milner to Chamberlain, 16 Nov. 1899, with enclosure, Ross to Milner, 4 Nov. 1899, and 6 Dec. 1899, with enclosures, Ross to Milner, 15 Nov. and 5 Dec. 1899; MS/PRO/DO 119/506, Ross diary (confidential), 14 and 22 Nov. 1899. See also Barwin 1952, p. 153. Another £750 was used to assist refugees while in Lourenço Marques. Any money spent on Indians was to be reimbursed by the India Office.

23. MS/JPL/ACPT, London letterbook, 27 Dec. 1899, regarding the Cape.

24. *Cape Times* (weekly) 11 Oct., 1 Nov. 1899; *S & D News,* 9 Oct. 1899; MS/PRO/CO 417/267, Milner to Chamberlain, 11 Oct. 1899, and lord mayor of London to Chamberlain, 11 Oct. 1899. For the enthusiasm for refugee relief in England, see MS/BOD/Violet Milner, VM 35/176/48, William St John Fremantle Brodrick to Violet Cecil, 17 Oct. 1899.

25. MS/PRO/CO 417/268, Milner to Chamberlain, 11 Oct. 1899 and 25 Oct. 1899. The men asked to sit on the committee included Sir J. H. de Villiers, Mr Justice Buchanan, the Hon. J. Rose Innes, Mr Mitchell, the mayors of Cape Town, Port Elizabeth and East London and the governor of Natal.

26. MS/PRO/CO 417/268, Milner to Chamberlain, 16 and 26 Oct. and 1 Nov. 1899; CO 417/285, Milner to Chamberlain, 17 Jan. 1900; CO 417/288, Milner to Chamberlain, 13 April 1900; MS/PRO/FO 2/405, report to FO, 23 April 1900, with enclosure, Milner to Chamberlain, 13 April 1900.

27. MS/PRO/CO 417/269, Milner to Chamberlain, 16 Nov. 1899, with enclosures, and Milner to Chamberlain, 20 Dec. 1899; MS/PRO/DO 119/432, deputy mayor of Durban to Milner, 24 Feb. 1900; *Cape Times* (weekly) 22 Nov. 1899; *Cape Times,* 6 March 1900.

28. MS/PRO/DO 119/435, 'Uitlander Committee at Cape Town, Rand relief, etc.' Wybergh, Forster and Buxton were active in the SAL, Anderson and van Hulsteyn in the Reform

Committee, Dalrymple in the UC, and Currey in local politics.

29. MS/UWL/Hills, diary vol. 1, 22 Sept. 1900; *Star*, 24 Feb. 1902; MS/PRO/CO 417/269, Milner to Chamberlain, 4 Oct. 1899, with enclosure from Caldecott to Milner, 20 Sept. 1899, re. Pietermaritzburg.

30. W. Wybergh to J. P. Fitzpatrick (confidential), 13 Dec. 1899, in Duminy and Guest (eds) 1976.

31. MS/PRO/CO 417/268, Milner to Chamberlain, 25 Oct. 1899; CO 417/285, Milner to Chamberlain, 17 Jan. 1900, with 'Statement receipts and disbursements of fund to 31 Dec. 1899'; *S & D News*, 2 Jan. 1900.

32. *African Review*, 22 (372) 6 Jan. 1900; *S & D News*, 21 Feb. 1900; MS/PRO/CO 417/285, Milner to Chamberlain, 17 Jan. 1900.

33. Regardless of press reports, Milner said only a very few were given funds (MS/PRO/CO 417/285, Milner to Chamberlain, 17 Jan. 1900).

34. MS/PRO/CO 417/268, with clipping from *Daily Mail*, 3 Feb. 1900; and see *S & D News*, 22 March 1900.

35. MS/PRO/CO 417/286, Milner to Chamberlain, 20 Feb. 1900; CO 417/287, Milner to Chamberlain, 24 March 1900; *S & D News*, 22 March 1900.

36. MS/PRO/CO 417/287, Milner to Chamberlain, 24 March 1900.

37. MS/PRO/CO 417/289, Milner to Chamberlain, 1 May 1900, with statement by L. L. Mitchell; MS/PRO/FO 2/405, report to FO, with enclosures, Milner to Chamberlain, 13 April 1900, and Chamberlain to Milner, 21 April 1900; MS/PRO/CO 417/288, Milner to Chamberlain, 13 April 1900.

38. *Cape Times*, 26 Sept. and 25 Dec. 1900; MS/TAD/GOV 215, Milner to Chamberlain (draft), 18 Sept. 1901, with report on Imperial Relief Fund, annexure 'C', 23 Feb. 1901.

39. MS/JPL/White, letter to 'My dear wife', 30 Aug. 1900.

40. MS/PRO/CO 417/289, Milner to Chamberlain, 1 May 1900, with statement by L. L. Mitchell; MS/TAD/GOV 327/40, report on 'Refugee relief: the work in Durban'.

41. MS/PRO/FO 2/405, FO to lord mayor of London (draft), 11 April 1900, with enclosures; F0 2/407, CO to FO, 17 May 1900, with enclosures; MS/PRO/CO 417/289, Milner to Chamberlain, 9 May 1900, with enclosures.

42. MS/PRO/FO 2/407, CO to FO, 8 May 1900, with enclosures, Milner to Chamberlain, 3 May 1900, internal memorandum, 8 May 1900, and FO to treasury (draft), 16 May 1900. See also FO 2/408, treasury to FO, 21 May 1900.

43. MS/PRO/FO 2/405, CO to FO, 23 April 1900, with enclosure, Milner to Chamberlain, 13 April 1900; MS/PRO/CO 417/288, Chamberlain to lord mayor of London (draft), 17 April 1900.

44. MS/PRO/DO 119/435, mayor of East London to Milner, 15 April 1900, and report on 'East London'. See also *African Review*, 24 (399) 14 July 1900, p. 52.

45. *S & D News*, 30 April 1900, citing *African Review*, n.d.

46. MS/PRO/CO 417/292, Milner to Chamberlain, 10 July 1900; CO 417/290, Milner to Chamberlain, 7 June 1900; *Cape Times*, 13 July 1900; *African Review*, 23 (394) 9 June 1900, p. 348; 24 (398) 7 July 1900, p. 14; (401) 28 July 1900, p. 128.

47. MS/UWL/Hills, diary, 4 July 1900; and see MS/PRO/CO 417/292, Milner to Chamberlain (confidential), 19 July 1900, with enclosure, resident commissioner at Salisbury to Milner, 19 July 1900; *African Review*, 24 (398) 7 July 1900, p. 14; (402) 4 Aug. 1900, pp. 151, 164; (417) 17 Nov. 1900, p. 235; (419) 1 Dec. 1900, p. 304; (402) 8 Dec. 1900, p. 345.

48. MS/NAM/Roberts, 'Letters from Milner, 1898–1920', Milner to Roberts, 23 Aug., 13 Sept. 1900. For worsening distress, see MS/PRO/CO 417/288, Milner to Chamberlain, 13 April 1900; and *African Review*, 24 (407) 8 Sept. 1900, p. 337.

49. MS/BOD/Mss. English, c. 687, extract from typescript letter, Milner to Lady Edward Cecil, 26 Oct. 1900. For a similar statement, see MS/BOD/Mss. Milner Dep. 170, private correspondence with Chamberlain, Milner to Chamberlain (confidential), 28 Oct. 1900.

50. MS/PRO/CO 417/295, Milner to Chamberlain (confidential), 7 Nov. 1900, with enclosure, Milner to chief of staff, 25 Oct. 1900. For Milner's fear of a 'pan-Afrikaner

conspiracy' at the Cape, see Galbraith 1983.

51. *Cape Times*, 31 May, 30 July, 25 Aug. 1900; MS/NAM/Roberts, Ms. letterbook from South Africa, vol. 2, Roberts to Milner, 31 May 1900; OP/CC/Cape Government Railways; Pakenham 1979, pp. 381—3, 422—3.

52. MS/PRO/FO 2/532, CO to FO, 12 Feb. 1901, with enclosure, Milner to Chamberlain, 9 Jan. 1901; MS/TAD/GOV 248/PS 18, Milner to Chamberlain (draft), 31 May 1901, with enclosure re. CRC by H. L. Omanney. The Chamber of Mines and the Chamber of Commerce paid the cost of registration and donated staff to the CRC.

53. For Mackenzie's views, see MS/TAD/PSY 49, military governor of Johannesburg to C-in-C, AHQ, 8 June 1900; MS/PRO/CO 417/290, Milner to Chamberlain, 13 June 1900, with enclosures, executive committee of Chamber of Mines to Milner, 31 May 1900, and Strange to imperial secretary, 31 May 1900; *African Review*, 23 (395) 16 June 1900, p. 386.

54. MS/PRO/CO 417/291, Milner to Chamberlain, 20 June 1900, with enclosure, Milner to Roberts, 17 June 1900; CO 417/292, Milner to Chamberlain, 27 June 1900, with enclosures, Roberts to Milner, 26 June 1900, and imperial secretary to Chamber of Mines, 27 June 1900. For the original list of 20 men, see MS/PRO/WO 105, Milner to Roberts (confidential), 27 June 1900; see also MS/JPL/ERPM, general manager, Hellman, to chairman and board of directors, 2 Aug. 1900, which provides a list of 20 men which differs somewhat from the one originally presented by the Chamber of Mines.

55. MS/BOD/Mss. Milner Dep. 230, Fiddes to Milner, 1 July 1900. The Railway Pioneer Regiment consisted of Rand workmen and artisans, men necessary to repair and extend the railway network.

56. Ibid.

57. MS/PRO/CO 417/292, Milner to Chamberlain, 11 July 1900, with enclosure, Milner to Roberts, 5 July 1900.

58. MS/NAM/Roberts, Ms. letterbook, vol. 3, Roberts to Milner, 6 July 1900.

59. MS/NAM/Roberts, Ms. letterbook, vol. 3, Roberts to Milner, 6 July 1900; and see MS/JPL/ERPM, miscellaneous correspondence, Mr Hellman to chairman of the board, 2 Aug. 1900.

60. MS/NAM/Roberts, 'Letters from Milner, 1898—1920', Milner to Roberts, 30 July 1900.

61. MS/PRO/CO 417/291, Milner to Chamberlain, 20 June 1900, with enclosures; *African Review*, 23 (395) 16 June 1900, p. 378; 24 (401) 28 July 1900, p. 133; (410) 29 Sept. 1900, p. 457. See also MS/PRO/CO 417/293, Milner to Chamberlain, 22 Aug. 1900, with enclosures; MS/TAD/PSY 49, Mackenzie to 'MS Chief, A Hdqs', 2 July 1900.

62. MS/PRO/CO 417/292, Milner to Chamberlain, 1 Aug. 1900, with enclosure, 'Circular A', 13 July 1900, which was sent to all Uitlander committees.

63. MS/PRO/CO 417/291, Milner to Chamberlain, with enclosure, Milner to governor of Natal, 16 June 1900.

64. MS/PRO/CO 417/292, Milner to Chamberlain, 1 Aug. 1900, with enclosure, private secretary of Natal to governor of Natal, 14 July 1900. See also CO 417/293, Milner to Chamberlain, 22 Aug. 1900, with enclosure, Milner to governor of Natal; *African Review*, 24 (410) 29 Sept. 1900, p. 443, where it notes that over 1,100 Indians had been registered in Durban by late August.

65. *Cape Times*, 31 Aug. 1900.

66. MS/PRO/CO 417/294, Milner to Chamberlain, 10 Oct. 1900, with enclosure, O. Walrond to Milner, forwarding 'High Commissioner's Circular D', 5 Oct. 1900. See also CO 417/292, Milner to Chamberlain, 1 Aug. 1900, with enclosure, secretary of Natal to governor of Natal (private), 14 July 1900; and *Cape Times*, 5 Oct. 1900.

67. MS/PRO/CO 417/292, Milner to Chamberlain, 1 Aug. 1900, with enclosures.

68. Johannesburg Gazette, 27 July 1900; OP/CC/Cape Government Railways, p. 3.

69. *Cape Times*, 1, 8, 9 and 10 Oct. 1900; MS/PRO/CO 417/295, Perry to Chamberlain (confidential), 31 Oct. 1900, with enclosure, proceedings of meeting of CRC, Cape Town, 9 Oct. 1900.

70. MS/PRO/CO 417/295, Perry to Chamberlain (confidential), 31 Oct. 1900, with

enclosure, proceedings of meeting of CRC, Cape Town, 9 Oct. 1900; CO 417/292, Milner to Chamberlain, 10 Oct. 1900, with enclosure, honorary secretary of central registration committee to Milner, 4 Oct. 1900. For registration, see *Cape Times*, 3 July, 8 Aug. and 8 Oct. 1900; and *African Review*, 24 (410) 29 Sept. 1900, p. 443.

71. MS/PRO/CO 417/295, Perry to Chamberlain (confidential), 31 Oct. 1900, with enclosure, Roberts to Milner, 13 Oct. 1900. This order was also sent to the governor of Natal, the directors of the railway at Cape Town and Natal, and GOC lines of communication, Natal and Cape Town. See MS/NAM/Roberts, Ms. letterbook, South Africa, 1899—1900, vol. 8.

Seven

The 'Johannesburg Republic'

*War is much too serious a thing
to be left to the military.*
Georges Clemenceau

On the eve of the conquest of the Rand, Milner at the Cape, and Roberts with his army poised to take the Transvaal, considered how best to set things in the new colony in the 'right direction'. For Milner this meant using the period of military rule to establish a new political and social order. 'The greatest advantage of conquest is that it gives you a clean slate', he wrote to Roberts on 25 May. 'The great advantage of the period of Military government . . . is that it gives us time to lay the foundations of that government, wh[ich] is to succeed it, carefully'.[1]

To set things in the 'right direction' on the Rand, it was necessary to appoint the right civilian advisers to assist the new military governor, Colin Mackenzie, for poor advisers could well give 'things a twist in the wrong direction'. Roberts suggested creating five departments and placing each under the leadership of an army officer, with a civilian adviser.[2] On 18 May, the director of military intelligence in the Transvaal, Major Francis Davies, wired the former president of the local South African League, J. Douglas Forster (now working in the civil branch of military intelligence in Cape Town) and asked him to come north. He was to bring with him Samuel Evans of Ecksteins (who had served Milner well in the early months of the war), as well as Wilfred Wybergh (another former president of the SAL), W. F. Monypenny of the *Star*, and a man named Linton.[3] Evans and Forster were on the Rand in time to negotiate the transfer of power between Dr Krause and General Lord Roberts.

While still at Kroonstad in the Free State, Roberts and his staff began to consider who should fill the posts at Johannesburg. Sam Evans was chosen as financial adviser; Wybergh as mining adviser; and Francis Davies would be left behind to head the Johannesburg police. Milner suggested appointing J. Emrys Evans, who had been vice-consul at Pretoria, as financial adviser instead of Sam Evans, and he was sent for by Roberts. Sam Evans then took the ill-defined post of civil commissioner. Monypenny became the director of civil supplies and Forster became Mackenzie's legal adviser.

Milner concurred with these appointments and in fact felt that these men would be 'excellent as originators', but, because they had 'great private interests to be looked after', they would not want to stay in government service after the war.

The high commissioner also suggested that A. Mackie Niven and St John Carr be sent for and that they, along with Sam Evans and W. Wybergh, serve Mackenzie in the capacity of a committee for municipal affairs. It was only when the new military governor asked for Friedrich Eckstein to be sent to Johannesburg that the high commissioner balked, arguing that he could not sanction it because other mining magnates had previously been denied permission to go north.[4]

The men chosen to help Mackenzie mould the new social order had all played prominent roles in the agitation and negotiations that led to the war, and all were willing to use the power vested in martial law to attain their long sought-after goals. They were also prepared to accept the posts because they were convinced that they were the best men for the jobs.

In the early months of the war the reformers, who had for years dreamed of little else than imperial rule in the Transvaal, imagined themselves and their colleagues installed in various posts expected to become available in the colonial administration. T. R. Dodd, a member of the SAL and secretary of the UC, informed Forster in January 1900 that, while it was 'rather sickening to have to speak of such things', the reformers had 'large claims' on the 'gratitude of the Country' and, therefore, had the right to discuss their futures in the Transvaal government. Wybergh concurred: 'The question of these appointments is . . . a very important one, and though of course it would be very improper to discuss these matters with an outsider, we need not be squeamish about speaking of them among ourselves'. And in the following months they did speak of such things, deciding who among them were fit to be advisers to the high commissioner and to sit in some future cabinet or legislative assembly. Wybergh suggested names for membership of a cabinet — Sam Evans, J. Douglas Forster, William Dalrymple, Thomas Dodd, William Hosken, William St John Carr, A. Mackie Niven, Charles Mullins, H. A. Rogers and himself — with Fitzpatrick as 'prime minister'. Although it was a cabinet that would have 'sufficient prestige and popular support', Wybergh felt that the bestowal of some 'alphabetical distinctions' upon its members would enhance their prestige with the 'multitude'. In planning their own futures, they firmly opposed recruiting 'distinguished men' from England to govern the Transvaal[5] — an option Milner later had no choice but to adopt.

While Milner was naïve to have believed that the 'great private interests' of these men would dampen their political ambition, he was suspicious enough of the military and its advisers to send his imperial secretary, Fiddes, to the Transvaal as Roberts's political adviser. The least he could do was be 'negatively useful' by 'preventing blunders and jobs',[6] though, on a more positive note, he was supposed to make recommendations on civilian matters.

By the time Roberts's army marched onto the Rand about 60,000 people, less than half of them white, were living between Krugersdorp and Boksburg. Probably half the whites lived in or near Johannesburg but, as a result of the series of deportations, very few were British. Instead, the white population consisted mostly of burghers and their dependants, refugees from the Cape and Orange Free State, and foreigners, some of whom entered the Republic after the war began to fight alongside the Boers. Of the blacks, close to 15,000 lived in or near the city, while about that number resided in the compounds of the now idle mines.[7] Most were still on the Rand because they had had no choice but to stay and work. Most too, expected a significant liberalization of 'native policy' with the arrival of the British army. The combination of oppression and raised expectations made them restive.

The transition from Boer to British rule had been relatively peaceful. Still the British were prepared for trouble, expecting to find the district peopled by a 'low class foreign element', riotous blacks and a volunteer special police force made up of criminals and potential traitors. The first order of business, then, was to ensure that law, order and peace prevailed. All arms were to be turned in — over 2,000 rifles were collected in the first weeks — residential passes secured, an oath of neutrality taken and a curfew observed.

Initially the special police were kept on, though as soon as possible the military commissioner of police, Davies, raised a temporary military police force from the battalions in town. The Fifteenth Brigade were assigned garrison duty for Johannesburg and its environs and implemented Davies's order to 'turn all [the] natives out of town and confine them to their locations and mine compounds'. On the reef the mine police continued to operate as before, maintaining order and peace. A military tribunal was established, under Major C. R. M. O'Brien of the East Lancashires, while a chief magistrates court was set up under Captain V. Ferguson of the South Wales Borderers. Between the two courts, over 1,300 cases were heard in the next ten months. In July a native court was created, which in the next few months heard over 1,400 cases and dispensed 'speedy justice'.

At the same time Major W. A. J. O'Meara, who had been intelligence officer in the besieged Kimberley, became acting burgomaster. Left £40,000 in debt by the departing Rust en Orde Commission, Johannesburg's financial future looked no rosier, for O'Meara was unable to enforce payment of debts and fines because there were no civil courts. Legally, too, tenants who refused to pay rent were covered by a proclamation announced at the beginning of the war by Kruger which was aimed at protecting the burgher poor from the *rentier* class. But to keep the situation from getting worse, Mackenzie ordered that vacant houses could no longer be occupied without the permission of the local authorities and that furniture — for which there had been a thriving market earlier — was not to be moved without the consent of its owner and the government. Meanwhile he confidentially instructed his legal adviser, J. D. Forster, to select the 'more pressing cases' of what he considered illegitimate house occupation, and he would have the squatters 'ejected . . . by military escort'.[8]

A second concern of the new administration was the provision of food, fuel and clothing for the civilian population, though the director of civil supplies, W. F. Monypenny, was at least as interested in helping British merchants re-establish themselves in Johannesburg. He began by setting maximum prices, issuing permits to market gardeners so that they could enter and leave the city, licensing businessmen and traders, and closing all bottle stores, 'kafir eating houses' and bars. He also ordered all customs duties on grain, meat, forage, vegetables, fruit, butter, sugar and preserves to be removed as soon as railway haulage limitations were lifted.[9] This latter measure was a direct descendant of the agitators' pre-war demand for the abolition of import duties on foodstuffs and other necessities, a reform predicated on the need to lower the cost of living, and the wages, of Randites.

By August Johannesburg had run out of supplies. Grain was being delivered from army headquarters in Pretoria and white residents were reduced to eating horse meat, which by September was 'exceedingly dear'. The Rand's shops were poorly stocked as a result of earlier looting and commandeering of goods, reluctance on the part of owners to reorder supplies, the disruption of production and distribution because of the war, and the earlier embargo on goods entering

Lourenço Marques. The shortage of supplies made it imperative that goods be brought up from the coast to feed the existing population, the military and any Randites who might be permitted to return. But not just any method of reprovisioning the district could be devised. Monypenny and his friends were anxious to formulate a scheme that would prevent 'foreign firms' becoming the beneficiaries of the reconstruction of the Rand.[10] This was certainly in keeping with the views of the British merchants in exile, who found the presence of Germans and Jews in business on the Rand particularly distasteful. They were also angry that the profits from the high price of goods in Johannesburg accrued to the non-British merchants who had stayed on, 'supplying the enemy' on the Rand, during the first eight months of war.[11]

Mackenzie and Monypenny would have acted upon this prejudice had they been given the chance. The military governor was quite willing to 'withdraw [the] trading licences' of any merchants who had traded with the Boers and were likely to benefit from the reopening of businesses when the refugees returned. Fiddes, however, pointed out to the Johannesburg administration that the companies in question had been well within their rights to carry on business during the period of Boer rule and could not, therefore, be legally interfered with. In the meantime, as soon as the railway lines were secured, three trains a week brought in food and rationing began.[12]

In order to re-supply the Rand so that the refugees could return and business and industry could reopen, Monypenny devised a plan whereby merchants at the ports would buy goods and turn them over to the Imperial Military Railway (IMR) for shipment inland. As they were expected to purchase the supplies with their own capital, the government planned to retail the goods quickly in order to reimburse the merchants who would otherwise develop cash-flow problems. It was estimated that it would take four to five weeks to get the required 6,000 tons of supplies into the district. Of this amount, 2,000 tons would go on sale immediately, while the rest would be stored in the city. This plan, then, was meant not only to resupply the district but to ensure that all the merchants would start business at the same time, thereby 'secur[ing] fair play to the refugee merchant[s]' at the coast.[13]

As the plan was implemented, it became even clearer that the scheme would be more than 'fair' to British merchants. For a start, trade was funnelled through colonial ports to bypass the wholesalers at Delagoa Bay, who had previously accumulated vast stockpiles of goods there on the assumption that the railway line between Lourenço Marques and Johannesburg would be the first to reopen. Furthermore, merchants resident in Johannesburg — and most were non-British — found it difficult to remit money to the coast, which was needed to buy a share of the 6,000 tons of supplies. The loyalist merchants at the coast had no such problem — a situation about which the administration privately expressed its pleasure.[14]

As the supplies were being shipped inland, Roberts's order to cancel the return of the refugees was issued. Monypenny's plan thus became obsolete. Now, instead of Uitlander merchants restarting operations, as expected, the military went into business supplying civilians, for the goods from the coast were 'taken over' and sent to military depots for distribution. Henceforth, the director of civil supplies became the purchaser of goods at the coast, though a few local merchants were licensed to import goods from the colonies. In the months this system operated, Monypenny managed to make a profit of £30,000 on sales of £140,000.[15]

Because the re-provision programmes were never very successful, food was both scarce and expensive throughout the rest of 1900 and well into 1901. An informal market thrived, with, it was said, only fresh milk being truly regulated by Monypenny's price controls. One measure devised to deal with this 'black market' was to fine, jail and/or deport any merchant discovered selling at prices above the official maxima.[16]

Another measure to regulate the movement of goods and prevent residents supplying Boer commandos in the countryside was to make it illegal to remove food from the city. Even mine officials were not permitted to take supplies beyond the city limit without permission. Later in 1900 the administration took this one step further by having a wire fence built around the city. By December it was complete: it was now 'impossible for anyone to take food to the enemy', a local correspondent for the *African Review* boasted that month. Soon, though, the futility of the effort became apparent. One of the 'funniest bit[s] of mis-calculation', wrote the correspondent in the new year, was the erection of the fence, whose various entrances were heavily guarded: as 'nobody . . . look[s] after the fence', all one had to do was throw things over it.[17]

Monypenny's provisioning scheme was neither popular nor effective, especially in the face of attacks on railways which disrupted resupply efforts. The reconstruction of the local economy was slowed because raw materials were scarce and inadequate supplies made it impossible for mine managers to employ men to 'de-water' the mines.[18] At the end of the year Mackenzie felt the situation was so bad that he had no option but to limit the distribution of food to burghers, foreign consuls and men in the Rand Rifles — a corps of civilian soldiers whose membership was restricted to British subjects. In other words, Government Notice 212 of 12 December 1900 meant that foreign civilians could no longer buy food at government-run shops. As a result the German consul at the Cape complained that all the Germans on the Rand — some 3,000 he estimated — would starve or be forced to leave. Because, in his words, they had 'very much furthered the British cause by helping to protect and keep intact the property of British subjects' on the Rand, he felt the action unjustifiable.[19]

In an attempt to pacify the 'outraged consuls', Fiddes had Lord Kitchener (who replaced Roberts as commander-in-chief in late November) modify the notice so that the 'privilege' of obtaining food was extended to foreigners who were certified by their consuls as being 'fit and proper persons to enjoy it'. The general was reluctant: had not the shortage of goods on the Rand developed because 'Peruvians' and 'foreign Jew ringleaders' had bought up the food in order to sell it 'when [the] railway failed'? In the end he changed the notice to include 'respectable' foreigners, but privately warned the consuls not to abuse their right to issue certificates of character, for if they did, they would debar themselves from making representations in the future. Fiddes doubted that Kitchener's warning would be taken seriously and felt that the 'object of the Proclamation [would become] nugatory'.[20]

Milner, who was more concerned about the complications which the war had brought with Germany, expressed his worries about the diplomatic ramifications which arose from Mackenzie's action. He wired Kitchener:

> It is difficult to think what imperative military reasons can exist for starving all foreigners out of Johannesburg, and unless there are such reasons it is most desirable to avoid the trouble in which the virtual expulsion will involve us. . . . Especially in view of the probable prolongation of the war it is most necessary to avoid causes of quarrel with Foreign Powers.[21]

And well Milner might have worried, for just as his warning was sent to Kitchener, the German government was making representations to Salisbury. It wanted more information about events in Johannesburg and implied that the military there wanted to see the whole German community deported. When these accusations reached Kitchener, he defended Mackenzie's action by stating that the Germans on the Rand were being treated no differently from any other group of people. In any case, the notice had been 'greatly modified' so as to provide food to the 'respectable foreign population'.[22]

And shortages continued. While Milner's staff may have believed that the British on the Rand suffered as much as the foreigners, it is unlikely that they did. Since all British men on the Rand were forced to join the Rand Rifles and since membership in the corps gave them access to government shops, it is more likely that it was the foreigners who went without, or paid extraordinarily high prices for what they found. When scarcity continued on into 1901, the German representative asked for an extension on the right to import food, but, because this went against an earlier policy designed to protect the interests of British merchants in exile, the request was denied.[23] Food, then, was a weapon used by the administration and its Uitlander advisers to remove people from the district who were deemed to be unfit and improper, and to assist in the formation of a new Anglo-Transvaal where British merchants would be pre-eminent.

The Rand administration also had to devise ways of dealing with the destitute. Charles Vincent, who had worked for the Temporary Relief Committee in Johannesburg throughout the first eight months of the war, was appointed to supervise all charitable aid. While the Temporary Relief Committee continued to assist the few British paupers who remained, the military took over the feeding of poor burghers, foreigners, and Boer refugees from the south. By July there were at least 5,000 families on the relief roll. Meanwhile in Johannesburg, as in Pretoria, the military began to make plans to return Republican sympathizers to their homes and to remove as many burgher dependants from the cities as possible.[24]

From the beginning, the reformers wanted someone other than Vincent to supervise aid. They suspected his politics because he remained (albeit feeding the British poor) on the Rand during the war. They also thought his aid 'too liberal' and believed that he 'pauperized' the burghers. Furthermore, his scheme was deemed too expensive, costing the military close to £2,500 a month to aid the destitute.[25] A campaign against him and his staff was begun. The press accused him of favouring the Boers because he had auctioned off unclaimed Uitlander goods for their benefit. That he had been ordered to do so by the military escaped attention. The press also complained that dependants of the enemy were receiving assistance while the British went without, but ignored the fact that Vincent had previously been concerned solely with the destitute British in Johannesburg and that the government, not him, had decided to provision burgher families. Soon he and his staff were forced to resign.[26]

While the Uitlander leadership would have preferred to have had Revd Kelly of the Present Help League brought to the Rand to take over relief, a military man, Major Cavaye, was appointed. Under his direction, relief rations were made 'just sufficient for health and no more'. People needing additional food were expected to purchase it, thus inducing them to 'work, to earn some money and so enabling them to live better than their less enterprising neighbours'.[27] Meanwhile, Vincent was given the job of escorting Boer dependants from the city and the few British still in need of aid were added to the military's relief roll. The demands on the new scheme continued to grow and the number of depots grew from two in Johannesburg in October 1900 to 13 along the reef by May the following year. From August 1900 to January 1901 inclusive, no less than 3,500 people received monthly assistance, though the figure climbed to over 5,000 in the following month. At the end of the period of British military rule, in May 1901, nearly 1,000 people were receiving aid each day.[28]

Public works projects were instituted for the destitute. One of the first of these was a clothing factory, where women sewed clothes which were sold to residents at cost price. By September the military had reopened the Masonic Hotel, which it ran primarily for the purpose of giving employment to the unemployed, but it soon began to take in civilian boarders. About the same time a job register was started to bring employers and job-seekers together. Meanwhile, private charity continued to assist the poor and concerts and other events were held in or near the city to raise money. Reports of these extravagances did not go unnoticed by the refugees at the Cape.[29]

The administration also turned its attention to crime and vice. Within weeks of taking office as legal adviser, Forster drafted a notice which made it punishable in terms of martial law to live off immoral earnings. Pursuing the goals of the social reformers of the pre-war years, Mackenzie now made it possible to imprison and deport pimps and prostitutes. The latter had little legal protection, for their expulsion from houses and from the city itself was justified as 'purely a military matter'.[30]

Upon taking control of the Rand, Mackenzie felt that his most serious problem was the 'native question'. In the following months he adopted the philosophy of the industrialists, taking a firm line with the black population. It was only months later that there was any liberalization of policy, but when that happened, it was accompanied by rationalization of the system of control.

The administration began by trying to pacify the riotous and looting Africans. The mine police, now under control of the British army, continued to operate as they had for the Boers. New passes were issued to Africans, as many had destroyed theirs when the British army marched onto the Rand. Government compounds were established to receive Africans without proper papers. There they worked for 9d a day, breaking stone in order to buy the 5s pass which would enable them to go out daily to look for other work. For a while the mines were able to recruit labour from the compounds, but soon Captain Baldwin (temporary superintendent of 'native affairs') put a stop to this because he felt it favoured some mines over others. Thereafter, most blacks went to the IMR, which was then constructing sidings and laying tracks along the reef.[31]

Like the earlier bosses and the Rust en Orde Commission, those now in power sought to eliminate the illicit liquor traffic. Mackenzie, adopting the view of his advisers, argued that the reason the trade had never been stamped out before was because the 'late Administration levied heavy fines and took an immense amount in bribes' from the dealers. Mackenzie's men would instead gaol the illicit liquor sellers. One man, for instance, was sentenced to six months' imprisonment for selling a bottle to a black man, while another was gaoled for two years for manufacturing alcohol.[32]

The administration also took the unusual and controversial step of importing special agents — previously members of the 'Illicit Liquor Gangs' — to trap dealers on the principle of 'converted poacher best gamekeeper'. The importation of Messrs Chadwick and Izdebski, experienced detectives from Kimberley, no doubt helped too. These measures, as well as the continued raids by the mine police on locations in search of 'kafir beer', resulted in some notable early successes.[33]

Meanwhile, the administration started a licensing system to control the licit sale of liquor to whites. A special commission, under Major Macpherson, was appointed to issue the licences and set prices — but it revealed its ignorance (or deceit) by giving the notorious 'illicit liquor king', Nathanson, a licence to sell in mid-1900. Restrictions on the sale of alcohol continued, though, for no beerhalls, pubs or bars were permitted a licence and, after 10 September, restrictions were imposed on the sale of liquor to non-commissioned officers and men. For those allowed to trade in alcohol, the overriding goal of Anglicizing the Rand was not to be ignored: Fiddes told the licensing commission in early 1901 that 'reliable British . . . firm[s]' were to be given preference.[34]

Obviously Mackenzie's duties extended to the mines as well. Wybergh was appointed mining engineer, while E.W. Buxton, ex-mining editor of the *Star*, was appointed mining commissioner at Krugersdorp. 'De-watering' was the first priority as the IMR began delivering coal to those mines needing it to run pumps. Most of the men working on the mines had been there during the Boer occupation, for no new or more 'loyal' men could be permitted to return from the coast as yet.[35]

The mine police force, too, was comprised of the same men as those who guarded the properties under the Boers. They seem to have easily shifted their allegiance, probably because they saw themselves as servants of the industry and not the government. For several weeks they continued to carry out their normal duties, adding to them the guarding of property threatened by looting British soldiers and volunteers.[36] No one doubted that they were still needed, yet the industrialists were no longer willing to foot the bill and, in July, a deputation from the industry met Mackenzie and asked for the cost of maintaining the police to be assumed by the army. The military declined and the mine police force was disbanded. Although mine owners in the outlying areas felt the need for protection most, by mid-July all the owners — who had been told that they were now responsible for policing their own properties — formed a new private force, which drew almost exclusively upon the membership of the old mine police. District leaders, such as Chevallier and Smith, were permitted to retain weapons in order to equip the new force. Meanwhile, the Railway Pioneer Regiment arrived and were divided into six units along the reef. In this manner, men with experience and familiarity with the mines and compounds served the industry as it waited to restart operations.[37]

Such were the more mundane matters with which the reformers had to deal. But these did not keep their minds sufficiently occupied and they began to concern themselves with long-term political changes. Intent upon implementing policies aimed at creating a city and society supportive of the mining industry and an Anglo-Transvaal, they used their positions in Mackenzie's administration and the powers vested in martial law to undertake reforms.

A few weeks after the reformers arrived in the Transvaal, Fiddes followed them north. At Elandsfontein he bought a copy of the recently-started *Johannesburg Gazette* and received his first inkling of what was happening. He wrote to Milner: 'It was a farce! Everything being started at once, anyhow, and in a big way. Customs duties to be suspended by a Mil[itary] Gov[ernor]; 3 courts constituted. Cape Law to be administered (and procl[a]m[ation] repealed on this point on the same day it was issued); a Star Chamber established with power to examine anyone on oath about anything.'[38]

Fiddes immediately began to do battle with the newly-established ruling clique in Johannesburg. One of his first acts was to induce Roberts to reverse a proclamation which placed a fine on burghers in districts where raids took place and which forced prominent burghers to ride back and forth along the railway line as hostages. H. C. Hull, a member of the UC and a recruiter for colonial regiments during the war, but now in the Transvaal, had apparently rushed through this order to 'make things hot' for Sammy Marks (a businessman who had made a fortune in Kruger's republic) and others whom the reformers disliked. Disgusted, Fiddes labelled the scheme 'not a military precaution, but a weapon for private spite'.[39] Immediately upon seeing Monypenny's pronouncement on the abolition of customs duties, Fiddes telegraphed Johannesburg to ask Mackenzie to suspend it. He then informed the high commissioner that he thought the 'extreme Uitlanders' were 'rushing things according to their wishes, having apparently captured the [Military] Governor'. He concluded by noting that they regarded the 'place as [the] Capital' and were acting as if 'Johannesburg [were an] independent state'.[40]

Fiddes soon discovered that the bone of contention between him and the reformers was that, in their eyes, he was a 'partisan of Pretoria'. Moreover, they saw his reversal of Monypenny's tariff policy — which he insisted upon, not because he or Milner opposed free trade, but because he was enforcing Milner's own order not to enact any long-term reforms immediately — as evidence that he thought Pretoria ought to remain the capital of the new Transvaal colony.[41]

From at least June the reformers pressed for the transfer of the capital to Johannesburg. Throughout the middle part of the year they canvassed support and sides were taken in the struggle over which city would be the capital of the colony and, ultimately, of a 'United South Africa'. The men surrounding Mackenzie, of whom the most outspoken were Monypenny and Sam Evans, favoured Johannesburg and argued the urgency of the matter: the 'plunge' must be taken now, not in six months, by which time it would be too late. Fitzpatrick advised them not to harass the authorities, for Chamberlain was about to fight an election campaign and was in no position to have people shouting anti-capitalist slogans and using this issue as an example of preferential treatment of the Randlords. Despite his urging, their scheming continued. Further, Evans tried to persuade Fitzpatrick to use his considerable influence with the high commissioner to force Fiddes to curtail his obstructive behaviour.[42]

Warned of Evans's request, Fiddes wrote a long telegraph to Milner, explaining his position and the situation as he saw it. Fiddes thought that Mackenzie's advisers would continue to press for the transfer of the capital and that they would continue to ask whether decisions were to be made in Johannesburg or Pretoria. He complained that Wybergh had been appointed acting commissioner of mines on the staff of the military governor of Johannesburg and had the 'verbal authority to organise [the] mining department as a whole'. Fiddes objected to this because he thought that such power, together with the power to make policy decisions on any matter of importance, should rest with Pretoria. He concluded his telegram by appealing to the high commissioner for his support and noting, probably with some regret, that 'at present everything points to our rule being inaugurated by a bitter fight'.[43] After having so clearly laid out his fears, worries and strategy, he gave his telegram to Francis Davies, the military commissioner of police, to send to Milner. But this telegram, important as it was, was mysteriously 'lost' and did not reach Milner for what, for Fiddes, must have been an agonizing week. In the meantime he continued to do battle against the 'Uitlander clique' on his own.

Fiddes met privately with Wybergh, who confided that he wanted to see the capital moved to facilitate the fulfilment of his own and the other reformers' political ambitions. Would it not be easier, he reasoned, for busy professional men in Johannesburg to take a more active role in the colonial government if Parliament were located on the Rand? Indeed! This is precisely why those opposed to the move felt that it should stay in Pretoria.[44]

With this knowledge, Fiddes then had discussions with Sam Evans and Monypenny in an attempt to resolve their differences. At the meeting Monypenny only made matters worse by antagonizing Fiddes and, ultimately, Milner: he warned the political secretary that even if every member of the British cabinet wanted the capital to stay in Pretoria, the men of Johannesburg could and would 'prevent it'. While the 'British Government could govern [the] Transvaal without [the] Dutch', he warned, 'it could not [do so] without Johannesburg'. When reporting these threats to Milner, Fiddes added that it seemed that the 'Johannesburg people expect to rule [the] whole show' and would treat with contempt anyone, including himself, who was 'unwilling to be completely subserving to them'.[45]

When Milner discovered what was happening, his reaction was firm: the 'high jinks' of the 'Uitlander *camarilla*' were natural enough at first, but they must be stopped, for this 'kind of thing is *not government*'. He disapproved of the reformers acting as though they could 'combine the role of government officials and political agitators'. He supported Fiddes's actions because he objected to any 'attempt to make great organic changes in the first moments of our occupation', but advised his secretary to avoid, as far as possible, any 'unpleasantness with worthy people who [are] temporarily too big for their boots'. Meanwhile, he called in Fitzpatrick and told him to 'get these people in hand and to sit on them'.[46]

The reformers thereupon tried to use their influence in London to induce *The Times* to agitate for the transfer of the capital to Johannesburg. But Milner, more adept at these power games, succeeded in persuading Chamberlain to give a 'hint' to *The Times* so that it would not play into the hands of the reformers and this hint was taken. But the Uitlanders did not give up. Next they persuaded Roberts to allow them to launch two local newspapers to publicize their cause. Milner, who chose not to explain his real reasons to Roberts, then asked that permission be rescinded, which it was. The issue of the capital reverberated for months, but as Evans and Monypenny predicted, a delay would ensure that the idea would be stillborn. 'I was only just in time to get the thing right: it was a close shave', Fiddes told Milner.[47]

This attempt to move the capital demonstrated clearly the extent of the reformers' quest for political power for their class. Milner and Fiddes's opposition was not based upon any hostility to Uitlander élite involvement in Transvaal politics. On the contrary they would come to depend on it. Instead, Milner was uncomfortable with military rule and the loss of control it meant to him. Martial law was to him both 'unintelligent and unpredictable' and the men who ran military government, 'very bad administrators'. Anxious to maintain control of the reconstruction process, he ordered that no major changes be implemented during the period of military rule and this would certainly have included a shift of the colonial capital. The 'longer they are at the helm the greater the mess we shall have to wipe up afterwards' was Milner's verdict on military government.[48]

Fiddes's victory in resisting the transfer of the capital was total and it made him powerful enemies. But this did not keep him from challenging other policies put forward by the reformers who were intent on consolidating Uitlander rule. In mid-July Monypenny and Sam Evans, 'who seem to hunt in couples', called on him with several proposals. One of their crucial schemes was based on the premise that, as they would cause 'great confusion', the old Republican political divisions should be abolished. Instead, the new colony ought to be redivided into four areas, each with its own administration. The first step toward implementing this new structure, they urged, was to place the gold districts under Mackenzie. As Fiddes later explained to the high commissioner, 'having failed to make Mackenzie Gov[ernor] of the whole of the Transvaal, they w[ou]ld like to make him gov[ernor] of the part wh[ich] interests them and the rest might rip'.[49]

Fiddes also decided to 'clip the wings' of the Uitlanders' 'Star Chamber', a body designed to enquire into 'acts of rascality — thieving, looting under the guise of commandeering and so forth' which occurred during the first eight months of war. While he might have tried to ensure that 'no political vengeance' was 'wreaked' by the court, it is certain that its members took up pre-war political issues and persecuted political enemies, such as Special Commandant Schutte.[50]

In most cases, it was the reformers' excesses, rather than their philosophy, to which Milner and Fiddes objected. For instance, they too supported the abolition of import duties on staples, but felt that Monypenny's decision was premature. The relegation of foreign merchants to a secondary position behind British merchants was an outcome they desired, but were unwilling to obtain by illegal means. Similarly, when the Johannesburg administration hit upon the idea of deportation as a solution to some of its thornier problems, both Milner and Fiddes favoured the scheme, though the high commissioner worried about its more serious diplomatic ramifications.

On the day Johannesburg fell to Lord Roberts, the railway employees in the city went on strike and one railway official notified the military that the men would not work for the British. Within hours it was decided that the striking workers and their families would be sent back to Europe and, within a week, notices were posted in the railway yard stating that the people would be given 72 hours to leave after being instructed to do so. In the following weeks, some 1,400 people were sent down to the coast and on to Europe. When the high commissioner heard of this he was 'delighted'. On the other hand, when the Foreign Office received its first complaint from the Austrian government, concern was expressed in Whitehall: 'this looks like the beginning of the trouble we are pretty certain to have over this matter'.[51]

Notes

1. MS/NAM/Roberts, 'Letters from Milner, 1898—1920', Milner to Roberts, 25 May 1900; and MS/NAM/Roberts, Ms. letterbook, South Africa, vol. 2.
2. MS/NAM/Roberts, Ms. letterbook, South Africa, vol. 2, Roberts to Milner, 24 May 1900. See also Samuel Evans to Fitzpatrick (private), 3 Nov. 1899, in Duminy and Guest (eds) 1976.
3. MS/JPL/Forster, Forster to Dalrymple, 8 Dec. 1900; for a slightly different list, see Amery (ed.), vol. 6, p. 588 ff.
4. MS/NAM/Roberts, 'Letters from Milner, 1898—1920', Milner to Roberts, 25 May 1900;

MS/NAM/Roberts, Ms. letterbook, South Africa, vol. 2, Roberts to Milner, 24 May 1900; MS/PRO/WO 105/34, Roberts to Milner, 4 June 1900 and WO 105/20, Milner to Roberts, 4 June 1900.

5. For this and other interesting exchanges, see Dodd to Forster, 3 Jan. 1900, Wybergh to Forster (confidential), 26 Feb. 1900, and Forster to Dalrymple, 6 March 1900, in MS/JPL/Forster. See also Wybergh to Fitzpatrick (confidential), 13 Dec. 1900, and Sam Evans to Fitzpatrick (private), 3 and 22 Nov. 1899, in Duminy and Guest (eds) 1976.

6. MS/BOD/Mss. Milner Dep. 170, Milner to Chamberlain (confidential), 27 June 1900, and Milner to Chamberlain, 6 June 1900. See also MS/NAM/Roberts, Ms. letterbook, South Africa, vol. 2, Roberts to Milner, 2 June 1900; MS/NAM/Roberts, 'Letters from Milner, 1898−1920', Milner to Roberts, 5 June 1900; and Fitzpatrick to Samuel Evans, 8 Aug. 1900, in Duminy and Guest (eds) 1976. Milner wanted at least 'one civilian with brains up there at the beginning of the new order'.

7. For population estimates, see MS/PRO/CO 417/296, Milner to Chamberlain (confidential), 5 Dec. 1900, with report from military governor of Johannesburg to political secretary, 26 Nov. 1900; MS/TAD/PSY 49, military governor to political secretary, 11 Oct. 1900; MS/RHO/O'Brien; African Review, 24 (403) 11 Aug. 1900, p. 191; MS/TAD/SNA/2, report of Johannesburg pass office for week ending 16 June 1900.

8. MS/TAD/LAJ 1/9, Mrs A. Badenhoop to Maj. C. R. M. O'Brien, 6 June 1900, and legal adviser to Mrs A. Badenhoop, 7 June 1900; LAJ 3/155, confidential circular signed by Mackenzie, 19 July 1900; LAJ 2/68; MS/TAD/PSY 52, Fiddes to Mackenzie; MS/NAM/Roberts, 'South African War, 1899−1900', vol. 1, Roberts to Marquess of Lansdowne (secret), 30 May 1900; African Review, 23 (390) 12 May 1900, p. 196; MS/BOD/Mss. Milner Dep. 175, Milner to Roberts (confidential), 10 May 1900 (copy), and Roberts to Milner, 16 May 1900.

9. Johannesburg Gazette, 4, 8, 15, 16 and 29 June and 2 July 1900.

10. MS/TAD/PSY 49, Mackenzie to 'MS Chief', 18 Aug. 1900; PSY 52, political secretary to military governor, 22 Aug. 1900. See also, MS/JPL/Johannesburg, correspondence 1900, file 3, sanitary superintendent of health inspector's department to acting burgomaster, 6 Sept. 1900; MS/NAM/Roberts, Ms. letterbook, South Africa, vol. 5, Roberts to Milner; Amery (ed.) 1900−9, vol. 6, p. 596.

11. African Review, 24 (407) 8 Sept. 1900, p. 335; (410) 29 Sept. 1900, p. 445. See also Fitzpatrick to Sam Evans, 8 Aug. 1900, in Duminy and Guest (eds) 1976.

12. MS/TAD/PSY 52, political secretary to military governor, 22 Aug. 1900; and see Amery (ed.) 1900−9, vol. 6, p. 596.

13. MS/TAD/PSY 49, Mackenzie to Fiddes, 8 Oct. 1900, and see Mackenzie to Fiddes, 11 Oct. 1899; MS/PRO/DO 119/469, Fiddes to Milner, 9 Oct. 1900, and Milner to Fiddes, 11 Oct. 1900; MS/PRO/FO 2/536, CO to FO, 14 May 1901, with enclosure, Milner to Chamberlain, 10 April 1901, with report by Mackenzie to secretary to Transvaal administration, 21 Feb. 1901; African Review, 25 (413) 20 Oct. 1900, p. 98; (416) 10 Nov. 1900, p. 211; Cape Times, 4 Oct. 1900, p. 4; and Fitzpatrick to Sam Evans, 8 Aug. 1900, in Duminy and Guest (eds) 1976.

14. MS/TAD/PSY 52, Fiddes to Mackenzie (confidential), 11 Oct. 1900 (draft); Cape Times, 27 Aug. 1900; African Review, 24 (410) 29 Sept. 1900, p. 457; 25 (412) 13 Oct. 1900, p. 52; (416) 10 Nov. 1900, p. 210. The problem remained, though, of how to ensure that the loyal British merchants at Delagoa Bay were not hindered by the new scheme and restrictions (MS/PRO/WO 105/34).

15. MS/PRO/FO 2/536, CO to FO, 14 May 1901, with enclosure, Milner to Chamberlain, 10 April 1901, forwarding report from Mackenzie to secretary to Transvaal administration, 21 Feb. 1901. See also for various restrictions on the sale of goods in Johannesburg, MS/TAD/LAJ 14/933; MS/PRO/FO 2/531, CO to FO, 29 Jan. 1901, with enclosures; Johannesburg Gazette, 2 Nov. 1900 and 15 Jan. 1901; African Review, 25 (415) 3 Nov. 1900, p. 172; (423) 29 Dec. 1900, p. 465; Amery 1900−9, vol. 6, p. 596.

16. MS/TAD/LAJ 1/34, legal adviser to Mackenzie, 30 June 1900 and Mackenzie to legal adviser, n.d. See also LAJ 4/232, legal adviser to Mark Odis; Johannesburg Gazette,

5 July 1900; *African Review*, 25 (413) 20 Oct. 1900, p. 98; and MS/PRO/DO 119/4, H. Strakosch to Milner, 13 July 1900, with enclosed letter from A. Brakhan, 30 June 1900.

17. *African Review*, 26 (427) 26 Jan. 1901; 25 (421) 15 Dec. 1900, p. 389; *Johannesburg Gazette*, 11 June, 2 and 28 July, 5 Sept., 2 and 13 Nov. 1900; MS/TAD/PSY 50, Mackenzie to chief of staff of Pretoria, 18 July 1900, for smuggling.

18. Fitzpatrick to Sam Evans, 8 Aug. 1900, in Duminy and Guest (eds) 1976; see also *Cape Times*, 10 and 17 Sept. and 22 Oct. 1900; *Johannesburg Gazette*, 4 Aug. 1900; *African Review*, 24 (409) 22 Sept. 1900, p. 418; 25 (411) 6 Oct. 1900, p. 26; and (423) 29 Dec. 1900, p. 465. C. Nina Boyle of St Monica's felt it was Monypenny's interference that 'nearly reduced the town to a state of famine'.

19. MS/PRO/FO 2/531, CO to FO, 29 Jan. 1901, with enclosure, Milner to Chamberlain (confidential), 27 Dec. 1900, forwarding correspondence, including consul-general for Germany at Cape Town to Milner, 18 Dec. 1900.

20. MS/PRO/FO 2/531, CO to FO, 29 Jan. 1901, with enclosure, Milner to Chamberlain (confidential), 3 Jan. 1901, forwarding letter from Kitchener to Milner, 21 Dec. 1900. See also enclosure, Milner to Chamberlain (confidential), 27 Dec. 1900, forwarding report from political secretary to Milner, 20 Dec. 1900. For further information on food shortages, see *Cape Times*, 23 Nov. 1900; and MS/NAM/Maxwell, P. Maxwell to father, 27 Dec. 1900.

21. MS/PRO/FO 2/531, CO to FO, 29 Jan. 1901, with enclosure, Milner to Chamberlain (confidential), 27 Dec. 1900, forwarding letter from Milner to Kitchener, 20 Dec. 1900, and Kitchener to Milner, 21 Jan. 1901. The Germans and British were already quarrelling. See Pakenham 1979, p. 253.

22. MS/PRO/FO 2/345, FO to Lascelles, 20 Dec. 1900 (draft); FO 2/418, FO to WO, 22 Dec. 1900 (draft), with letters between WO and Kitchener, 17, 18, 28 and 29 Dec. 1900, and Milner to Chamberlain (copy), 29 Dec. 1900. See also FO 2/531, CO to FO, 29 Jan. 1901, with enclosures. On the other hand, Kitchener denied seeing the proclamation before Mackenzie had issued it and when he did he thought it 'unwise'.

23. MS/PRO/FO 2/534, CO to FO Office, 2 April 1901, with enclosures; and see MS/NAM/Maxwell, P. Maxwell to mother, 25 Jan. 1901.

24. MS/NAM/Roberts, Ms. letterbook, South Africa, vol. 4, Roberts to Botha, 20 July and 23 Aug. 1900. For more on the movement of burgher dependants, see Pakenham 1979, pp. 449–50; MS/PRO/WO 105/28, 'A list of families sent from [Johannesburg] 8 Aug. to 10 Aug. 1900'; *Cape Times*, 23 Nov. 1900; *Johannesburg Gazette*, 15 Aug. 1900. See also MS/BOD/Mss. Milner Dep. 230, Fiddes to Milner (private), 5 Aug. 1900; MS/TAD/PSY 49, military governor of Johannesburg to C-in-C, 18 June 1900, with notes on file.

25. MS/PRO/FO 2/536, CO to FO Office, 14 May 1901, with enclosure, from Milner to Chamberlain, 10 April 1901, forwarding report from Mackenzie to secretary to Transvaal administration, 21 Feb. 1901; MS/BOD/Mss. Milner Dep. 230, Fiddes to Milner (private), 5 Aug. 1900; *Cape Times*, 22 Aug. 1900.

26. *Cape Times*, 22 Aug. and 22 Oct. 1900; MS/TAD/PSY 49, military governor of Johannesburg to C-in-C, 18 June 1900, with notes on file.

27. MS/PRO/FO 2/536, CO to FO Office, 14 May 1901, with enclosure, Milner to Chamberlain, 10 April 1901, forwarding report from Mackenzie to secretary to Transvaal administration, 21 Feb. 1901; MS/BOD/Mss. Milner Dep. 230, Fiddes to Milner (private), 5 Aug. 1900.

28. *Cape Times*, 22 Oct. 1900; MS/PRO/FO 2/536, CO to FO, 14 May 1901, with enclosure, Milner to Chamberlain, 10 April 1901; Amery 1900–9, vol. 6, pp. 596–7.

29. *Johannesburg Gazette*, 4, 20, 24 and 27 July, 24 Aug., 4, 6 and 7 Sept. and 7 Nov. 1900. For refugees' complaints, see *Cape Times*, 17 Aug. and 2 Nov. 1900.

30. MS/TAD/LAJ 4/200, draft 'VR Notice' with comments; and LAJ 2/88, legal assistant to Mackenzie and Mackenzie to legal assistant, 15 July 1900.

31. MS/TAD/PSY 52, Capt Baldwin to military governor, 7 Nov. 1900; *Johannesburg Gazette*, 18 June 1900; Warwick 1983, p. 133.

32. MS/RHO/O'Brien, vol. 1, p. 134, 22 June 1900; MS/TAD/LAJ 1/34, Regina vs. Schwaff;

LAJ 17/1053, F. Nielson to military governor.

33. MS/BOD/Mss. Milner Dep. 183, Milner to Fiddes (private), 25 June 1900, (typescript copy); MS/RHO/O'Brien, vol. 2, p. 7, 12 July 1900; Amery 1900—9, vol. 6, p. 591.

34. MS/TAD/PSY 53, Fiddes to Lieut. Kersey, 5 Jan. 1901. See also *Johannesburg Gazette*, 4 and 5 June, 18 July and 10 Sept 1900; *Cape Times*, 23 July 1900; and *African Review*, 24 (401) 28 July 1900, p. 128. For licensing see MS/TAD/LAJ 6/413, president of liquor commission to legal adviser, 6 Sept. 1900, and confidential circular from legal adviser to all magistrates, 11 Oct. 1900. For complaints re Nathanson, see MS/TAD/PSY 52, Mackenzie to Fiddes, 10 Aug. 1900, and notes on file.

35. *Johannesburg Gazette*, 5 June, 3 July 1900; *Cape Times*, 6 July 1900; *African Review*, 24 (400) 28 July 1900, p. 128.

36. For looting by British, see MS/JPL/Mine Police, 'Rapports quotidiens', esp. 17, 20—22 and 30 June 1900.

37. MS/JPL/Mine Police, 'Correspondance des chefs de groupes, no.6', 7—9 July 1900; 'Rapports quotidiens', 10 July 1900; *Johannesburg Gazette*, 12, 13 and 25 July 1900; *Cape Times*, 17 July 1900; MS/TAD/PSY 49, Mackenzie to C-in-C, n.d. See also Amery 1900—9, vol. 6, p. 391.

38. MS/BOD/Mss. Milner Dep. 230, Fiddes to Milner, 1 July 1900.

39. Ibid. Ironically, Marks had played some part in halting the destruction of the mines.

40. MS/BOD/Mss. Milner Dep. 230, Fiddes to Milner, 24 June 1900.

41. MS/BOD/Mss. Milner Dep. 230, Fiddes to Milner, 1 July 1900.

42. MS/PRO/DO 119/446, H. W. Struben to Milner, 9 June 1900, and secretary to the HC to Struben, 15 June 1900; MS/BOD/Mss. Milner Dep. 230, Fiddes to Milner, 4 July 1900 (originally sent 27 June 1900); and see Sam Evans to Fitzpatrick, 22 Nov. 1899, Fitzpatrick to Monypenny, 16 July 1900, Fitzpatrick to Evans, 18 July 1900, and Fitzpatrick to F. Eckstein, 26 May 1900, in Duminy and Guest (eds) 1976.

43. MS/BOD/Mss. Milner Dep. 230, Fiddes to Milner, 4 July 1900 (originally sent 27 June 1900).

44. MS/BOD/Mss. Milner Dep. 230, Fiddes to Milner, 1 July 1900, Milner to Mackenzie, 2 July 1900. See also Fitzpatrick to Monypenny, 16 July 1900, in Duminy and Guest (eds) 1976. For the opposition argument, see MS/PRO/DO 119/446, H. W. Struben to Milner, 9 June 1900.

45. MS/PRO/DO 119/469, Fiddes to Milner, 29 June 1900. See also Fitzpatrick to Wernher, 4 July 1900, in Duminy and Guest (eds) 1976.

46. MS/BOD/Mss. Milner Dep. 183, Milner to Fiddes (private), 25 June 1900 (typescript copy).

47. MS/BOD/Mss. Milner Dep. 230, Fiddes to Milner (confidential), 13 July 1900. See also MS/PRO/CO 417/291, Milner to Chamberlain, 6 July 1900, and Chamberlain to Milner (draft), 15 July 1900; MS/PRO/DO 119/469, Fiddes to Milner, 7 July 1900, and Milner to Fiddes, 8 July 1900; DO 11/510, Milner to Roberts, 13 July 1900, and Roberts to Milner, 13 July 1900. See also Fitzpatrick to Evans (private), 18 July 1900, in Duminy and Guest (eds) 1976; *The Times* (London) 6 April 1901; MS/RHO/O'Brien, vol. 2, p. 33, 7 Sept. 1900, for further discussions of the capital.

48. Milner to Mrs Montefiore, 22 Aug. 1900, cited in Galbraith 1983, p. 75.

49. MS/BOD/Mss. Milner Dep. 230, Fiddes to Milner (confidential), 13 July 1900.

50. MS/BOD/Mss. Milner Dep. 230, Fiddes to Milner (confidential), 13 July 1900; for 'Committee of investigation assembled at Johannesburg', see MS/TAD/PSY 50 and PSY 73.

51. MS/PRO/FO 2/326, Milbanke to FO (confidential), 23 Aug. 1900, with notes on file. For deportation of NZASM workers, see FO 2/413; OP/GB/Deportation Commission, FO 881/7619X; MS/PRO/WO 105/15 and WO 105/27.

Eight

Anglicizing the Rand

What have I done for you,
England, my England?
W. E. Henley

It was a cold winter's eve in June 1900 when engine driver R. H. Baragwanath and his fellow Cornishman, Richard Williams, sat at dinner at Moss's Grill Room in central Johannesburg. Baragwanath had come to the city from Heidelberg the previous day to buy supplies for the mine where he worked as a caretaker. He was tired and no doubt frustrated, having discovered that although he could purchase supplies, he was not permitted to remove them from town. Two British soldiers entered the café and demanded to see the papers of the 40 or so men in the room. After the soldiers left, Baragwanath and Williams thought no more about the incident until they left the café and were met in the street by a dozen soldiers who ordered them to halt and remain where they were. As the rest of the diners left the restaurant, most were ordered to join the Cornishmen and all were marched off to gaol.[1]

About the same time, Mr Atlas, a Russian grocer and building caretaker, was preparing for bed. He had been a special policeman in Doornfontein when the Rust en Orde Commission governed the city, but now he was back at home in Fordsburg. He was tired, partially undressed and anxious to get to bed, when he heard a noise in the road. On leaving his house to investigate, he was ordered by a British soldier to remain where he was in the street. After 15 minutes in the cold night air without a shirt or jacket, he was allowed to re-enter his house to get a coat and was then marched off to Market Square to join the 200 or so restless and cold prisoners gathered there.[2]

That night and the next, all over the city — though mainly in the central district and western suburbs where the working poor and foreigners lived — men faced similar treatment at the hands of British soldiers. The vast majority of the 450 or so men arrested on those two nights were foreigners. In fact, it seems that Baragwanath and Williams were the only British subjects held and that their detention was a mistake caused by the former's foreign-sounding name. The rest were Italian, Austro-Hungarian, German and Russian, with a few Swiss, Greeks, Scandinavians and Americans thrown in. Some had been roused from their homes by a knock on the door, while others had been arrested in the street. No explanation had been offered as they were hauled away; some were not even asked their names.[3]

British soldiers at Johannesburg captured and broke up Boer weapons, yet continued to feel unsafe. This picture was taken in July 1900, the month of the Racecourse Plot and subsequent deportations (*Africana Museum, Johannesburg*)

With the fall of Johannesburg, pro-Boers were sent to the coast by train (*Africana Museum, Johannesburg*)

Colin MacKenzie, military governor of Johannesburg, with his staff and advisers, 1900 (*Africana Museum, Johannesburg*)

After the fall of Johannesburg, a concentration camp for Boers was opened at the racecourse nearby (*Africana Museum, Johannesburg*)

Some months later Mackenzie justified the action of his men by explaining that there were some 20,000 people in the city who were 'in the main markedly hostile'. Mackenzie went on to explain that:

> many men had come to the Transvaal during the war and been armed by the Boers, and with the lower class of adventurer and rabble inseparable from the mining community already in town, formed a most dangerous element, which was ripe for rising. To cope with this state of affairs there was not one policeman. British soldiers, drawn from the garrison, hastily improvised as police, with a few ex-Transvaal detectives, had to be depended upon to watch the attitude of that hostile population.[4]

The military commissioner of police, Francis Davies, reported that a man named Lorenz, supposedly a leader of a movement aimed at overpowering the British garrison, was in hiding in Johannesburg. The 'rising' was to take place on 14 July, while the British officers were at a race meeting to celebrate Bastille Day.[5] Hence, the 'racecourse plot'.

Captain Astell, head of the CID, explained that the conspirators planned to hide in the trees surrounding the grandstand with the intention of killing all the officers and men in attendance. The shooting was to be a signal to the rest of the conspirators to rush the police stations and government buildings in town, to rob the banks and to pillage Johannesburg.[6]

Following their arrests, the men were marched to gaol. Many were without a change of clothes, some suffered from the cold, but no one was allowed to return home to collect his things. There they remained with poor sanitation and crude sleeping arrangements. Food consisted of bread and water and a plate of soup for dinner. When individuals asked to see their consuls, they were laughed at and their requests denied.[7]

While the men were being held, Davies called together the consuls of the United States, Germany, France, Sweden and Norway. Each was furnished with a short statement of the 'facts of the case' and they seem to have agreed that the military's action was warranted. They were asked to vouch for any men they considered trustworthy and of good character and some 75 detainees were duly released.[8] That more were not released was the result of bad luck and careful planning.

Because it was wartime, some consuls were absent and many men were represented by consuls other than their own. For example, the Russians and Greeks were under the care of the French consul, while his Austrian counterpart represented the Italians. When he left the city in the midst of these proceedings, the Italians and Austrians were passed over to the German consul. As a result, the consuls were unfamiliar with many of the men in their care and were, therefore, unable to vouch for their good character. Similarly, many of the names presented to the consuls were unclear or incomplete. The sergeant who took the names of the Italians did not, for example, understand that it was their custom to provide their surnames first, so a name such as Bruno Giuseppe appeared on the list as Giuseppe B., with dozens of other Giuseppes, Giacomos and Giorgios.

In other cases the names of suspected conspirators never reached the lists at all. For instance, the Danish consul, Baersveldt, who was in charge of the Belgians, Hollanders and Danes, was not notified when the Dane, Andersen (a member of the mine police), was picked up. For this reason, the consul did not attend Davies's meeting with government representatives. Later when he was told that a Hollander had been arrested, he went to Davies's office and checked the list 'carefully'. Andersen's name did not appear and other names on the list, he claimed, were 'distorted and unintelligible'. Andersen's case was not unique, for the names of a number of those arrested were left off the list, thus making it impossible for their representatives to intercede for them.[9]

There is also reason to believe that some consuls were willing to go along with the administration's plans. For instance, when the German consul visited the gaol and was asked by some Austro—Hungarians to do what he could to have them released, he told them that only Englishmen and Frenchmen were eligible for release — a story which was inconsistent with Davies's statement that consuls had the power to have anyone of good character freed. Similarly, the French consul gave the fairly far-fetched excuse to the Russian prisoners that he had no time to deal with them after handling the Frenchmen's cases.[10]

On Sunday 15 June, those men who had not been released were marched to the railway station under the gaze of soldiers with fixed bayonets. A few found third-class compartments but the majority were placed in open cattle cars. They were given no covering and had only bread and tinned meat to eat during their four-day journey to East London. All were anxious about their personal effects — which were left behind — and many about their families who remained on the Rand without any means of subsistence. The journey, and particularly the cold, nearly killed some of the men.[11]

At East London they were classified according to nationality and by their ability to support themselves. Some, such as Baragwanath and Williams, were temporarily paroled and allowed to move about freely. Some were provided with assistance, which angered the refugees who had recently been removed from the relief rolls.[12] But 250 were less fortunate: they were loaded onto a barge, covered with a tarpaulin and put aboard the *Hawarden Castle*.

The *Hawarden Castle* left East London on 19 June with about 750 people — some of them Dutch families expelled because of their connection with NZASM. The ship sailed to Simonsbay, where it remained for four days. While it was at anchor, many of the men wrote to the high commissioner to beg for his assistance. Some 30 Russians complained to 'Millner' that they had been arrested without explanation and had been denied the opportunity to prove their innocence. Another group of about 60, most with Italian names, wrote a similar letter: they had been arrested without being informed of the cause, and had been sent away from Johannesburg even though 'nearly all of us have got their [sic] families'. They explained that they were in the 'saddest position', not knowing their fate and being 'pennyless [sic] and without any clothes'. 'We are innocent and fathers of families', they concluded. The Dane, Andersen, took this opportunity to write to his consul at the Cape, but it was several days before the letter was received and by that time the ship had sailed for Europe. Nothing was done for the men aboard the *Hawarden Castle* when it was at the Cape, though one consul had managed to convince the ship's captain that the passengers ought to be allowed the use of cutlery, a luxury previously denied them.[13]

Upon reaching Flushing in the Netherlands, the majority of the deportees disembarked. Most had only the clothes on their backs. About 160 men were taken on to London, where the ship was met by 50 men and officers of the Horse Artillery and another 25 from the Metropolitan Police. For some hours they attempted to block the entry of the 'undesirables'. Eventually they were allowed to enter and were escorted as far as the dock gates before being permitted to pass on into the city. Before their arrival, the Colonial and Foreign Offices had renounced all responsibility for them and the Home Office had made it clear that it was not going to use 'coercive measures' to force them to leave the country. But most of them eventually did leave, though the handful who did not were kept under surveillance by the police for as long as they remained in the country.[14] Within a few weeks the other Johannesburg deportees arrived in Europe. Five entered Britain aboard the *Manhattan* and the only two to leave the *Braemar Castle* in England in September were Baragwanath and his friend Williams.[15]

Deportations continued. There was a second sweep of the town between 21 and 25 July, when men were again detained without explanation and given no time to collect their property. After waiting in gaol for about two weeks, they were among the 80 or so men who were deported from southern Africa and sent to Europe in August. At least ten such ships landed in Europe in September, all of which carried 'undesirables' in addition to people expelled because of their NZASM connection.[16] About the same time some notorious Boers and pro-Boers were rounded up and sent away. Emmanuel Mendelssohn, the proprietor, and W. Bruce, the managing director of the *Standard and Diggers' News*, as well as Leo Weinthal, who was also associated with the newspaper, and ex-commandants Schutte and Krause, were all sent south.[17]

Milner was ambivalent about the deportations: 'I don't mind how many ruffians are sent to Europe', he wrote to Fiddes in late July, 'though even this, I think, might be done a little more systematically'. What he did not like was being 'suddenly . . . called to say what is to be done with 50 Italians, who have been sent down, and put on board, mixed up with Netherlands Railway people, and who protested loudly, and very naturally, against being landed at Amsterdam'. His main concern, though, was to have the people in the Transvaal devise a better way of deciding just who was to be sent down. 'My view', he explained, 'is that, if a man is so dangerous that he cannot be left at liberty in the Transvaal, he ought either to be in choko there, or if a foreigner, sent to Europe'.[18] Milner, already full of pan-Afrikaner conspiracies, did not want them at the coast, where he thought they would have a deleterious effect on the Boer population. Burghers ought to be kept under surveillance in the Transvaal and away from the inflammable Cape population, he explained. 'Even the atmosphere of East London is beginning to be infected', he told Fiddes in mid-August. 'Do you think you have trustworthy advisers as to who is, and who is not, dangerous?' he asked.[19]

In response to Milner's concerns, Fiddes had a word with Roberts, Mackenzie and Maj. Gen. J. G. Maxwell, the military governor of Pretoria. Thereafter Maxwell sent a list of people he wanted to deport to Fiddes before implementing the expulsion orders. As for Mackenzie and his men, their methods of choosing who to deport seem to have remained much the same. Turning to the issue generally, Fiddes tried to explain to the high commissioner that:

> the question is difficult; for in the future interests of the country we ought to clear out a lot of the foreigners, and the actual pretext for doing so in many cases is not easy to find. In fact, we must use the arbitrary will of the Military for the purpose. They mean well according to their lights, and are, as they think, playing up to us; so it wouldn't do to discourage them or find too much fault with their proceedings.[20]

No one in the administration, from Milner downwards, seems to have questioned the morality of such social engineering. Indeed, the only concerns raised were how to avoid complications at the Cape and how to deal with the diplomatic ramifications in Europe. As the high commissioner explained to Fiddes:

It is impossible to conceive [of] anything more haphazard than the way in which several hundred foreigners were bundled out of Johannesburg on the 13th [sic] of July. We shall, I expect, hear more of this when [the] 'Hawarden Castle' gets to Europe. It is of course most desirable to get rid of the foreign riff-raff, but we must not have European complications over it.[21]

Indeed, foreign complications soon began to arise. While no one questioned Roberts's right to rid his battlefield of dangerous individuals, the press and governments on the continent and in the United States did feel that the methods used had been unduly harsh. Consequently, soon after the ships reached Europe, formal complaints and requests for compensation were presented to the British government. Adding to the confusion was the claim made by many on the *Hawarden Castle* that they were British subjects. The War Office wanted Milner and Roberts to forward 'full details' about the circumstances under which these people had been deported.[22]

Roberts then asked Mackenzie and others in the new colonies to forward 'accurate details' to him as the War Office commanded. In the meantime, Roberts proposed telling London that the military had only done what was necessary: 'the men were too dangerous to be left in the Transvaal and Orange River Colony, and . . . the High Commissioner objected to having them in the Cape Colony'. Even while diplomatic pressure mounted in London, Whitehall had to be content with Roberts's assurance that no one had been sent away 'without good cause'.[23]

On 30 August a memorandum was prepared in the Foreign Office which outlined the information that had been gathered about the deportations thus far: more ships carrying deportees were due to land in Europe soon and claims from exiles already landed were reaching the Foreign Office daily. Meanwhile the Colonial Office repudiated any share of responsibility for the affair. Most distressing for all the officials at home was the fact that they had 'no statement of why the military deported them'. Already the War Office was coming to realize that it would probably have to pay compensation to some exiles and had begun to consider the creation of a commission to adjudicate claims.[24]

As complaints continued to come in, the War Office again asked Roberts to supply details: 'We understand privately that [a] certain proportion of undesirables were expelled from South Africa for being mixed up in a plot against [the] Government [which] was discovered at Johannesburg in July last. If so furnish details.'[25] The cable was again forwarded to Mackenzie, who was requested to provide the War Office with an immediate answer. At the same time the men on the Rand were expected to provide full details about individual cases of deportation.[26]

Finally, on 17 September, Roberts sent his formal report to the War Office. This report of the 'plot' differs little from the evidence the military later presented to the Compensation Commission; it referred to the conspirators' plans to capture the garrison, to the military's moves to thwart the plan, to the foreign consuls' coordinated approval and to the immediacy of the need to deport the men. Roberts explained that the high commissioner had been kept fully informed of events. While a letter with fuller details was forwarded by mail, this report was meant to satisfy the War Office. In the interim Roberts assured London that he fully supported the action taken and that the 'precautions' had met with the 'hearty approval' of people living in Johannesburg.[27]

The wire was forwarded to the Foreign Office for the information of the staff who had to deal with the complaints being filed by the deportees and their governments. Later, when Roberts's full report (which included statements by Mackenzie and Davies) arrived, it too was forwarded to the Foreign Office. It was only then, three full months after the event, that the officials at home were to learn that the 'plot' had been, according to Davies, 'engineered principally by certain foreigners of the lower class and by well known agitators of socialist tendencies, who acted in concert with the Transvaalers still on commando. The agitation extended to the Dutch of Fordsburg and Vrededorp who, though personally not so active as the lower foreign element, were certainly prepared to join any rising which might take place.' The men in Whitehall now also learned that the police had been told by their supervisors to arrest anyone suspected of being implicated in the plot as well as any who were 'known to be in Johannesburg without any visible means of support or settled occupation'. They were told that the consuls had been forewarned by the Johannesburg administration that 'certain persons who were known to be disaffected' were going to be arrested.[28]

Meanwhile, deportations continued and complaints and requests for information and compensation continued to arrive at the Foreign Office. In November Baragwanath's MP threatened to take up the matter in parliament, but held off until he could get more information about the Cornishman's case.[29] With pressure mounting and with Roberts's, Mackenzie's and Davies's reports in hand, the imperial government privately debated how to handle the affair.

In late October Chamberlain expressed his view that publishing a report about the plot would serve no useful purpose. Salisbury disagreed: the German government intended to press for compensation for its people, who, it appeared had been expelled for no apparent reason. Therefore, the prime minister argued, it would be in Britain's interest to explain fully the reasons for their deportations.[30]

Chamberlain's reluctance may have been motivated in part by a report written by H. Bertie in the Foreign Office, which argued that the military's statement about the affair read as though the deportations had been 'rather lightly treated'. Bertie went on:

> One of the main complaints of the expelled people is that they had no kind of trial and therefore [had] no means of showing that they were harmless; but the [military's] report says that all who might be able to give a satisfactory account of themselves were to be released. There is [also] a gradual passage in the report from the arrest of conspirators firstly to that of 'undesirables' generally, and secondly to that of all persons without settled occupation or visible means of support. The notice to the Consuls speaks of the 'disaffected'.[31]

Chamberlain may also have been reluctant to publish details of the plot, for he had known since early July that the military, 'for political as well as military reasons', intended to 'deport certain indigent persons and suspicious characters whose presence in South Africa constituted a source of danger'.[32] Nevertheless, Lansdowne at the Foreign Office agreed with Salisbury that publicizing the plot would act as a defence against claims for compensation. In mid-December a parliamentary paper appeared giving details of events in Johannesburg on Bastille Day 1900.[33]

While officials in London tried to deal with the problems created by Mackenzie's deportations, events in the Transvaal continued to provide an excuse for more deportations. In Pretoria in early August a plot to kidnap Roberts was foiled by the military. The intention had been to turn him over to a Boer commando. While Roberts informed the high commissioner that he should not be alarmed, Milner was explaining to Fiddes that he hoped that it would give them an 'opportunity of putting under lock and key some of the worst rascals'. Few, though, were arrested, and only Hans Cordua, the suspected ringleader, was tried, found guilty and shot.[34]

Three months later another conspiracy was discovered in Johannesburg, this time to murder Roberts and his officers while attending a Sunday service at St Mary's. Historians tend to agree with the Italian consul who described it as a 'tragic comic story of a plot'.[35] Nonetheless, it served a purpose. While evidence suggests that the ringleaders were Austrians and Germans who worked on the Robinson mine,[36] when the arrests were made, five Italians, four Greeks, one Frenchman and one Russian were held. One, Mr Gambini, reportedly already known for his Anglophobia, was, according to Police Commissioner Davies, the 'principal mover'. The Italian consul thought the police's theories doubtful and felt instead that it was the administration's general distrust of Italians that was behind the arrests. No bombs were found, there was too little evidence to take them to trial, so the suspects were not held. They were deported instead.[37]

By Christmas it had been decided in London to form a commission to deal with the claims of the deportees and their representatives. While the German government wanted an international board of inquiry to be established, the Foreign Office chose instead to appoint a committee made up of military men, a lawyer and the only British member of the Republican Volksraad, R. K. Loveday. The 'South African Deportation by the Military Authorities Compensation Commission' came into being in April 1901 and the Foreign Office warned prospective claimants that they should submit their requests for compensation by the 25th of that month.[38]

Behind the scenes preparations were underway. Roberts, upon his return to England, brought a full list of names of people thus far deported. As the claims were received, they were processed by the Foreign Office which sent the names of the claimants to South Africa where, it was expected, the military would prepare formal reports explaining why each individual had been expelled. The War Office, Foreign Office, Colonial Office and the commissioners assumed that the Commission would travel to Southern Africa to collect evidence, but Roberts and Kitchener opposed the idea and subsequently convinced the government of their view.[39]

From the first public sitting on 30 April, the Commission made it clear that a man's guilt was proven by his having been deported, otherwise, it argued, his consul would have attested to his good character and he would not have been expelled. In other words, a man was assumed guilty unless he could prove otherwise. Similarly, some deportations were assumed to have been justified because of the jobs the deportees held in Johannesburg. For instance, if a man were employed on the railway or at Begbie's armaments factory, he was presumed to be a belligerent and justifiably deportable. A man working on a mine operated *by* the Republic (such as the Robinson, the Bonanza or the Ferreira Deep) was assumed to be hostile to the British cause, while a man working on a mine operated *for* the Republic — i.e. under company management, such as the Wemmer, the Village Main Reef or the Ferreira — was not. A man who served in the special police force in town or the mine police as a protector of British property was not deemed to be hostile and was, therefore, not automatically deportable. Such principles were established only as the Commission took evidence and so claimants' requests for compensation were discounted only as they were presented.[40]

Between 30 April and 5 September there were 60 public sittings, followed by a recess of nearly two months, and then five sittings, the last held on 14 November. There were over 1,600 claims for compensation submitted, nearly 100 of which requested no specific amount of money. Many wanted compensation for unnecessarily harsh treatment while others sought money for loss of wages and liberty. The total amount claimed by deportees was nearly £1.3 million.[41]

As a result of problems arising from, first, the difficulty of collecting details from the military about individual deportations (not surprising considering such details had not really concerned the administration); secondly, the inability of claimants to travel to England to testify because of their poverty and the distance involved; and, thirdly, Maj. Gen. Sir John Ardagh's probable doubts (as prosecutor for the military) about the motives underlying the mass deportations, the Commission decided during the recess to settle a lump sum upon each government. In September Ardagh, who was also director of military intelligence in the War Office, initiated negotiations with the states involved and, by the end of October, the awards had been made. The total amounted to about 10 per cent of the original claim.[42]

Although the British government eventually paid over £100,000 to deportees' governments, this did not mean that the British government, the military or the Johannesburg administration publicly accepted any wrongdoing. The compensation, as Ardagh explained when awarding the money, was an act of grace on the part of the government. Had the 'plot' been allowed to ripen, he went on, there would have been wholesale bloodshed and, for that reason, the civilized world ought to be thankful that the men were deported. The Commission's report echoed his words: the Johannesburg authorities had 'reasonable ground[s]' for deporting those suspected of involvement in the various conspiracies.[43]

Publicly Mackenzie and his advisers had been exonerated. But privately there were, and remain, serious doubts about the existence of the racecourse plot. Certainly the deportees denied any knowledge of it, claiming that they had not even heard of the plot until they reached the Cape aboard the *Hawarden Castle*. The deportees' representatives before the Commission also questioned its existence. Dr Bisschop, representative of The Netherlands government, protested that not even Roberts's testimony provided the 'slightest proof' of its existence. Mr Lousada, the Austro—Hungarian representative, alleged that the only grounds for the arrests were that those arrested were foreigners. What sort of plot could it have been, he asked, when the 'knowledge of [it] was suspected to be in the possession of 374 persons?' It was a 'vaudeville plot' he told the commissioners.[44]

Even the Foreign Office and the Commission's prosecutor had serious doubts. Only in the case of Baragwanath, wrote a member of the Foreign Office staff, had 'reasonable grounds' for believing in the existence of a plot been established and, in that case, 'they are so weak that the War Office are quite ready to pay compensation equal to one-half the man's Rand earnings for the whole time the expulsion lasts'.[45] Ardagh could not have agreed more. In a secret minute he declared that he had never received any evidence of a plot, nor any information to suggest that, if a plot existed, 'any one person of those arrested was concerned in it'. In his 'private opinion', the accused had been treated with 'unjustifiable harshness' and deserved compensation, even though he argued against this before the Commission. For this reason, he found his position 'embarrassing'.[46]

On the one hand, there is reason to believe that a Boer commando was in the district in mid-July as asserted. It may or may not have been in communication with people in the city, though Boers certainly moved in and out of Johannesburg secretly throughout these months. Certainly, too, some officials in the city held a 'very blue view' of the British position there, worrying about 'anarchist plots for clearing off all the high officials'.[47]

On the other hand, there were other reasons for the administration wishing to be rid of as many 'undesirables' as possible. Certainly there was a scarcity of food, as Mackenzie reported. And, as Mr Lousada argued before the Commission, it was quite understandable that the military 'considered it desirable to reduce the number of the surplus population' on account of this 'insufficiency of food'. Ardagh agreed: when speaking of some deported miners he stated that they were 'simply devouring food, which was difficult to procure. It was a perfectly natural thing', he continued, 'for the military authorities at Johannesburg to get rid of all those indigent aliens'.[48]

Yet the administration had other, longer-term reasons for deporting Johannesburg's undesirables. From June 1900 onwards, Mackenzie's staff used deportation as a means of removing particular groups of people from the city and its environs. Quite naturally Boer agitators were marked for removal. Criminals were also dealt with by being sent south. But destitute foreigners, especially East-European and Russian Jews, were the primary targets. Had Mackenzie had his way, all 'four year burghers' — i.e. those men who had obtained burgher rights after the Jameson Raid — would have been sent away. He proposed that by removing them he could rid the city of 'some two thousand Peruvians and other low-class Jews', or 'in fact, all the criminal class'.

Instead of denouncing his anti-Semitism and his plan, Fiddes and Roberts concurred so long as it did not appear to be 'class legislation'. Fiddes explained to Mackenzie that the general thought that:

> no action should be taken against the Jewish population as a class nor indeed need the word 'Jew' be mentioned. But there is no doubt that the 'peruvians' are a wholly objectionable element, and the more of them that can be sent down the better. It is a matter for the Military and wherever you have reasonable grounds for suspicion against individuals they should be deported. . . . This measure and possible deportations under the head of 'military exigencies' ought to rid us of a considerable portion.[49]

From August onwards the local Transvaal administrations were expected to follow guidelines laid down by Milner. First, the cooperation of foreign consuls was to be obtained whenever possible, for surely they could not 'want to retain disreputable nationals. Failing this,' the high commissioner instructed, 'we must have [a] good prima-facie case for expelling any noxious individual'. Further, he wanted all deportees sent to their countries of origin, wished families to be kept intact, and asked for pregnant women to be excluded from deportation orders. He wanted the deportees to be given sufficient time to pack their things before being sent away and ordered the authorities to ship them down to the coast in batches, whenever possible. He also wanted advance warning of their arrival, so that his staff could arrange for their immediate transport to Europe. Again Milner was motivated by diplomatic considerations.[50]

Hence, all levels of the civil and military administrations seem to have agreed that deportation was a most effective way of ridding the Rand and, to a lesser extent, Pretoria, of the dangerous classes. Wartime conditions provided the excuse and the method with which to carry out these mass expulsions, a method peacetime could not have so easily provided. The apparent ease with which over 400 men had been removed in July gave impetus to the deportation movement, for those expulsions were only the beginning.

In January 1901 reports of mass deportations from Johannesburg again reached the outside world and at least 60 'deported foreigners' reached Durban that month. This was reportedly part of a 'general clearance' then under way in Johannesburg, and records indicate a sharp rise in the number of non-Hollander aliens arriving in Europe the following month.[51]

Estimates vary on how many people were actually deported in 1900/1. At one point, at the end of August 1900, there were reportedly 20 people expelled from the Rand daily. On the other hand, police commissioner Davies reported that only 48 people were deported from the city after mid-July. The other 1,300 who left in the latter part of the year were supposed to have done so voluntarily and with their consuls' approval. Similarly, Kitchener claimed that from the new year onwards there were no deportations from the Transvaal: after that date, all those leaving had to sign a declaration stating that they had no claims on the British government, a declaration which was meant to prove their willingness to leave.[52]

The whole concept of voluntary exile from the Rand at this point in time might be questioned. The case of Giovanni Bartulovich, a former employee at the munitions factory, serves as an example. While he apparently signed Kitchener's declaration upon leaving the colony, he later changed his mind and informed the British government that he wanted to qualify his statement. In fact, he asserted, he had been 'forced to leave' the Rand because he had found it impossible to find food. Davies responded by arguing that Bartulovich's departure had been the result of his consul not recommending that he be allowed to buy food. And, Davies added, 'there is no doubt that the Consul had good reasons for refusing'. But in the light of Kitchener's warning to consuls about their attesting to a man's good character, it is easy to believe that the decision to remain or to leave rested not with the individual or his consul, but with the military administration.[53] Also, it is difficult to understand why any large number of people wished to leave either the Rand or southern Africa, for neither the coast nor Europe offered a better alternative. Indeed, the refugees stuck at the coast were clammering to be allowed to go inland, and those who had previously gone to Europe were coming back. In fact, Milner was undoubtedly correct when he stated that their leaving the Rand because of restrictions on food sales in this period was 'virtual expulsion'.[54]

By and large Milner and Fiddes approved of the changes sought by Mackenzie and his advisers, from deporting undesirables to anglicizing Johannesburg commerce, but objected to their timing, their methods and, on occasions, their personalities and behaviour. Very early on Fiddes decided that, to gain control of the reconstruction process, he had to remove the Uitlander advisers from Mackenzie's administration. He began with Forster, the legal adviser. Milner agreed that Forster — not the most popular or trusted of men — had been a ludicrous choice as a legal adviser and, in July, Fiddes devised a scheme whereby Forster could be dismissed on the pretext that, since Roberts had recently acquired his own legal adviser, Mackenzie no longer needed one. Mackenzie was unwilling to follow Fiddes's instructions to 'get rid of Forster' and Fiddes had to write a letter explaining the new appointment himself. Fiddes's plan included getting Forster to return to the Cape, but he managed to remain in Johannesburg where he continued to serve as the vociferously anti-Boer correspondent for the *Pall Mall Gazette*.

Fiddes also wanted to rid the administration of Francis Davies, whom he suspected of devious behaviour in the 'lost' telegram episode in June 1900. He informed Milner that Davies ought to be released as soon as possible and replaced by E. R. Henry 'or any decent official'. In fact, Henry became director of civil intelligence, and later commissioner of police in the period of quasi-civil rule, or crown government, which followed Mackenzie's departure in May 1901.

Fiddes was not opposed to Wybergh's continued employment in the administration, but would have preferred him to have been transferred from Mackenzie's to Roberts's staff. A compromise was reached when Wybergh became acting commissioner of mines, for this was a post in the central administration but with its headquarters in Johannesburg.

Furthermore, if Fiddes was to gain control of the Johannesburg administration, he had to '[get] hold of the revenues'. 'We can't', he explained to the high commissioner, 'have the Republic of Johannesburg . . . administer its own finances and keep its balances, or her poorer sisters w[oul]d be very badly off'. He began by placing J. Emrys Evans in charge of finances, and later, when the post of 'collector of revenue' was created, it was placed under the control of Pretoria. Fiddes set about trying to find a 'business soldier-man' rather than an Uitlander to fill the post.

In August, Fiddes raised the question of Sam Evans's appointment with both Milner and Mackenzie. It was suggested that Evans be replaced by an appointee from Pretoria, but Mackenzie refused. Word must have reached Evans that Fiddes was proposing to replace him, for Evans soon approached Fiddes and explained that he did not particularly want to retain the post of civil commissioner. Fiddes agreed that it was best for Evans to resign and for the post to be abolished, so that it did not appear as though he had been dismissed.[55]

As the warm weather once again returned to the highveld, only three short months after the 'extreme Uitlander clique' had come to power, Fiddes managed to gain control of Mackenzie's administration. As he put it to the high commissioner: now 'Lord Roberts is at least Suzerain of the Johannesburg Republic and I am his "grand Vizier"'.[56] Yet these men, who had been active in pre-war politics and who helped Mackenzie for such a short time, had already established a tone of government (and initiated a programme) that reflected their pre-war goals and their willingness to use means justified by the ends. By the time they returned to private life, they had gone a long way towards Anglicizing Rand commerce, fostering industrial development, protecting the sanctity of private property and public morality, and creating a new society devoid of paupers, Jews and foreigners. These few months of Uitlander rule in the winter of 1900 were to leave a lasting mark on Johannesburg's 'clean slate'.

Notes

1. MS/PRO/FO 2/533, CO to FO, 25 March 1901, with affidavit from R. H. Baragwanath, 12 Oct. 1900. For the raid on Moss's Grill Room, see *The Times* (London) 14 Nov. 1901.
2. OP/GB/Deportation Commission, pp. 254—68.
3. *The Times* (London) 14 Nov. 1901. According to Maj. Luard, an 'exceptionally large number of persons were arrested in Fordsberg [sic], because that contained the largest

population of the poorest classes of foreign subjects and unskilled Boer labourers . .. It had a total population of 6,000, less than 100 of whom were British born'.

4. *The Times* (London) 14 Nov. 1901.

5. *The Times* (London) 14 Nov. 1901. In fact, Jan Saral August Lorenz and Marinus Johannes van Hoogestraten were captured along with 35 or so other men in the vicinity in this period. See MS/PRO/WO 108/303, Transvaal lists, nos. 3272—3499; and WO 108/304.

6. *The Times* (London) 14 Nov. 1901. There were various reports of how the police supposedly learned about the plot. The favoured explanation was that a girl, while secretly pro-British, was wooed by a burgher boy who told her of the plan. She then informed the local police. See *Cape Times*, 18 July 1900; and MS/RHO/O'Brien, vol. 2, 15 July 1900.

7. MS/PRO/CO 291/304, FO to CO, with enclosures; OP/GB/Deportation Commission, evidence, *passim*, MS/PRO/FO 2/533, CO to FO, 25 March 1901, with enclosures, and WO to FO, 2 March 1901, with report from Davies to Mackenzie. See also, FO 2/961, with report by Edward Rothfuch; and FO 2/414, with press reports from Vienna.

8. MS/PRO/WO 105/32, Roberts to secretary of state for war, 17 Sept. 1900 (draft), and see MS/PRO/FO 2/416, WO to FO, 17 Oct. 1900, which forwards reports from Roberts and Davies, with annexure 'C', 'Memorandum to consuls', 14 July 1900. See also *The Times* (London) 14 Nov. 1901, for the men released.

9. OP/GB/Deportation Commission, evidence, *passim*; MS/LHC/Edmonds, Box V/3/3, 'Memoirs: the intelligence division: the South African War, 1899—1902', p. 14; MS/PRO/FO 2/535, CO to FO, 25 April 1901, report by Con. Baersveldt, 13 Feb. 1901 (transcript). For at least two other cases of distorted spellings, see FO 2/961, WO to FO, 28 March 1902 re. Edward Rothfuch (Rutlifuch) and OP/GB/Deportation Commission, p. 284, Frederich Czapek (Burdrich Capek). See also *The Times* (London) 25 July 1901.

10. OP/GB/Deportation Commission, evidence, pp. 254—68, 279. See also, for consuls, MS/PRO/WO 32/8773, confidential memorandum, 11 Sept. 1900, with enclosures from Milner to Mackenzie, 12, 13 and 17 July 1900, and French consul-general to consul at Johannesburg (copy), 17 July 1900.

11. For scenes at the station, see OP/GB/Deportation Commission, evidence, pp. 172, 254—68; MS/PRO/FO 2/414, with enclosed press cutting; FO 2/533, WO to FO, 2 March 1901, with enclosure; FO 2/413, memorandum by F. Bertie, 29 Aug. 1900, re. 'Norwegians expelled from S. Africa'; FO 2/823, Edmonds to FO, 7 Sept. 1902, with enclosure; MS/RHO/O'Brien, vol. 2, 15 July 1900.

12. OP/GB/Deportation Commission, evidence, pp. 172, 259. Also MS/PRO/FO 2/533, CO to FO, 25 March 1901, with Baragwanath affidavit; FO 2/532, WO to FO, 14 Feb. 1901, with enclosed, commandant of East London to military secretary, AHQ, Pretoria, 7 Jan. 1901. For complaints, see MS/PRO/CO 417/293, Milner to Chamberlain, 22 Aug. 1900, with enclosure, Carter of Uitlander Committee at East London to private secretary to Milner, 15 Aug. 1900.

13. MS/PRO/FO 2/533, WO to FO, 2 March 1901, with enclosure, GOC lines of communication with South Africa to WO, 5 Jan. 1901, forwarding report from principal transport officer of naval transport, South Africa, 6 Jan. 1901. For letters and complaints, see MS/PRO/DO 119/414, 'Hawarden Castle' file; MS/PRO/FO 2/415, correspondence between Milner and consul-general for The Netherlands at Cape Town; OP/GB/Deportation Commission, evidence, p. 172.

14. For the voyage, see MS/PRO/FO 2/533, WO to FO, 2 March 1901, with enclosures; FO 2/414, enclosing press report from Vienna; for their arrival at Flushing, see FO 2/533, WO to FO, 2 March 1901, with enclosed report by J. C. Oughterson, 20 Sept. 1900; for their arrival in England, see *The Times* (London) 24 August 1900. For statements by the WO, HO and FO, see F0 2/413, HO to FO, 21 Aug. 1900, with enclosure, HO to WO, 21 Aug. 1900, urgent; and MS/PRO/WO 32/8773, confidential memorandum, 11 Sept. 1900. For those who remained in Britain, see MS/PRO/FO 2/413, HO to FO, 23 Aug. 1900, and FO 2/414, FO 2/415 and FO 2/416, forwarding police reports to FO.

15. MS/PRO/FO 2/414, HO to FO, with enclosure, New Scotland Yard to HO, 15 Sept. 1900; and FO 2/415, HO to FO, 25 Sept. 1900, with enclosure, chief constable's office in Bargate to HO, 21 Sept. 1900.

16. MS/PRO/CO 291/304, FO to CO, 22 Nov. 1900, with enclosed claims by three Austro-Hungarians; MS/PRO/FO 2/535, CO to FO, 25 April 1901, with enclosure, Milner to Chamberlain, 22 March 1901, forwarding memorandum from Davies to Mackenzie, 26 Feb. 1901; and FO 2/371, Mr Wolff to FO, 1 Oct. 1900, with enclosed letter from F. Mata, 30 Sept. 1900. For the arrivals and departures until August 1901, and information about deportees, see MS/PRO/WO 32/8773; MS/PRO/FO 2/413—18; FO 2/531—8; and FO 2/540.

17. MS/PRO/DO 119/469, Milner to Fiddes, 13 Aug. 1900; MS/PRO/WO 105/27, with enclosure, Roberts to secretary of state for war, 13 Sept. 1900. See also *The Times* (London) 18 Jan. 1902 for the trial of Dr Krause.

18. MS/BOD/Mss. Milner Dep. 184, Milner to Fiddes (private and confidential), 23 July 1900, (typescript copy).

19. MS/PRO/DO 119/469, Milner to Fiddes, 13 Aug. 1900; and see Fitzpatrick to Sam Evans, 8 Aug. 1900, in Duminy and Guest (eds) 1976. For Milner's fears of a pan-Afrikaner conspiracy, see Galbraith 1983. See also MS/BOD/Mss. Milner Dep. 184, Milner to Fiddes (private and confidential), 23 July 1900, (typescript copy).

20. Fiddes added, 'There is one difficulty on which I am going to write tomorrow for your advice and, I hope, assistance. We have a considerable number of Russian Jews with a sprinkling of foreigners other than Hollanders who certainly ought to be sent out of the country . . . [and] a small number of Italians who[m] we wish to get rid of'. See MS/BOD/Mss. Milner Dep. 230, Fiddes to Milner (private), 5 Aug. 1900. For Maxwell, see MS/PRO/DO 119/469, Milner to Fiddes, 13 Aug. 1900; and MS/BOD/Mss. Milner Dep. 230, Fiddes to Milner (private).

21. MS/PRO/FO 2/416, CO to FO, 25 Oct. 1900, with enclosure, Milner to Chamberlain (confidential), 3 Oct. 1900, forwarding Milner to Fiddes, 12 Aug. 1900.

22. MS/TAD/HC 79, file 131—2, secretary of state for war to the general in Cape Town, 24 Aug. 1900, with copy sent to the military secretary in Cape Town, 27 Aug. 1900. For claims and complaints, see *African Review*, 24 (413) 20 Oct. 1900, p. 84; 25 (422) 22 Dec. 1900, p. 422; *The Times* (London) 28 Aug. 1900; MS/PRO/FO 2/326, Milbanke to FO, 30 Aug. 1900; FO 2/413, memorandum by H. B., 28 Aug. 1900, and FO to WO, 28 Aug. 1900 (draft); MS/PRO/FO 2/416, FO to WO, 31 Oct. 1899 (draft); MS/PRO/WO 32/8773, memorandum and correspondence concerning deportation of undesirable aliens from South Africa, appendix 2, F. H. de Villiers, under-secretary of state in WO, to FO, 28 Aug. 1900; MS/NAM/Roberts, Ms. letterbook, South Africa, vol. 7, Roberts to Mackenzie, 17 Sept. 1900.

23. MS/NAM/Roberts, Ms. letterbook, South Africa, vol. 6, Roberts to military governors, Pretoria and Johannesburg, and GOC lines of communication, Cape Town, 27 Aug. 1900; MS/TAD/HC 79, file 131—2, 'Undesirable foreigners deportation', with enclosed, Lord Roberts to HC, 27 Aug. 1900; and see MS/PRO/WO 32/8772, Roberts to secretary of state for war, 27 Aug. 1900. Milner, of course, knew exactly what was going on in Johannesburg (WO 105/32, Roberts to secretary of state for war, 17 Sept. 1900, enclosing a report to Milner, 22 July 1900).

24. MS/PRO/FO 2/423, memorandum, 30 Aug. 1900.

25. MS/PRO/WO 105/27, WO to Roberts, 14 Sept. 1900.

26. MS/NAM/Roberts, Ms. letterbook, South Africa, vol. 7, Roberts to military governors, Johannesburg and Pretoria, 15 Sept. 1900, and Roberts to Mackenzie, 17 Sept. 1900.

27. MS/PRO/WO 105/32, Roberts to secretary of state for war, 17 Sept. 1900.

28. MS/PRO/FO 2/416, WO to FO, 17 Oct. 1900, with enclosure, Roberts to WO, 17 Sept. 1900, which forwards Mackenzie to Roberts, 17 July 1900, and Davies to Mackenzie, 17 July 1900.

29. MS/PRO/FO 2/533, CO to FO, 25 March, with enclosures.

30. MS/PRO/FO 2/417, FO to CO, 12 Nov. 1900 (draft).

31. MS/PRO/FO 2/417, memorandum by H. B[ertie].
32. MS/PRO/WO 32/8773, confidential memorandum, 11 Sept. 1900, with enclosure, Milner to Chamberlain, 5 July 1900.
33. MS/PRO/FO 2/417, memorandum by H. B[ertie].; and see *The Times* (London) 15 Dec. 1900 for the 'Johannesburg conspiracy'.
34. MS/PRO/DO 119/469, Milner to Fiddes, 13 Aug. 1900, in a 'personal and private' postscript. For the Cordua plot, see Spies 1977, pp. 161—2.
35. MS/PRO/WO 105/25, 'Johannesburg conspiracy', enclosing letter from Italian consul in Pretoria to Davies, 24 Nov. 1900.
36. MS/LHC/Covernton, 'Fifty odd years of memoirs, 1893—1945', pp. 36—7. His information was supplied to him by a German who spied for British military intelligence.
37. MS/PRO/WO 105/25, 'Johannesburg conspiracy', report by Davies, 27 Nov. 1900; *African Review*, 25 (420) 8 Dec. 1900; Spies 1977, p. 162.
38. MS/PRO/FO 2/345, FO to Lascelles, 20 Nov. 1900 (draft); FO 2/964, memorandum, 22 Sept. 1900, and FO to *London Gazette*, 8 April 1901 (draft). The members of the commission were: Thomas Milvain, Esq. KC, chancellor of the County Palatin of Durham (chairman), Maj. Gen. J. Upton Prior, Maj. Gen. the Hon. H. F. Eaton, C. A. Wilkins, Esq., former judge of the High Court, Calcutta, and R. K. Loveday, formerly member of the SAR Volksraad. Maj. Gen. Sir John C. Ardagh, Royal Engineers and military intelligence presented the case for the military, while Mr J. P. Foster was the secretary to the commission. See also *Cape Times*, 15 Dec. 1900.
39. MS/PRO/WO 105/27, file 81; and MS/PRO/FO 2/535, WO to FO, 30 April 1901, with enclosures; and FO 2/538, WO to FO, 12 July 1901. See also FO 2/964, Kitchener to secretary of state for war (secret), 29 March 1901; MS/PRO/PRO 30/57, vol. 20, 'Roberts to Kitchener, 1900—2', Roberts to Kitchener (private), 27 April 1901.
40. *The Times* (London) 1 and 8 May, 23 and 24 July, 27 and 29 Aug. 1901; OP/GB/Deportation Commission, evidence, FO 881/7619X, *passim*, and FO 2/696 on 'the decision of the commission concerning the employees of The Netherlands South African Railway Company'.
41. OP/GB/Deportation Commission, report, pp. iii—iv. The claims broke down as follows:

National Origin	Number of Claimants	Amount (£)
USA	13	49,609
Austria—Hungary	115	59,174
Belgium	6	6,046
Denmark	3	890
France	1	20,000
Germany	206	253,635
Greece	1	616
Italy	128	52,860
The Netherlands	1,146	718,146
Russia	35	125,329
Spain	2	520
Sweden and Norway	12	6,094
Switzerland	5	851
Unknown	1	446

The total is 1,674 claims and £1,294,216.
42. OP/GB/Deportation Commission, report, p. vi. The awards were as follows: Germany (£30,000), Austria—Hungary (£15,000), Italy (£12,000), USA (£6,000), Russia (£4,100), Sweden and Norway (£1,000), Belgium (£800), Denmark (£250), Switzerland (£250), and Spain (£150). The total was £69,550, but in November The Netherlands government agreed to accept £37,500 and other governments, £7,950. A suspense account was created from which further claims could be paid. See MS/PRO/CO 291/41, Milner to Chamberlain, 1 Sept. 1902, where Milner states that as of that date, £107,750 had been paid to foreigners who had been deported from the Transvaal by the military. For the later Claims' Board, see MS/PRO/FO 2/823; FO 2/962; and FO 403/324. For

Ardagh's comments regarding the settlement, see FO 2/696, memorandum, 13 Dec. 1901.

43. *The Times* (London) 29 Oct. 1901. Privately Ardagh felt that the commissioners had set a 'slight value on the alleged loss and suffering of the deported foreigners [and] . . . [w]here any award has been made, sums of £5 and £10 are of the most frequent occurrence'. These amounts, to Ardagh's mind, were 'wholly illusory' (MS/PRO/PRO 30/40, vol. 17, claims' commission papers, 1901, private and secret memorandum, 23 Sept. 1901).

44. OP/GB/Deportation Commission, evidence, FO 881/7619X, pp. 175, 256; *The Times* (London) 24 and 25 July and 16 Aug. 1901.

45. MS/PRO/FO 2/538, minute by H. F., 12 July 1901. Baragwanath was reportedly arrested because he was in the company of Williams, a 'dangerous person'. Later, according to this file, this reason was in doubt: 'even now it does not appear to be known why Mr Williams was considered "dangerous"'. See FO 2/533.

46. MS/PRO/PRO 30/40, vol. 17, claims' commission papers, 1901, private and secret memorandum, 23 Sept. 1901. See also in this same volume his confidential memorandum, 9 Nov. 1901, and another handwritten memorandum, n.d..

47. MS/RHO/O'Brien, vol. 2, 15 July 1900; MS/JPL/Potts, pp. 98–9, for rumours of commandos entering the city.

48. *The Times* (London) 20 Aug. 1901; for a statement by Mackenzie which supports this view, see MS/TAD/PSY 49, Mackenzie to C-in-C, Pretoria, 21 July 1900.

49. MS/TAD/PSY 52, Fiddes to Mackenzie, 9 July 1900 and, for Mackenzie's suggestion, see MS/PRO/WO 105/27, with Mackenzie to Roberts, 3 July 1900, and Fiddes to Mackenzie, 18 July 1900, which notes, 'Chief fully approves proposal to deport indigent foreigners'.

50. MS/PRO/FO 2/416, CO to FO, 25 Oct. 1900, with enclosure, Milner to Chamberlain (confidential), 3 Oct. 1900, forwarding Milner to Fiddes, 12 and 25 Aug. 1900.

51. MS/TAD/HC 143, 'Deportation of undesirable foreigners from the Transvaal in 1900'; *Cape Times*, 11 and 30 Jan. 1901; *African Review*, 26 (426) 19 Jan 1901; for ships' arrivals, see n. 16, ch. 8, above.

52. The August 1900 figure may include burgher dependants being sent out of the city. See *Cape Times*, 5 Dec. 1900 and 25 July 1901; MS/PRO/FO 2/537, WO to FO, 1 and 21 June 1901, with enclosure, Kitchener to secretary of state for war, 2 June 1901. For other estimates, see Spies 1977, pp. 163–4; Amery 1900–9, vol. 6, p. 593.

53. MS/PRO/FO 2/538, WO to FO, 25 July 1901, with enclosure, Kitchener to under-secretary of state for war, 27 June 1901, with report from Davies, 20 June 1901. For a similar case, see FO 2/830. For Kitchener's admonition, see n. 20, ch. 7 above.

54. For the deportees' difficulties in re-establishing themselves in Europe, see OP/GB/Deportation Commission, evidence, FO 881/7619X, *passim*. For Milner's comment, see n. 21, ch. 7 above.

55. For these dismissals, see MS/PRO/CO 417/292; CO 291/27; CO 293/2; MS/PRO/DO 119/510; MS/BOD/Mss. Milner Dep. 230, Fiddes to Milner, 13 July, 5 Aug. 1900. See also *The Times* (London) 18 Jan. 1902; *African Review*, 26 (429) 9 Feb. 1901; 25 (416) 10 Nov. 1900, p. 197; MS/TAD/PSY 52, Fiddes to Mackenzie, 2 Aug. 1900; and MS/BOD/Mss. Milner Dep. 226, Milner to military governor (copy), 30 April 1901. For Wybergh's view of the dismissals, see Wybergh to Fitzpatrick, 14 Aug. 1900, in Duminy and Guest (eds) 1976; for Forster's critical views, see MS/JPL/Forster, Forster to Dalrymple, 8 Dec. 1900.

56. MS/BOD/Mss. Milner Dep. 230, Fiddes to Milner, 5 Aug. 1900.

Nine

Going Home

He which hath no stomach to this fight,
Let him depart
William Shakespeare

When the Uitlander refugees boarded the train bound for the coast, most of them thought that the war would be over in a few months, by Christmas perhaps. But all Christmas 1900 brought was news of Boer victories. Now, months later, with their savings exhausted by the high cost of living, by rapacious landlords and by shopkeepers intent on making a profit from the war, the refugees had become restless. Many had lost track of their loved-ones. Fathers and sons were at the front; some were missing, others dead. The jingoistic fervour which swept through Britain in late 1899 had raised money to feed and clothe the refugees, but, as this abated, money had run out and the able-bodied were ordered off the rolls. Meanwhile the capitalists were consolidating their rule of Johannesburg — or so it seemed to many of the refugees who read of Mackenzie's appointments. Tired of waiting at the coast, all clamoured to return home to the Rand, to claim their possessions and to begin work again.

While the refugees blamed Milner and his advisers for the delay, the high commissioner blamed the army. When Roberts postponed the refugees' departure set for 13 October 1900, Milner was clearly upset and made sure that Mackenzie was made aware of the situation at the coast. 'I think,' wrote Milner:

> it has perhaps not been quite recognized . . . how great our difficulties in the Colony have been with regard to the refugees. There are between thirty and forty thousand people, who had been exiled from Johannesburg for more than a year, many of them getting to the end of their tether in regard to means. They have been extraordinarily patient, and have behaved, on the whole, wonderfully well, but are now getting 'hard up' . . . and, in their idleness and disappointment, they are becoming prey to a number of agitators, who seize on every occasion . . . to make trouble. It is extremely important to get these people back to their business as soon as possible.[1]

The postponement of the refugees' return was the result of two problems: the first, though the less significant, was that it was difficult to provision the city. The second was that the 'Irregulars' had threatened to mutiny again. Milner expressed his frustration to his confidante, Violet Cecil: the troops were sick to death of this protracted war and the 'Irregulars', whether African or oversea[s, are] semi-mutinous. . . . One form the mutinousness of the S.A. Colonials takes is to refuse to fight longer if the Refugees return to Johannesburg. . . . The Refugees *ought* to return . . . and I had promised them so, under a distinct pledge from headquarters. Now they are definitely delayed, owing to the protest of their fellows in the field, and in return are *threatening themselves to rebel* (nice kettle of fish and edifying spectacle for the 'Loyal Dutch').[2]

While the volunteers' grievances were much more complicated than a simple desire to protect their old jobs on the Rand, certainly the Uitlanders-under-arms were worried that the Uitlanders at the coast, as well as any newcomers to the scene, would be allowed to return to the Rand before them. Milner sent Fitzpatrick to meet them and to get them to take a more 'reasonable' view of the situation: they had to understand that until 2,000 or 3,000 were allowed to return, the economic life of the Rand would not be regenerated and no one — refugee or volunteer — would be able to return.[3]

The return, though, was postponed indefinitely and it was this that gave impetus to the growing discontent among coastal refugees. Meetings, petitions and deputations resulted, and several groups, standing in opposition to the original Uitlander refugee committees, sprang into existence. The Refugee Committee, Cape Town, was the most vociferous and organized. It was, according to Milner, comprised of 'genuine working men' — miners and artisans. But, as it became more critical and obstreperous, Milner accused the men of having fallen into the hands of 'professional agitators' who used the organization to air the refugees' grievances in a 'regular campaign of public meetings and articles in the public press'.[4]

In an effort to regain control of the refugees and to counteract the outpourings of the rowdiest element, Milner formed a 'Consultative Committee' to advise him on issues affecting Uitlanders. As the high commissioner later explained to Chamberlain, he appointed 'prominent men of all classes' to the committee, including three from the 'so-called' Refugee Committee, Cape Town. Milner was chairman of the committee, and W. H. Rogers, 'a gentleman of large interests in the Transvaal', was his deputy. The honorary secretary was the vociferous editor, Pakeman, while also on the committee were Harold Strange, E. P. Solomon, J. Dale Lace and H. Graumann, among others. Having in this way attempted to co-opt the leadership of the articulate working-class refugees, he thereafter had little to do with the alternative refugee movement, refusing to see its delegations and mislaying its petitions.[5] Had Milner been more receptive to the complaints of this section of the refugees, he may have been better able to allay further discontent. As it was, his ploy failed and refugee unrest continued. Grievances were not confined to the issue of their return, but extended to a wide range of refugee concerns.

Pauperism among refugees had become much worse by the last quarter of 1900 and the burden on the relief rolls continued to grow. In November Milner cabled Chamberlain, explaining that earlier the 'large financial houses' had donated nearly £30,000 for refugee aid, but that he now had enough money for only two more months. Only women, children and 'decrepits' were in receipt of assistance and the rest were in 'great distress'.[6]

By Christmas he was ready to propose a radical solution. He wanted to borrow from the banks to keep up the work of the Lord Mayor's Fund and to help support 'better class' people who now found themselves without money. The collateral for the loan of an initial £100,000 was to be his pledge that the new colonial governments, when fully established, would repay it. Chamberlain responded with a different idea: the Treasury Chest officer at the Cape had been instructed to give Milner up to £50,000 for refugee relief, on condition that those who received aid were 'unable to maintain themselves'. He was especially adamant that no man between the ages of 16 and 60, who was fit enough to be employed by the colonial or military authorities, should receive assistance.[7]

The Consultative Committee found Chamberlain's proposal 'highly unsatisfactory', but after Milner reinterpreted the colonial secretary's instruction by 'read[ing] between the lines with my official experience', the new scheme was introduced. Some of the money went into the Imperial Relief Fund, which assisted 'people of a high social stratum' who were assumed to have property in the Transvaal. The remaining amount augmented the Lord Mayor's Fund. Women, children and, in some cases, able-bodied men were assisted. It was hoped that some would eventually repay the money given to them under this scheme, but the Committee felt that it could not bind people to do so.[8]

While Milner was thus able to extend his relief efforts, the local authorities undermined his efforts to some extent by beginning to reduce their contribution to refugee assistance. For instance, in January 1901 the Durban authorities decided that half the men working on public relief projects were fit enough to join the volunteers and that they ought to do so. As for the rest, the Durban Corporation thought they could learn to live on a lower 'living wage'. In Port Elizabeth the relief committee stopped aiding those it felt were becoming demoralized by charity and losing their independent spirit.[9] Hence, just as the imperial government finally took a step toward directly aiding the refugees, the local officials began to shed their responsibilities. No doubt the refugees felt as insecure as ever. In any event, unrest continued.

Besides matters of relief and the postponement of the return of the refugees, the Uitlanders articulated a wide range of grievances. These arose from living conditions along the coast, as well as from events in the Transvaal. Some reflected fears common to all the refugees, while others more clearly demonstrated the class consciousness of the working people in exile. The working class was worried about events on the Rand (and the machinations of the Uitlander advisers there) and feared that the alliance of capital and the military would work against the interests of the common man.

Refugees at the coast complained about the high cost of living, particularly about the profiteers and *rentiers* who took advantage of their forced exile to make huge profits. Those who were employed protested about low wages and racially-mixed work teams, while those without work complained that there were not enough jobs to go around. The plague broke out on the coast in the early months of 1901 and this added to everyone's worries. The refugees became more urgent in their appeals. As one mother wrote: let us go back before 'ourselves and families are carted away in those dreadful wagons'.[10]

The Uitlanders were also unhappy about the fine treatment, as they saw it, handed out to the Boer refugees and foreign deportees. The president of the Guild of Loyal Women of South Africa wrote to Milner in mid-1901 to register the Johannesburg branch of the Guild's protest that the British government looked after the Boers better than it did its own people and to argue that the money, food, and educational and medical facilities provided for the Boers in the concentration camps ought to be 'equally available for loyal refugees'. In a similar vein, a 'refugee for twenty months' wrote to the *Cape Times* in mid-1901:

> I desire to tender my thanks to Mr Lindley [with the Lord Mayor's Fund] for drawing attention to the sickly sentimentality over the alleged woes of the Boer refugees. It more than disgusts one to know that thousands of British refugees . . . are living in absolute want . . . while the families of our enemies . . . are being kept in ease and — what is to them — luxury.[11]

Milner, back from London and lengthy policy discussions, noted publicly that concentration camps were a military exercise and in no way benefited the Boers at the expense of loyalist refugees.[12] In much the same manner complaints had been registered earlier about the men who had been deported from Johannesburg in July 1900, of whom some had stayed on in East London and received 3s a day while the able-bodied refugees received nothing.[13]

All the refugees worried about the reported looting and damage to their properties in Johannesburg, but only the middle class actually organized a petition asking for a special commission to be formed to inquire into the losses sustained because of the war and for a procedure to be established to enable the Uitlanders to gain compensation for their losses. Members of the working class were, however, no less concerned about their few possessions — particularly their clothes, furnishings and tools — and A. S. Raitt (the jingoist trade unionist and a member of the Uitlander Council) suggested to A. Mackie Niven that a separate category for 'indirect claims' be created by the commission to help people without property make bids for compensation for losses resulting from the war. As it turned out, working people suffered significant losses in Johannesburg and along the Rand and, by the end of the war, there was a definite need for a system whereby men could obtain small loans to buy more tools and equipment in order to start work again.[14]

The working-class refugees thus shared a wide range of concerns with the Uitlander middle class. On the other hand, there were certain grievances that specifically concerned working people. These centred upon issues which arose during the course of the war, but became coloured by the fears and suspicions carried south from the Rand by the refugees. Working people were particularly afraid of capitalist rule being initiated on the Rand; much of their concern focused on the power of the mining élite in the new order and they grumbled about the unrepresentative nature of Milner's committees. For instance, George Kent, while not an artisan, reflected the view of many refugees when he complained to the high commissioner in May 1901 that 'we do not have a single representative near you — the Gentlemen on your Advisory Board were not elected by, neither do they represent, us'. Had this been otherwise, he continued, 'your Excellency would have known long ere this . . . of the dissatisfaction amongst the masses'. More to the point, a year later he reminded Milner that only a portion of the Uitlanders had 'personal access' to him, 'as for instance, certain members of the Chamber of Mines and their representatives'.[15]

Although Milner was accused of favouritism, of more concern at that moment were events taking place in Pretoria and Johannesburg under the military rule of Colin Mackenzie. At a large meeting of refugees in Cape Town in late September 1900, a resolution was adopted which complained of the 'many appointments under the new administration of the Transvaal of . . . former representatives of interested corporations'. As a result, the resolution continued, the administration lacked the public's confidence. In its manifesto the radical Refugee Committee, Cape Town, outlined its views more thoroughly:

> With the knowledge possessed by all Uitlander residents of the Transvaal of the past history, policy and definite methods of the great financial houses, they are becoming alarmed at the rapid increase in the wealth, influence, and unrelenting enterprise of the latter.
>
> Their 'freezing-out' tactics, and their formidable secrecy in operation are thoroughly well-known to Johannesburg residents, of whom a large number hail from the Kimberley of the early days.
>
> The alarm became consternation when it became known that the representatives of the great mining interests, who for years 'persuaded' the Pretoria Government, are now surrounding the new Administration of the Transvaal.

Further criticism of 'capitalistic appointments' was made part of a petition to the queen from Cape Town refugees in November: we 'protest against the civil appointments of the best character being given to the nominees of the capitalist groups'. The goal of Mackenzie's advisers, it was argued, was to carry out 'financial monopolistic schemes'. Meanwhile the military was exonerated, for the refugees felt it did not know what it was doing when it appointed these men to positions of authority, having been duped by the manipulators of power.[16]

While the working class feared a coordinated assault on white wages as well as the introduction of cheap imported labour by the Randlords upon their return to Johannesburg, they also attributed to the capitalists a scheme for creating a compound system for whites on the Rand mines. Possibly as rumours of the formation of the Witwatersrand Native Labour Association (WNLA) circulated, they fuelled pre-existing fears. In any event, a connection was made between the postponement of the return of the refugees and the much-hated compound scheme: 'Upon what plan is the slow return being conducted? . . . A 'huge scheme' has been floated . . . [and my] contention is that the scheme . . . is nothing else but the awful compound system . . . and they . . . want to get through before we get back in numbers, for they would not dare to attempt it when we are in Johannesburg in force'.[17]

Milner had no sympathy with such views and told London that it was a 'small but noisy gang of Radical agitators amongst the refugees carefully nursed by the "SA News" and our Colonial rebels generally' who were causing the trouble. They were, he continued, 'fishing in troubled waters and trying to get up our "anti-capitalism" now on this occasion'. No doubt Milner thought, as did the chief intelligence officer in Cape Town, Captain Ross, that this was also part of the rampant 'Fenianism' of the place. In any case, such anti-capitalist sentiment fed into the pro-Boer movement in Britain during this period when the 'Khaki election' dominated the news.[18]

Another of the refugees' complaints was the so-called 'rent issue'. This one problem epitomized for many the dangers which faced the exiled working class. It began in October 1899 when Kruger proclaimed that, as long as martial law was in force, property owners had no right to demand rent from tenants, though the lessee of a business property, if it were still being used as such, had to pay half rent to the owner. Furthermore, the interest due on unpaid mortgages, or on loans that used property as collateral, could not be collected by the bondholder during the period of martial law. In proclaiming this *besluit* (decision), it was Kruger's intent to protect commandos and their families (who were in no position to meet their financial commitments) from *rentiers*, leading land companies and mortgage institutions. Needless to say, those dependent upon rents for their livelihood were not pleased, but the landlords had no choice but to accept the pronouncement.[19] The proclamation went into effect at the beginning of the war and this is how matters stood when the British took over the administration of Johannesburg on the last day of May 1900.

Within a few weeks of the transfer of power, Forster, as Mackenzie's legal adviser, expressed his opinion that a 'considerable amount of injustice was being suffered by owners of property' as a result of the proclamation. It was particularly distressing to him that tenants actually claimed the right to remain in occupation of buildings without paying rent and rejected the landlords' right to eject them for non-payment. While Mackenzie dealt with these cases with the power vested in him by martial law, Fiddes urged that the whole issue be investigated. Hence, the military governor appointed a 'Rent and Interest Committee' which consisted of two majors as well as several civilians, *inter alia*: Messrs. J. A. Hamilton, A. Brakhan, H. L. Lindsay, J. N. de Jongh, and a Mr Pizzighelli. All these men, with the exception of Lindsay, who was an attorney and a member of the Uitlander Council, were representatives of major mining and landholding companies in Johannesburg.[20]

Immediately the composition of the committee became public, a cry of outrage was heard all along the coast. The refugees believed that the military authorities were about to rescind Kruger's proclamation and that they would all be faced with months of back rent and interest due when they returned to the Rand.[21] Milner's response was to try to convince them that the committee had been created to investigate the situation, not to decide the issue.[22] But Roberts's Proclamation no. 13 of 1900, which appeared in August, only worsened the situation, as it stated that taxes, revenues, licence fees, etc. which would normally be due to the Republican government were now to be paid to the military authorities instead. And though this proclamation did not deal with rents or interest, or even with private contracts, the refugees feared that it set a precedent regarding the back-payment of rents. Refugees also saw this as a means of depriving small-claims holders of their property, for they (unlike the large mining companies' representatives), were unable to return to the Rand to pay their back taxes.[23]

This proclamation, coming as it did on top of the creation of the rent committee, fuelled the anti-capitalist fire. The views of the people were made known to the colonial secretary when the vice-chairman of the Refugee Committee, Cape Town, met him in London in early September. When raising the question of the rent issue, P. G. Shepherd argued that it seemed clear that the Johannesburg administration was determined to rescind the *besluit*. He used as evidence the 'one-sided commission' appointed by Mackenzie, which was 'made up solely of representatives of big corporations which stood in the positions of landlords and mortgagees'. Also, he told Chamberlain that the 'circular issued by the Consolidated Investment Company, showing that they expected to be able to exact payment of their arrear rents and interests' indicated even more clearly the intention of Johannesburg's élite. Shepherd also raised the issue of civil appointments with Chamberlain, asking him for some assurance that, when the permanent civil appointments were made, the imperial government would not permit the 'large financial corporations to control the civil administration by giving their representatives the position of heads of departments as was the case in the temporary appointments by the military authorities'. Chamberlain, much to

Shepherd's pleasure, guaranteed that such practices were now a 'thing of the past'.[24]

Upon returning to the Cape, Shepherd told a meeting of refugees that it was not the military that was responsible for the 'proclamation regarding rents and interest', but the 'impure atmosphere' which surrounded the administration.

> It was the gentlemen on the Rand who had been so closely connected with the big [mining] groups in whose interests these two proclamations had been issued. What could be more monstrous than the constitution of the commission, consisting as it did of landlords and mortgagees who advised the military Governor of Johannesburg whether mortgages or rents and interest should be paid.[25]

While the rent committee's recommendations, presented to the military governor early in the new year, differed little from the position taken by the disgruntled refugees, the latter continued to worry and to think that landlords intended to collect rents (on properties they had not even seen for over a year) and enforce contracts.[26]

In October 1901 the rent issue was temporarily resolved. The Consultative Committee recommended that, after a certain date, tenants in 'beneficial occupation' would pay rent and that interest would begin to accrue on unpaid mortgages. Milner agreed and Proclamation no. 27 of 1901 carried this into effect, setting the deadline at 9 October. This was not to affect the refugees still at the coast, for they were not in beneficial occupation, but was aimed at people who remained on the Rand or who had returned there after the war began. Still, the Uitlanders at the coast were uncertain of their liabilities. For instance, was a refugee family that had left its furnishings in a rented home considered to be in beneficial occupation and thus liable for rent? When these refugees returned to the Rand they found that the Personal Property Enquiry Department had attempted to avert such trouble (and had facilitated the rerenting of property) by removing such furniture and storing it in central warehouses in Johannesburg.[27] There the matter rested for some months.

The return of the refugees was seen as a solution to most of these problems, for people thought they could protect their interests better and find work more easily if they were on the Rand. They had been frustrated by the order to delay their return. With news of a mutiny suppressed, though speculated on in the press, they were told that the postponement was due to problems of supply. Soon the people at the coast began to question whether Johannesburg really had supply problems and, to support their views, cited news reports of banquets and balls held on the Rand. Nor did they believe the claim that it was unsafe to pass through the open countryside by train, for if individual refugees — and women and children at that — could travel north by rail, why could not the mass of people?[28]

After the postponement of October 1900, the work of registering refugees continued under the leadership of Milner's private secretary, M. S. O. Walrond, and the CRC. In the new year, a special secretary in the high commissioner's office was appointed with the sole task of dealing with refugee permits and devising, with the assistance of the CRC, a policy to govern the refugees' return. H. T. Ommanney, previously a civil servant in the India Office, took up this post.[29]

The policy adopted sought to return British refugees first, though a few foreigners, particularly any who were deemed necessary to reconstruction because of their business connections or professional qualifications, were allowed to go back early. This policy remained in force until October 1901, when the military ordered that no non-British refugees were to be allowed to return, except those with special permits from army intelligence. By mid-1902, former residents of the Transvaal who carried French passports were permitted to return at a rate of 15 a month. Two months later permits were being issued to 20 Italians a month, but always subject to the provost marshall's approval. This was in keeping with Milner's expressed desire to restrict the entry of foreigners to the Transvaal colony.[30]

The administration did not ignore the destitute or the 'undesirables'. Those who had earlier been deported by the military were expressly forbidden re-entry until after the war. This is not to say that those who had been sent to Europe were kept there, for many managed to return to southern Africa. Yet the imperial government tried to control their re-immigration and, in October 1901, the Currie line closed its bookings to persons previously deported from southern Africa following a government pronouncement that such persons would not be allowed to land there.[31]

Keeping 'undesirables', paupers and deportees out of the port cities was one thing; keeping them off the Rand was another. Martial law, the permit system and control over the railways made it relatively easy to guard the Rand from an onslaught of such people. But decisions still had to be made about who was to be given a permit. On the Rand, Mackenzie's legal adviser, Forster, compiled at least two lists, which were used to exclude those whom the reformers thought unfit to return. The first, a 'list of persons who on no account should be authorized to come up at present' — i.e. in mid-1900 — included some 100 people, many of whom were Randlords such as George Albu, Harry Solomon, S. Baumann, Julius and Carl Jeppe and Harry Graumann. The second list, somewhat shorter but more comprehensive, was labelled 'people who should not be allowed to Johannesburg now' and included members of the defunct town council, the stock exchange, some burghers, 'Russian Jews (including Peruvians), liquor dealers, jewellers and Italians'. A third list, which appears to have originated in Milner's office and bears the stamp of his own Uitlander advisers, was also used to exclude people. It was a list of supposed 'anti-British schemers of the more modern and ambitious type' and included J. H. Munnik, the former assistant state mining engineer, James Hay, a former president of the Chamber of Mines, as well as most of the mining inspectors who worked for the Republican government. Both the 'Illicit Liquor Gang' and the 'Illicit Gold Gang' were included, as was Dr N. Mansvelt, previously superintendent of education, and Schutte, ex-special commandant of the Witwatersrand. Mendelssohn and Bruce of the defunct *Standard and Diggers' News* were enumerated, along with over 100 other people, including the whole of the Volksraad (except six members) and all the justices of the peace listed in the *State Almanac*.[32] In addition to these enumerated individuals, there were another 4,000 'undesirables' at the ports to whom the CRC barred re-entry. If these lists were not enough to keep out those who might upset the new social order, the Uitlanders on the CRC and the refugee committees along the coast had the power to eliminate any others.[33]

After Roberts postponed the return of refugees in October 1900, only essential personnel were allowed to go north. With the new year these restrictions were eased and, in January, permits were granted to a few mine managers on condition they returned to the coast after inspecting their properties. Not long afterwards about 100 managers and engineers were given permission to return permanently to begin preparations for restarting the mines. Naturally the merchant community demanded similar treatment and about 100 representatives were granted permission to return to the Rand for two weeks only, though some managed to remain permanently. Permits for representatives of insurance companies and officers of building societies were distributed in early 1901 to enable them to go inland to inspect the damage done to clients' properties. Another select few, including pharmacists, were chosen to go north because of their expertise. A list of other essential personnel was also prepared, which included telegraphists, dentists, and hotel and boarding-house keepers.[34]

The permit office granted just over 200 permits to civilians in 1900 and, between New Year's Day and 30 April 1901, another 1,400 men and 200 women went to the colony, the vast majority to the Rand. In the second quarter of 1901, Ommanney's permit office moved to Johannesburg and the refugees at the coast soon began to complain that the process had become overly centralized. To placate the opposition Milner added three more men to his CRC, all chosen from Uitlander committees at the coast. This served to quiet dissent while ensuring that the decision-making process remained firmly in the administration's hands. After May more complaints were expressed, for it appeared to people at the coast that the CRC had been disbanded and that all decisions were being made by Ommanney in Johannesburg. While this was not the case, it is certain that the process of choosing who would return to the Rand had grown no more democratic.[35]

In May 1901, after months of quiet, Johannesburg changed. The executive committee of the Chamber of Mines returned in April, as did the staffs of many mining houses. Vacant streets began to fill with people and more shops, some closed for over 20 months, now reopened. In the first week of May three mines opened and the sound of stamps pounding once again reverberated along the reef. This meant the reintroduction of 300 white mine workers, as well as boarding-house keepers and their staffs to serve them. This steady flow of population, in addition to the arrival of some 1,500 guards since February, led all to believe that the Rand's British population was returning home.[36] But in June the whole process once again ground to a halt.

Rumours purporting to explain why the flow of refugees had stopped spread quickly. The city's poor sanitation was blamed, as was the inadequate supply of water, though neither seem to have been the primary cause. Instead, the problem seems to have been that some 'undesirables' had reached the city, including one family of 'notoriously bad repute'. The police informed Kitchener that additional policemen were needed to meet the problems likely to arise with the increased population and the commander-in-chief ordered that when permits were issued again, they were to be given only to individuals sanctioned by headquarters.[37]

Return of Refugees to the Transvaal
May 1901—May 1902

1901		1902	
May—July	1,485	January	5,492
August	648	February	6,581
September	2,164	March	6,833
October	1,849	April	5,419
November	2,626	May	4,865
December	4,752		

After a brief interval, refugees once again began to flow inland in ever increasing numbers. The vast majority of the 42,000 who returned to the Transvaal between May 1901 and May 1902 inclusive, headed for the Rand.[38] As early as January 1901 the white working class made its reappearance in Johannesburg and, by the end of the year, a few Asians and non-white servants were seen on incoming trains. In early 1902 Ommanney suggested that, because some whites of the 'poor or working class' had been admitted along with some Indians, perhaps some Cape Coloureds 'of the better class' should be allowed to return. The secretary of the Native Affairs Department agreed as it would 'supply a want in the shape of labour'. And in April 1902, as if to reassemble British society on the Rand fully, the wholesale importation of indigent British refugees began.[39] Select foreigners also began to make a reappearance.

To facilitate the refugees' reintegration into the community, several organizations were created. One of these was the Personal Property Enquiry Department, which answered queries about lost property on the Rand. In November 1900 it added to its duties investigations of commandeered and looted property and the collection of documents, evidence and books that might 'affect the private rights of individuals in regard to their property'. The head of the department was eventually appointed assistant commissioner of police and given the power to recover stolen and commandeered property, where before he had to rely upon 'moral suasion' only. Since he could now start criminal proceedings against people in possession of illegally acquired goods, the amount of property recovered rose dramatically.

The department also collected and stored absent tenants' furniture and private property. This was placed in two large warehouses which were open to refugees upon their arrival from the coast. After Proclamation no. 27 of 1901 (which made tenants in beneficial occupation liable for rent) the department received an increasing number of requests to collect and store furniture from refugees, who were then expected to pay a small fee.[40]

In August 1901 leading Uitlanders in Johannesburg formed the Refugee Aid Committee. At its first public meeting speakers recalled the past philanthropic endeavours of the Johannesburg community, especially the 'capitalistic Altruists' who gave so generously during the war. It was noted with some dismay that while the imperial government and the people of Britain had been generous to the Boer women and children in the concentration camps, the Uitlanders had received relatively little. It was necessary, therefore, to create an organization that would serve the refugees upon their return from the coast.

Soon the committee had grown to include hundreds of leading men and women, while a sub-committee of 16 people was elected to consider policy. A delegation was sent to Milner, who was now in residence in Johannesburg, to seek financial assistance from the government. In response he suggested that the committee confine its work to Rand refugees of all nationalities rather than British refugees throughout the whole of the colony, and that it should not concern itself with the severely destitute, for they would not be permitted to return for some time. He concluded by telling them that he could not promise financial assistance until a public subscription had been tried. After the public had donated the government might assist.

Since many committee members felt strongly that the Uitlanders deserved the support of the imperial government, the committee divided between those who agreed with Milner's proposal and those who did not. Thus divided, it was unable to move any further. When the disagreement was reported to the high commissioner, he agreed to fund the committee's work on condition it was formally reconstituted and placed under government direction. Hence the committee became a department, though it retained the active support of the beneficient community along the Rand.[41]

By 1902 the Refugee Aid Department had branches throughout the colony. In Johannesburg it gave railway tickets to the poor, lent money to people to set up homes and provided horses and wagons on credit to tradesmen and contractors who needed them to begin work again. It also imported and sold furniture at cost price, provided temporary shelter in its five houses, and distributed rations and meat coupons to the needy. When the CRC disbanded in June 1902, it took over the task of handling the remaining permit applications. As a community-based and politicized organization, it also took upon itself the task of investigating issues it thought vital to the Rand community, such as the Gold Law, claim licensing, and rents and interest due. Concerning these and other municipal matters, it petitioned and advised the high commissioner.[42]

An offshoot of the department was the Labour Bureau founded in January 1902. Under the direction of Revd Kelly, a favourite of the Johannesburg benevolent community, it found work for men discharged from the volunteer corps and for refugees who were unable to return from the coast because of their inability to support themselves once on the Rand. Keeping in touch with the Uitlander committees at the coast, it managed to channel the working class home. Preference was given to former members of one of the Irregular Corps, a policy which conformed to that set by the permit office and to promises made to men upon their enlistment and while in the field.

Market Square in central Johannesburg, 1901. Returning uitlander refugees could buy goods here to start life anew (*Africana Museum, Johannesburg*)

Between January and November 1902 the bureau found work for some 4,500 white men, of whom 3,700 were ex-volunteers, another 400 reservists or regulars, and the remainder, civilians. Some 1,200 former Irregulars took work from the Rand Mines Limited, where they received 5s a day plus rations and lodging. All in all, over 60 per cent of the men applying for jobs with the bureau found work and were able to leave the coast before it closed its doors and the Refugee Aid Department took over its work in late 1902.[43]

At the end of the war some 10,000 refugees remained at the coast, mostly 'British subjects of bad character and . . . foreigners who . . . had themselves naturalized' in the colonies. There were, of course, other Randites there who had settled down and chose to remain. There was far less economic distress, for work was more easily obtained and the destitute who had wanted to return had done so.[44] The crisis was over, after two-and-a-half years of poverty and frustration. The presence of tens of thousands of Randites had caused considerable alarm among both local and imperial officials, but Milner led the way and had dealt with them as any pragmatic administrator might. He attempted to divert and suppress criticism, to co-opt and quieten leaders of the opposition and to eliminate as far as possible the causes of discontent. He had relied upon the 'better class of Uitlanders' to assist him in this, especially J. P. Fitzpatrick and other prominent Rand businessmen and reformers. Aware of the growing partnership between the administration and the 'better class' of Randites, the working class formed alternative organizations, which articulated its own grievances and championed issues through the press, through petitions and public meetings, and through representations to the government. The white working class, though exiled by war, had not forgotten the distinct and clear warnings given by radicals before the war, warnings which foretold of the disastrous consequences that would befall white labour if the mining industrialists and their colleagues ever took over the reins of political power in the Transvaal.

Notes

1. MS/TAD/PSY 52, memorandum entitled 'Refugees: memo HC views convey verbally to MG', n.d., though probably between 13 and 20 Oct. 1900. See also MS/PRO/CO 417/295, Perry to Chamberlain (confidential), 31 Oct. 1900, with enclosures, Milner (on tour) to private secretary, 21 and 27 Oct. 1900, for further reactions by Milner to the postponement.
2. MS/BOD/Mss. English History, c. 687, Milner to Lady Edward Cecil, typescript extract, 26 Oct. 1900. For concerns about inadequate provisioning, see MS/PRO/CO 417/295, Perry to Chamberlain (confidential), 31 Oct. 1899, with enclosure, Milner to private secretary, 21 Oct. 1900; and Milner to Fitzpatrick (confidential), 25 Oct. 1900, in Duminy and Guest (eds) 1976.
3. MS/PRO/CO 417/295, Perry to Chamberlain (confidential), 31 Oct. 1900, with enclosure, Milner to private secretary, 27 Oct. 1900, Milner to Chamberlain (confidential), 7 Nov. 1900, with enclosures, Milner to chief-of-staff, 25 Oct. 1900, and political secretary to Milner, 31 Oct. 1900, and private secretary to Milner, 2 Nov. 1900. See also, Fitzpatrick to Beit (private and confidential), 7 Nov. 1900, for a fuller discussion of their grievances, in Duminy and Guest (eds) 1976; *Cape Times*, 16 Oct. 1900.
4. MS/PRO/CO 291/30, Milner to Chamberlain, 6 Dec. 1901.

5. MS/TAD/GOV 213/PS 6, minutes of meeting of consultative committee held 7 Oct. 1901; *Cape Times*, MS/PRO/FO 2/532, CO to FO, 12 Feb. 1901, with enclosure, Milner to Chamberlain, 9 Jan. 1901. For Milner's relations with the Refugee Committee, Cape Town, see MS/PRO/CO 291/30, Milner to Chamberlain (confidential), 7 Nov. 1900, with enclosure, political secretary to Milner, 31 Oct. 1900; MS/BOD/Mss. English History, c. 687, Milner to Lady Edward Cecil, typescript extract, 26 Oct. 1900.

6. MS/PRO/CO 417/295, Milner to Chamberlain, 3 Nov. 1900; MS/TAD/GOV 215, Hely Hutchinson to Milner, 18 Sept. 1901, with enclosed report by J. B. Lindley, secretary of the Mansion House Fund central committee, to chairman of the Imperial Relief Committee, 17 Sept. 1901.

7. MS/TAD/GOV 215, 'The Imperial Relief Fund', pp. 2–3, for Milner to Chamberlain, 25 Dec. 1900, and Chamberlain's reply, 28 Jan. 1901. See also MS/PRO/CO 417/296 and MS/PRO/FO 2/532.

8. MS/TAD/GOV 215, 'The Imperial Relief Fund', pp. 2–4, 'His Excellency's interpretation'. For concern with the middle-class poor, see MS/PRO/CO 417/289; OP/GB/Cd. 903 (1902), Milner to Chamberlain, 15 Nov. 1901.

9. *Cape Times*, 8 Jan. 1901; *Johannesburg Gazette*, 23 April 1901, and see 12 Jan. 1901.

10. For profiteers, see *Cape Times*, 25 Sept. 1900; MS/UWL/Hills, diary, 7 Aug. 1901; Froes 1899, p. 26; MS/JPL/Cockerill, 28 July 1900. For discussion of work, see *Cape Times*, 20 Aug., 23 Oct. and 25 Dec. 1900 and 17 May 1901. For this appeal from 'a mother of four', see *Cape Times*, 29 April 1901. For the plague generally, see the Cape press for March–May 1901; MS/PRO/FO 2/269; MS/PRO/CO 291/301; *African Review*, 23 (392) 26 May 1900, p. 267; 24 (433) 9 March 1901, p. 333; MS/USPG/14885, 'Association in aid of the diocese of Cape Town, report and account 1901', essay V, 'Reminiscences of uitvlugt during the outbreak of the plague in Cape Town, 1901'.

11. *Cape Times*, 22 July 1901; and see MS/PRO/CO 291/29, Milner to Chamberlain, 20 Sept. 1901, with enclosure, president of guild of Loyal Women of South Africa to Milner, 28 Aug. 1901; for a similar complaint from the Uitlander Committee at Pietermaritzburg, see *African Review*, 25 (423) 29 Dec. 1900, p. 463.

12. For Milner's view of the camps, see *Cape Times*, 12 Sept. 1901; *Johannesburg Gazette*, 9 Sept. 1901; Pakenham 1979, ch. 39; Spies 1977, *passim*.

13. MS/PRO/CO 417/293, Milner to Chamberlain, 22 Aug. 1900, with enclosure, Carter, Uitlander Committee at East London to private secretary to Milner, 15 Aug. 1900.

14. *Cape Times*, 4 April 1900; MS/PRO/DO 119/412, H. Solomon to Milner, 9 July 1900, with a copy of a petition. See also MS/PRO/CO 417/292, Milner to Chamberlain, 16 July 1900, with enclosure, E. C. Lowe, secretary to the Johannesburg Chamber of Commerce to Milner, 30 June 1900; MS/TAD/GOV 213/PS 6, A. S. Raitt to A. Mackie Niven, chairman of the Uitlander Committee, 6 May 1901; *The Times* (London) 1 Sept. 1902. For further information about the losses sustained by the working class, see PRO/CO 291/39, Milner to Chamberlain, 8 May 1902, with enclosed report about the work of the 'Refugees' Aid Department', 1 May 1902; CO 291/37 and CO 291/39.

15. MS/JPL/Kent, 27 May 1901 and 25 Aug. 1902. Kent was a surveyor and a supervisor of titles.

16. For the meeting, see Farrelly 1900, pp. 7–8; *Cape Times*, 24 Sept. 1900. The manifesto may be found in MacDonald n.d., pp. 104–5; for the petition see *African Review*, 24 (415) 3 Nov. 1900, p. 168; and (416) 10 Nov. 1900, p. 200; for concerns about Mackenzie's advisers, see Refugee Committee, Cape Town 1900, p. 3; Ross n.d., pp. 5, 82; *Cape Times*, 29 Oct. and 1 Nov. 1900.

17. *Cape Times*, 31 May 1901. For expressions of fear of an assault on wages, see *African Review*, 24 (410) 29 Sept. 1900. This fear was not without foundation (MS/BOD/Monk Bretton, 91, Lord Harris to Lord Monk Bretton, 13 Nov. 1902, with enclosure, H. H. Webb to C. D. Rudd, 1 Oct. 1902).

18. MS/BOD/Mss. Milner Dep. 170, Milner to Chamberlain (confidential), 28 Oct. 1900 (copy). For Ross and Milner's fear of radicalism at the Cape, see Galbraith 1983, p. 77; for the impact these sorts of arguments had in Britain, see Price 1972; for Fitzpatrick's

view of Milner's stance, see Fitzpatrick to Sam Evans (private), 18 July 1900, in Duminy and Guest (eds) 1976.

19. *S & D News*, 26 Oct. and 22 and 30 Nov. 1899; *Cape Times*, 25 Aug. 1900; *Star*, 27 Sept. 1899; MS/JPL/ACPT, London letterbook, p. 393. On the other hand, houses had little rental value during the period anyway and, in some cases, people were paid to occupy them. See MS/PRO/CO 291/27, Milner to Chamberlain, 27 Feb. 1901, enclosing a letter to the rent and interest committee from J. A. Hamilton of the Johannesburg Consolidated Investment Co.

20. MS/TAD/LAJ 2/68, legal adviser to Mackenzie, 6 July 1900, and Mackenzie to legal adviser, 6 July 1900. For composition of the committee, see MS/TAD/PSY 52, Fiddes to Mackenzie, 27 July 1900; *Cape Times*, 15 Aug. 1900; *African Review*, 24 (409) 22 Sept. 1900, p. 403.

21. *Cape Times*, 6, 20 and 21 Aug. and 24 Sept. 1900; MS/PRO/CO 417/293, Milner to Chamberlain, 22 Aug. 1900, with enclosure, Carter to Milner's private secretary, 15 Aug. 1900.

22. MS/PRO/CO 417/293, Milner to Chamberlain, 22 Aug. 1900, with enclosure, Milner's private secretary to Carter, 15 Aug. 1900; and see *Johannesburg Gazette*, 28 Aug. 1900.

23. *Johannesburg Gazette*, 24 Aug. 1900; *Cape Times*, 24 Sept. 1900.

24. *Cape Times*, 5 Sept. 1901.

25. *Cape Times*, 24 Sept. 1901.

26. MS/PRO/CO 291/27, Milner to Chamberlain, 27 Feb. 1901; and compare Farrelly 1900, p. 15; MS/JPL/Kent, 'The [Durban sub-] committee report upon the subject matter referred', n.d. (*c*. Aug. 1900). For the refugees' continued fears, see *Cape Times*, 29 July and 5 Sept. 1901.

27. MS/TAD/GOV 213/PS 6, minutes of a meeting of HE's consultative committee, 7 Oct. 1901; MS/PRO/CO 291/29, Milner to Chamberlain, 18 Oct. 1901, with enclosure; CO 291/39, Milner to Chamberlain, 7 May 1902, with report by H. Roberts on the 'Personal & Property Enquiry Department'; and *Cape Times*, 15 Aug. 1900.

28. MS/PRO/CO 417/295, Milner to Chamberlain, 7 Nov. 1900, with enclosure, political secretary to private secretary, 26 Oct. 1900. See also, *African Review*, 25 (416) 10 Nov. 1900; *Cape Times*, 26 Oct., 2 Nov. 1900.

29. MS/TAD/GOV 248/PS 19, Milner to Chamberlain (draft), 31 May 1901, with enclosure, memorandum by H. T. Ommanney, and report about CRC, n.d.

30. MS/TAD/GOV 248/PS 19, Milner to Chamberlain (draft), 31 May 1901, with enclosure, memorandum by H. T. Ommanney, and report about CRC, n.d.; and see MS/PRO/CO 291/30, Milner to Chamberlain (confidential), 7 Dec. 1901, with enclosures, report by Ommanney, 5 Dec. 1901, and H. F. S. S[trange] to O. Walrond, 6 Dec. 1901; CO 291/37, Milner to Chamberlain, 11 Feb. 1902; CO 291/41, Milner to Chamberlain, 31 Aug. 1902; and CO 291/42, Milner to Chamberlain, 29 Sept. 1902.

31. MS/PRO/FO 2/347, information received from WO written on file. See also FO 2/531, 25 Jan. 1901; and FO 2/651, CO to FO, with enclosures; MS/PRO/WO 32/8773, 'Return of "undesirables" in Union Castle steamers to Cape', 29 July 1901. And see *Johannesburg Gazette*, 29 Oct. 1901. See also MS/PRO/CO 291/307, note on file in response to WO query, 19 Dec. 1900: 'it will be a long time before the destitute refugee is wanted back in South Africa'. For restrictions on their return, see MS/PRO/WO 108/96, Kitchener to GOC, Natal and Cape Town, 9 Nov. 1901.

32. MS/TAD/LAJ 2/115, 14 July 1900; MS/PRO/WO 105/24, 'Black list: names of Boers and others of the Transvaal who should not be given employment in the new territories', forwarded by Milner to Roberts (confidential and private), 23 Aug. 1900.

33. Ommanney 'relied largely on the [CRC's] knowledge of the late inhabitants in discriminating between applicants'. See MS/TAD/GOV 248/PS 19, Milner to Chamberlain, with enclosed report by Ommanney, p. 2. See also MS/PRO/CO 291/29, Milner to Chamberlain, 27 Sept. 1901, with enclosure, Strange to Milner, 10 Sept. 1901, with memorandum, 23 Aug. 1901.

34. OP/CM 1900/1, p. 45; *African Review*, 24 (433) 9 March 1901, p. 351; *Cape Times*, 31 Jan.

1901. See also MS/PRO/CO 291/27, Milner to Chamberlain, 30 Jan. 1901; CO 291/29, Milner to Chamberlain, 27 Sept. 1901, with enclosed report by Ommanney; MS/TAD/PSY 50, Mackenzie to political secretary, 3 Jan. 1901; and MS/TAD/GOV 248/PS 19, Milner to Chamberlain (draft), 31 May 1901, with enclosed report by Ommanney, p. 5.

35. MS/PRO/CO 291/29, Milner to Chamberlain, 27 Sept. 1901, with enclosures, report by Ommanney, 27 Sept. 1901, Strange to Milner, 19 Sept. 1901, forwarding report by Ommanney to CRC, 20 June 1901, and memorandum by CRC to Ommanney, 17 July 1901. See also MS/JPL/Kent, 'Report of the sub-committee re. governor's letter, 25 June 1901 — Uitlander Committee [Durban]'; *Johannesburg Gazette*, 6 May 1901. This may have been in response to Kitchener's restrictions on the issuance of permits: see below.

36. MS/PRO/CO 291/29, Milner to Chamberlain, 27 Sept. 1901, with enclosure, Strange to Milner, 10 Sept. 1901, forwarding report by Ommanney to CRC, 20 June 1901; OP/CM 1900/1, pp. 21, 45, 54; *African Review*, 27 (437) 6 April 1901, p. 23; (438) 13 April 1901, p. 49. See also MS/NAM/Bernstein, J. M. Bernstein to parents, 4 May 1901.

37. *Cape Times*, 5 July 1901; MS/PRO/CO 610, minutes of the seventh ordinary meeting of the Johannesburg town council, 26 June 1901, and minutes of the tenth ordinary meeting of the Johannesburg town council, 10 July 1901, with a report from Fiddes, secretary to the Transvaal administration, 25 June 1901; and MS/PRO/CO 291/29, Milner to Chamberlain, 27 Sept. 1901, with enclosed report by Ommanney, 27 Sept. 1901.

38. The figures are taken from MS/PRO/CO 291/29; CO 291/30; CO 291/37; OP/GB/Cd. 1163 (1902), nos. 28, 35, 50.

39. MS/PRO/CO 291/39, Milner to Chamberlain, 8 May 1902, with report by Sommerville, 1 May 1902; CO 291/30, Milner to Chamberlain (confidential), 7 Dec. 1901; CO 291/38, Milner to Chamberlain, 30 April 1902. See also MS/TAD/SNA/13, Ommanney to secretary of Native Affairs, 14 Jan. 1902, and secretary of Native Affairs to Ommanney, 17 Jan. 1902; OP/GB/Cd. 1163 (1902), no. 36, Milner to Chamberlain, 25 April 1902; *Johannesburg Gazette*, 25, 26 and 29 Oct. 1901; *Star*, 9 April 1902.

40. OP/GB/Cd. 903 (1902), no. 64, Milner to Chamberlain, 14 Dec. 1901, with enclosure, H. J. Roberts, head of the personal and property enquiry department, 11 Dec. 1901; MS/PRO/CO 291/29, Milner to Chamberlain, 17 May 1902, with enclosure, H. J. Roberts, assistant commissioner of police, Johannesburg, to Milner, 1 May 1902.

41. *Johannesburg Gazette*, 21 and 30 Aug. and 16, 22 and 29 Oct. 1901. See also MS/PRO/CO 291/29, Milner to Chamberlain, 18 Oct. 1901, with enclosures, J. Moon, secretary to Refugee Aid Committee, to Milner, 6 Sept. 1901, and minutes of a meeting between Milner and a deputation of the Refugee Aid Committee, 14 Oct. 1901.

42. MS/PRO/CO 291/39, Milner to Chamberlain, 8 May 1902, with report by J. Sommerville, secretary to Refugee Aid Committee, 1 May 1902; CO 291/41, Milner to Chamberlain, 25 Aug. 1902, forwarding report by Sommerville, 8 Aug. 1902; *Star*, 24 Feb. and 21 April 1902; OP/GB/Cd. 1163 (1902), no. 41, Milner to Chamberlain, 10 May 1902. For the disbandment of the CRC, see MS/PRO/CO 291/39, Milner to Chamberlain (confidential), 21 June 1902, with enclosures. The final meeting was held on 21 June 1902. There had been a total of 285 meetings and 33 different men had sat on the committee at some point during its operation. There were 23 men on the committee when it disbanded, growing from 13 at its inception. Only three men sat on the committee for its full term.

43. *Star*, 28 Feb. 1902; OP/GB/Cd. 1463 (1903), no. 20, Milner to Chamberlain, 1 Dec. 1902, with enclosures; OP/TVL/Transvaal Labour Commission, pp. 659—60.

44. MS/PRO/FO 2/651, CO to FO, 4 Aug. 1902, with enclosure, Milner to Chamberlain, 23 June 1902; MS/PRO/CO 291/41, Milner to Chamberlain, 25 Aug. 1902, with report by J. Sommerville, 8 Aug. 1902.

Ten

Preparing for Peace

You cannot fight against the future.
William Gladstone

The complacency which had grown up over the months since Roberts's army marched onto the Rand was shattered on Boxing Day 1900 when a Boer commando attacked the New Kleinfontein mine, some 18 miles east of the city. Led by General Piet Viljoen, a mining commissioner at Heidelberg before the war, the commando did over £200,000 worth of damage. It also destroyed buildings on the Benoni, the Chimes West and the Kleinfontein Central mines nearby.[1]

A week later several of the industry's representatives managed to see Lord Kitchener and asked him to allow them to select from the loyalists at the coast a mine guard which they would import and pay themselves. The general, while admitting his surprise at (and the army's lack of preparation for) the destruction of the mine buildings and equipment, was disinclined to give special protection to the industry. Still, he was willing to consider their proposal.

This is just what the Chamber of Mines at the Cape had hoped for. The situation on the Rand was bad. There had been no formal guard on the mines since the mine police had been disbanded some months earlier and replaced by an informal guard on several properties. Matters were made worse by the fact that, on the now pumping mines, working men 'in sympathy with the enemy' had been hired because there were no more loyal men available. The Chamber soon prepared a formal proposal, which included a request that the nucleus of any mine guard include the Railway Pioneer Regiment, largely made up of Rand artisans and miners. That the men of the regiment, when not on guard duty, could replace the suspect mine-workers and 'de-water' the mines and build coal bins was an added bonus which did not go unnoticed. Finally, but importantly, the Chamber of Mines asked the military to foot the bill.

The commander-in-chief, upon reading the proposal, was not pleased. After several days of negotiations with the representatives of the industry, he crisply informed the high commissioner (who, unlike the general, felt that the mines warranted special protection) that it had been the industrialists, not he, who had first broached the subject of a guard and that, if the Chamber was not prepared to accept the financial burden, it should follow its own course.[2]

Left to its own devices, the Chamber of Mines set about the task. Soon a guard was formed, drawing over 1,000 civilians from the Cape and another 450 from Port

Elizabeth, East London and Durban. The men were to be paid 5s a day and were promised that they would not be used away from the mines — a condition stipulated by the Chamber of Mines when it agreed that the industry would pay the bill. By the end of January 1901 the first contingent of what was to become the Mines Division of the pre-existing Rand Rifles was drilling at the Cape.[3]

In the interim the Boers stayed busy. On 20 January the Rand Central Electric Company at Brakpan on the east Rand was attacked by about 200 commandos, at least five of whom were recognized as ex-employees. While little damage was done, the attack disrupted pumping and reconstruction work on several mines and placed parts of the district in darkness for some time. In the same period several other mines were attacked, with damage running into tens of thousands of pounds sterling. It was becoming imperative that the new guard be sent north.[4]

But, as might be expected, the news of the importation of men onto the Rand created discontent elsewhere. The commercial community in exile, for instance, complained that businessmen were not permitted to join the new guard unit, and suggested that they form their own guard so that some of its own people could go home. More worrying was the 'considerable discontent' expressed by men in the 'Colonial Corps'. They had two basic grievances. First, they were upset that the new guards were going to be paid 5s while men in the field, including a substantial portion of the Railway Pioneers, earned only 4s a day and rations. Secondly, they thought it 'most unjust' that civilians were being allowed to 'go straight up to [the] mines where [they would be] in [the] best position to get future employment' while some 200 Railway Pioneers, who had served for nearly a year, had just been discharged and sent back to the coast.[5]

Their discontent, according to Mackenzie, was exacerbated by the fact that some 900 white men were then working the pumps on the mines, earning four to five times the pay of the corps. He warned the high commissioner that if, in the opinion of the military, this became detrimental to the recruitment of more volunteers or bred further discontent among men already in the field, he would have no choice but to order all work on the mines to stop. He suggested that the Chamber consider the problem and, in the meantime, he offered his own solution: pay all the men on the mines the same as the volunteers in the Colonial Corps and put the balance of their wages into a fund which could be used for some charity. This latter provision, he acknowledged, was necessary to avoid the appearance that the Chamber of Mines was taking advantage of the situation to reduce the price of labour.[6]

The Chamber responded by reminding Milner that twice previously it had publicly pledged to reserve jobs for ex-volunteers for a month after their discharge or after the end of the war. And, more to the point, it had suggested using the Railway Pioneers as the core of the new guard in an effort to forestall just such criticism from the volunteers as now existed. As for the fund, the Chamber pointed out that in January, during negotiations about the formation of a mine guard, it had suggested (again in an effort to avoid such problems) that a special fund be created from workers' wages for the widows and orphans of Rand men killed during the war, but that the high commissioner had rejected the scheme, arguing that it would cause 'complications'. On the other hand, the Chamber felt that it could not pay the new guard unit less than it had promised. At the same time it feared that the men currently working on the mines would not work for lower wages or on the terms suggested by Mackenzie. Nor would closing the mines be a reasonable alternative.[7] There was, then, no immediate solution and there the matter rested for a time.

Nonetheless, the first instalment of the guards arrived in mid-February, with the mines furthest from the city taking the highest proportion of the force. While fortunate to be among the earliest arrivals of civilians on the Rand, the men were still dissatisfied with their lot, and especially their pay. One guardsman expressed their frustration in much the same terms as the refugees at the coast did: 'In many cases the wives of men are suffering severely from want, and the contrast of the treatment meted out to the wives and families of the enemy as compared to that meted out to the families of these men needs no comment. It really seems that the surrendered burgher is better off than the fighting British subject.'[8]

By the end of the year, as the military situation improved, the need for the guard diminished and it was disbanded. It had cost the industrialists over £130,000, money considered to have been well-spent in this period of guerilla warfare. When this unit folded, a few companies owning outlying mines remained concerned about security and grouped together to form another corps, the 'Mines Defence Force', consisting of several hundred men, many of whom had served in one of the previous guard units.[9] This was the last of the four different corps raised since the beginning of the war especially to protect the mines, and paid for by the industrialists throughout. The total cost climbed to probably £250,000 and, naturally, the Randlords were anxious to recover their losses.

Since at least May 1900 the Chamber of Mines had been prepared to send men back to the Rand with a view to restarting the mines. But its scheme collapsed along with the high commissioner's plan to return refugees in October of that year. After that the most companies could do was hire men already on the Rand to pump water and make essential repairs. But, in February 1901, Mackenzie provided the impe'us for reopening the mines with the startling news that African workers, most of whom had been at work since the war began, were leaving the Rand.

On 18 February Mackenzie wrote to Milner to say that in the previous eight months the 'wastage' resulting from mining company lay-offs had been about 6,000 blacks. The Ferreira mine, for instance, had reduced its complement by half. But, he continued, the IMR had needed labour and had taken the Africans on, which not only kept the men on the Rand but spared the industry the expense of feeding them. The problem, he continued, was what to do with them when the railway no longer needed them? There will be no 'suitable' work available, he explained to the high commissioner, to justify their being kept on the Rand. Even if a public road project were underwritten by the imperial treasury, it was unlikely that that would dissuade them from going home.[10]

The Chamber of Mines, upon hearing the news, renewed its efforts to restart work on the mines. Looking forward to the post-war years, it feared that the 'difficulties which, in any case, the industry [would] later on have to face in procuring an adequate supply of labour [would] be materially increased' if the Africans already there were allowed to leave. Milner agreed and in his attempt to convince Kitchener of his view, added a political dimension to the argument:

> *If it were possible, without in any way increasing the difficulties of supply,* to set a few of the Mines working, it would, I believe, have a great effect in discouraging the Boers still in the Field and hastening a collapse. . . . If [the Africans] could be engaged by the Mines as the IMR dismisses them, they would suffice to start work on two or three of the central Mines along the

outcrop. Not only would this mean a certain amount of business, a certain amount of revenue, at once, but it would *keep the natives on the spot*.[11]

Kitchener gave his approval, but listed five conditions, one of which, not surprisingly, was that the rate of pay for whites working on the newly-opened mines was not to exceed that of the colonial volunteers still in the field. While the Chamber had reservations about paying skilled miners 5s a day, it fully recognized that if this were not done the 'old question of dissatisfaction about [the] irregular corps' could arise again. Hence, the industrialists suggested once again that excess wages be placed in a fund for widows and orphans of Rand volunteers. Eventually, though, it was decided that the fund's beneficiaries were to be the families of the mine guards, of the men working on the mines, and of ex-mine workers serving in the volunteer corps.[12]

On 1 June 1901 the 'Mines Fund' became operational, with a committee of nine men (representing the Chamber of Mines, the men in the field and the mine employees) formed to administer it. It distributed money at a daily rate of 1s per adult and 6d per child for each day worked or served by the breadwinner. But soon the amount disbursed far exceeded estimates previously made. This was because the list of dependants continued to grow. Eventually more distant relatives, such as aunts and cousins, were disqualified as dependants, thus reducing the drain on the fund.[13] Although imperfect, the scheme served its purpose, for even the promise of its creation stifled dissent in the Colonial Corps long enough to get the mines started.

At 4.15 on the afternoon of 4 May 1901, Mrs Wybergh, wife of the acting commissioner of mines, broke a bottle of champagne against the stamps at the Meyer & Charlton mine and the industry was once again set in motion. It was a day of speeches, with George Albu setting the tone by listing the reforms sought by the industrialists before the war, and noting with pleasure the advent of the new 'enlightened administration'. He praised the government for its awareness that the 'interests of the mining industry and the country in general [were] identical' and for designing its policy accordingly. Two days later, at the reopening of the Robinson mine, it was the turn of the administration in the person of Mackenzie to praise the industrialists: 'If the Chamber of Mines in future dealings with the Government shows itself as public-spirited and as disinterested as many members of that Chamber and gentlemen connected with the mining industry have shown towards the local Military Administration, I am sure the future Government will have in the Chamber a very able and a very valuable support.'[14]

With the stage set for close cooperation between the industrialists and the government, the Rand mines began working again. The first seven mines, with a total of 350 stamps, were operating by 4 June. In August another mine was added, in November, three more and, in December, four. The gold output rose accordingly: in May 1901 a meagre 7,439 oz. was won, but by November the output had risen to over 32,000 oz. per month. Gold valued at about one million pounds sterling was taken from the ground in 1901.[15]

Although the high commissioner and the Randlords continued to worry about the industry's recovery being hindered by an inadequate supply of black labour, the number of Africans on the mines rose from 9,000 in May 1901 to over 18,000 by the end of the year.[16] This was partly the result of an agreement reached between the Chamber of Mines and Kitchener, whereby blacks who were discharged by the Railways were held in Johannesburg, to be engaged by WNLA for work on the mines. African mine-workers were paid 30s a month, or 10s more than they received from the Boers, but at least 20s less than they had been paid immediately prior to the war. As before the war when the wages were lowered, the result was desertion. Little other black industrial unrest was recorded before the end of the war.[17]

This, though, was not the case among white workers, who continued to complain about the 5s a day rate of pay. As new miners and guards were taken on, they had to sign an agreement accepting the terms of pay on offer. Yet it was the men who had remained on the mines drawing good wages during the war and who now had to accept the 5s a day to keep their jobs who were of more concern to the industrialists and the administration. To ensure compliance with the regulations while maintaining peace among the volunteers and productivity along the reef, Francis Davies, the acting commissioner of police, promised to deport any man who refused to work for the rate of pay on offer.[18]

By the end of July, less than three months after the mines reopened, the men were grumbling. On the 29th they sent a deputation to the Chamber of Mines with a petition signed by representatives of six working mines. It outlined their grievances:

> The clause in our agreement that full pay may not be given until the majority of Colonial irregular forces have been disbanded, should no longer be a reason for existing circumstances, owing to the fact that great numbers of discharged volunteers have elected to remain at the coast towns in preference to returning to work on the mines under the present system, while others still remaining in the field, although benefiting by the fund created, view our action with the greatest disfavour, dubbing us 'black legs', etc. . . . [A]fter three months' trial of our present system . . . we find that it is a matter of impossibility to meet the expenses incurred in supporting families and dependants, while at the same time providing necessaries for ourselves. . . . [W]hile firms in town are permitted to employ hands at the old rate of wages, we, the mine employees (the majority of us being discharged volunteers), are compelled to continue working for 5s per day and rations.[19]

The men asked the Chamber to use its influence with Kitchener to get him to review the situation and approve a wage reform.

When the commander-in-chief received the news he expressed his sympathy but stated that, in time of war, the burden had to be shared by all the people in the empire and that Rand miners had to be as prepared as the rest to 'display the necessary self-sacrifice and patriotism'. The Chamber of Mines therefore advised the men to be patient. But 60 of the 95 men on the May Consolidated mine were unmoved by such reasoning and decided to strike for full wages. Francis Davies thereupon reiterated his earlier threat, warning them that he would expel anyone who refused to work. But 35 remained obdurate, and they were escorted to the railway station and placed aboard a train bound for the coast. Not surprisingly, locals felt that 'present indications are that none of the employees of the other [mining] properties will resort to the ill-advised course adopted by the May workmen'. The fact that unemployed men from the city were hired to replace the strikers emphasized the point.[20]

The strike and the 'widespread discontent' displayed by mine-workers on other properties convinced the Chamber that the men would leave rather than continue working for such low wages. Its representatives voiced its fears to Kitchener,

Cooperation between the uitlander elite and the British administration led to the re-opening of the mines. Mrs Wybergh, in the centrre of this picture and the wife of the acting-Commandant of Mines, re-opened the Meyer and Charlton Mine in May 1901 by smashing a bottle of champagne on the stamps (*Africana Museum, Johannesburg*)

The re-opening of the Meyer and Charlton Mine, 4 May 1901: George Albu delivering his address (*Africana Museum, Johannesburg*)

adding that if the men left, it would mean reclosing the mines. When faced with this alternative — and all its political and military implications — Kitchener relented, telling the companies that after 1 November they could 'do as they wished' so long as the families of the former mine employees still with the Irregular Corps continued to recieve aid from the Mines Fund.[21] By the end of 1901, then, the mining industry was well on its way toward recovery.

To return Johannesburg to a state of near normality it was necessary to resurrect civil government. Both the colonial secretary and the high commissioner were anxious to see an end to military government[22] and, in early 1901, Milner appointed a commission to facilitate the transfer of power. In mid-March, Lionel Curtis (previously private secretary to the chairman of the London County Council and a man well versed in social engineering of the urban poor) was appointed secretary to the commission. Curtis, like the Uitlander advisers before him, was well aware of the unique power at hand: 'one gets things done at the stroke of a pen that in England would entail an Act of Parliament and an exhaustive Parliamentary enquiry'. He was anxious to get started. Soon the commission's proposals were ready: an early return to civil government, with the formation of a nominated town council and the appointment of a town clerk to formulate a new system of government. Both Curtis and the report found favour with Fiddes and Milner and he was appointed acting town clerk of Johannesburg.[23]

Milner worked closely with the local military administration when planning the transition to civil rule. He and Mackenzie agreed that a military governor would no longer be necessary, especially as many of the duties for which he was responsible were to be allocated to others. Some continuity was ensured, though, as Major W. A. J. O'Meara, who had acted as burgomaster during the period of military rule, was to become the acting mayor and the *ex-officio* chairman of the nominated town council. An engineer and intelligence officer who had served as chief staff officer in Kimberley during the siege there, O'Meara had his own ideas about Johannesburg's future and the role he and his town council were to play in it. He felt, for instance, that the city boundary ought to be extended and that the centrally-located areas, overpopulated with the working poor of all colours, had to be cleared in order to foster urban development. To undertake these and other tasks, the town council had to have ample power: for example, it needed the right to take over government lands for public use, to establish health and sanitation measures and to control local trade.[24] Another to remain in the administration was Francis Davies, as acting commissioner of police. Wybergh became the acting commissioner of mines and had 'Native Affairs' temporarily under his control. Fiddes remained as secretary to the Transvaal administration.

The choice of who was to sit on this increasingly powerful city council was left to Milner. Although he publicly declared that there was a 'super abundance' of qualified men from whom to choose, privately he despaired of the 'great unwillingness' on the part of the 'best men' to serve, for they were all too busy.[25] Seemingly he was reluctant to appoint men who had served as Mackenzie's advisers. No doubt too, they were wary of offering to join an administration in which Fiddes, and other men from England, played a major role. In any case, none appeared on Milner's list of choices: *inter alia*, W. St John Carr, W. Dalrymple, W. Hosken, J. W. Quinn, W. Rogers, R. Shanks, A. Epler, H. Lindsay, and H. F. E. Pistorius.[26]

While contemporaries praised the councillors for being men of integrity and ability and the town council as a whole for being 'representative of every shade of opinion', it is obvious that pre-war political reformers dominated it. For instance, of the first six men listed above, only Rogers was not a member of the pre-war Uitlander Council. As the town council grew, still other reformers joined it: in August 1901, A. A. Noble, another member of the Consultative Committee; in September W. T. A. Davies, of the earlier Reform Committee; and in early 1902, A. Mackie Niven. Not surprisingly, local labour leaders were suspicious of its make-up, referring to it as a 'wonderful tribute to Eckstein power.[27] Indeed, it did display a definite ethnic purity and a middle-class bias. In addition, though these men varied widely in their skills, personalities and charm,[28] they held generally similar political and economic views, at least until the post-war period when major issues, such as the importation of Chinese labour or the formation of responsible government, divided them. But now, at the end of the war, combined as they were, with Milner's support, and in the absence of any organized opposition, they were vested with great power, which they used to implement policies designed to create on the Rand a society that would assist the industry's growth while anglicizing the Transvaal.

The first problem facing the council was a fiscal one. The city's expenditure far exceeded its revenues, largely because rates had not been collected for some months. Furthermore, there were no plans to collect taxes until a decision could be reached regarding the full impact of the Kruger rent proclamation upon assessment rates. Therefore, to put the city on its feet, the high commissioner lent it £100,000 to pay its debts and to meet any expenses incurred in its first six months of life.[29]

When in the following months it set about devising a system of municipal taxation, it decided to assess land and ignore improvements. This scheme was aimed at speculative landowners — many of whom, having made their money before the war, had dubious political sympathies — for by increasing their tax burden they could well be forced to put some of their vacant land onto the market. No doubt councillors hoped that the development of vacant stands would result (thereby easing the worsening housing crisis) and ultimately allow for a reduction in the high cost of living and in the salaries of white workers. But the scheme also worked in the interest of aspiring landowners, men who could now firmly plant their feet on the Rand.

One of those who had managed to buy vast tracts of land along the reef before the war was J. B. Robinson, who was now vociferous in his opposition to the plan, calling it 'spoilation' and accusing the council of pushing it through even though it was not what the community as a whole wanted. This, he argued, was because the council did not represent the community, not having been elected, and because too few property owners had been allowed to return from exile. So, even though the majority of the councillors approved the scheme, in the end Milner refused to sanction it because opposition was so fierce. Thereafter, both land and improvements were assessed, though separate rolls were kept for each.[30]

Meanwhile, the town council also faced a multitude of personnel decisions as it began to hire men to fill vacant municipal posts. Not surprisingly, it chose men who had proven their loyalty and trustworthiness by serving in the British army or a volunteer corps, and refused positions to men who had served under the Rust en Orde Commission. Furthermore, the council was not averse to hiring men nominally for one position, when in reality they were employed to spy for the acting police commissioner, Davies.[31]

In keeping with the administration's desire to create a modern city on the Rand, and one that gained directly from having the industry and industrialists close at hand, the town council was called upon in late 1901 to bring the mining district into the urban area. This entailed pushing out the city limit much further than the earlier extension, which had enlarged the pre-war city of five square miles to nine. Now, this second and far more ambitious plan — to enlarge the city to 82 square miles — pitted the generally reluctant industrialists against Milner and his local administrators.

Not all the industrialists were so single-minded and apolitical as to shun involvement in local politics, but Fitzpatrick does seem to have been the most exceptional. Way back in 1898, for instance, he felt that the industrialists owed the Rand community something: 'fortune after fortune is made out of the place', he complained, 'and yet nothing worth speaking of is put back except as reinvestment for a bigger profit'. Milner felt much the same about the place: the mine owners, he told Chamberlain, reject any municipal responsibility, but seek to keep the mining district as a 'little Kingdom of their own whose inhabitants have no civic rights or duties and are exempt, except in the last resort, from civic oversight'. What is needed, he explained to Fitzpatrick, was for the Randlords to take an active interest in municipal affairs. 'It is quite as much to your advantage as to that of the community that you should take a hand', he assured him. Moreover, the administration felt that if the owners were allowed to maintain a separate identity, divorced from urban affairs, it would be damaging to the creation of a 'single corporate whole'.[32]

In the ensuing effort to get the Chamber of Mines to agree to incorporation, the 'carrot and stick' approach was called for. Curtis, trying to make the extension as acceptable to the companies as possible, proposed that city rates be assessed on land and on commercial and residential buildings only, and that underground values and mining machinery not be taxed. This 'sort of bribe to the mines', to use Basil Williams's phrase, meant that only the areas where miners' houses were located and leaseland held for commercial purposes were eventually assessed for purposes of municipal taxation.[33]

Milner made it clear to the industrialists that he wanted them to receive what he called 'fair treatment'. 'I will give you a charter now', he told the Chamber of Mines in February 1902, 'which will safeguard you in the future . . . and will be very difficult to alter later on. . . . The terms will be very much better for you than any you can hope to get from the Public', he warned them. And he kept his word, for, in 1902, an ordinance was enacted which provided that any law the town council wished to pass that would affect the industry or any specific company, had to be submitted to the Chamber for consideration. Afterwards, the lieutenant governor and the mining commissioner would review the Chamber's recommendation and only then could the town council proceed.[34]

Milner's aim was not only to drag the Randlords into municipal affairs, but also to widen the local tax base and to ensure that the miners living along the reef became active in the political life of the district. Milner's overriding goal as far as southern Africa was concerned was to 'strengthen and hearten the British element, and to envelop South Africa, as far as possible, in a British atmosphere'. Only then did he feel he could allow its residents to go to the ballot box to decide their political future. The Rand, with its modern industrial economy, was important to his plan and he had urged, since at least 1900, that a large British population be encouraged to settle there. Incorporation of the mines into

Johannesburg was only a small part of the plan: though few in number, the miners who lived along the reef were skilled, well-paid and primarily British, and must therefore be represented at a local level.[35]

For some months the matter of incorporation was quietly discussed in town. The Chamber of Mines presented its objections, arguing that 'harmony' would best be maintained if the administration of the mines and the city were kept separate. Milner and his people were unconvinced. Matters were finally brought to a head in January 1902 when the 'Health Board' at Germiston attempted to levy a tax upon property and buildings of one of the nearby mines. This provided Milner with the opportunity to act, for when he now announced that the municipal boundary was to be extended, it was 'welcomed' by the Chamber as 'evidence of the intention of the government to deal with the central mines as a whole, through a body on which they could be represented, rather than leave them, as they [were] inclined to imagine, to the caprices of a number of insignificant local authorities'. This threat, as well as his visit to the Chamber of Mines' meeting the following month, where he made it clear that he had 'backing from the Home Government and the Home public' on this issue and where he promised the industrialists 'safeguards', won the day.[36]

Milner, the Randlords and the local administration shared many ideas about what Rand society ought to be like. Basically, they supported measures which were designed, as Charles van Onselen puts it, to 'help stabilize the Rand's skilled white proletariat, secure British hegemony, and facilitate social control by separating the labouring classes from the dangerous classes'. In an effort to achieve these goals, Mackenzie and his Uitlanders had used martial law. Now Milner, assisted by his 'kindergarten' and his nominated councillors, used the power of Crown government to rectify the perceived 'shortcomings of fifteen years'.[37] To foster controlled growth, the city council tackled the town's poorly developed infrastructure, improving the city's lighting and its sewage system, while assisting the development of an electric-tram system which became operational in early 1906. Most importantly, the administration turned its attention to the area just west of the city centre, where Mackenzie's soldiers had earlier swooped to arrest men in the 'racecourse plot' and where, over the years, a slum had developed which was populated by poor families of all colours.

Before the war, the burgher working poor and unemployed had moved into the area — into the Brickfields, Vrededorp and Burgersdorp — encouraged to settle there by Paul Kruger. At about the same time, efforts began to be made to remove the nearby 'coolie location', that 'fever-breeding' 'eyesore', to an area outside the city. But in the late 1890s, the British government, seeking any issue 'to beat Kruger with', opposed moving the Asians to a more distant location on the grounds that their removal was designed only to permit the transfer of valuable inner-city stands to political favourites.[38] Now in power, the British administration viewed the situation in quite a different light.

The need to relocate the Asian location had not escaped Mackenzie's notice earlier, but he was unable to do anything about it unless he could justify the move on sanitary grounds. Well aware that the British government would oppose any 'class legislation' — measures aimed at one ethnic or national group — he never tried. Even so the return of the Asian refugees was slowed down to give the administration more time to consider the problem.[39]

Later, when the town council was considering how to improve the city's infrastructure, police commissioner Davies drew Lionel Curtis's attention to the western suburbs generally. The area of the Brickfields, Aaron's Ground and the 'coolie location', he wrote, 'is so laid out in a network of passages and dens as to form a refuge for the criminal class most difficult for the Police to control . . . and is a permanent menace to the safety of the Town'. He asked that these 'dens of iniquity' be swept away and the 'slum' moved from the business section of town. Now, with the inclusion of these white suburbs, populated by the poor of all nationalities, any objections to removing the 'coolie location' were eliminated. No longer could the scheme be considered 'class legislation' in the sense meant by the imperial government.[40] Hence, the 'Insanitary Area Scheme' was born, with its joint goal of ridding the city of Asians and of white 'undesirables'.

The town council took the initiative. In June 1901 the Health & Measures sub-committee reported that there was a:

> great risk to the health of the town arising from the present state and position of the Coolie Location, especially in view of the imminent possibility of an outbreak of bubonic plague. We recommend: That the attention of the Government be drawn to the urgent necessity of taking in hand the removal of the locations with the least possible delay.[41]

By October the white slum areas were included in the scheme, though the plan to improve drainage in the area was not formally placed before the town council until 19 February the following year. By this time the council had already sought Milner's support, for it was afraid of being accused of being unrepresentative of the community at large because it had been appointed and not elected. Milner felt sure that it was both strong and representative enough to carry the scheme through.[42] By this time, too, the town valuer had estimated that the drain-building programme would cost £750,000 and would generate a profit of £80,000 for the city.[43]

The administration was now ready to present the scheme to the public. When placed before the council in February it naturally generated a great deal of concern among property owners and residents in the area. On the 25th, a meeting of 'standholders' who lived within the proscribed area was chaired by Harry Solomon, a stockbroker of some importance but a man whom most reformers disliked. The owners and occupiers based their opposition to the plan, first, on its timing: could not the council wait until more refugees had returned so that they might have a say in an affair which directly affected them? Secondly, they argued that the council did not have to appropriate the whole area just to build drains, but could tear down single buildings on individual stands where needed. The owners, Solomon assured the council, would be 'only too glad to erect new buildings'.[44] Clearly, though, this was not what the administration had in mind, for it certainly did not want paupers, criminals and people of colour to return to the area once drains were built.

Milner, though, had to appear to be just and, because of this and other opposition, he appointed a committee to investigate the district, to decide whether any of it was a health hazard and to determine what course should be taken if this were the case. Evidence was again collected and presented to the public: high mortality rates, overcrowding, interracial living, immorality and crime. These factors, in addition to the crucial one of the area's central location, were again weighed.[45]

As it became clear to owners that the expropriation of the area could not be stopped, the opposition shifted its focus to the price that would be paid and to the manner in which the area would be assessed for purposes of compensation. As negotiations continued, the date of the land's valuation was extended, thereby adding to the price of the land. In the meantime, the council agreed to pay for the cost of removal and the 'loss of goodwill', both of which added to the price of expropriation.[46]

In September 1903, the 'Insanitary Area' — some 188 acres — was expropriated. The overcrowded area of the Brickfields and to the west, which 'contained dangerous spots of insanitation' and 'narrow streets' laid out on 'chaotic plans which . . . made proper sanitation impossible', could now be cleared. All the buildings were to be removed and new streets added, with two major roads — Jeppe and Bree — pushed through the area. Proper drainage was to be constructed and the land resurveyed into large and regular blocks.[47] Nevertheless, after expropriation, residents continued to live in the area as tenants of the city, though no attempts were made to improve conditions.

In fact, whereas before expropriation every standholder in the 'coolie location' had been responsible for the cleanliness of his property (every stand had a 'topaz', or caretaker, assigned to it) now, according to Mohandas Gandhi, 'the owners were not allowed to have any say either as to the manner in which the stands were kept, or as to the tenants that were received'. Furthermore, the population continued to grow and conditions worsened, while, according to Riva Krut, the municipality turned a blind eye and used racial categories to allocate blame.[48]

In March 1904, 20 cases of plague were diagnosed in the Asian quarter and, by the end of the month, 88 people in the 'Insanitary Area' had died. It was only when the non-white residents of the area were segregated by race and relocated in 'temporary dwellings' near Klipspruit Sewage Farm south-west of Johannesburg, part of the vacated area fenced to prevent rats from escaping and enclosed buildings razed to the ground, that the plague abated.[49] The area, with its new markets, widened streets and square blocks was, by 1908, 'Newtown': much later, the 'temporary' locations to the south-west were to become Soweto.

While the mines reopened and civil government was re-established in the first half of 1901, the city did not begin to return to normal until later that year. Only when the 'civilian element' returned in large numbers and when the barricades were removed from the rest of the shops, offices and homes did the town assume a normal appearance, albeit 'to a modified degree'.[50] While the railway lines were now secure and licensed traders could import certain goods into the city, there continued to be shortages of food from time to time. Furthermore, there was the 'Racecourse Concentration Camp' nearby which provided clear evidence that the war continued, as did the presence of several camps along the reef for Africans who had been 'collected together' from their kraals and sent there.[51]

Furthermore, British men were still forced to join the Rand Rifles upon their arrival. Many disliked the duty, complaining that being 'shoved into the King's uniform' was only the 'thin edge of the wedge of conscription'. Nonetheless, their duties were usually confined to drilling about the city. In April 1901 they had been tested, and found wanting, when Kitchener ordered them to Springs to protect several mines. Mackenzie suggested that the order be changed, explaining that it promised to create 'great discontent' among the citizen-soldiers and that only 10 per cent would probably comply. They would defend the town, he later told the high commissioner, but would do little more.[52]

Returning Uitlanders also faced a housing crisis upon their arrival. With mass transport to the outlying areas nonexistent, suburban development had been hindered. With chambers in town being transformed into offices and the cost of buying land and building a house prohibitive for the working man, family housing was in short supply. The war made matters worse, for houses remained off the rental market because they were still barricaded or because they had been ransacked at some point during the war and had yet to be refurbished (and this was delayed because of the high cost of building materials and labour). As a consequence rents were high. The working class was naturally bitter. One resident explained to the press in 1902 that for two and a half years he had served in the volunteer corps while his wife and children lived on the beach. Now, when he returned to the Rand to begin life anew, he found it virtually impossible to live on a wage of 5s a day. Even later, when wages rose, an artisan would find that rents had risen 300 per cent since before the war and that he was paying over three-quarters of his salary for a three- or four-roomed cottage.[53]

In early 1902 residents put forward several radical solutions to the housing problem. For example, they asked the military to commandeer hotels to house British women as it had done for Boer families. They also asked the military to control rents as it did the price of food and liquor. One 'victim' explained that the city needed restrictions similar to those in the Orange River Colony, where the 'same evil' had 'taken root'. There the administration promptly issued a proclamation barring any landlord from raising the rent or attempting to remove a tenant without the provost marshall's approval. Other residents proposed placing the people who were being forced into the less expensive western suburbs in vacant houses owned by absent refugees, or in temporary shelters erected solely for that purpose. Such radical solutions, which impinged on the sanctity of private property, found no favour with successive local governments, and Johannesburg continued to be notoriously short of cheap housing and an 'impossible place' in which to find homes.[54]

The solution to the housing crisis, investigated thoroughly by the Housing Commission of 1903, had to wait for some time. First, new suburbs had to be developed, which was possible only with the advent of mass public transport in the form of the electric tram. Construction costs had to come down, and housing had to be provided for working men and their families on the mine properties. Yet, before all this was accomplished, the Rand suffered a serious socio-political setback. The housing crisis forced British artisans — the population upon whom Milner hoped to build his Anglo—Transvaal — to send their families home. As many as a third of the Rand's artisans repatriated their dependants in this period and, 'instead of making their home' on the Rand, they continued to look 'upon this place as one in which to make money as speedily as they can and then to get out of it'.[55]

Before Roberts entered the Rand in May 1900, the high commissioner had spoken of Johannesburg as a 'clean slate'. Now the administration saw it as what Curtis described as a 'dirty canvas to clean and mend before you can begin painting' on it again.[56] The 'cleaning and mending' had been going on for some time, since Mackenzie and his advisers used 'military exigencies' as justification for deportations and abuses of martial law. The O'Meara administration in the last year of the war used Crown government powers to enlarge the city to allow it room to absorb a newly-settled white work-force, and to incorporate the mines and their owners and managers into a power structure. If it were to contribute to Milner's overall plan to attract British settlers to the Transvaal, it had to become a viable economic and political nucleus. Somehow, though, over the next few years (as depression dogged the city and industry, and anglicization of the Transvaal proved illusory), the whole scheme seemed to go awry.

Notes

1. OP/CM 1900/1, p. 2; MS/TAD/GOV 280, New Kleinfontein Company Ltd to CO (copy), 15 March 1901; *African Review*, 25 (423) 29 Dec. 1900, pp. 459, 469; and 24 (435) 23 March 1901, p. 430.
2. OP/CM 1900/1, pp. 2–9; MS/PRO/CO 291/27, Milner to Chamberlain (confidential), 8 Jan. 1901, with enclosures, Milner to Kitchener, 4 and 7 Jan. 1901, and Kitchener to Milner, 5 Jan. 1901, and Milner to Chamberlain (confidential), 17 Jan. 1901, with enclosure, Kitchener to Milner, 8 Jan. 1901. See also MS/BOD/Mss. English History, c. 687, Milner to Maj. Goold Adams (typescript copy), 'Doubtless the Rand District has the first claim to absolute protection'. For concerns about the loyalty of the men already on the mines, see MS/PRO/CO 291/27, Milner to Chamberlain (confidential), 17 Jan. 1901, with enclosure, Mackenzie to Milner, 12 Jan. 1901.
3. OP/CM 1900/1, pp. 8–16; MS/PRO/CO 291/27, Milner to Chamberlain (confidential), 17, 22 and 30 Jan. 1901, with enclosures. See also *Johannesburg Gazette*, 21 and 24 Jan. and 5 and 7 Feb. 1901; *The Times* (London) 31 Jan. 1901.
4. OP/CM 1900/1, pp. 15–16; MS/PRO/CO 291/27, Milner to Chamberlain (confidential), 30 Jan., 20 Feb. 1901, with enclosures; MS/TAD/GOV 280; MS/PRO/FO 2/985, WO to FO, 3 April 1903.
5. For complaints from the business community, see MS/TAD/GOV 282, mayor and council of Kimberley to Milner, 7 Feb. 1901 and Chamber of Commerce, Kimberley, to Milner, 14 Feb. 1901, in same file. See also, MS/PRO/CO 291/27, Milner to Chamberlain (confidential), 20 Feb. 1901, with enclosure, private secretary to mayor of Kimberley, 13 Feb. 1901; and *Johannesburg Gazette*, 24 Jan. 1901. For complaints from the colonial corps, see CO 291/27, Milner to Chamberlain, 6 Feb. 1901, with enclosure, Mackenzie to Milner, 4 Feb. 1901.
6. MS/PRO/CO 291/27, Milner to Chamberlain, confidential, 6 Feb. 1901, with enclosure, Mackenzie to Milner, 4 Feb. 1901. See also OP/CM 1900/1, pp. 17–18, 21.
7. OP/CM 1900/1, pp. 5, 7, 17–21. See also MS/PRO/WO 105/20, Milner to Roberts (confidential), 10 July 1900; *Johannesburg Gazette*, 12 Dec. 1900; MS/PRO/CO 291/27, Milner to Chamberlain (confidential), with enclosure, Milner to Mackenzie, 7 Feb. 1901.
8. MS/TAD/GOV 283, extract from anonymous letter from Johannesburg, 24 June 1901. For disposition of the guards, see MS/TAD/Rand Rifles, 'Old nominal rolls'; OP/CM 1900/1, pp. 16–17; MS/TAD/GOV 283, James Law to Walrond, 22 Jan. 1901; *Cape Times*, 14 May 1901.
9. OP/CM 1900/1, pp. 24–6, 28. See also *Star*, 1 May 1902.
10. MS/TAD/GOV 248/PS 18, Mackenzie to Milner (copy), 18 Feb. 1901. On 3 Dec. 1900, Mackenzie informed Milner (GOV 316/PS 31) that 'in many mines the native food supply is almost completely exhausted'. For conscription of Africans for work on the railway, see *Star*, 9 April 1902; MS/JPL/ERPM, Hellman to chairman and board of directors, 2 Aug. 1900; *African Review*, 26 (431) 23 Feb. 1901, pp. 275–6; and Warwick 1983, pp. 133–5.
11. MS/TAD/GOV 248/PS 18, Milner to Kitchener (confidential), 18 Feb. 1901 (copy); OP/CM 1900/1, p. 48.
12. OP/CM 1900/1, p. 50, citing Mackenzie to Chamber of Mines, 12 March 1901, which lists Kitchener's conditions, and see also pp. 50–4, and report of the executive committee, p. xxxvi; and MS/TAD/MGP 113, 10299 A, Commander Nigel, mine guards to military governor, Pretoria, 10 Aug. 1901; *Johannesburg Gazette*, 2 May 1901.

13. MS/JPL/ERPM, H. W. P. Steeds to ERPM, 1 and 10 July 1901, and L. B. Chesterton to ERPM, 1 Oct. 1901. See also *Cape Times*, 30 July 1901; MS/TAD/MGP 113, 10299 A, Commander Nigel, mine guards to military governor, Pretoria, 10 Aug. 1901; *Johannesburg Gazette*, 2 May 1901.

14. *Johannesburg Gazette*, 6 and 7 May 1901.

15. OP/CM 1900/1, p. 63; OP/GB/Cd. 1163 (1902), no. 30, Milner to Chamberlain, 5 April 1902.

16. OP/GB/Cd. 903 (1902), no. 61, Milner to Chamberlain, 14 Dec. 1901, with report from the mining commissioner; and Cd. 1163 (1902), no. 30, Milner to Chamberlain, 5 April 1902. See also *Johannesburg Gazette*, 5 June 1901; and MS/BOD/Mss. Milner Dep. 72, diary, 24 April 1901, where Milner notes that Nourse of Native Affairs told him that, 'unless a great additional supply [of black labour] is obtained from the Portuguese territory, business will be greatly blocked, on the cessation of hostilities'. For statistics, see MS/TAD/SNA/13, secretary of WNLA to Lagden of Native Affairs, 20 Jan. 1902, and OP/GB/Cd. 1551 (1903), no. 3, Milner to Chamberlain, 7 April 1903, annexure 3.

17. OP/CM 1900/1, pp. 51—2; MS/PRO/CO 293/2, minutes of a meeting of the executive council, 24 July 1901, p. 67; MS/TAD/SNA/9, report of the commissioner for Native Affairs, 12 Dec. 1901; *African Review*, 24 (411) 28 July 1900, pp. 128, 130—1; and 24 (419) 22 Sept. 1900, p. 424; *Johannesburg Gazette*, 4 July 1901. Those discharged from the railways for future work on the mines were kept by the Native Department in Johannesburg, and their upkeep paid for by WNLA and the government. Basil Williams notes in his diary on 17 Feb. 1902 that he had been told that Kitchener refused to allow the blacks who had completed their contracts to leave the Rand. He added that, '"Native Affairs" want them to be kept practically as forced labour to keep them out of mischief'. The black mine-workers were to be kept on the spot even if it meant 'strain[ing] the law', to use Williams's words. See MS/RHO/Williams, vol. 1.

18. OP/CM 1900/1, pp. 55, 57.

19. Ibid., pp. 57—8. For the white working-class's view of this scheme and the men employed in it, see Cope 1943, pp. 59—60.

20. OP/CM 1900/1, p. 60; *Cape Times*, 20 Aug. 1901.

21. OP/CM 1900/1, pp. 30—3, 60—2. See also MS/JPL/ERPM, L. B. Chesterton to ERPM, 1 Nov. 1901.

22. MS/BOD/Mss. English History, c. 687, Milner to Lady Edward Cecil, typescript extract, 23 Oct. 1901; and, for Chamberlain's distrust of military administration, see MS/BOD/Mss. Milner Dep. 170, Chamberlain to Milner (private), 22 Dec. 1901. See also Galbraith 1983, p. 75.

23. Krut 1979, citing Curtis, 25 April 1901. See also Nimocks 1968, p. 30; MS/RHO/Williams, vol. 1, entries 13—23 Jan. 1902.

24. Krut 1979, p. 50; MS/BOD/Mss. Milner Dep. 72, diary, 23 April 1901.

25. For his public view, see OP/GB/Cd. 903 (1902), no. 17, Milner to Chamberlain, 8 May 1901; and, for his private view, see MS/BOD/Mss. Milner Dep. 72, diary, 25 April 1901. See also Fitzpatrick's view of the obligations of the 'best men', Fitzpatrick to J. Wernher, 7 March 1902, in Duminy and Guest (eds) 1976.

26. OP/GB/Cd. 903 (1902), no. 17, Milner to Chamberlain, 8 May 1901. The other three appointed but not listed in the text were W. E. Hoy, W. McCallum and W. A. Martin. For the formal transition of power, see *Johannesburg Gazette*, 14, 16 and 18 May 1901.

27. MS/JPL/Leslie(a), p. 143 for the comment concerning the whole council. For information regarding the men listed, see MS/TAD/GOV 213/PS 6; *Cape Times*, 30 Aug. 1901; Leyds 1964, p. 278; MS/RHO/Williams, vol. 1, entries 13—23 Jan. 1902. For the comments of labour leaders, see MacDonald n.d., p. 105. Ms L. Kennedy, librarian of the Johannesburg Public Library supplied further information to the author in a letter dated 11 May 1981.

28. MS/RHO/Williams, vol. 1, entries 13—23 Jan. 1902, notes about the town councillors that Quinn was 'shrewd rather radical ... very sensible and quick at seizing a point'. St John Carr was a 'very honest hard working man, but not brilliant and rather quick

tempered'. Mackie Niven he thought 'one of the ablest men on [the] Council and quick and practical with a will of his own'. Noble was a 'very solid reliable man', though Lindsay was 'a radical pigheaded cantankerous lawyer' and Shanks, the 'working man member, rather a fool'.

29. *Johannesburg Gazette*, 17 July 1901.

30. MS/PRO/CO 291/38, Milner to Chamberlain (confidential), 6 March 1902, with enclosures, Robinson to Milner, 3 and 5 March 1902. Milner notes privately that Robinson was 'the worst type of moneyed man pure and simple with no idea beyond his personal interest'. See also Maud 1938, pp. 54—5.

31. *Johannesburg Gazette*, 6 June 1901; MS/LHC/Covernton, 'Fifty odd years of memoirs, 1893—1945', p. 40; MS/RHO/Williams, vol. 1.

32. Fitzpatrick to S. J. Jennings, 26 Sept. 1898, and Fitzpatrick to J. Wernher, 7 March 1902, citing Milner, in Duminy and Guest (eds) 1976; MS/PRO/CO 291/29, Milner to Chamberlain (confidential), 11 Oct. 1901. For Milner's view of the capitalists on the Rand, see Milner 1906, pp. 215—16. For the underlying philosophy of Johannesburg reconstruction, see MS/PRO/CO 291/29, Milner to Chamberlain (confidential), 27 Sept. 1901, with memorandum from Lionel Curtis, n.d.

33. MS/PRO/CO 291/29, Milner to Chamberlain (confidential), 27 Sept. 1901, with memorandum from Lionel Curtis, n.d.; MS/RHO/Williams, letters (strictly confidential), vol. 2, 23 April 1902. For the justification of this measure, see MS/PRO/CO 291/38, Milner to Chamberlain, 6 March 1902, with enclosures. See also Denoon 1968, esp. p. 310.

34. Fitzpatrick to J. Wernher, 7 March 1902, citing Milner at the Chamber of Mines meeting, in Duminy and Guest (eds) 1976. Maud 1938, pp. 56, 61—2, outlines the legislation that enacted this policy.

35. Milner 1906, p. 212; Krut 1979, p. 14; MS/PRO/CO 291/29, Milner to Chamberlain (confidential), 11 Oct. 1901.

36. MS/PRO/CO 291/29, Milner to Chamberlain (confidential), 1 Oct. 1901, forwarding Chamber of Mines memorandum, 1 Oct. 1901. See also CO 291/38, Milner to Chamberlain (confidential), 12 April 1902, with enclosure, Mr Goldring of the Chamber of Mines to Milner, 29 Jan. 1902, forwarding a letter to the Chamber from the Consolidated Gold Fields of South Africa, 22 Jan. 1902. For his visit to the Chamber of Mines, see Fitzpatrick to J. Wernher, 7 March 1902, in Duminy and Guest (eds) 1976.

37. Van Onselen 1982, vol. 1, pp. 28, 30—31. See also Krut 1979, p. 50, citing the town council.

38. *Star*, 14 Dec. 1897 and see 6 Dec. 1897, 18 Nov. 1898, 14 Feb., 24 Aug. 1899; MS/PRO/CO 417/263, Milner to Chamberlain, 5 and 18 July, with enclosures. For additional observations, see Fitzpatrick 1899, pp. 322—3; and MS/JPL/ACPT, London letterbook, 14 Nov. 1899, which links J. B. Robinson to the shifting of the locations.

39. PRO/CO 291/37, Milner to Chamberlain, 3 Jan. 1902, with enclosed, W. A. J. O'Meara to Fiddes, 17 Oct. 1901, which lays out Mackenzie's views.

40. PRO/CO 291/37, Milner to Chamberlain, 3 Jan. 1902, with enclosed, Davies to town clerk (confidential), n.d.. Later police commissioner Showers adopted this view (van Onselen 1982, vol. 1, p. 27). In PRO/CO 291/37, Milner to Chamberlain, 3 Jan. 1902, with enclosed, O'Meara to Fiddes, 17 Oct. 1901, O'Meara notes that with the 'incorporation of other insanitary areas inhabited by a European population' into the scheme, 'the main objection . . . made by me to Colonel Mackenzie' had been removed.

41. *Johannesburg Gazette*, 6 June 1901.

42. OP/GB/Cd. 2482 (1905), Milner to Lyttleton, 23 Jan. 1904, forwarding report from the law department for the year ending 30 Aug. 1903; and PRO/CO 291/37, Milner to Chamberlain, 3 Jan. 1902, with enclosure, O'Meara to Fiddes, 17 Oct. 1901.

43. PRO/CO 291/37, Milner to Chamberlain, 3 Jan. 1902, with enclosure, Curtis to O'Meara, 15 Oct. 1901, which forwards a preliminary report by Richard Currie, the town valuer, n.d.

44. *Star*, 20, 24, 26 and 27 Feb. 1902. And see, MS/RHO/Williams, vol. 1, 26 Feb. 1902.

45. OP/TVL/Johannesburg Insanitary Area Improvement Scheme. See also the *Star* in late February 1902; and Maud 1938, p. 63.
46. MS/RHO/Williams, letters, vol. 2, 11 Jan. 1903.
47. Krut 1979, p. 53, citing town council report of work for 1903.
48. Krut 1979, p. 54.
49. Ibid., pp. 55—6; Swan 1985, pp. 107—8; Leyds 1964, p. 171; Maud 1938, p. 70. For a first-hand account of the burning of the area, see MS/LHC/Covernton, pp. 41—2. It has been noted that the arrival of the plague was not entirely unwelcomed by the white community (Denoon 1973, p. 115).
50. *Cape Times*, 6 Sept. 1901. By April 1902 there were about 45,000 whites in the city (MS/PRO/CO 610, 53rd meeting of the Johannesburg town council, 18 June 1902).
51. Spies 1977, pp. 193—201, 217, 225; Warwick 1983, *passim*; and, for trade, see *Cape Times*, 5, 10, 15 and 23 July 1901; *Johannesburg Gazette*, 3 Oct. 1901; *Star* 25 Feb. 1902.
52. MS/NAM/Maxwell, 10 March 1901; and see, for a similar dislike of duty in the Rand Rifles, MS/UWL/Hills, diary, vol. 2, 14 May 1902. Mackenzie took delight in calling it, 'compulsory volunteering' (*Johannesburg Gazette*, 1 Dec. 1900). For the April 1901 fiasco, see MS/TAD/GOV 468, Mackenzie to Milner, 10 April 1901, and Mackenzie to Kitchener, 10 April 1901. See also *Johannesburg Gazette*, 23 April 1901; *Star*, 1 May 1902; and OP/CM 1900/1, p. 27.
53. *Star*, 1 March 1901; Krut 1979, p. 28 citing Raitt.
54. For these complaints and suggestions, see *Star*, 15 March, 22 April, 13 May 1902, and the *Star* editorial, 11 April 1902. For a thorough discussion of the post-war housing crisis, see Krut 1979.
55. Krut 1979, p. 39, citing H. Hamilton, and p. 31, citing Raitt.
56. Ibid., p. 49, citing Curtis in March 1901.

Eleven

A New 'Social Order'

And to make an end is to make a beginning.
T. S. Eliot

Exactly two years after Lord Roberts marched into Johannesburg, the war in South Africa came to a close. In the city peace was greeted with indifference, for its inhabitants had already returned to their infamous preoccupation with 'making a pile' and gave scant attention to grander political moments. Only in 'club land' was there any revelry in the the 'time honoured fashion', but this might have been expected, for it was the men with the resources to frequent Johannesburg's clubs who were most likely to benefit from Milner's peace. So, while the town council might have proclaimed a public holiday, it did not. While parades and celebrations might have been organized by the city fathers, they were not. Instead, shops and offices remained open as usual and Johannesburg's streets were practically empty as men and women, bundled against the bitterly cold wind, trudged back and forth to work.[1]

While few ordinary residents gave much thought to the distant future, the high commissioner — in residence since March 1901 at Hermann Eckstein's 'Sunnyside' in the northern suburbs — and his aloof and unpopular young advisers, his 'kindergarten', were making plans. Over the previous two years a scheme had unfolded, a scheme which was to mould the four colonies into an Anglicized and prosperous federated dominion within the British Empire. The success of Milner's plan depended in large part upon the mining industry, for it was expected to generate the 'overspill' which would finance the resettlement of the Boers on their farms, the modernization of agricultural production, and the establishment of British and colonial families on the land. It was to draw to Johannesburg and other towns along the reef skilled British workmen and their families, to promote secondary industrial and commercial growth, and to provide the revenue with which to run the colonial administration. Only with the near doubling of the English-speaking population — which Milner expected would happen in the following five years — would there be a sufficiently large British community to ensure the domination of British culture, values and institutions, and a pro-British victory in any future elections.[2]

In so far as the Rand was concerned, Milner's plans meant, first, putting the industry on a sound footing, and secondly creating an administration, a society, and an infrastructure which would support the growth of both the industry and a permanent British population. At the same time, it also meant discouraging the settlement and enfranchisement of individuals considered detrimental to the creation of this new society. Some progress had been made since June 1900 in ridding the Rand of paupers and foreigners, and those now in power were not about to allow the community to be overrun once again. As long as Johannesburg was nominally within the battle zone, the administration had little to fear.

Until the end of 1901, there were few restrictions aimed at keeping the coast clear of 'undesirable' immigrants. But, after some controversy, martial law was finally extended to the colonial port cities and, after New Year's Day 1902, anyone wishing to travel to the Cape Colony or Natal had to apply for a permit in Britain. To obtain it, applicants had to provide proof of their good character and had to have £100 or evidence that they could maintain themselves once in southern Africa. A person who had previously been deported as an undesirable or had been expelled as indigent could not apply for re-entry.[3] Once the immigrants managed to get to the colonies, their names were added to the list of refugees seeking permission to move inland, a list which was thoroughly scrutinized for undesirables by the Uitlander bureaucracy set up in 1899/1900.

When it became obvious that peace was finally at hand, the administration began to worry about what it would do to protect Rand society after martial law there was rescinded. Specifically, how was it to deal with the influx of 'foreigners, especially Russian and Polish Jews . . . [which was] certain to be great'? In March 1902 Milner complained that the administration would 'not be able . . . to exclude even the most undesirable of these immigrants'.[4] But by the time martial law was repealed, Milner's people were prepared and the Indemnity & Peace Preservation Act took its place. Now any person who wished to enter the new colony had to have been a resident there on 31 May 1902 and not since expelled, or had to acquire a permit to enter. There was no doubt about the purpose of the act. It was 'to protect the new Colonies against the influx of persons socially, and in some cases, politically undesirable, before we have time to settle down and complete a social order which will be able to absorb the influx'.[5]

To keep 'undesirables' from piling up at the coast, the Cape Colony passed the Cape Alien's Act in early 1903. It placed the responsibility for immigrants arriving without permits on ships' captains. 'Coolies' were a favoured target of the new act, but so were whites of 'no occupation', and 'Polish Jews', who earned their living as 'petty traders' or who worked in the 'sweating trades, ousting colonials from the trades in towns'. These people were thought to do 'nothing to develop the country'.[6]

At the beginning, having been refused entry to the colony, hundreds of aliens were held aboard incoming ships. Soon, though, would-be immigrants who could not qualify for a permit were barred access to ships at ports of departure, which made things easier for the Cape port authorities. Nonetheless, unqualified immigrants did manage to evade the law and slip into the colony. In February 1903, for instance, it was reported that 'Russian and Polish Jews' — who supposedly formed the 'majority of the undesirables' — circumvented the act by borrowing money from a fund set up by coastal Jews to help their poorer brethren prove their financial independence. Less organized immigrants, such as those from India or Madeira, were not as successful.[7]

With immigration more or less under control at the coast, foreigners, paupers and the criminal class came under attack in the Transvaal. On the Rand, the Peace Preservation Act was used to remove residents suspected of turning the district into a 'resort of political intriguers and undesirable immigrants'. The lieutenant governor had the power to deport anyone he considered undesirable, or a danger to the peace and good order of the society, including anyone who had managed to sneak into the colony without the required permit. Also, from mid-1903 onwards, a new morality act was on the books for use against anyone living from immoral earnings. Nevertheless, the majority of pimps and prostitutes on the Rand managed to remain there until 1906, when Milner's successor, Lord Selbourne (who was less tolerant of vice than Milner), ordered the local police to clear the city of these 'vice merchants'.[8]

In an effort to foster Milner's version of the perfect British colonial society, the administration was anxious to avoid extending political rights to foreigners. Early on, Fiddes wrote to the law officers (who were then drafting the proclamation that would annex the two new colonies) to ask them if they really meant that all Free State and Republican residents would become British subjects upon annexation. 'The term "inhabitant"', he pointed out, 'would include foreigners, Peruvian Jews and other undesirables'. Could not the word 'inhabitant' be substituted by 'subjects of the late Republic' or 'full burghers?' he asked.[9] In the same vein, that leading 'British race patriot', Milner, was concerned because people living in the coastal colonies during the war had become naturalized British subjects after only a short term of residence, without being able to speak English and without becoming acquainted with British customs. He was relieved to learn that their naturalization did not give them the right to move into the new colonies as British subjects.[10]

While not about to allow a similar situation to develop in the Transvaal, Milner felt bound by the franchise negotiations he had undertaken on behalf of the Uitlanders before the war, and now supported a five-year residency requirement for any person wishing to apply for British citizenship in the new colony. Ordinance 46 of 1902 carried this policy into effect, with aliens of demonstrated good character and five years' residence eligible to apply for citizenship. Still, the lieutenant governor had the power to reject any application for the 'public good'. He did not have to explain his reasons, nor was an appeal possible. Apparently, though, the administration felt this measure too lax, for, within a year, the Ordinance was amended to allow the residential requirement to be extended to ten years.[11] How ironic considering this was the issue which, four years before, Milner had pushed to the point of war.

The Municipal Ordinance Act of 1903, which gave the municipal vote to white British subjects only, was another piece of legislation aimed at protecting the Rand from undesirable influences. Men and women who owned property valued at over £100, or who occupied property for which they paid at least £24 a year, were enfranchised. This excluded dependants (such as wives and sons) and a three-month tenure requirement eliminated the transient. While the imperial government supported a class-based and colour-blind franchise (which would have given educated and 'civilized' non-white British subjects the vote), the non-official, nominated local members of the Transvaal legislature (with one exception) opposed the enfranchisement of these people. On the other hand, government members, who were in the majority, supported the motion. Nonetheless, in the face of this local racialist opposition, the attorney general withdrew his motion for a colour-blind franchise.[12]

At the same time there was a 'strong body of opinion' in favour of the municipal vote being extended to alien whites. But the administration, which had bowed to the wishes of the local community regarding non-whites, now decided to ignore its views and stated that it would be impossible to enfranchise aliens while leaving non-white British subjects unenfranchised. The end result: only white Britons could vote. Asians and Coloureds expressed their dissatisfaction with the legislation and accused the government of taking a 'retrogressive step'; aliens complained of being put on the same footing as non-whites and pointed out that, since 40 per cent of the white population was foreign, a 'new Uitlander question' was in the making.[13]

Milner's effort to determine artificially the composition of the Rand was in keeping with similar moves undertaken previously. For instance, Kruger's Aliens Expulsion Act in 1897 was aimed at removing racially, politically and socially undesirable people. Similarly, the Rust en Orde Commission went to considerable trouble in 1899/1900 to rid the district of criminals, surplus non-whites and foreign paupers. Mackenzie and his Uitlander advisers used martial law to deport 'undesirables' and justified the removal of prostitutes, political opponents and the poor in terms of 'military exigencies'. By 1902 the Rand administration's methods and goals were well established. The dangerous classes were shifted away from the city centre; Jews, Asians, paupers and others labelled undesirable were barred re-entry to the district; and political power was vested in white British subjects. The creation of a rational, ordered and, above all, British society meant minimizing alien influences and eliminating any elements that might stand in the way of maximum labour productivity and social peace.

A different aspect of Milner's social policy was his attempt to create a stable British working-class community, united politically with the British professional, commercial and industrial élite. To institute such a society, the high commissioner relied upon the industrialists. Back in early 1902, he had explained to the Chamber of Mines that he was 'not afraid to be called a friend to the Capitalists' and, over the next four years, had proved it by granting almost any concession to help companies dig low-grade ore and develop deep-level mines.[14] He began by rectifying the grievances articulated repeatedly by the reformers before the war.

For instance, the dynamite excise was reduced and the coal distribution network extended. The reduction of railway tariffs and the abolition of custom duties, two major pre-war issues, were initiated in this period. And even as the imperial government deliberated on how to tax the industry, it was concerned that it should not over-tax it and 'kill the goose that lays the golden eggs'.[15] In the week after peace a 10 per cent tax on profits was introduced, a tax the industrialists thought onerous but which few others felt unduly heavy.[16]

The administration then turned to the problem of how to reduce black labour costs, which had been of overriding concern to the industrialists ever since the first spade had cut soil on the reef. Lowering costs did not only mean lowering cash wages, which the Chamber did before the end of the war, but also meant increasing labour productivity. This was in part achieved by the development of what the industrialists had longed for — a supportive 'centralized and coercive state apparatus',[17] which would improve the enforcement of more rationalized pass and liquor laws.

From the inception of British rule, the administration had followed the lead of the Randlords when it came to matters of black labour, arguing that the best weapon to combat desertion was the pass law. Milner agreed — the 'root idea' of the old Republican pass law was 'not a wrong one' — and believed that such legislation was necessary to regulate the flow of Africans into white areas, thereby avoiding 'pandemonium'.[18] What was needed, then, was not laxity, but a more efficient implementation of the law. The pass office was duly reorganized and expanded, its legal procedures improved to deal with breaches of contract under the Master & Servants Act, and a finger-printing office opened to identify deserters more easily.[19]

Also in an effort to raise labour productivity, the administration supported the owners' attempts to reduce the African workers' consumption of alcohol. This might be seen as part of the government's quest to improve living and working conditions on the mines and to reduce the outrageously high level of disease and death, but reform was also of direct benefit to the employers. In 1901 Milner proclaimed a new liquor law (reminiscent of Kruger's 1896 law) which encompassed the principle of total prohibition for Africans. The following year the high commissioner outlawed the distillation of alcohol for commercial purposes and soon the mining industry began to reap the benefit. Before the war up to 30 per cent of the African work-force was incapacitated by liquor at any one time, whereas now this figure was closer to 7 per cent and dropping.[20]

To complete his aid package for the industry, Milner sought to increase the supply of black labour. In 1901 he negotiated the *modus vivendi* with Portuguese Mozambique which gave Transvaal labour agents the right to recruit Africans from Mozambique in return for the preferential right of entry into the Transvaal of goods grown or produced in the Portuguese colony. In addition, Milner agreed that at least 50 per cent of the Transvaal's trade would pass through the port at Delagoa Bay. WNLA subsequently negotiated a secret agreement with the Portuguese, an agreement the Transvaal government knew about and approved of, which gave WNLA a 'near monopoly' of recruitment in the colony. In this effort to help the industrialists, Milner traded away a good deal, for in the following years, the amount of goods which flowed through the colonial ports, along colonial railways and through the hands of colonial wholesalers was significantly reduced.[21]

If Milner's short-term goal was to create an economically vibrant, pro-British community in the Transvaal, then it is clear that even before the end of the war his plan had begun to go awry. In the countryside a series of droughts beginning in 1902 made it difficult to resettle Boers on the land or to draw new British families to the rural areas. The provision established by the Land Settlement Commission that new settler families had to be able to invest £300 of their own money in their farms, limited the number of British farmers and ex-soldiers who could afford to take advantage of the scheme. Furthermore, there was little agricultural land near the towns, where new farmers might expect to find markets for their produce. The result was the failure to establish a significant immigrant British settler population on the land, or to curtial the drift of the poor, landless Boers into the towns, there to swell the ranks of the dangerous classes.

In the longer term, though, Milner's policy was a success. A new rural bureaucracy was introduced in these years which brought technological and scientific knowledge to a community which had little before. This revolutionized the way in which animal disease was handled and contributed to the increase in production of maize and beef, which within a few years meant that the more progressive farmers were searching for new export markets. After 1907 the precedent set by Milner's bureaucracy was extended, for the state continued to act in support of the capitalization of agriculture and in the interest of white farmers over black.[22]

While hoping to establish British farmers on the land, the high commissioner was also counting on the formation in Johannesburg and along the reef of a skilled, educated and stable British work-force. In theory, the Randlords supported his policy, advocating that family men bring their children to the Rand with them, to be 'developed from the apprentice stage'.[23] In reality, though, many of the policies adopted and the actions taken by the mining companies and other employers at the end of the war discouraged the growth of just such a community. Class conflict, never far below the surface on the Rand, re-emerged and undermined Milner's carefully-laid plans.

For a start, workers' wages were under attack. In this period, when the cost of living was more than 200 per cent higher than pre-war levels, money wages of skilled mine-workers, with few exceptions, were much the same as they had been during the depression year of 1898.[24] Hand in hand with maintaining low wages went the long-awaited offensive on trade unionism, with companies refusing to deal with union representatives during strikes, saying that they would negotiate with their employees only. Similarly, managements sought to impose tame labour leaders on incipient unions, thereby discouraging militants and confusing the rank and file. There was also a concerted effort on the part of some companies to import skilled labour from continental Europe, while trade unionists along the reef, well aware of the high rate of local unemployment, argued against it. Among themselves the Randlords were explicit about their reasons for importing foreigners: they wished to break the 'near monopoly' of British workmen in the rock-drilling sector. Local trade unionists, long accustomed to dealing with Rand capitalists, were fully conscious of what was going on and knew that the effort to import foreigners was part of a larger plan to crush the unions and to lower white wages generally.[25]

Not surprisingly, 1902 was a year of labour unrest, for this was when the conflict between capital and labour (put on the back-burner during the war) began to work itself out once again. The first significant strike by whites took place early in the year when over half the carpenters and joiners in the city refused to accept the pre-war rate of £1 a day, arguing that another 2s 6d was needed to meet the rising cost of living. Two months later, the management of the Crown Reef mine tried to force several groups of artisans to adopt a piece-work system. The goal, according to a consulting engineer, was to increase their productivity. All you had to do, he said, was watch the drill sharpeners at work: 'They start as soon as the hooter blows, and never cease until the hooter gives the signal. . . . [Y]ou will observe they never lose a step, or give an unnecessary blow in their work. See how they perspire! — a fact which shows they utilise every second of their time. This is how we wish the men to work.'[26]

Working men along the full length of the reef believed that if the piece-work system were introduced on the Crown Reef mine, it would be imposed by managements from Springs to Randfontein. Consequently, the striking workers gained widespread support, which resulted in the formation of a United Trades' Societies Committee. This represented the various workmen on strike and strengthened their resolve. On losing the strike, the management scrapped the proposed piece-work system. The action on the Crown Reef had two other long-term consequences: the Transvaal Miners' Association was formed and the Johannesburg (later the Witwatersrand) Trades & Labour Council was revived.[27]

Within a month the struggle shifted back into the city, where journeymen tailors went on strike in a defensive action against wage cuts. Like the one before the war, this strike in May 1902 focused on the payment of wages as set in the industry's 'log'. As the men talked of starting their own union shops, they called on 'Christian' tailors to support their action, thereby hinting at the very real possibility that cheap Jewish labour was being used to undermine the position of unionized workers. Similarly, in September, the Argus company (owner of the local *Star*, among other African newspapers), fired strikers who advocated a wage increase and sent their names to other printing works, in the hope that they would be blacklisted throughout the city. Non-union labour was hired to replace them and, until 1919, the *Star* (the spokesman of capital on the Rand) remained a non-union shop.[28]

Also in September a major strike took place on the Village Main Reef mine. The manager, Frederick Creswell, with at least the initial support of Fitzpatrick, placed four white unskilled rock drillers — instead of the customary five Africans — on two rock drills under the supervision of one fully-trained white miner. The scheme, as proposed by Creswell, was to foster the use of unskilled British ex-soldiers, thus encouraging them to settle permanently in the Transvaal, while at the same time releasing blacks for other jobs. These unskilled men, who had no formal training, received 5s a day. But when taking into account their room and board, the cost to the company per man was computed to be 10s a day. Therefore, to lower costs, Creswell ordered each skilled miner to supervise six unskilled whites, using three drills, for no extra wage.

Although the skilled and experienced miners were only vaguely aware of the larger issues at stake — the fragmentation of jobs with the deskilling of previously skilled tasks, which made fully-trained miners less necessary to the industry — they knew that the 'cheap white labour' policy was a threat. Trained miners went on strike saying that supervising the additional machines meant more likelihood of their contracting miners' phthisis and that the 5s wage was going to lead to an industry-wide reduction in pay in that these unskilled miners (who — unlike Africans — could not be denied access to skilled jobs because of their colour) would become skilled but would refuse to join a union and would continue to work for lower wages. The strike, which was particularly acrimonious, was won by the men and the cheap white-labour policy was scrapped. By that time the Chamber of Mines had taken a stand against Creswell, arguing that unskilled white labour was too expensive and inefficient.[29] That is to say, unskilled whites could not be controlled or exploited to the same extent as blacks. So, unwilling to use unskilled whites and with black labourers preferring to work for higher wages elsewhere in the colonies, the Randlords turned to China for their unskilled labour-force and, within a few months, the first steps towards 'celestializing the Rand' had been taken. Then the white miners really had reason to fear for their privileged positions.

The Randlords were worried, not only about the power of organized labour in the work place, but also about the role white workers might play in the political arena. While Milner was anxious to avoid the creation of a 'white proletariat', unskilled and relegated to manual labour, he did want to see the growth of an educated and skilled urbanized British work-force, which would vote when the time came for thoroughly British candidates. The leaders of the industry, even those most in tune with Milner's vision, were less sure. Fitzpatrick, for example, reflected the fears of his class when he explained to J. Wernher in August 1902 how appalling it would be if there were to develop on the Rand a strong labour movement: a 'working man's paradise'.[30] Percy Tarbutt, chairman of the Village

Main Reef mine, elaborated on the theme about the same time. Expressing the anxiety of his associates at Wernher, Beit & Company, as well as those at Consolidated Gold Fields, he said that their commonly-held view was:

> one of fear that if a large number of white men are employed on the Rand in the position of labourers . . . the combination will become so strong as to be able, more or less, to dictate, not only on the question of wages, but also on political questions by the power of the vote when a representative government is established.[31]

Charles Rudd of the Gold Fields emphasized the point nearly a year later when he wrote to oppose the suggestion that 200,000 'native workers' be replaced by 100,000 unskilled whites. 'They would simply hold the government of the country in the hollow of their hands', he lamented.[32]

Unwilling to take its lead from the Randlords, the articulate white labour-force set its own agenda, which grew from its suspicion of mining capitalists. This suspicion, which had emerged before the war as a result of events on the reef, had led many workers to view Kruger as a friend of the working man. After the war, organized labour continued to feel much the same. In 1904, for instance, the South African Typographical Union placed a wreath on Kruger's grave, no meaningless gesture at the time, for it demonstrated its appreciation of the president's support in comparison with Milner's reluctance to protect local printers from outside competition.

During the war the anti-capitalist conviction of many Uitlanders-in-exile continued to grow, fuelled by the 'rent issue', by appointments at Johannesburg, by a belief that an offensive on wages was to begin at the close of the war, and even by rumours that the industrialists intended to import Chinese labour. The fears, arguments and accusations expressed by radical Randites found their way into print through the press and the pamphlets of the Refugee Committee at Cape Town, as well as in the writings of J. A. Hobson. The pro-Boers in Britain, S. C. Cronwright-Schreiner and others on the lecture circuit, picked up their arguments and spread them the length and breadth of the country.

Soon after the war a list of workers' demands surfaced, demands that grew out of the Rand situation but also demonstrated how much the British and colonial experience had moulded the South African labour movement. The list included requests for white male suffrage; the secret ballot; payment of members of the legislation; government administration of public services; access to free, secular and compulsory education; and electoral districts divided equally among the white population. Economic demands included an eight-hour workday for govern-ment employees, an end to the 'sweating' and 'subletting' systems of work, a variety of health and safety measures for the mines, compulsory arbitration of labour disputes, and minimum wages for both black and white labour. Organized labour also advocated a graduated income tax on all wages over £500 a year (skilled working men then made about £300 a year), a tax on land irrespective of improvements, the prohibition of Asiatic labour importation, and the 'inalienable right of the people to the unearned increment of all'.[33]

As labour leaders returned to the Rand from the coast and Europe and as the number of strikes grew, the labour movement began to take an interest in local political affairs. But, because the labour movement and its leadership were splintered by personal animosities and by arguments over tactics and theoretical underpinnings, it was unable to consolidate its support.[34] Yet Milner was still unable to convert the innate conservatism of many Rand workers into support for the Randlords or for what were to become the 'progressives', for workers continued to be wary of the machinations of owners and managers. They blamed them for the post-war industrial depression and accused them of deliberately holding back African workers to justify importing Chinese. The white working class was also displeased with Milner, for he had permitted the importation of Asians, had concurred with the repayment of wartime rents and mortgage interest, had refused to intervene in strikes, and had abolished protective tariffs. They felt there was little chance that unfair labour contracts would be overturned in such a political climate or that an eight-hour bill would be passed while Milner remained in power. The high commissioner, they believed, was 'under the thumb of the mine owners'.[35]

The alliance between Milner and the mining capitalists has been the subject of much speculation and analysis,[36] mostly because it was a complex relationship and one which does not lend itself to simplistic explanations. Before the war Milner's close relationship with the leaders of the reform movement, which included industrialists (albeit sometimes secretly) from the onset, was the result of their need for one another. Without the support of the high commissioner, the reformers' grievances would have remained obscure and their cause unknown. In fact, without his cooperation, their position would have been much the same as that of Mackenzie's advisers in 1900 when they tried to pressure the imperial government into moving the Transvaal capital to Johannesburg.

At the same time, Milner needed the reformers. If he was to 'work up a crisis', then he needed it to appear as though the 'helots' at Johannesburg were united in

The new Johannesburg. Lord Milner at Sir Percy Fitzpatrick's garden party, 1903 (*Africana Museum, Johannesburg*)

their opposition to Kruger. In this the Uitlander Council and the South African League were crucial, as their task was to mobilize public opinion where possible, and equally important, to create an appearance of unity by stifling any real dissent and discrediting the opposition. In this they were a success, as any reading of the British command papers or of traditional British histories of the Anglo—Boer war will show. And during the war the alliance held, for Milner depended upon this 'better class' of men to govern the increasingly vociferous Uitlander refugees. The military depended upon them for civilian intelligence and Mackenzie, especially, used their advice to rule the Rand. When various of the reformers disappointed Milner — as they did several times during the war — he kept it to himself, refusing to express divisions publicly and garnering the goodwill and support of the Randlords and the business community for use after the war.

From 1902 onwards the Randlords and their colleagues were important to Milner because it was these men, the leaders of industry and commerce, who were to generate the wealth upon which his reconstruction programme depended. Many continued to serve him and his colonial administrators as advisers, while reformers who had been active in the various wartime agencies now took part in local politics. At the lower levels of the bureaucracy, the dividing line between the industry and the state tended to blur as men with company experience took up posts in the colonial administration and ex-colonial bureaucrats took more lucrative positions in the industry. From that time forward the state devised and implemented policies aimed at assisting the Rand industry.[37]

'Johannesburg', as Winston Churchill once noted, 'is the great stage upon which all South African dramas are played out'.[38] Not only have the Rand goldfields been a key factor in the economic development, and underdevelopment, of the whole subcontinent, but events there have played an important part in determining political alignments within South Africa in the twentieth century. Furthermore, Johannesburg and the industry upon which it is based have been vital to developments in another fundamentally South African way.

Racialism, not new to southern Africa when the mines were discovered, had its roots in the seventeenth century. Fostered by the importation of slaves from the East Indies and indentured labour from India, by Calvinist doctrine and the trek north, it was well established in the Republic by 1886. Racialist practices had emerged as a consequence of the superiority of European weaponry, of the need to run herds of cattle, to manage homes devoid of labour-saving devices, to do backbreaking work in the pits of Kimberley or the fields of the Cape, at the smith's anvil or the cobbler's bench, and in kitchens throughout the subcontinent.

But racialism along the reef came to mean something quite different. No longer was it a paternalistic, face-to-face experience between master and man, madam and maid, subject to the nuances of personality. Now racialism, like the economy, was to be rationalized, efficient and impersonal. When custom was not strong enough to remould age-old practices to fit the needs of the new society, legislation was used. Colour in the industrial economy was to bar a man from advancement, limit his wages, determine his living conditions, his recruitment and dismissal procedures, his hours and length of service, and his relationship with his co-workers and employer. Rapid economic transformation made access to skills and training essential, yet colour restricted entry to training schemes, technical schools and apprenticeship programmes.

While many of these practices were rooted in the past, more importantly they were now a part of the future. As a result, racialist practices were firmly integrated into the rapidly changing socio-economic system. Had the relationship between farmer and servant, artisan and assistant, been allowed to die with the passing of the old way of life, race relations in South Africa would have been different today. But industrial capitalism, initiated on the Rand before the Anglo—Boer war and on a smaller scale at Kimberley even earlier, along with the state which supported it, ensured that colour would be maintained as a dominant divisive factor in southern African society. At the stopes and in the mills this new industrial relationship was created. From there it was taken into the compounds and hostels. It was facilitated by monopsonistic labour recruitment and pass laws, by restrictions on mobility and advancement, and has generated group areas and homelands, population registration and security restrictions. From the discovery of gold in the hills of the Witwatersrand in 1886 until the present day, the economic miracle of South African development has meant one thing for non-whites: the rationalization of their oppression.

Johannesburg, which recently celebrated its hundredth birthday, is long past the days of dusty streets and city centre slums. Today it is a modern city with a skyline as impressive as any in the world. Its wide, shop-lined streets are filled with bustling crowds of businessmen, shoppers and workers. Its sprawling suburbs have large and lovely homes and gardens bespeckled with shimmering pools and servants' quarters. But as proud as it is of its development, its wealth and its beauty, the city retains the characteristics given to it at the turn of the century, characteristics which detract mightily from its glory. For instance, anti-Semitism, an active force in the early years, periodically rears its ugly head as synagogues and Jews become targets of the far right. Harassment of black trade unionists is an outgrowth of the fear of African advancement, a fear expressed in a hundred different ways at the turn of the century and today. The long haul by bus or taxi which commuters from Soweto make daily is a direct result of successful early efforts to rid the city of Asians and blacks. Jokes about 'van der Merwe', heard in the best restaurants and boardrooms of the city, reflect the prejudice of Randites who grew up watching the *arme burgher* struggle without an education or skills, dispossessed and marginalized. Johannesburg had a second chance — something rarely given to a city or society — yet avarice and prejudice, the twin pillars of Rand society, soon blemished the 'clean slate' the British conquest had provided for the twentieth century.

Notes

1. *Star*, 2 June 1902.
2. For post-war policy, see Katzenellenbogen 1980, pp. 341—62; Marks and Trapido 1979, p. 54. For the kindergarten and how it was viewed locally, see MS/RHO/Williams, vol. 1, entries for 13—23 Jan. 1902; MS/LHC/Covernton, p. 40.
3. OP/GB/Cd. 903 (1902), no. 52, Chamberlain to Hely Hutchinson, 2 Feb. 1901; Headlam (ed.) 1933, pp. 270—81; Le May 1965, pp. 120—1; Galbraith 1983, pp. 75—80.
4. MS/PRO/CO 291/38, Milner to Chamberlain (confidential), 4 March 1902.
5. Milner to Hely Hutchinson, 15 Nov. 1902, in Headlam (ed.) 1933. See also *The Times* (London) 18, 20 Sept., 3, 6 and 9 Oct. and 21 Nov. 1902; OP/GB/Cd. 1553 (1903), Ordinance no. 38 of 1902.

6. *The Times* (London) 12 Feb. 1903.
7. *The Times* (London) 7, 10, 12 and 27 Feb., 13 March 1903 and 31 March 1904.
8. *The Times* (London) 21 Nov., 1 Dec. 1902, 13 March 1903; Scully 1911, p. 200; van Onselen 1982, vol. 1, pp. 134—5. See also Milner to Hely Hutchinson, 15 Nov. 1902, in Headlam (ed.) 1933, for the citation.
9. MS/PRO/DO 119/499, political secretary to imperial secretary, 13 Dec. [1900].
10. MS/PRO/CO 291/38, Milner to Chamberlain (confidential), 4 March 1902, with enclosure, Hely Hutchinson to Milner, 17 Feb. 1902. His concern was based upon statistics which indicated that about two-thirds of the people naturalized in the Cape Colony in 1901 bore 'Jewish names' and were from Russia or Poland. See also van-Helten and Williams 1983, p. 26.
11. MS/PRO/CO 291/38, Milner to Chamberlain (confidential), 4 March 1902; OP/GB/Cd. 1553 (1903); Cd. 1903/189 (1904).
12. OP/GB/Cd. 2104 (1904), no. 11, Milner to Lyttleton, 16 May 1904, with enclosure, lieut. governor to Milner, 14 May 1904; Cd. 2482 (1905), Milner to Lyttleton, 23 Jan. 1904, report from law department for year ending 30 July 1904. Also OP/TVL/Municipal; *The Times* (London) 4 June 1903.
13. OP/GB/Cd. 2104 (1904), no. 11, Milner to Lyttleton, 16 May 1904, with enclosure, lieut. governor to Milner, 14 May 1904; *The Times* (London) 11 June 1903; Pillay 1976, p. 153; Warwick 1983, pp. 174—8.
14. Fitzpatrick to A. Beit, 15 Jan. 1902, citing Milner, in Duminy and Guest (eds) 1976. Churchill once stated that, the 'mining interests were . . . the only friends upon whom [Milner] could rely, and to preserve that allegiance scarcely any expedient seemed too desperate' (Denoon 1973, p. 236). For a more thorough discussion of Milner's alliance, see Bozzoli 1975, esp. pp. 46—9.
15. MS/BOD/Mss. Milner Dep. 170, Chamberlain to Milner (confidential), 18 June 1900. See also OP/CM 1900/1, pp. xliii, xlviii; Denoon 1973, pp. 71—2; Thompson 1961, pp. 54—5; *Cape Times*, 23 July, 6 Sept. 1901; MS/PRO/DO 119/448, Johannesburg Chamber of Commerce to imperial secretary, 13 Aug. 1900; OP/TVL/Transvaal Indigency Commission, evidence, pp. 71, 94—7; Warwick, Introduction to the 'Aftermath of war', in Warwick and Spies (eds) 1980.
16. Fitzpatrick to A. Beit, 15 Jan. 1902, in Duminy and Guest (eds) 1976; and see Denoon 1968, p. 308; and Mawby 1974, pp. 398—401.
17. Marks and Trapido 1979, p. 60.
18. MS/PRO/CO 291/30, Milner to Chamberlain, 6 Dec. 1901.
19. *Cape Times* (weekly) 18 Dec. 1901; Jeeves 1975, esp. p. 12; Warwick 1983, pp. 171—4.
20. van Onselen 1982, vol. 1, pp. 89—92; OP/CM 1900/1, pp. xli—xlii; OP/TVL/Transvaal Labour Commission, p. 685; Worsfold 1906, p. 529; and see MS/PRO/CO 291/30, Milner to Chamberlain, 6 Dec. 1901; Jeeves 1975, pp. 16—18.
21. Jeeves 1975, pp. 18—28; Denoon 1973, pp. 129—30; Duffy 1961, pp. 170—1; Hammond 1966, p. 327. In November 1902, 79 per cent of Transvaal trade went through British South African ports, whereas four years later the figure had dropped to 44 per cent.
22. Katzenellenbogen 1980, pp. 342—50; Marks and Trapido 1979, pp. 68—71.
23. OP/CM 1902, annexure, p. 16.
24. Ibid., p. 15 and exhibit 14; and OP/TVL/Transvaal Mines Department, statistics for the half year ending Dec. 1902, table 5, and government mining engineer's annual report for the half year ending 30 June 1904, table 9.
25. Katz 1976, pp. 48—51, 66—7, 69; Cope 1943, pp. 49—51, 65; Denoon 1973, pp. 147—8.
26. For the carpenters and joiners' strike, see *Star*, 26 and 27 Feb. and 7 March 1902. For the consulting engineer's comment, see Gitsham and Trembath 1926, p. 26; Katz 1976, pp. 47—51; *Star*, 8, 10, 12, 22, 28 April 1902.
27. Katz 1976, pp. 47—51; Cope 1943, p. 65; Walker and Weinbren n.d., pp. 11—13.
28. For the tailors' strike, see *Star*, 10, 12, 13, 14 and 19 May 1902. For the shutout at the *Star*, see Katz 1976, pp. 52—4.
29. Creswell n.d.; Katz 1976, pp. 79—85; Fitzpatrick to A. Beit, 15 June 1902, in Duminy

and Guest (eds) 1976.

30. 'I know ... the appalling position that we should be in if we were to work towards Mr Seddon's New Zealand ideal' (Fitzpatrick to J. Wernher, 23 Aug. 1902, in Duminy and Guest (eds) 1976). See also Marks and Trapido 1979, p. 66.
31. This note was dated 3 July 1902 and may be found in Gluckstein and Saxby 1904, p. 53.
32. Katz 1976, p. 120.
33. For the state's dispute with printers, see *Star*, 17 March 1902; MS/TAD/CT 255, T. G. Town, SATU, to Milner, 29 Jan. 1902; OP/TVL/Transvaal Indigency Commission, evidence, p. 94; and Katz 1976, pp. 61–2. For a discussion of the post-war labour movement and its political aspirations, see Katz 1976, esp. pp. 47, 58–63, 191. For this list of demands, see *The Times* (London) 4 Aug. 1902.
34. Katz 1976, pp. 185–91.
35. MacDonald n.d., pp. 105–7, citing a trade union secretary. In Nov. 1902, the Kruger rent proclamation was declared *ultra vires* by the Supreme Court in the case of Crow and Crow vs. Aronson. Tenants in beneficial occupation could be forced to pay rent in arrears as well as interest on mortgages. The Supreme Court argued that this would not affect many residents, as most cases of rent-due had been settled amicably and out of court. Yet some 2,200 cases of mortgages and innumerable cases of rent were known to be unresolved when the proclamation was rescinded. The issue continued to generate working class anger into the new year. See Krut 1979, pp. 44–6.
36. For instance, see Denoon 1968; Mawby 1974; Marks and Trapido 1979; Jeeves 1973.
37. Jeeves 1975, p. 14.
38. Winston S. Churchill, 22 Feb. 1906, House of Commons, Great Britain, in James (ed.) 1974, vol. 1.

Bibliography

Primary Sources

MANUSCRIPTS (MS)

(BOD) BODLEIAN LIBRARY, OXFORD
Monk Bretton Papers
Alfred Milner Papers (Mss. Milner Dep.)
Mss. English History, Additional Milner
Violet Milner Papers

(JPL) JOHANNESBURG PUBLIC LIBRARY, STRANGE
LIBRARY OF AFRICANA, JOHANNESBURG

African City Properties Trust Limited (ACPT) 274 vols. letterbooks, day books, cash books, ledgers, rent rolls, financial statements, minute books, 1893-1963
Auson, H. H., 'Foreign volunteer corps, 1899-1902'
Battle of Johannesburg, 'The Battle of Johannesburg, collection of documents'
Cockerill, John, 'Letters, June 1900—February 1905', 3 vols.
East Rand Proprietary Mines Ltd (ERPM), three boxes of miscellaneous correspondence
Forster, [J.] Douglas, 'Papers, miscellaneous letters and documents relating to the Anglo-Boer War and the Uitlander Council, 1899—1900'
Johannesburg City Archive
Kearns, C. W., 'Johannesburg during the Anglo—Boer War'
Kent, George, 'Miscellaneous papers and letters'
Krause, F. E. T. (a), 'A glimpse into the past: a memorandum dealing with some historical events before and after the surrender of Johannesburg on the 31st of May 1900'
— (b), 'Kennisgewig and notice issued by Dr F. E. T. Krause announcing to the burghers of the Witwatersrand and Johannesburg the terms of surrender of Johannesburg, 30th May 1900'
Lennard, E. Ada N., 'Diary of the doings of Ada Lennard during the war between

England and the two republics'

Leslie, T. N. (a), 'Casual memories of an octogenarian'

— (b), 'Diary kept during the Anglo-Boer War', 2 vols

Mann, Ethel, 'Things I remember'

Mine Police, 'Records of the Witwatersrand special police appointed by F. E. T. Krause [sic: D. E. Schutte] to guard the mines in the South African War', 7 vols.

Potts, Margaret, 'A nursing sister's diary of events in the Transvaal in the early days'

Roos, J. C., 'Half a century ago: Anglo—Boer War, 1899-1902. The surrender of Johannesburg, 31st May 1900. How the mines were saved'

van der Horst, A. C. 'The lost republic'

White, Walter C. H., 'Letters written by W. C. H. White, dated Johannesburg 1894 and Durban 1900'

(LHC) LIDDELL HART CENTRE FOR MILITARY ARCHIVES, KING'S COLLEGE, UNIVERSITY OF LONDON, LONDON

Brig.-Gen. Sir James Edward Edmonds Papers

Capt Ralph H. Covernton Papers

(NAM) NATIONAL ARMY MUSEUM, LONDON

Bernstein, Julius M., 'Letters' (7706—51)

Jourdain, Col. H. G. W., 'Nine diaries kept by Col. Jourdain' (5603—10)

Maxwell, Patrick, 'Letters' (7402—33)

Lord Rawlinson Papers (5201—33)

Field Marshal Lord Roberts Papers (7101—23)

(PRO) PUBLIC RECORDS OFFICE

Colonial Office (CO)

    CO 291   Transvaal dispatches, correspondence

    CO 293   Transvaal sessional papers, executive council, Transvaal minutes

    CO 417   Correspondence, 1884—1910 from Colonial Office to Foreign Office, War Office and miscellaneous offices

    CO 610   Minutes, Johannesburg Town Council

Dominions Office (DO)

    DO 119   Papers of the High Commissioner, South Africa

Foreign Office (FO)

    FO 2   General correspondence, Africa

    FO 403   Confidential print, Africa

    FO 804   Register of correspondence, Africa, 1897—1902

Public Records Office (PRO)

    PRO 30/40   John C. Ardagh Papers

    PRO 30/57   Lord Kitchener Papers

War Office (WO)

    WO 32   South Africa, Boer War

    WO 105   Field Marshal Lord Roberts Papers

    WO 108   South African War Papers

Bibliography

(RHO) RHODES HOUSE, OXFORD
O'Brien, Charles Richard M., 'Letters in diary form, 1900–1902' (Micr. Afr. s. 425–430)
Williams, [Arthur Frederick] Basil, 'Diaries, travel notes, letters, South Africa, 1900–1946', 6 vols (Mss. Afr. s. 130–135)

(SN) SISTERS OF NAZARETH, LONDON
Letters from Johannesburg and Durban to Nazareth House, London 1899–1900

(TAD) TRANSVAAL ARCHIVES DEPOT, PRETORIA
Colonial Treasurer (CT)
255 D 1146/02   Printing workers' petition, 1902

High Commissioner, South Africa (HC)
    79   Deportations
    143   Deportations, undesirables, NZASM

F. E. T. Krause Collection (KC)
Legal Assistant to the Military Governor, Johannesburg (LAJ)
    1–22   Correspondence, June 1900 to May 1901

Lieutenant Governor of the Transvaal (LtG)
    40/43   Refugee aid

Military Governor, Pretoria (MGP)
    113   Mine guard, 1901
    205   Foreigners, nationality

Political Secretary to the Field Marshal Commander-in-Chief of Her Majesty's Force in South Africa (PSY)
    49–51   Incoming correspondence from Johannesburg, 1900–01
    52–53   Outgoing correspondence to Johannesburg, 1900–10
    73   Looting, commandeering, mining in Johannesburg, 1900

Rand Rifles
Old nominal rolls of Rand Rifles, Mines Division

Rust en Orde: Johannesburg Archives: Government Committee, Witwatersrand Goldfields, Department of Peace & Order (Rus en Orde) (R&O)
    515   Minutes of meetings, 2–12 October 1899
    516–18   Incoming correspondence
    522–23   Letterbooks, March–May 1900
    528–30   Minutes registers, 1899–1900
    532   Special police, incoming correspondence, 1899–1900
    536   Special police, letterbook of commandant, Oct. 1899–May 1900
    540–47   Permits and incoming correspondence
    548   Minutes of permits commission, Oct. 1899 and January 1900

Secretary to the Governor of the Transvaal (GOV)
213 PS   6   Destruction of mining property
215 PS   13   Relief for refugees
248 PS   18   Resumption of mining
248 PS   19   Permits

280 PS	23	Damage to mining properties
327 PS	40	Uitlander committees, 1901—03
468 PS	102	Rand Rifles fund

Secretary for Native Affairs (SNA)
1—14   Correspondence, reports, etc.

(USL) UNIVERSITY OF STELLENBOSCH, CARNEGIE
LIBRARY, STELLENBOSCH
Lipp, Isabella, 'My diary: fact, fiction and fancy'

(USPG) UNITED SOCIETY FOR THE PROPAGATION
OF THE GOSPEL, LONDON
Bound pamphlets: Africa, general I, 1898—1901 (14885)
Letters received, 1897—1902

(UWL) UNIVERSITY OF THE WITWATERSRAND LIBRARY,
JOHANNESBURG
Hills, William, 'Diaries and miscellaneous papers, 1876—1960' (A618)
Law, Thomas, 'Diary', in Henry Nourse family papers (A743)
Walker, Ann Low, 'Autobiography, 1856—1936' (A722)

OFFICIAL PUBLICATIONS AND PRINTED SOURCES (OP)

(CC) CAPE COLONY
Cape Government Railways (1900) Notice no. 1034, 'Return of the refugees to the Transvaal' (directions and information issued by the Chief Traffic Manager's Office, Cape Town, 19 Oct. 1900), with appendix: high commissioner's in- structions in connection with the return of refugees to the Transvaal.

(CM) CHAMBER OF MINES
Annual Reports for the years 1900/01, 1902

(GB) GREAT BRITAIN
Parliamentary Papers published by Command of the Government

C.	8423	(1897)	Further correspondence re. affairs in the South African Republic
C.	9345	(1899)	Papers re. complaints of British subjects in the South African Republic
Cd.	33	(1900)	'Brundsrath', 'Hertzog', and 'General' (German mail steamers). Action of British naval authorities.
Cd.	43	(1900)	Events in South Africa from March 1899 to January 1900
Cd.	903	(1902)	Further correspondence re. affairs in South Africa
Cd.	1163	(1902)	Further correspondence re. affairs in South Africa
Cd.	1463	(1903)	Further correspondence re. affairs in South Africa
Cd.	1551	(1903)	Papers re. the progress of administration in the Transvaal and Orange River Colony
Cd.	1553	(1903)	Papers re. finance of the Transvaal and Orange River colony

Bibliography

Cd. 1903/189 (1904)   Aliens, naturalisation: Transvaal and Orange River Colony

Cd. 2104   (1904)   Correspondence re. affairs in the Transvaal and Orange River Colony

Cd. 2482   (1905)   Further correspondence re. affairs in the Transvaal and Orange River Colony

Deportation Commission, South Africa,'Report of the South African deportation by the military authorities compensation commission, dated 10 December 1901', and minutes of evidence in FO 2/696 and FO 881/7619X.

(JHB) JOHANNESBURG
Johannesburg Gezondheid Comite, Sanitary Department (1896) 'Census, 15 July 1896. Report of the Director of Census', Johannesburg: Standard & Diggers' News Printing & Publishing Company

(SAR) SOUTH AFRICAN REPUBLIC
Mining Industry (1897) 'Evidence and report of the Industrial Commission of Inquiry, 1897', Johannesburg: Witwatersrand Chambers of Mines and the Times Printing Works
Rapports van den Staats-Mijningengenieur, 1893—8.

(TVL) TRANSVAAL
Johannesburg Insanitary Area Improvement Scheme (1903) 'Report of the Johannesburg Insanitary Area Improvement Scheme, 1902—1903, with minutes of evidence, and annexures. Presented to His Excellency the Governor of the Transvaal, March 1903', Johannesburg: Transvaal Leader Office

Mining Industry Commission (1908) 'Report of the Mining Industry Commission and minutes of evidence with appendices and index, Parts I—IV. Presented to both Houses of Parliament by command of His Excellency the Governor', Pretoria: Government Printing & Stationery Office

Municipal Elections Ordinance no. 38 of 1903

Transvaal Indigency Commission (1908) 'Report of the Transvaal Indigency Commission 1906—1908. Presented to both Houses of Parliament by Command of His Excellency the Governor', Pretoria: Government Printing & Stationery Office

Transvaal Labour Commission (1903) 'Report of the Transvaal Labour Commission, together with minority report, minutes of proceedings and evidence. Presented to His Excellency the lieutenant-governor', Johannesburg: The Argus Printing & Publishing Company Ltd.

Transvaal Mines Department (1901—1910) 'Half—yearly and yearly reports of the government mining engineer'

Secondary Sources

BOOKS, ARTICLES AND THESES

Amery, L. S. (ed) (1900–9) *The Times history of the war in South Africa, 1899–1902,* 7 vols, London: Sampson Low, Marston & Co. Ltd.

[Anon.] (1901) 'With the fleet at Delagoa Bay', *Blackwood's Magazine,* 170, November.

Ashe, E. Oliver (1900) *Besieged by the Boers: a diary of life and events in Kimberley during the siege,* London: Hutchinson & Co.

Barwin, Victor (1952) *Millionaires and tatterdemalions: stories of Jewish life in South Africa,* London: Edward Goldston & Son Ltd.

Bitensky [Katzen], M. F. (1950) 'The South African League: British imperialist organisation in South Africa, 1896–1899', M.A. thesis, University of the Witwatersrand.

Blake, Colonel J. Y. F. (1903) *A west pointer with the Boers,* Boston: Angel Guardian Press.

Blore, Harold (1900) *An imperial light horseman,* London: C. A. Pearson.

Bozzoli, Belinda (1975) 'The roots of hegemony: ideologies, interest and the legitimation of South African capitalism, 1890–1940', D. Phil dissertation, University of Sussex.

Butler, Lieut-General, the Rt Hon. Sir W. F. (1911) *Sir William Butler: an autobiography,* London: Constable & Co. Ltd.

Castledown, Lord (1923) *'Ego': random records of sport, service and travel in many lands,* London: John Murray.

Chilvers, Hedley A. (1936) *The yellow man looks on: being the story of the Anglo–Dutch conflict in South Africa and its interest for the people of Asia,* London: Cassell & Co. Ltd.

[Cleaver, Mrs] (1913) *A young South African: a memoir of Ferrar Reginald Mostyn Cleaver,* advocate and veldcornet, Johannesburg: W. E. Horton & Co. Ltd.

Cope, Robert K. (1943) *Comrade Bill: the life and times of W. H. Andrews, workers' leader,* Cape Town: Stewart.

Davies, Robert (1978) 'The 1922 strike on the Rand: white labour and the political economy of South Africa', in Gutkind et al.

Davis, Webster (1901) *John Bull's crime of assaults on republics,* London and New York: Abbey Press.

de Kock, M. H. (1924) Selected subjects in the economic history of South Africa, Cape Town: Juta & Co. Ltd.

Denoon, D. J. N. (1968) ' "Capitalist influence" and the Transvaal government during the Crown Colony period, 1900–06', *Historical Journal,* 11 (2) pp. 301–31.

— (1973) *A grand illusion: the failure of imperial policy in the Transvaal colony during the period of reconstruction, 1900–1905,* London: Longman.

Downes, A. J. (1952) *Printers' saga, being a history of the South African Typographical Union,* Johannesburg: South African Typographical Union.

Duffy, James (1961) *Portuguese Africa,* Cambridge: Harvard University Press.

Duminy, A. H. and Guest, W. R. (eds) (1976) *Fitzpatrick, South African politician, selected papers, 1888–1906,* Johannesburg: McGraw-Hill Book Co.

[Farrelly, M. J.] (1900) *The capitalists and the empire in the Transvaal,* n.p.: Cape

Town Refugee Committee of the Uitlanders.

Fitzpatrick, J. P. (1899) *The Transvaal from within: a private record of public affairs*, London: William Heinemann.

Fraser, Maryna and Alan Jeeves (eds) (1977) *All that glittered: selected correspondence of Lionel Phillips, 1890–1924*, Cape Town: Oxford University Press.

Froes, T. (1899) *Expelled from the Randt: notes before and after leaving Johannesburg, with experience at Delagoa Bay*, Cape Town: William Taylor.

Galbraith, J. S. (1983) 'British war measures in Cape Colony, 1900–1902: a study in miscalculations and mismanagement', *South African Historical Journal*, 15, November, pp. 68–84.

Gitsham, Ernest and James F. Trembath (1926) *A first account of labour organisation in South Africa*, Durban: E. P. & Commercial Printing.

Grobler, F. J. (1968) 'Die invloed op die Suid-Afrikaanse politiek, 1886–1924', Ph.D. dissertation, University of Potschefstroom.

Gutkind, Peter C. W. et al. (1978) *African labour history*, vol. 2, Beverly Hills and London: Sage Press.

Hammond, R. J. (1966) *Portugal and Africa, 1815–1910: a study in uneconomic imperialism*, Stanford: Stanford University Press.

Hancock, W. K. and Jean van der Poel (eds) (1966) *Selection from the Smuts papers, volume I: June 1886–May 1902*, Cambridge: Cambridge University Press.

Harris, Revd J. C. (1901) *Refugees and relief*, London: Imperial South African Association.

Headlam, Cecil (ed) *The Milner papers: South Africa, 1899–1905*, 2 vols, London: Cassell & Co. Ltd.

Hennessy, Maurice N. (1973) *The wild geese: the Irish soldier in exile*, London: Sidgwick & Jackson.

Hillegas, Howard C. (1900) *With the Boer forces*, London: Methum & Co.

Hobson, J. A. (1969) *The war in South Africa: its causes and effects*, New York: Howard Fetig.

James, Robert Rhodes (ed) (1974) *Winston S. Churchill: his complete speeches, 1874–1965*, 8 vols, vol. 1: 1897–1908, New York: Chelsea House Publishers.

Jeeves, Alan (1973) 'The Rand capitalists and the coming of the South African War, 1896–1899', Canadian Historical Association, *Historical Papers*, pp. 61–83.

— (1975) 'The control of migratory labour on the South African gold mines in the era of Kruger and Milner', *Journal of Southern African Studies*, 2 (1) October, pp. 380–98.

Jenkin, T. Nicol (1902) *Report of the general trades of South Africa (excluding engineering and textiles)*, London: P. S. King & Son.

Katz, Elaine N. (1976) *A trade union aristocracy: a history of white workers in the Transvaal and the general strike of 1913*, Johannesburg: University of the Witwatersrand, African Studies Institute.

Katzen, Leo (1964) *Gold and the South African economy: the influence of the gold-mining industry on business cycles and economic growth in South Africa, 1886–1961*, Cape Town and Amsterdam: A. A. Balkema.

Katzenellenbogen, S. E. (1980) 'Reconstruction in the Transvaal', in Warwick and Spies (eds).

Krut, Riva M. (1979) ' "A quart into a pint pot": the white working class and the housing shortage in Johannesburg, 1896–1906', B.A. thesis, University of the Witwatersrand.

Kubicek, Robert V. (1979) *Economic imperialism in theory and practice: the case of South African gold mining finance, 1886—1914*, Durham, NC: Duke University Press.

Le May, G. H. L. (1965) *British supremacy in South Africa, 1899—1907*, London: Oxford University Press.

Leyds, G. A. (1964) *The history of Johannesburg, the early years*, Cape Town: Nasionale Boekhandel Beperk.

Lynch, Arthur (1924) *My life story*, London: John Long Ltd.

MacDonald, J. Ramsay (n.d.) *What I saw in South Africa, September—October 1902*, London: The 'Echo'.

MacNab, Roy (1975) *The French colonel Villebois-Mareuil and the Boers, 1899—1900*, London: Oxford University Press.

Malherbe, Ernst Gideon (1925) *Education in South Africa, 1652—1922*, Cape Town and Johannesburg: Juta & Co.

Marais, J. S. (1961) *The fall of Kruger's republic*, Oxford: Clarendon Press.

Marks, Shula and Stanley Trapido (1979) 'Lord Milner and the South African state', *History Workshop*, 8, Autumn, pp. 50—80.

Maud, John P. R. (1938) *City government: the Johannesburg experiment*, Oxford: Clarendon Press.

Mawby, A. A. (1974) 'Capital, government and politics in the Transvaal, 1900—1907, a revision and a reversion', *Historical Journal*, 17 (2) pp. 387—415.

May, Henry John (ed.) (1970) *Music of the guns: based on two journals of the Boer War*, London: Jarrolds Publishers Ltd.

Milner, A. (1906) 'Great Britain and South Africa', *National and English Review*, April, pp. 209—18.

Moody, Henry John (trans and ed.) (1977) *Sophia Izendinova: a few months with the Boers. The war reminiscences of a Russian nursing sister*, Johannesburg: Perskor Publications.

Neame, L. E. (ed.) *Today's news today: the story of the Argus Company*, Johannesburg: Argus Printing & Publishing Co.

Nimocks, Walter (1968) *Milner's young men: the 'kindergarten' in Edwardian imperial affairs*, Durham, NC: Duke University Press.

Noer, Thomas J. (1978) *Britain, Boer and Yankee, the United States and South Africa, 1870—1914*, Kent, Ohio: Kent State University Press.

Ovendale, Ritchie (1980) 'Profit or patriotism: Natal, the Transvaal, and the coming of the second Anglo—Boer War', *Journal of Imperial and Commonwealth History*, 8 (3) May, pp. 209—34.

Pakenham, Thomas (1979) *The Boer War*, London: Weidenfeld & Nicolson.

Pillay, Bala (1976) *British Indians in the Transvaal: trade, politics and imperial relations, 1885—1906*, London: Longman.

Rabinowitz, L. I. (1989) 'The Jewish Ambulance Unit', *Jewish Affairs*, November.

Refugee Committee, Cape Town (1900) *Protest of the Refugee Committee, Cape Town, against capitalistic legislation in the Transvaal*, Cape Town: Townshed, Taylor & Snashall.

Reitz, Deneys (1940) *Commando: a Boer journal of the Boer War*, London: Faber & Faber.

Richardson, Peter and Jean Jacques van—Helten (1980) 'The gold mining industry in the Transvaal, 1886—99', in Warwick and Spies (eds).

Roos, J. C. (1949) 'Johannesburg en die tweede vryheidsoorlog, Oktober 1899—Mei 1900', D.Litt. dissertation, University of the Orange Free State.

Rose, E. B. (1902) *The truth about the Transvaal: a record of facts based on 12 years residence in the country*, London: E. B. Rose & the 'Morning Leader' Publishing Department.

Ross, G. (n.d.) *The South African all-absorbing sham and a remedy*, n.p.: n.p.

Ruda, Richard (1974) 'The Irish Transvaal Brigades', *The Irish Sword*, 11 (45) pp. 201—11.

Scully, William Charles (1911) *The ridge of white waters (Witwatersrand) or impressions of a visit to Johannesburg with some notes on Durban, Delagoa Bay and the Low Country*, London: Stanley, Paul & Company.

Siwundhla, Hulme T. (1977) 'The participation of non-Europeans in the Anglo—Boer War, 1899—1902', Ph.D. dissertation, Claremont Graduate School.

[Smuts, J. C.] (1899) *A century of wrong*, issued by F. Reitz, London: 'Review of Review' Office.

Spies, S. B. (1977) *Methods of barbarism? Roberts and Kitchener and civilians in the Boer republics*, January 1900—May 1902, Cape Town and Pretoria: Human & Rousseau.

Swan, Maureen (1985) *Gandhi: the South African experience*, Johannesburg: Ravan Press.

Thompson, L. M. (1961) *The unification of South Africa, 1902—1910*, London: Oxford University Press.

Ticktin, David (n.d.) 'White labour's attitude, 1902—1904: towards the importation of indentured Chinese labourers by the Transvaal Chamber of Mines', (17) p. 250.

'Uitlander' (1899) 'The Transvaal crisis: a voice from the Rand', *Fortnightly Review*, (71), pp. 1,038—47.

van den Bergh, Gert Nicholaas (1972) 'Die polisiediens in die Zuid-Afrikaansche republiek', D. Litt. dissertation, University of Potschefstroom.

van Helten, J. J. and Keith Williams (1983) 'The crying need of South Africa: the emigration of single British women to the Transvaal, 1901—1910, *Journal of Southern African Studies*, 10 (1) October, pp. 17—38.

van Heyningen, E. (1978) *The relations between Sir Alfred Milner and W. P. Schreiner's ministry, 1898—1900*, Pretoria: RSA Archives Year Book, Government Printer.

van Onselen, Charles (1982) *Studies in the social and economic history of the Witwatersrand, 1886—1914*, 2 vols, Johannesburg: Ravan Press.

— (1982a) 'Prostitutes and proletarians, 1886—1914', in van Onselen 1982, vol. 1.

— (1982b) 'Randlords and rotgut, 1886—1903', in van Onselen 1982, vol. 1.

— (1982c) 'The world the mine owners made: social themes in the economic transformation of the Witwatersrand, 1886—1914', in van Onselen 1982, vol. 1.

— (1982d) 'The regiment of the hills — Umkosi Wezintaba', in van Onselen 1982, vol. 2.

— (1982e) 'The main reef road into the working class: proletarianisation, unemployment and class consciousness amongst Johannesburg's Afrikaner poor, 1890—1914', in van Onselen 1982, vol. 2.

Vera, Vicente (1902) *Un viaje al Transvaal durante la guerra*, Madrid: Impr. de Fortanet.

Walker, Ivan L. and Ben Weinbren (n.d.) *2000 casualties: a history of the trade unions and the labour movement in the Union of South Africa*, Johannesburg: South African Typographical Union.

Warwick, Peter (1978) 'African societies and the South African War, 1899—1902',

D. Phil. dissertation, University of York.

— (1983) *Black people and the South African war, 1899—1902*, Johannesburg: Ravan Press.

Warwick, Peter and S. B. Spies (eds) (1980) *The South African War: the Anglo—Boer War, 1899—1902*, London: Longman Group Ltd.

Wheatcroft, Geoffrey (1985) *The Randlords: the men who made South Africa*, London: Weidenfeld & Nicholson.

Worsfold, Basil (1906) *Lord Milner's work in South Africa from its commencement in 1897 to the peace of Vereeniging in 1902*, London: John Murray.

NEWSPAPERS, GAZETTES AND PERIODICALS.

African Review
Cape Times
Cape Times (weekly)
Comet (Johannesburg)
Johannesburg Gazette
Pretoria Friend
South African Mining Journal [and Financial News]
Standard and Diggers' News (Johannesburg) (*S & D News*)
Star (Johannesburg)
The Times (London)
Transvaal Critic (Johannesburg)

Index